Colors of a Different Horse

Colors of a Different Horse

Rethinking Creative Writing Theory and Pedagogy

Edited by

Wendy Bishop
Florida State University

Hans Ostrom
University of Puget Sound

National Council of Teachers of English
1111 W. Kenyon Road, Urbana, Illinois 61801-1096

Manuscript Editor: William Tucker

Production Editor: Michael G. Ryan

Interior Design: Tom Kovacs for TGK Graphics

Cover Design: Doug Burnett

NCTE Stock Number 07168-3050

Library of Congress Cataloging-in-Publication Data

Colors of a different horse : rethinking creative writing theory and pedagogy / edited by Wendy Bishop, Hans Ostrom.
p. cm.
Includes bibliographical references (p.) and index.
"NCTE stock number 07168-3050"—T.p. verso.
1. English language—Rhetoric—Study and teaching—Theory, etc. 2. Creative writing—Study and teaching—Theory, etc. I. Bishop, Wendy. II. Ostrom, Hans A.
PE1404.C617 1994
808′.042′07—dc20 94-7323
CIP

Contents

Acknowledgments

The contributors to this book would like to thank the teachers, theorists, students, and writers who have contributed to this project in ways and forms too numerous to name here. Since we had to limit the number of names suggested in each category, we also want to thank the *many* additional unnamed individuals who contributed to our development.

Teachers: Barry Bauska, Elizabeth Browning Anderson, Will Baker, Richard Bausch, Robert Bausch, Wendy Bishop, Vance Bourjaily, Fred Busch, Francois Camoin, Sandra Cisneros, the Cleveland State University Poetry Forum, Beverly Conner, Sally Creviston, George Cuomo, Tracy Daugherty, Kate Daniels, Lynn H. Elliott, Eugene Garber, Robert Gibbs, Albert Guerard, Ehud Havazelet, Bill Hotchkiss, David Huddle, John D. Husband, Judith Johnson, Hank Lazer, Ursula K. Le Guin, Miss Kirtzenknobbe, Ivan Kolpacoff, Carl Klaus, Larry Levis, Susan Lohafer, Andrea Lunsford, Don McAndrew, Hans Ostrom, Linda Pastan, Sheila Roberts, Lex Runciman, George Sessions, Karl Shapiro, Elaine Showalter, Janice Silverman, Myra Sklarew, Eugene Smith, Jerome Stern, Mike Thompson, Alberta Turner, Ellen Bryant Voigt, Esther Wagner, Rudy Wiebe, writer's group members—Helen Cooper, Kate Ellis, Susan Nash, Alicia Ostriker.

Theorists: Chris Anderson, Roland Barthes, Rachel Blau Du Plessis, Wendy Bishop, James Britton, Robert Brooke, Stanley Cavell, Jacques Derrida, Terrence Des Pres, Peter Elbow, Judith Fetterly, Stanley Fish, Michel Foucault, Paulo Freire, H. G. Gadamer, John Gardner, Louise Glück, Susan Griffin, Seamus Heaney, Ernest Hemingway, bell hooks, Wolfgang Iser, Julia Kristeva, William Labov, Jacques Lacan, Richard Lanham, Willie Mays, Katherine Mattern, Dan Moshenberg, Tillie Olsen, Louise Phelps, Adrienne Rich, Gabrielle Rico, Elaine Showalter, Claude Levi-Strauss, Joseph Williams, Virginia Woolf.

Students: Sarah Arnette, Dennis Bennett, Laura Besaw, Matt Carey, Lawrence Carnahan, Gay Lynn Crossley, Hope Daniels, Megan Emery, Fish, Dan Gorlick, Cynde Gregory, Carol Hayes, Sue Helmer, Steve Horn, Mona Houghton, Wenda Jansen, Will Jennings, Ashley Johnson, Dan Jones, Nancy Krusoe, Monifa Love, Mary Ann Martorelli, Abby Mates, Rick Miller, Daniel Monk, Emily Moran, Imani Morgan, Fatima

Myers, John Pelz, David Pritchard, Jan Ramjerdi, Marc Reyes-Conner, Hadley Richards, Danielle Rymer, Gordon Scott, Jennifer Shea, Emanuel Shepherd, Janice Sherburne, Contessa Small, Andy Sugg, Sandra Teichmann, Sara Warner.

Writers: Louisa May Alcott, Matsuo Basho, Jo Ann Beard, Elizabeth Bishop, Jorge Luis Borges, Jane Bowles, Robert Browning, Robert Bly, Isak Dinesen, F. Scott Fitzgerald, Carolyn Forche, Albert Goldbarth, Patricia Hampl, William Heyen, Geoffrey Hill, Richard Hugo, Langston Hughes, Zora Neale Hurston, James Joyce, Philip Larkin, Daphne Marlatt, William Matthews, John McPhee, Herman Melville, W. S. Merwin, Toni Morrison, Alice Munro, Leslie Norris, Flannery O'Connor, Mary Oliver, George Orwell, Pattiann Rogers, Leslie Marmon Silko, Gilbert Sorrentino, William Stafford, Gertrude Stein, Laurence Sterne, David St. John, Anne Tyler, Ellen Bryant Voigt, Eudora Welty, Virginia Woolf, women's writers, group members (Louise Ben, Gloria Dyal, Ramona Long, Nancy Schrencongost), W. B. Yeats.

Special thanks go to Jacquelyn Bacon Ostrom for the title, *Colors of a Different Horse.*

In addition, the editors, Wendy Bishop and Hans Ostrom, would like to thank Michael Spooner (senior editor for publications at NCTE), the NCTE editorial and production staffs, NCTE anonymous reviewers, and the NCTE Editorial Review Board for their comments on, faith in, and support for this project. Additional appreciation goes to Spencer, Jackie, Sven, Ike, Morgan, Tait and Marvin, without whom our work would be impossible.

Permissions

Several of these essays appeared in slightly different versions in the following journals and magazines. We thank the editors for the opportunity to reprint this work:

R. M. Berry's "Theory, Creative Writing, and the Impertinence of History" in *The Centennial Review* (36.2 [Spring 1992]: 243–64) under the title: "Literary History, Theory and Practice."

Wendy Bishop's "Crossing the Lines: On Creative Composition and Composing Creative Writing" in *Writing on the Edge* (forthcoming).

Maxine Clair's "Oral Literature in the Teaching of Creative Writing" in *AWP Chronicle* (24.2 [Oct./Nov. 1991]: 1–3).

Robert Coover's "The End of Books" in *The New York Times Book Review* (June 21, 1992: 1, 23–25) is reprinted with permission of the author and Georges Borchardt, Inc.

Carl Leggo's "Voice(s) in Writing: Symphony and/or Cacophony" in *Rhetoric Review* (10.1 [Fall 1991]: 143–52) under the title: "Questions I Need to Ask before I Advise My Students to Write in Their Own Voices."

Jay Parini's "Literary Theory and the Writer" in *The Chronicle of Higher Education* (September 9, 1992: B1–under the title: "The Theory and Practice of Literature: A New Dialogue?")

Introduction: Of Radishes and Shadows, Theory and Pedagogy

Hans Ostrom
University of Puget Sound

An Abundance of Radishes

The man pulling radishes
pointed the way
with a radish.

This little poem by the late eighteenth- and early nineteenth-century Japanese poet, Issa, serves as an allegory for the several ways we teachers consider the subjects of theory and pedagogy.

When someone asks us to say how we think creative writing, composition, or literature should be taught, we point the way with a pedagogical epistemology to which we're committed—the radish we're pulling up. Some of us may even have an epistemology that sees "creative writing," "composition," and "literature" as false distinctions, that sees all text making and text interpreting as a single process within which exist only illusory boundaries. Others of us, unsure about the idea of theory, might insist the radish is a radish, not a theory.

In any case, our explanations of what we do in the classroom are driven by our beliefs about what we teach. And our beliefs are one kind of theory. We can hold conflicting beliefs or abandon old beliefs as we develop new ones, just as we do with our explicit theories.

At the moment there seems to be an abundance of radishes pointing in all directions: tradition(s), canon(s), formalism, feminism, nationalism, Marxism, semiology, cultural studies, cognitive theories, discourse theories, ethnic studies, writing across the curriculum, ethnography, deconstruction, postmodernism, cyberpunk, artificial intelligence, lesbian and gay studies, new historicism, post-colonialism, post-symbolism, dialogism. . . .

Competing and Retreating

College teachers react in a variety of ways to this wealth of perspectives, but at least two ways stand out. At a minimum, some teachers compete. They seize on a theory, advocate for it, let it inform their teaching—although some theories implicitly trivialize teaching, in which case "inform" is not the right word.

Meanwhile, other teachers retreat, seeing the wealth of perspectives not as a wealth but as a confusion-producing impoverishment. They may fall back on how they have always operated in the classroom, doing whatever seems to work, imagining themselves to be theory-free—and glad to be so—because they rarely attend colloquia, read a journal, or go to a conference. They take what they assume to be a commonsensical, jargon-free approach to their everyday work.

Those who seize on theory can seem officious, offering up the newest, the best, the ONLY radish, seemingly talking always and only about radishes—when those around them want only to get on with it. Those who retreat, however, can be just as alarming. For they revel in what they imagine to be their theory-free status (no radishes, no radishes at all) but may in fact operate on the basis of strongly held, if unacknowledged, theoretical assumptions.

Teachers of "creative writing," as the subject is generally defined, may well make up a disproportionate share of those who retreat from theory. I want to turn now to explore some causes and effects of such retreat.

Wendy Bishop's and my perceptions about this retreat, its causes, and its effects spring from our own experiences teaching literature, composition, and creative writing for some fifteen years each at a variety of universities in California, Florida, Alaska, Washington, Arizona—as well as in Nigeria and Germany. They also result from our experience with a Special Interest Group and postconvention workshops at CCCC during the past several years. They come from the process of soliciting material for this collection and arise out of reading essays and books in an area of inquiry that integrates creative writing, pedagogy, rhetoric, composition studies, literary theories, and cultural studies. (We have included a substantial bibliography that suggests the contours of this blending.)

Our sense is that the retreat from—or at least resistance to—theory may spring in part from teachers seeing themselves as writers first and teachers second: a distant second, as in "it (teaching) pays the bills." If pedagogy is not considered important enough to conceptualize—to bother with intellectually—then the notion of theory is in a sense rendered negligible at the outset: "Out of my way—I have classes to get through and novels to write."

Also, perhaps as much as anyone in the academy, teachers of creative writing are likely to rely on validation through performance ("I write poetry successfully") and testimony ("Here's how I wrote the stories I've had published"). One probable reason for this reliance is that such teachers are much less likely than their counterparts in literature and composition to experience organized training to teach what they teach; performance and testimony are natural fallback positions in the absence of training.

However, if as teachers we value performance and testimony exclusively, then we silence alternate ways of knowing, such as theory-building, research, and cognate, cross-disciplinary thinking. We may also idealize published writers as "those who know best." But when only the "best" writers know best, then the world of successful creative writers—those who gain tenure-earning jobs, or publication, or enough publication to scorn tenure-earning jobs—becomes inbred, elite, and reactionary. Why? Because "best" often means only those like us, and because "best" may be contingent on a range of biases, patterns and accidents of history, and social constructs.

Further, when only those like us can offer reliable testimony, then the unpublished underclass of laboring teacher-writers who prepare students for higher levels of initiation have no place in the teaching of literary art. Indeed, such teacher-writers are often suspect not only because they have published little but also because they mix with literary theorists, rhetoricians, and linguists, thereby endangering the distinctiveness—the purity, if you will—of "creative writing."

The fact that creative writers and teachers of creative writing often constitute a small, embattled part of the English studies family only exacerbates elitism, inbreeding, suspicion, and unproductive conflict. The creative writers often feel underappreciated, even scorned, by those in "literature" and challenged by those in composition and cultural studies. The academic creative writer often feels aggrieved, always waiting to "arrive," fantasizing a major transformation into canonized, revered text making—while having to mix with and teach the under-appreciative undergraduate, the sophomoric English major, the uppity, competitive MFA student.

In addition, academic writers participate in a publishing world that offers lottery-like odds of success. For each book that wins a contest or finds an agent, there are thousands of "losing" manuscripts, and it's only getting worse—that is, more arbitrary, more crass. It is also a world that asks writers to take risks within a conservative text tradition:

the tradition says, "Write something original, but make sure it's marketable," or it says, "Write what you know and find your own voice but pay homage to Great Books and Great Writers." The message in the context of the National Endowment for the Arts seems to be "Write something original, but make sure it's not offensive." In such a world of mixed messages, recognition comes mainly from naive acolytes and from rare live readings in which fifty other aspiring, competitive human beings finally listen to them for fifty minutes.

It should be no surprise that many writer-teachers turn from this world of contesting for grants and competing to get published to the classroom, seeking their best—most in-control—hours, but finding only more disappointment: What group of students can provide the recognition such writer-teachers crave? And to what extent does the craving itself pollute teachers' perceptions of themselves and their classrooms?

These, then, are some of the reasons that writer-teachers may retreat from theory and, more particularly, from conceptualizing pedagogy. Now let's take a look at some effects of the retreat.

Worn-Out Workshops, and Theories That Leave No Room for Pedagogy

Most probably, those who retreat from theory and pedagogy are likely to fall back on the workshop in its simplest form: "going over" poems and stories in a big circle, holding forth from time to time, pretending to have read the material carefully, breaking up squabbles like a hall monitor, marking time.

Moreover, to maintain the prestige of their topsy-turvy world—in which "writing" is valuable, especially when it is "Literature," but in which "writers" are undervalued—writer-teachers may be tempted to follow protective lines of reasoning, variations on George Bernard Shaw's "Those who can, do; those who cannot, teach": "Those who can write, do; those who can't, theorize." Or, "Those who can write poetry can teach poetry; those who theorize about teaching poetry probably can't write it." These rationales are extremely efficient because in one way they give the writer-teacher great authority but in another way provide an avenue for exerting minimal effort teaching. The rationales also produce at least one paradox: The teacher is important, authoritative, powerful; teaching, though, is finally incidental.

Does this particular kind of resistance to theory have to be driven by cloaked theory? Probably. It certainly has been driven by reactions and overreactions to historical developments within English departments, writing programs, and colleges during the last five decades. I am thinking of such issues as open enrollments, the rapid development of MFA programs; fundamental redefinitions of interpretation, text, and canon; the rise of composition and first-year writing as areas of inquiry; and so forth. And those reactions, in turn, result from the rise and fall (or the illusory fall) of different theories of reading and writing.

For example, we might trace some of the resistance to conceptualizing teaching back to resilient Romantic theory (Blake, Wordsworth, Coleridge, Keats, Emerson, Whitman, Ginsberg)—"Romantic" in this sense: The writer is perceived to be an isolated author whose spirit breathes life into an organic art form, and when native talent or "genius" meets solitude, good artistic things happen. Pedagogy and theory become incidental at best in the egotistically sublime pedagogy of the self. The author, as defined in Romantic terms, has no particular use for teachers or workshops; "he" was born with author-ity, with authorizing talent, with genius, with a potency, with a "repetition in the finite mind" (as Coleridge would have it) "of the Infinite I Am." He is godlike—Dionysian, Promethean, mercurial. He is gifted and blessed; he's got what it takes.

Of course, many authors who have perceived authorship in these terms have held appointments at universities, for, after all, the contemporary Prometheus requires health benefits, a pension, and the prestige of a professorship. These writers have "taught," if only in a manner of speaking and regardless of whether their perceptions of authorship honor the efficacy of teaching.

At another extreme, postmodern theorists appear to cut the writer loose from all moorings, sanctioning an anything-goes classroom. As with any new theories, those grouped as postmodern sometimes seem to be advocated by in-groups, members of elite guilds who rush ahead of the novice theorist, wagging fingers. Novices are sure they can never catch up, learn the code, and be accepted.

Consider, too, how resilient New Criticism has been; to a large extent, it still dictates the terminology—and the view of the text as verbal icon—in workshops, anthologies, reviews, and books on writing. Though numerous other theories of interpretation have supposedly replaced it, New Criticism thrives. And to a degree, New Criticism is based on equally durable Aristotelian aesthetic ideas.

Whether they are Romantic, postmodern, New Critical, or Aristotelian in origin, unexamined, received teaching practices complement the besieged outlook many writer-teachers may have as they are raised in the dysfunctional English studies family. That is, they may think, "It's damned hard to write, damned hard to publish, win fellowships, earn a living through writing. I can't afford the time to 'theorize' about teaching, even if I wanted to. What I desperately need is some luck, some time to write, and the courage to keep writing, none of which 'theory' can give me."

The situation becomes even more complicated when parents and children of the dysfunctional English studies family mix it up. Literature faculty often dislike the apparent isolation of creative writing teachers and then do much to insure that the isolation will harden. They objectify creative writing by naming it "anti-intellectual" or "touchy-feely," then dismiss it—a process of bigotry that is not so different from racism, which always finds the enemy it seeks.

Meanwhile, a growing rank of research- and theory-trained rhetoricians may be widening old divisions, perhaps unwittingly: Those who study "writing" without adjectives (just plain writing processes, not "creative" or "imaginative" or "art" writing) are eager to study creative writers—in part to determine whether "creative" is a useful adjective. With their very attitude toward the writing they wish to study, they thereby threaten to demystify an entire domain, or at least to demystify that crucial adjective, "creative."

Directors of writing programs often—and understandably, given university politics—put most of their energy into training graduate students to teach first-year writing; directors may tolerate the presence of undergraduate creative writing courses, but training someone to teach the courses or reconceptualizing the role of creative writing is rarely a priority.

In such situations, departmental division can create all kinds of distaste or hatred, and in this atmosphere the writer-teachers may feel obliged to return hatred of critical and pedagogical theory in kind. Meanwhile, the composition constituency—those who teach plain vanilla first-year college writing and who don't write much because they are overworked, underpaid, and not encouraged—may look on "creative writing" and "literature" constituencies as two similar varieties of privilege.

There are, of course, many reasonable questions that each constituency may ask of the others. Critical theorists can point out that resistance to theory is itself a theory, as I have suggested here. They can also point out that an a priori dismissal of theory coincidentally saves the dismisser from having to do a lot of reading. Creative writers can suggest that the theories seem to neutralize each other, to bring forth a mouse, and that much theoretical writing is so dull, so heavy, so narrow in its conception of its audience as to beg not to be read. Dedicated composition teachers can rightly ask writer-teachers who disdain pedagogy how such disdain can be anything but dishonest and corrosive. But even if these and other questions are worthy ones, they serve chiefly to feed a destructive professional atmosphere.

Meeting the Shadow of Theory Halfway

Thus far I have sketched out some of the environmental and behavioral causes as well as some effects of the retreat from theory and pedagogy. Now I'd like to consider some ways in which teachers of creative writing might negotiate zones of conflict in the profession and to make productive use of theory and pedagogy.

Obviously, Wendy Bishop and I believe teachers of creative writing should perceive theory and pedagogy to be interdependent; otherwise, we wouldn't have undertaken to collect these essays. And while we ourselves have experienced writing, reading, theory, and practice disharmoniously within a variety of departments, we feel compelled to consider these issues together in order to conceptualize what we believe to be a common enterprise.

The following suggestions, however, are informed by our being aware of how problematic and unappealing the move toward linking pedagogy, theory, and creative writing can be for many teachers, and for many writers.

One different and potentially more productive approach to take is to redefine arguments across boundaries as dialogues with the self. What if we see the conflicts between literature, composition, rhetoric, and creative writing in vaguely Jungian terms ("vaguely Jungian," perhaps, being a redundancy)? This approach would have to do with the Jungian shadow and with theory being a kind of Other.

In a rudimentary form, the approach works this way: A teacher of creative writing may loathe a colleague in her department—a critical theorist. Her reasons? She can't understand a word he says about literature. She'd like to see what he would come up with if he tried to write a poem or a story, meaning she suspects she would see garbage. To her he seems smug, sexist, pompous—not to mention a dyed-in-the-polyester postmodernist. Let us, for the moment, grant her these reasons for disliking him.

One day, however, while granting herself her legitimate reasons for disliking him and his ideas, she goes on to probe what seems to be her overreaction. Why does her dislike turn into fear or hatred? Does he, she wonders, have daydreams about being in a writing workshop and having his sorry poems torn apart? Does she tear apart poems in the same way he tears apart "creativity"—that is, reactively?

In essence, this creative writing teacher might ask what it is about her critical-theory "enemy" that contains some of her shadow—that is, something in herself, her writing, or her teaching which she has not examined, but which exerts power over her. Only she would know the answer, but here are some possibilities: She might have a certain smugness herself—about being a writer, when the rest of her family is more "ordinary"; or about being a much better writer than her students and her much-celebrated literary colleagues who seem to have the system rigged to disguise their inability to write a sentence. Worse, there might be a part of her that is an abstract thinker, a part that revels in generalities, a part that shows up sometimes in her short fiction, a part of her short fiction that she always edits out later because it isn't "vivid" in the old show versus tell way it "should" be. (Workshops and writing groups have been known to be hostile toward Big Ideas and abstract thinkers.)

Thinking seriously—or better yet, playfully—about this invention, her shadow, could enhance her writing and teaching. She can observe a certain smugness that creeps into her tone when she talks to students in class or conferences. Or she can say, "Ah, what the hell, I'm going to write the 'abstract' story everyone has always warned me off and refused to publish. I'm going to wallow in it. I'm going to tell, not show. I'm going to mess with the conventions; I'm going to deconstruct them."

Or she can look with less resistance at the territory (writings) of the critical theorist. Reading these writings for her own purposes, in her own way, she can bring to class a paragraph from a theoretical article. Perhaps she can see it as simply thought provoking, without the need for its full context. Or she can view it as theoretical self-parody, or as an exotic cluster of words, a little buzzing, exotic theory hive. She might have her writing class "strip the paragraph for parts" (to borrow Richard Hugo's term) and write a poem, or invent the "character" who wrote the paragraph.

Even in this rudimentary form of shadow work, the creative writing teacher's relationship to theory and the enemy theorist becomes more playful, more improvisational, more energetic, more like jazz. If the challenge resides in high literary art, then she can put high and low art in dialogue; she can become a signifying monkey. She can, in the end, defang theory. Theory can become a goofy guest in her classroom, a vaudevillian parody of Professor Patriarch. Or—more soberly—perhaps connecting with a broader "family of thought" in English studies is like participating in a productive discussion, as in those best late-night conversations with friends, the ones that spark ideas and help us remember the extent to which our enterprise is mutual: the conversations that brought her, that brought most of us, into English studies in the first place.

Such shadow work is but one of many methods with which she can reveal a potentially useful secret: Theory can result in new creative products, in honorable teaching practices, in classroom events that electrify pedagogy, in intellectual refurbishment. By talking with, through, around, beside theory, she becomes better grounded in her own institutional history—less defensive, combative, or ill at ease. She will be more easy, familiar, and supportive with students, more likely to invite them into her own evolving doubts and beliefs about reading, writing, and literary conventions. If she approaches theory on her own terms, she will be more likely to change the institution, to shift paradigms, to dismantle the ancient hierarchies that even the most avant-garde critical theories seem, subtextually, to preserve. Best of all, she can still have "differences" with her colleague and his ideas—and even with herself. She hasn't sold out or gone over to the other side, assuming the bifurcation still seems necessary to her.

It doesn't make sense for teachers of creative writing to compete with literary theorists solely on the literary theorists' terms; the rewards of such competition have so little value in most epistemologies of creative writing teachers. But retreat from theory and from examined pedagogy cannot be seen as a legitimate alternative either, for such retreat is corrosive, cynical, and entropic. We need to seek alternatives to competing and retreating. In addition to the improvisational "shadow work" suggested above, here are a few more alternatives, some of which are expanded upon in the essays we have collected.

Pedagogy à la Carte

If taking on theory, as such, seems too daunting or too monolithic a task (even in playful Jungian terms), perhaps reconceptualizing only one area of pedagogy will seem more productive and practical to many. For example, all of us could probably benefit from taking a hard look at precisely how "the workshop" functions in our classrooms. What are our guidelines, and what assumptions underlie them? How explicitly do we probe the criteria for assessing work-in-progress? What is our role in workshops and group work, and how productive has this role been? What other roles might we experiment with? What else should go on in a workshop besides the workshop? To what extent are we "playing the old tapes" of workshops we took? What do we know about group dynamics, and what should we know? Who gets silenced in our workshops and why? How often do we/should we revise our workshop methods? When are the conversations in our workshops most productive and why? What might be gained by dismantling the workshop model altogether and starting from scratch?

If such a microcosmic approach might be appealing to some, a macrocosmic, curricular approach might work for others but still seem less exotic than the aforementioned shadowboxing. What seems to be the function(s) of creative writing in our particular curriculum at our particular institution? How does the subject mesh with the English major, the rest of the writing program, and/or the ethos of the institution? What sorts of reading do we/should we assign in the courses and to what purpose? Who takes creative writing courses and why? What do students think they're getting out of such courses? What do we think they're getting out of them? Who teaches the courses at different levels and why? What opportunities does the department or the institution provide for rethinking pedagogy or training new teachers? What is the relationship between "creative" writing and "basic" writing? How does creative writing fit into the narrative histories of rhetoric, literature, and criticism that our profession has constructed and continues to revise?

One other area of inquiry that might be both attractive and pleasantly terrifying to some of us is that of "assessment" or "evaluation." How do we respond to students' poems, stories, and works-in-progress? To what extent do we "see" these texts differently from (or the same as) students'expository essays? What is the rhetoric of our responses? How are we implicitly shaping students' assessments of their colleagues' writing—implanting critical theory? Should creative writing be graded? What are some reasonable ways of structuring the grading in these courses? What are students' expectations concerning evaluation, assessment, and "performance"? To what extent do our colleagues see students' poems and stories in a much different light than students' essays? What happens when we get together with colleagues and evaluate a student's story? What arguments ensue, and what literary values and attitudes toward students emerge?

A fourth and final topic to consider is "authorship." Given all of the developments in feminist criticism, discourse and social-constructionist theory, and interactive fiction, to what extent should our definitions of "author" and "authorship" change? To what extent does the idea of solitary authorship still drive our ideas about writing and teaching? In the postmodern carnival, what does "originality" mean? Are more us of becoming collaborative writers? What role should collaboration play in our creative writing classes? Can we identify key cultural attitudes toward artistic collaboration and intellectual property?

These are but four of numerous productive ways each of us might enter the fray and begin to rethink the ways we teach this oft-maligned, strangely defined, but ironically robust subject called "creative writing."

In reexamining how we teach the subject, we should probably let ourselves be guided in part by the idea that connecting theory and pedagogy in itself suggests that students are worth the trouble—that, to a certain extent, theorizing pedagogy honors the students and our profession. As we pursue the reexamination, we might also consider the function of creative writing in universities of the twenty-first century. The subjects/concepts of "basic writing" and "composition" have undergone and continue to undergo close scrutiny and redefinition in our profession and at institutions. It may well be that (so-called) imaginative writing has a greater role to play in (so-called) basic and first-year writing; one old assumption is that students had to master skills before they produced literary art, but increasingly it seems as if the connections among skills, mastery, creativity, and so forth are more complicated and less linear than we have assumed. Such phenomena as computer-assisted writing and the ever-evolving ethnic and linguistic make-up of American society only complicate the connections further.

We might also ponder the "uselessness" of creative writing. That is, if courses in creative writing do not serve the university or the economy in the same way first-year writing or business writing courses do, then why are they so popular, what are students drawing from them, how do administrators view them, what kinds of treatment do they get in curricular debates, and what will happen to them if the society demands with increasing insistence that universities concentrate on "educating the workforce" and "keeping America competitive"? In other words, what is the status of creative writing in the evolving political economy of American universities, and how is that status determined?

We Are Not Indispensable

As we ponder the place of creative writing in the academy, we may also need regularly to remind ourselves that, regardless of what happens in the academy, imaginative writing will continue to exist—that our college courses are hardly the only writing venue in town. Writers who share their work with only one or two people, private writing groups, writing conferences, arts colonies and writers' retreats, writing in prisons, neighborhood arts groups, writing groups springing from small presses and magazines, writers in women's shelters, the culture of rap and hip-hop, electronic mail networks, the culture of writing contests: Remembering such examples indicates just how much creative, linguistic, and sociopolitical energy exists off campus, far from the Registrar's Office, MLA, NCTE, AWP, and CCCC. Remembering may also prevent us from making our professional arguments too claustrophobic, too insular—and from allowing an academic arrogance to overcome us.

Moreover, as with boundaries of genre, we might also begin to question the boundaries between the Academy and The World Out There—as Richard Hugo did in his *The Triggering Town,* blowing up the myth that the University was somehow not a real world. How can college teachers draw on the energy of writing and writers in the community? What can college students learn not just from published writers on reading tours but from ordinary working stiffs who also write and publish? How can we use our classrooms to link community and college?

What will ethnographies of extra-academic writing groups add to our pedagogical and theoretical inquiries? What can we learn from the "rhetorics" of community writing—books such as Kenneth Koch's *Wishes, Lies, and Dreams* and *Rose, Where'd You Get That Red?* or Natalie Goldberg's *Writing Down the Bones?* Particularly in the context of Mike Rose's *Lives On the Boundary,* to what degree are basic writing and creative writing important links between the street and the academy? What do we have to offer to these groups and they to us? Who among us is already inviting rap, hip-hop, performance poetry, and other so-called popular sources of compositional improvisation into our workshop? How does this happen, and what is its effect?

What the Thunder Said

Instinctively, teachers of creative writing know the radish they have pulled up is different from other radishes in English studies. But they have not always pointed the way with it, and they have even less frequently followed the way it points.

The essays that follow suggest a uniform alternative "way" only in the following implicit sense: With all that has taken place culturally, critically, technologically, and socially in the late twentieth century, we must reexamine what takes place in creative-writing classrooms, why it takes place, what exactly "creative writing classrooms" are, and so forth.

After tacitly agreeing that fundamental reexamination is necessary, however, the essays proceed to collide, connect, overlap, rebound, contradict, and chemically react. One overall effect of the collection may be carnivalesque, raising as many—if not more—questions than it answers. We know this.

Further, in the book, in our profession, in our culture, fundamental disagreements about writing persist and should not be glossed over. Defining "voice," "author," and the writer's "self" has become an enormously contentious enterprise, with significant consequences for teaching, writing, and the politics of literacy. That is, the extent to which we believe in or discount an autonomous writer's self and a unique writer's voice will determine numerous decisions and responses we make as teachers, writers, readers, and creators of curricula.

Similarly, many approaches to cultural studies erase differences not just between low and high art but between literary art and other writings: a text is a text is a text. The implications of such erasures are enormous because English departments and writing programs—not to mention the literary marketplace and bourgeois, post-industrial culture—have defined themselves, in part, based on hierarchies of genre, codes of taste, and rigid rankings of cultural documents. Computer technology and predictions about the advent of a "post-symbolic age" impinge on issues of voice, genre, art, and text making, as well.

While Wendy Bishop and I wanted the ethos of this book to be one of affirmation, generosity, and exploration, we did not set out to pretend that many confounding and some explosive issues do not exist. Implicitly, however, the book argues against allowing such issues to paralyze us or to fragment our profession even further. The book also provides many vantage points from which to view the issues that divide us; sometimes perspective on disagreement is the next best thing to resolution.

Indeed, we hope the collection creates a sense of expansiveness and possibility—rejuvenation, if you will; or what Professor Judith Johnson of SUNY Albany, during a recent CCCC meeting, called "the poetics of possibility," a sense of amplitude. At this stage of inquiry, exuberance is more important than uniformity, not to mention easier to achieve. And the conversations among us—teachers of creative writing—may need to be simultaneous, perhaps a little raucous, and to some degree deliberately inconclusive, speculative, provisional, maddening, and pleasurable, as they are here, as you join in.

I Reconsidering the Workshop

1. The Workshop and Its Discontents

François Camoin
University of Utah

We're puzzled by all this talk about critical theory. We ask our colleagues across the hall for advice. We open a book; we begin to read. We are frightened by the words. Structuralism. Semiotics. Poststructuralism. Deconstruction. And those legions of French authors: Barthes, Todorov, Levi-Strauss, Genette, Foucault, Cixous, Irigaray. Worst of all, le grand Jacques—Derrida with his impenetrable prose. Logocentrism. Traces. The supplement. What does the simple act of writing fictions or poems have to do with all this?

We engage in a politics of retreat. "We'll write the stuff," we say. "Let the others (those across the hall, the critics) talk about it."

Of course, since we are most of us teaching workshops full of students who want to know how to make their writing better, we must talk about it too. Like our critical colleagues, we are faced with texts, and silence is not an option. But we have our own stock of critical terms, familiar and non-threatening. Round and flat characters. Point of view. Narrative persona. Flashbacks. Showing versus telling. If our stock seems a little depleted, the shelves bare, if the little tin cans with the picture of E. M. Forster or Henry James on the label smell musty when we open them in front of our students, and taste like dust and ashes in the mouth, we can retreat into the Orphic and the ineffable. We can teach by example—flap our poems and fictions at the students and say, "Just be like me. Write." We can embrace our role as the exotica of English departments. Be the goats and monkeys. Wear funny clothes. Get drunk in public. Step into the bathroom at parties to do a little dope. Trail our disorderly personal lives in front of everybody by way of demonstrating that we are in close contact with the gods. We can give way to the peculiarly American shame a writer feels if somebody calls him intellectual. I remember watching William Least Heat Moon take off his boots at a convention in St. Louis and talk about squelching his feet into the mud of life. Who would ever have thought that he had a Ph.D. in Renaissance Lit.? Who'd have thought that he would be so ashamed of it? One of my students a couple of years ago published a novel and was fool enough to admit on the book jacket that he had studied narrative theory. He was savaged in a subsequent *New York Times* review as being an academic and therefore, by implication, certainly not entitled to call himself a writer. Better if he'd said he belonged to a motorcycle gang.

I would like to argue, I think, that just as war is too important to be left to the generals, so critical theory is too important to be left entirely to the critics. Their enterprise is, for the most part, opposed to ours. They want to make fiction safe; we try to keep it disturbing, dangerous, misunderstood. Like the makers of armor and the makers of cannons, we need each other; we live by the opposition, but that doesn't make us friends. We coexist uncomfortably in the same departments, pretending that what we both do can be subsumed under the larger rubric of education, but nobody's fooled. They interrogate texts; we try to make stories and poems that will remain stubbornly silent under the most rigorous questioning. And what we do inside the schoolhouse, in the company of students, does not, finally, much resemble what they do.

The workshop may take place in the same classroom as the literature course, but what goes on there is a scandal, an affront to the English department. Imagine a class in which the teacher is, for the most part, silent. Imagine texts which deny their own authority. (For it is the Law of the Workshop, as powerful as the law of incest is in the culture at large, that *the author must not speak.* This fundamental Law shapes the workshop, makes it what it is.) Imagine a place in which fictions are not studied, but written. It denies everything, this place. Most of all it contradicts the metaphysics of literary study, which asserts that there is a place outside of texts where the scholar, the critic, can stand, and, like Aristotle's God, comment without being commented upon. In the workshop there is no outside; we speak and everything changes. We suggest a new narrative sequence, the collapsing of two characters into one, the elimination of a third, a new ending. Everything is different now; the text under study is no longer the text under study. We are always inside the text, working feverishly to make it different, to make it more complex, to change it. Nothing in the workshop is *less* sacred than the text.

But isn't this precisely what critical theory teaches us? That writing can no longer be thought as a capitalist enterprise in which the author produces and the reader consumes? That reading is, after all, a kind of writing? That the *I* who reads is not the originary, homogeneous, fixed self I would like to honor and cherish, but is itself textual in nature, a loose galaxy of half-remembered narratives inside which, by means of which, I constitute my self?

If the workshop is different from the literature class, it is nevertheless a place where texts are in question, and we must speak, without authority perhaps, but still speak. It's not a question of teaching without theory—we can be goats and monkeys in the halls and at department parties, but in workshops the students want more from us than "Be like me. Write" (which is not very useful advice, finally). The theory (whether we want to call it that or not) is always there, though it's often suppressed, disguised as craft, or common sense, or literary taste, or *what-I-have-learned-in-twenty-years-of-being-a-writer.* But, finally, it comes down to speaking about how texts mean, what they do, how they exist in the world, how they function. We can look into our hearts all we want; what we will find there will always be somebody else—Henry James or Percy Lubbock or E. M. Forster. Or Barthes, Kristeva, Irigaray.

Nevertheless the workshop is not the literature class, and the Todorov or Barthes I read is not the same one my critical colleagues read. For one thing, I read theory the way I read fiction, unencumbered by the irritable desire to understand, to make sense of everything, to see clearly. It's partly a matter of metaphysics—critics see the world of writing as a rational continent dotted with little enclaves of the uncanny which they have not yet reduced to a civilized condition. Writers, I think, live in a different country: a country more like William Bradford's Massachusetts, "a hideous and desolate wilderness, populated by savage beasts and savage men." Here and there a fortified village where Reason rules, a little territory which I will defend with more or less passion, depending on whether I'm John Gardner or William Gass.

And I turn what I read to different ends. The conditions under which I must use critical concepts are not the same. My colleagues talk about the absence of the author, the disappearance of intention—every day, I walk into a workshop and deal with living writers who are full of as many intentions as anyone can stand, and then some. The Law of the Workshop, which does not allow them to speak, is both necessary and terrible.

It's not a bad thing, this critical theory. It gives us a vocabulary, a stock of metaphors, with which we can think about poetry and fiction, and talk about writing. It allows us to think about fiction as something other than the imitation of life. It gives us a way to talk to ourselves when the Orphic fever has died down, the first draft is done, and we're faced with the problems of craft. The student who learns that he has no intentions worth talking about—that he has nothing to say when he sits down at the typewriter, only something to make—will write much better fiction. The student who thinks about narrative logic, writing strategies, the foregrounding or erasing of the narrating act, who has learned that writing fiction consists largely of putting off telling a story, (that in fact the ingenious devices by which she delays the story *are,* in the end, the story) will write better fiction than when she is trying to make the reader feel what she felt when her aunt Maggie died. The reader will still weep, if weeping is called for.

Students need to learn from us that reading is only a preliminary to further writing, that a text is a moveable thing. They need to learn the difference between the probabilities of life and the necessities of narrative logic.

I wake up in the morning, stare at myself in the bathroom mirror—it's me all right, a little older than I remembered, but not looking too bad. Only there's this lump below the jaw, on the right side, which I haven't seen before.

Say for now that this is a novel and I'm a fictional character—if I don't worry about the lump, I'm probably done for, I've got cancer. Otherwise what's the lump doing there, not on my neck, where it could mean nothing, but in the narrative, where it must? If I do worry about it, then my chances are fifty-fifty. Maybe it's there simply to make me worry, and there's no need for narrative logic to kill me off. Or maybe it's cancer. But within this (rather traditional) narrative, if I worry I've at least got a chance. (There is, naturally, a third option. A novel in which I stare at the mirror and think, "If this were a novel I'd be done for; since it isn't, the lump doesn't mean anything—it's just a lump—no more, no less." This obstinate assertion that what I'm reading is life and not narrative discourse is, of course, the basic strategy of realism, which is more complicated than we dreamed of.)

I'm writing the story—I've got my character in front of the mirror, he's just noticed the lump. I have options. The question is how to think about them in such a way as to write a better story. Or else I'm reading the story in a workshop, and the question then is how to talk about the options effectively.

Naturally when we're working on the first draft we don't think like this. We dig blindly. One word leads to the next. We follow a vein, it peters out, we turn back and follow another. It's catch-as-catch-can, no-holds-barred, and gouging discretionary. (Or maybe we do think like this after all. First drafts are already always second drafts, revisions. We hear a sentence in our head, change it, write down something that resembles it. All writing is rewriting. The fabled first draft, like Derrida's

God, is never there when we look close enough.) In any case when the fever dies down and we come to the end, or *an* end, we stop to read what we've written and the questions have to be asked. What does this story do? How does it mean? What can I do to make it work? Does it need a sex scene here between pages 5 and 6? And if so who should be doing what to whom?

My critical colleagues—it's not a fault, it's the nature of what they do—never see the text at that instant where it must become something else. Sometimes they burrow through the special collections and come upon first drafts, or incomplete attempts, but those are texts already frozen, traces of a process always already completed.

Am I setting up a false opposition here? It's become fashionable to say that, after all, there's no difference, really, between criticism and fiction or poetry. "We all write poetry," the critics say. Or some of them. And it's true that some critics write like angels. Barthes. Derrida. And that some of their work is as complex, as uncanny as a poem. And their intentions, if we can momentarily reinscribe intention here in its naive sense, can be every bit as shabby or as laudable as ours. They want to be rich. They want to be famous. They want to be loved. They want to do something with their empty lives.

But no, it's not the same enterprise, and though it's possible to talk about it as if it were, it's probably not a good idea. Critical texts exist in the world in a manner different from poetry and fiction. A critical text presents itself as *about* something. It inscribes itself as a passion to communicate, an obsession to be understood. Poets and critics share a common language, but put it to different uses.

So. I wake up in the morning, stare at myself in the bathroom mirror—it's me all right, a little older than I remembered, but not too bad. Only there's this lump below the jaw, on the right side, which I haven't seen before.

I walk down the hall in the English Department. A critical colleague asks (hostility barely disguised as curiosity) "What really goes on in the workshop, anyway? What do you *do* in there?"

"I have this lump under my jaw," I tell him. I point. "Look, right there."

"God," he says. "You writers. Always making a tragedy out of your lives. What are you doing, working on a novel? Is it about cancer? Middle age? Death?"

2 Reflections on the Teaching of Creative Writing: A Correspondence

Eugene Garber
SUNY at Albany

Jan Ramjerdi
California State University, Northridge

June 7, 1991

Dear Jan,

I want to begin our correspondence on the creative writing workshop inductively and historically and more or less personally.

I have taught fiction workshops pretty steadily from the late fifties to now, about thirty years. For all but the last two or three, my experiences with them tended not to be very variable. Fiction writers sat in a circle and commented on each other's stories. They tended to be kind and helpful and generally insightful. They had clearly joined together to help each other make their stories better. They seemed sincerely delighted when fellow students got stories published or presented them successfully at public readings. We virtually never talked theoretically, though there was often conversation about types of stories and influences.

What unspoken principles were we proceeding from? I think they were something like this (though of course I can't be sure): All writers were granted the uncontested right to produce any kinds of stories they wanted to, using any subject matter. It was the business of commentators to help the writers make their stories better stories of the kind they were writing. I believe, therefore, that commentators proceeded from mostly unspoken judgments about whether writers successfully used conventions and generic expectations. Of course commentators might be delighted when these expectations were defeated—parodically, innovatively, whatever—but I think that what gave these conversations their communal element was a set of, again often unspoken, shared perceptions about the possibilities of the "game of fiction" as it was being played at any given moment. At various times there were more favored types—well made, lyrical, metafictional, experimental, etc.—as

I recall we stayed pretty open to any choice writers wanted to make. But as a result of these shared perceptions commentators could attempt to point out to writers where they were successful, or unsuccessful, in the generic terms, or rules of the game, they had set out to explore. Thus conversations were always aimed toward revision.

A few years ago the workshops changed, at least in my experience. My question for you, as one who has taken a number of workshops recently, is this: What exactly has changed? Workshops now seem more interesting, but also more contentious and problematical. I would never want to go back to the days of gentle formalism that I tried to describe above, but I feel the need to understand much better than I do the new teaching scene that pertains today.

Let me speculate just for a little bit about what may have changed, giving you, if nothing else, some misconceptions to correct. Feminist criticism has changed things, I think. Though feminist critics are attentive to every aspect of a literary work, they often take a very strong interest in thematics and in the rhetorical properties of a work, what it tries to get readers to believe or even do—the illocutionary and perlocutionary of speech act theory. Such interests obviously are not to be satisfied with commentary that confines its interest to the writers' successes and failures within the conventions and genres they have chosen. This same point could be made in regard to any kind of thematic, culture criticism, whether Marxist-oriented or otherwise. It will not be satisfied with judgments based essentially on intrinsic properties. I think this is a change from my old days.

Here's one more stab. Poststructuralist criticism has invaded the workshop differentially. Some have it. Some don't. Those who have it will be likely to be skeptical about our ability to judge others' writing accurately or fairly. They will not easily assent to claims of objectivity and disinterestedness. They will have a strong impulse to unmask the ideological allegiances of commentators, to point out the lack of or the inadequacy of the critical and theoretical grounds from which particular comments and judgments come.

In other words, I'm suggesting that the old agreements, however fractional and constraining one may judge them to have been, did at least make a communal discourse possible. In the absence of such agreements, even with a pluralism of possible agreements, conversation may become inchoate, sometimes contentious. Anyway, I will be grateful if you can shed some light on the current condition of workshops from your perspective as a frequent student in them. I look forward to hearing from you.

Sincerely,

Gene

June 13, 1991

Dear Gene,

The workshops of the past you describe these nostalgic days of gentle formalism that is those days when you could know what type of story you were reading you could as a reader know this you knew how to read this and that type of story you could name each type and its conventions and you could know success and failure and how to remedy failure. Everyone could agree on this everyone could read and everyone could write within a frame then, it was separate from a wall that surrounded it and within that specific frame (everyone could name them, everyone could agree on them) there were rules of composition you could agree on rules of the game that were shared. This seems a happy social homogeneity in which the rules of the workshop were generic conventions you knew what to say within this agreed-upon frame, there was a frame for discourse, it was stable, it was grounded on something outside of itself, some well-known conventions (they are implicit) and of course it did not vary very much—it was stable, it was static.

What has changed?

(Would you say the creative writing workshop is the last bastion of formalism? That, by its very status as marginal to the academic enterprise, it is the last to respond to the radical changes in literary theory?)

What has changed?

Number one I'd venture is the shift in focus from the text as autonomous object to text as a construction of the reader. Here the focus is on the reader and as you focus on the reader constructing a text, a whole new set of considerations emerge that were suppressed in a formalist perspective. Virtually all post-formalist theories have contributed to this elevation and redefinition of the role of the reader from a neutral observer to an active participant.

The reading model assumed in your former workshops is a limited, specific case of reading as production: reader's expectations are defined as generic conventions to be met or overturned, a particular convention of reading too limited to address the more interesting questions contemporary literary theorists would ask, like "Who defined these genres?" A loaded question that suddenly expands the field of critical vision from the neat isolation of the work by itself, its rules and conventions (this provides a common ground for us to frame our workshop discourse), a whole field of vision formalist strategies evaded, that is the focus of contemporary theories, all the political and ideological issues that emerge when we can no longer isolate the text as object, its boundaries are no longer clearly there, its aesthetic autonomy is no longer viable in today's critical climate. Even something so seemingly neutral and stable as generic conventions are not safe: Where do they come from? Most everyone would agree they come from us (Who are we?) agreeing they are there and then we name them, but we only name those we can agree on (Who are we?) so that those that are there are those we can agree on and we name them. Those that we cannot agree on, then, do not exist. Marxists, feminists, Afro-centrists, gay and lesbian critics can tell us why they are not there: the forms we choose to name are the forms that reflect and support the dominant ideology and those that are not named are those that undermine it, and Foucault tells us how this is all about power.

The neutral model of reading you describe in the old workshops is not something students exposed to contemporary criticisms are willing to accept. What happens when there are no commonly agreed-upon conventions for reading? When there is no shared set of external conventions that gives the workshop a common ground for discussion? How do we talk to each other when we cannot agree on a basis for evaluating the work?

It's helpful, it's instructive if readers can articulate their responses in the language of a critical perspective other members of the workshop understand (the workshop is an ideal place to examine and test contemporary theories against contemporary texts) but given the proliferation of critical perspectives, a common body of knowledge cannot be assumed. Does this make communal discourse impossible? No, I think underlying the sometimes contentious clash of alternative readings is the fact that there is a real dialogue in process, it is happening that readers are saying what they have to say about their construction of a text including things that were suppressed in the benign workshops you describe, like "This is white racist shit and I refuse to read it." (Is that a genre?)

Just as contemporary theory poses a threat to the autonomy as well as the status of the literary text as an aesthetic object, it also poses a threat to the autonomy of the already marginalized creative writing workshop. It seems we ought to articulate what we think are the roles of creative writing workshops within a graduate academic program now.

Sincerely,

Jan

June 21, 1991

Dear Jan,

I liked your letter of the 13th a lot. I liked the Steinian rhythms that punctuated some of your observations about the old benign workshops. I liked the way your discussion of that now impossible old model comes around at the end to the question not only of textual autonomy but also of the autonomy of the creative writing workshop—as a practice, I'm going to add—in the context of our graduate program (and of programs in other places).

Well, I'm guessing you'll agree that the workshop can't claim autonomy any more than texts can. Workshops are, in a way, texts, discourses, and as such are invaded on every border by ideologies, reading practices, goings-on in the department, in the discipline, in the profession, etc. The question is one of usefulness and intellectual energy, not autonomy. So, just for the heck of it, I'm going to take two opposite positions, leaving myself open to charges of dichotomous thinking, rhetorical disingenousness, etc., etc. (One can't say anything nowadays without stumbling across a thousand poststructuralist taboos—polarity, hierarchy, logocentrism, phallocentricism, any kind of center, essentialism, foundationalism, HUMANISM, etc.)

Position #1 (Prone) Workshops Are the Worst Place to Encourage Responsible Talk About Writing and Ought to Be Banished. *They have developed no publicly examinable practice or discourse, statements about themselves (in AWP Bulletins, Teachers Collaborative, etc.) constitute the most lugubrious species of touchy-feelies, guru-ism, magic intuitions, etc. (although they are covertly vulnerable to every fad in the markets, whether lit mag or NYC publishing). At the same time they are critical troglodytes, hanging on tenaciously, as you suggested, to the tenets of a long-dead formalism. Their marginalization is self-inflicted, a misguided insistence on isolating themselves from the evil influences of the academy of which they are a part, on claiming for MFA studio degrees education sufficient for college teaching. Maybe all this comes from the Romantic mystique about the inviolable soul of the artist—as dangerous a hyperbole in its own way as the disappeared author in Foucault, Barthes, Machery, et al. Anyway, workshops create a company of know-nothing navel-gazing isolates. Put them in the third book of* Gulliver's Travels *with instructions to the flappers never to awaken them again.*

Position #2 (Supine) Workshops Are the Best Place to Encourage Serious Talk About Writing and Must Be Kept as an Integral Part of Any Good Grad Program. *Workshops save us from the inadequacies and the RELENTLESS TENDENTIOUSNESS of academic theory and discourse. (Often especially tendentious are those that are supposed to liberate us—Marxism, some feminisms, deconstruction, psychoanalysis—but that's a horse from another opera.) Creative writing workshops glory in the idiosyncrasies and particularities that escape the nets of critical paradigms and thereby keep us human and individuated. Workshops are piratical, eclectic, pragmatic, care nothing for theoretical consistency, create camaraderie and support, help people, and WORK LIKE NO OTHER ACADEMIC ENTERPRISE WORKS. (I have heard convincing descriptions of some communal feminist classes that really work. They sound a lot like workshops.)*

Well, trashy exaggerations for rhetorical effect, you might be thinking. Maybe. But I claim that these two thumbnails actually come from experience. I have been in workshops where the commentary was so groundless, stupid, and hurtful that I swore I'd never have anything to do with another one. I've been in workshops where the commentary was so brilliant and helpful that you could veritably feel writers expanding their sense of the possibilities of fiction. I think you and I have been together in those two very different rooms. Anyway, if there are these two divergent tendencies in workshops, then we, as serious pedagogues, ought to be thinking about how to make the better happen more consistently. Tell me how.

A postscript on the relationship of workshops to the grad program. My pitch has been that workshops ought not to be enclaves, safe havens, but ought to be as dynamically related to the rest of the program as possible, the various discourses flowing freely and encountering each other at every corner, mutually enriching. But some have said that this will only make a muddle, and we will lose distinct flavors. Maybe, but my feeling, at least at the moment (and these propositions are always local and historical, never universal), is that the workshops need more rigor and the "academic" classes need more freedom and imagination. What do you think? Your experience in workshops and in academic classes is much richer than mine.

Look forward to hearing from you.

As ever,

Gene

June 28, 1991

Dear Gene,

Yes, I've been in those two seemingly different rooms you describe, but I'm less inclined to see these two divergent tendencies in the workshop as antithetical. What most characterizes the workshops, distinguishing them from academic classrooms, is their INTENSITY, deriving, I think, from the fact that MORE IS AT STAKE IN THE WORKSHOP THAN IN THE ACADEMIC CLASSROOM. Why? Well you could explain this by saying writers are a bunch of oversensitive, navel-gazers, and this would lead us to your Position #1: the workshop is a safe place for writers to hide from the cold, hard gaze of academic scrutiny—but I don't believe this. The writers I've encountered here are not interested in hiding in workshops, they are far from anti-intellectual, they are in fact among the best students in all academic classes, with a healthy interest in theory and criticism to the extent it is useful, i.e., can be plowed back into their own work.

I'd argue that the reason for the high level of intensity in the workshop, and this is what makes it different from the academic classroom, is that there is no object of study that filters, directs, constrains, and distances response as there is in academic classes. The existence of an object of study, as nebulous as this may be (as, say, in Don Byrd's Spring 91 workshop/class "Models of History in Literary Criticism"), and its embodiment in a set of texts creates a circumscribed context with boundaries for response even when the mode of discourse is open, even when the focus is on student-written texts. Still there is that filter, that object of study, that other thing to come back to that circumscribes the discourse, that is one step removed from me responding directly to your text, if I respond (and this is a problem in workshop classes, often we don't prepare a response to each other's work, that is student-written texts are not taken as seriously as assigned texts are in academic classes) I am responding to your response to the assigned text we both read, which is a very different form of response than in workshops where it is me responding with all my unarticulated ideological, personal biographical, psychological baggage as well as my literary prejudices and, maybe, a critical tool or two. (Of course I have all this baggage when I respond to any text, but with an accredited, assigned text between us we have a common, distanced object we can talk about.) This is not the model of response literary scholars use to respond to texts. What was most apparent to me in Judy Johnson's Spring workshop/class (where visiting faculty members discussed student-written work using their critical perspective) should have been that writers do not respond to texts the same way as literary scholars do. What we are willing to call a response, literary scholars would call an initial personal response which then requires a standing back, the insertion of critical distance, the use of a critical lens which turns the text into an object of academic study rather than a nebulous encounter, a blur really, of personal and ideological texts, yours and mine. (Hence, more is at stake.)

When you say that workshops should become more rigorous, I imagine what you are concerned with is this: most of what is said in workshops is a reflection of pretty elementary reader responses, responses you'd submit to a bit more scrutiny if you were contributing them in an academic class, and unfortunately the level of discussion often stays here, a series of unexamined first-level reader responses. When the discussion gets interesting what is generally going on is that the text is clashing with a reader's ideology and/or poetics and there is a good likelihood that as this reader develops her response as she speaks and others listen and respond, a conflict will emerge. This is good and shouldn't be suppressed (as often happens in the interest of keeping things nice). This conflict, as well as its flip-side counterpart (though primarily this conflict), is what we spend hours discussing in bars for weeks afterwards. Where there is this high level of energy generated (think of Charles Olson's poetics of the transfer of energy from writer through reader by means of the text) here the energy is unmediated by a discipline, a defined, necessarily limiting constraint of boundaries of what is "in" the class and what is "out."

What we need are pedagogical methods that bring more of the workshop energy into the academic classroom and more of the high-level reading practices of the academic classroom into the workshop, a classroom/workshop in which the student-written text is the object of academic study. So far, the moves in this direction have been made by the creative writing faculty, faculty accustomed to centering the focus on student-written texts. What if we had creative writing workshops taught by other faculty members? Is there some reason why workshops should be taught by writers? (I'm fishing for something we can argue about—we're agreeing too much.)

Sincerely,

Jan

July 8, 1991

Dear Jan,

I'm going to skip a couple of inviting topics that your last letter offered: Why does the presence of the "object of study" in the ordinary academic class tend to de-energize through its mediation? Why do writers respond to texts differently from scholars? Instead, I'm going to the question of energy and contention. You say that workshops get serious and energetic when discussions enlist animated, even clashing, values—ideologies, poetics, subjectivities, etc. And, yes, I did suggest that I, as teacher, was willing to trade contentiousness for niceness. I want now to liberate myself from that position.

When do workshops get really interesting and energetic? I've got an idea. I'll be interested to see if you find it at all convincing. First, a case. You remember the night we discussed your story about three or four women and their dippy boyfriends, how they all get pregnant, and end up taking care of their babies in a serio-comic quasi-heroic world of single parenthood—a story of considerable charm, at once light and serious. And you remember the outburst from the young men in the class. Denigrated they were, and the women heroized beyond all belief. A regular ideological/feminist melodrama you had written. And the women in the class, by and large, while not upset by the alleged theme of female super-independence, gave you lots of advice about how to get the plot working better, i.e., create better narrative drive, crises, resolutions, etc. What the hell was going on, you and I wondered together the next day in my office. Oh well, threatened young men . . .

I want to introduce the notion of master narratives, the seminal (*examine this word) stories a culture has to have in order to teach its patterns and values, the ones that in the West have been loaded in the direction of the male at least since Lascaux, the ones some poststructuralists say we have to get rid of altogether if we want to be free, etc. (*Pace *Jameson, Lyotard, et al.) I want to suggest that the workshop gets interesting (like the infamous night of your husbandless mothers) when a master plot gets traduced. Most of the time we read in workshops, even with students as good as ours, what Jauss calls culinary works—standard fare made according to the best traditional recipes, tasty, undisturbing, made to order for cookbook advice: a dash more plot, a little more yeasting of this character's background, some sentence/seasonings that need correcting, etc. These are writings that do the work of reproducing the master narratives in that ritual campfire repetition that keeps our lives meaningful, i.e., patterned by paradigmatic stories. The discussions of such writings are, as you would say, bound to be nice, peaceable, a celebration, mostly not conscious, of the way things are.*

So, an energetic disturbance happens when a piece alters the counters (characters, symbols, ethics) of a master narrative: when instead of boy meets girl, boy gets girl, boy loses girl, boy probably regains girl, we have girl gets boy, girl gets baby, girl ditches boy. The young men raise hell. Low-grade energy, but energy nevertheless. More critical is the kind of crisis-less round you created for the women, interlacing their lives: row row row your boat, get get get your man, get get get his seed, toss toss toss the husk. I mean the more serious disturbance, probably even in the bowels of our young bucks, was not the gender-dependence switcheroo, but the refusal to follow structure. Tell us that our narrative counters are in the wrong place, their valences confused, and we can defend ourselves against this traducing of the master narratives, because it's all hanging out there for everybody to see. Or, better yet, being bona fide youthful radicals, we can value this kind of writing as aiming to right wrongs, provide a more flexible and capacious set of counters. But, if you tell us that we don't know how to tell stories, that all our equipment of rise and fall, of excitement, expenditure, and relaxation, all our sense of seasonal and sexual rhythm, our sense of ending and closure, has got to be changed, why then all hell breaks loose. Now we have high-level energy. Even the sisterhood deserted you.

But, you're going to say, I've offered really far-out pieces to workshops and commentators have responded favorably. *Yes, because of two things. One, it's just too square to fail to appreciate the avant-garde, even if it's threatening. More important, the avant-garde is easy to deal with precisely because it is far-out, out there, wonderful crazy aleatory shit, miles from real life, caring nothing for representation, can't hurt anybody. But if you write a piece that is, I'll say, contiguous to the master narrative, that is a plot "about" women and men and babies and the economics of family, stuff that ought to fit the master narrative but does not, now you've got disturbance.*

Oversimplified summary. In the workshop, discussions of culinary writings are nice and easy and enervated. Discussions of far-out works are engaged and lively, but finally not serious because they don't really get to the profound cultural, epistemological, maybe even ontological challenge that the works represent, if they're any good. Discussions of works that appear to be representational but don't represent correctly (i.e., re-represent the master narratives) will be the most energetic because people will see that the counters and structures of master narratives are really being challenged.

Couldn't quite do it in 3 pages this time. Take it away.

As ever,

Gene

July 12, 1991

Dear Gene,

Master narrative: Once upon a time character X was in global state A. Event μ happened to him and he was thrown into transitory state not-A. As a result of actions $\tau_{1,t}, \ldots \tau_{n,t+p}$, aided or thwarted by characters $Y_1, \ldots, Y_k$ (human or not), X, passing through transitory states $a_{1,t}, \ldots, a_{n,t+p}$ arrives at a new global state A which is a transmutation of original state Â; X, the wiser for having passed through states $a_{1,t}, \ldots, a_{n,t+p}$.

Is this a fair description of the master narrative? Is this not a description of the structure of my story "The Three of Us"? Isn't my story a master narrative? What I'm getting at is this, what you assume in your concept of master narrative is it is a fixed thing we can point to it, it is what is supporting the dominant ideology and when it does not it is not a master narrative. That is denying the master narrative is subject to revision, to my vision of the same master narrative only with another master, not a male, not even an individual, but three women (none of them characters in the traditional sense). In sum, the story is a master narrative usurped by a multi-headed female monster/hero. What is so threatening is the question of who is master here?

I want to push a bit more your concept of master narrative and the idea that it is either used to support the dominant ideology or it is traduced and thus a threat to those who respond in workshops by defending the master narrative. This, as a model, does not take into account the possibility that the master narrative exists as a structural form, as any generic form exists, *because* it can be transformed, that is it exists because it is revealed to us by the unexpected deviation that provokes its exceptions to itself and in so revealing its limits reveals itself as such, the master narrative is alive, can live because it is subject to alteration from the outside, the non-master, asserting her right to a form that has never been used to tell her story, this story, for instance, of three women.

The workshop reaction to the story was an attempt to regain control of the master narrative, of saying you can't do this (*you,* meaning me, a woman), you can't use the master narrative in this way, you must not use so many lists (lists are not narrative), you can't tell this all in summary (more plot, more scene, more dialogue), you can't make two-dimensional male characters, you can't have women who are saints (you must not valorize your female characters). The workshop response to stories like mine that claim the master narrative, that aim to expand its range of vocalizers, is to silence them with disapproval couched in technical terms. I have seen this in every workshop I have attended (and here is a place for some enlightened pedagogy).

Always part of what a workshop does is enforce a social censor on the work. Always there is a chorus of voices saying, "No, you can't do this, this is not allowed, that is not the way to write, you have violated some social norm," and because it is fiction workshop we will talk about this as a violation of narrative conventions and this is thinly veiled criticism, what is violated is not a narrative convention but a social convention in narrative form and more so, as you say, if the piece is representational it is what we are most vulnerable to, what is most realistically depicted we must causally connect the actions in the narrative as we would in real life if they happened to a friend or us and here the ideological clash of hypothesized connections we construct as readers of representational work does or does not conflict with the ideological values we use to causally connect real events in the nonfictional world we are living in. There is reason for more energy released (as you say) in representational narratives that "misrepresent" the determinism of the structure of the plot that underlies the master narrative.

I would argue that virtually all works that are read in fiction workshops now are at the same time repetitions of antitheses of gradations of a master narrative, that is how can we write or speak at all without invoking a master narrative that is how can we communicate at all without reference to the prevailing economic and social relations that is all we know we exist inside them and outside them both depending on when we are who we are and what are the prevailing rules for when we are who we are being outside and inside. Now they are undecidable. That means representational writing and nonrepresentational writing are not so easily distinguishable and deterministic positions are not so determinant. In writing fiction today there is not any writing I can see that is so clearly representational to a reader reading now that is not just appearing to be representation, that is it is using the literary conventions of representation to evoke representation, but it is not representing anything but writing that is representational writing which the reader recognizes as representational writing, and that is how we read now, or I do anyway, so there is not much difference to me between a so-called representational piece like "The Three of Us" and a less representational piece like "Inhabiting the Yoni."

To come back to the creative writing workshop, I am, as a writer, interested in the defensive operations of readers reading fictions that openly challenge their reading conventions, but also, as a reader, I am interested in being challenged and so I look for whatever seems not quite right to my own reading conventions. I think this is what is most interesting in writing workshops: the unexpected, the aberration, the deviation from conventional narrative norms that necessarily points to itself and the convention it violates is then more known than it was before when it was not consciously known, only vaguely in the way of unquestioned myth and so not accessible to transformation.

And this to me is what is most valuable about the writing workshop: in reading and discussing contemporary work, the boundaries of what is and is not "doable" now according to different writers and readers is sketched out as a map of narrative possibilities. We could never define and name them as generic categories, so mutable are the boundaries that apply it seems here to one reader, one writer, and the paths we make within these boundaries, across boundaries is what has in their *difference* created for me an opening, a breech in what I had thought was a firmly structured concrete thing, a master narrative somebody else owned and I was to learn how to tell it right, and what I learned instead was that there were only conventional ways in which language is worked to be a narrative and so readers read them in conventional ways and you can use them any way you want and some people will listen, some will object, many will say you can't do that.

Over the course of this correspondence (I've just reread what we've written so far), I see two threads we are weaving, or trying, to weave. Maybe they are opposing points of view or maybe they can work together. What do you think?

1. You want textual boundary definitions (the desire for firm ground): a vocabulary, a set of defined concepts we can use as a basis for the discussion in workshops, e.g. generic definitions, the master narrative.
2. I resist the above for an equally limiting point of view, call it fluid, multiple, it is not definable, it gels in conflict sometimes, but generally it is content to be rigorously amorphous, resistant to rigid structuration, structure imposing itself, nonetheless, it can exist outside form because form structures it outside itself.

Looking forward to hearing from you.

Sincerely,

Jan

August 1, 1991

Dear Jan,

Here is my last shot. I was really interested in the things you said about master narratives in your last letter, and for a while I thought I would write again about that, e.g., do writers really have the power to revise the master narratives of a culture? Are all fictions inevitably located somewhere in relation to the master narratives? Can a significant deviation from a master narrative be effected without changing the structure of the narrative? Is a master narrative as much a set of reading conventions as it is a set of textual conventions? Is the disturbance of a deviation from a master narrative greater if the deviation remains ostensibly representational? (Is serious representational fiction impossible now—all ostensibly representational fictions being essentially self-reflections on the nature of representation?) These are fascinating questions, but I'm not sure I have much more to say about them. And anyway, I want to turn to the crux you've located in our correspondence: the matter of a firm ground for workshop discourse.

To begin, judgment is everywhere. Reviewers make judgments, teachers in choosing texts, editors, etc., etc. We could take the position that judgment is only a necessary evil, like death, so that there will be room, a life, instead of an inchoate mass of organisms. It would be better kept out of workshops, where we would limit ourselves to descriptions that clarify for writers their choices. If we let judgment into workshops at all, it should be limited to advice about current publication preferences and markets, i.e., the dominant literary ideology, making no pretense of speaking aesthetic value. Such a position would find favor with critics and theorists who trace judgment to ideology and who therefore embrace a sort of democratic pluralism and relativism.

The position has its attractions, but I find that it does not satisfy me—my experience, my intuitions, or my sense of literary value. All of which, of course, may be maskings of ideology, but I'm going to argue that they're not. I'm going to argue that you and I and any perceptive reader can make suggestions that will really help writers make their fictions better. Conversely, bad commentators will make suggestions that are irrelevant or might actually make fictions inferior. How can I make this claim, knowing that we are prisoners of history, culture, world view, etc., etc.? Do I claim that we can escape, transcend? No. What I claim is that good reader/commentators can make shrewd judgments about where writers in given pieces are locating themselves in the world of language games called contemporary fiction. Having made that estimation, they can say interesting things about what moves are likely to be effective in just that place, in this culture, at this time.

In Just Gaming, *Jean-Francois Lyotard claims that one's discourse is always a set of complex moves cutting across several games. I think so. Thus every fictive utterance is always at once strategic and tactical—strategically locating itself at the juncture of several games, tactically making moves just there that have never been made before. To what purpose? Formal inventiveness? Not ultimately. Innovation in language games is eminently practical, says Lyotard. I think that he means that the world is, to a large extent, discourse. Who changes the language games changes life. The world is everything that is the case, says Wittgenstein in the* Tractatus, *i.e., everything that can be said. Of course, near the end, as I recall, he says that what can't be spoken of must be passed over in silence. I don't quite agree, but I agree plenty enough to believe that good commentators can report to writers pretty accurately where they are in the universe of propositions that make the "cases" that are the world. Can tell writers when a piece is simply not located; when it is located simplistically where several games cross, looking at a stone when all the sky is above; when it slavishly rehearses moves already made many times; when it vauntingly, like a mad transcendentalist, claims to locate itself outside the universe of discourse; when, conversely, it says that the game is a closed immutable system, "life is like that," etc.*

Take your *fictions. In them, you say, you want to achieve a marked deviation from the norm, want to achieve what you call a rigorous amorphousness. What a wonderful oxymoron. Well, I claim that you didn't need to tell me this, that I was able to discern where you had located yourself, and even that I was able to offer you some useful comments—that in one story, having established by imitation Stein's moves of rhythmic repetition, you didn't offer us enough variation of your own; that in another the amorphousness was so extreme and antic that it ceased to be an interesting commentary on its other, form; that in another you had assembled a wonderfully rich mise-en-scène, inviting complex moves, and done very little with it; etc.*

Well, maybe these evaluations (dread word!) were wrong. I still would claim that they were to the point. They were there at the node of the language games where you had chosen to locate yourself. They engaged you where you were, or at least very near where you were, and so could be of use to you as you made your fictive decisions.

So I argue that evaluative commentary in workshops does not have to be destructive (ideological proscriptions masquerading as aesthetic judgments—a very shrewd observation on your part). If commentators join writers where they have chosen to be, join the dance, then commentators can help writers find effective moves.

I look forward to your response. I look back over what I've written and immediately have doubts. Your responses help me go on, point out turns I must make to avoid pits .

AA
aa
hh hh
h
,

As ever,

Gene

August 6, 1991

Dear Gene,

On Location:
The Vacant Room.
Why is anything vacant? (Stein "Rooms")

Speaking as an economist: A portion of vacancy is caused by temporary dislocation. It is a structural vacancy. It is always there, and because of movement there are always vacant rooms. (Also, some structural vacancy is explained by the need to maintain and repair the existing stock.) Structural vacancy is a necessary cost of the reasonably unlimited mobility our society assumes. Or, there is vacancy because there are more rooms than there are people who can afford to inhabit them. This is an economic problem: the number of rooms > the number of potential occupants because the affordability of rooms exceeds effective demand, that is, supply > demand.

Who is not in the Vacant Room?

On Location:

You raise the problem of location, location of writers' texts on the map of charted discourse; the location function the workshop reader plays ideally in pointing to that place that the text is wanting to occupy. This is the ideal evaluation/judgment.

On Location:

We're sitting around a table in the Humanities Lounge. It's an editorial meeting for *The Little Magazine.* We are reading a poem about a black man in a dashiki, he has a grocery bag of posters that say, "White people don't fuck with me," etc. and he is the Jesus Man, we stand him in the corners of our eyes "cruxifixed in cross hairs."

This is a problem of location.

We are all white women. Lori, the poetry editor, likes the poem, wants it in *The Little Magazine*, but I am saying, but do we know this, but do we know: Is this poet a Black Man?

I am saying this is a problem of location.

"Where in this universe of propositions that make the 'cases' that are the world," where on this map of what is said can be said can we place this?

On Location:

A center of activity or concentration.

Act so that there is no use in a center. (Stein "Rooms")

The concept of a centered structure . . . beyond the reach of play.(Derrida)

To begin the placing there is no wagon. (Stein "Rooms")

Where we write is in the spaces we can find to occupy, either those left uninhabited or uninhabitable, outside of presentable discourse. Is this "transcendental madness?" What is madness? A principle of exclusion, says Foucault. What is transcendental? A principle of exclusion: outside (beyond), and inside (here, really).

Judgment undertakes to justify the taboo—you can't say that location, there is no such place.

If it were placed there would not be any doubt. (Stein "Rooms")

How do I know where I am? The text tells me, here you are here. What you see is where. Where I am taking myself to. I am looking for a place to inhabit: "Inhabiting the Yoni."

On Location:

The Chessboard and the Vacant Room

"Every fictive utterance is always at once strategic and tactical."

The game analog (from Saussure) goes like this: The rules of the game (*langue*), like grammar and syntax (let's extend them to include generic forms), are fixed and determined independent of our playing of the game. The game, as played by individual players playing by the rules, has a wide range of possible moves (*parole:* individual enactments of these rules) and they are interactive.

This is a zero-sum game, that is, I win/you lose, or you win/I lose; and I win and you win are two mutually exclusive events. It is assumed that we are each playing to win. What if I am not playing to win? What if I am playing just to play, in which case my goal is not to win but to keep you playing (here I am the writer writing and you the reader reading). I will adhere to the rules of the game just sufficiently to keep you thinking you are playing the game you think you are playing, the one you know the rules to.

But in fact I am playing another game! This!

It is an endless game in which no one ever wins or loses, we just keep moving, making moves (Is this strategic?) through a space that you are looking at and what you see is a map of red and black squares, a grid of determinate locations with counters in or not in each.

I am looking at the Vacant Room.

The walls are white. I have the Queen in my hands and I know I have to move her, move my arm, place her, where. You move a pawn closer to me and this I can see even in the Vacant Room there are other people, people who suggest moves, constrain moves, and, my arm, the way it operates, has its range of movement, this I have in common with all these people that inhabit any sort of room, even chessboards.

So I move my arm and the Queen changes locations. It feels good to move like this. This is the value of exercise I think and I change. I occupy another corner of the room. (Is this strategic?)

If you define a move for me, if you say, what you are doing is moving from one corner to the next diagonally, for instance, then along the North wall to cross diagonally again, this is helpful because perhaps I am concentrating on how I am moving each move rather than where I am (the problem of location) The patterns my movements and where I am arriving may be difficult to discern without a reader of my movements. So what you can say that is helpful is, "I was able to discern where you had located yourself," (yes, I didn't know where I was), "having established by imitation Stein's move of rhythmic repetition" (here, I knew I was repeating for a reason of resemblance), "the amorphousness was so extreme and antic," (I'd become a hyperactive jellyfish), "you had assembled a wonderfully rich mise-en-scène," (dinner, seven courses, linen napkins folded in crystal goblets).

On Location:

You may say this vacant room does not exist, everything is furnished with discourse (Does she furnish a house as well?" Stein "Four Religions") like chairs there are couches, chesterfields, ottomans, Castro convertibles, sectionals (are you still in the market for a couch?) These are locations which you can occupy (here you are with a stable point of view) and you can say this style calls for that, a matching chair or one that formally juxtaposed still coheres.

On Location:

Perhaps my myth of the Vacant Room is just that, a myth, an enabling myth of a space in which I can speak my own locations. An unlocated site, a gap between all the walls that have ever been built (there are so many). Temporally, that is historically, it does not exist; topographically, it is spreading; economically, it is what has no exchange value; socially, it is what evades the principle of exclusion; philosophically, it is the question of: Can one angel illuminate another (Is it one kind of religion if there is any kind of disciplined kneeling)?; sexually, it, the female orgasm, is multiclimactic, it, the location, is never resting; psychologically, it is the post-Freudian, post-Lacanian anti-oral/anal/genital drive to furnish a room as well; institutionally, it has padded walls; epistemologically, but this could be extensively debated, it is: I could agree with this couch you said and I could not agree with this couch and I could agree with this not-couch you said and I could agree with this couch not-you said; academically it is possible, if it can exist at all, it is possible if the workshop does not have padded walls (this could be dangerous!), it could not have walls at all, if there is a great deal of NOISE, NOISE of all types critical, ideological, academic, pots and pans clattering against each other (I could do without the sorority girls down the hall), I mean INTENSE NOISE, discursive noise that is what hears the Vacant Room in between, the space in which I can speak or write at all.

To end: let's have lunch in some quiet restaurant.

Sincerely,

Jan

3 The Body of My Work Is Not Just a Metaphor

Lynn Domina
SUNY at Stony Brook

I'm not much of an athlete, but I do like to swim. I like gathering my courage for the cold shock, then the water opening in welcome. When it is cold enough, it is always too cold until I begin to breathe, and then it is perfectly chilly. Some days I feel graceful right from the start, as if the water renders me invisible; other days grace hovers ahead of me through twenty lengths, or thirty. The water pulls me forward and my body cooperates: up, turn, back; stroke, stroke, breathe, stroke.

I love best the edge of cold along a line that begins at my underarm and stretches crescent-like to my shoulder. Rhythm established, I might think of the properties of that line, remembering words like *arc* and *slope* and *point,* then of dots and dashes, Morse code, of political boundaries cartographers design to resemble code. The cold will remind me of Canada, where I imagine everyone is always in love. This will remind me of novels, especially British novels, wherein few characters swim. Which is fine, as I am not an imagined character, I tell myself. My hand slaps the edge and I count *fifty* and stop. Pulling myself up into mortal air, I take pleasure in the sensation of my arms knowing themselves in their fatigue as arms. They have it right who baptized by immersion and thence recollect no need for absolution.

We, though, who teach writing have need of absolution. I wish I believed that, leaving our writing classes, students felt this cleanly exhausted. I suspect, rather, that by the end of a typical workshop, too many students taste something fetid at the back of their mouths which won't dissolve no matter how many times they spit. This is true in other classes, too, of course, but in writing classes students lack the defense a disengaged-receptor-mode allows. Within the time-lapse nature of my memory, these scenes occur in rapid succession:

—My classmates and I are given an assignment to write a poem which addresses the mythology of our sexuality, though throughout the course the instructor has expressed disdain for any activity which isn't explicitly heterosexual.

—At a post-reading reception, faculty members drink very dry wine, lounge on large pillows before a fireplace, and complain that a student has been admitted to the program solely because she is black.

—In a cafe over cheesecake, a friend vents her frustration after a semester throughout which the male instructor referred to comments from men by beginning "as John said" or "as Michael said" but referred to comments from women with the phrase "as someone said."

—Later, another classmate approaches, and as we sit outside on an uncomfortable porch, she worries that because one of the characters in her story is a lesbian, people will speculate about her own identity.

—A teacher now, I am meeting with a student who discounts her considerable talent and rich perceptions because she is a "non-traditional student," because her first language is not English and she struggles with its syntax.

Whether through malicious or inadvertent means, each student in these situations discovers herself in a situation which erodes the foundation of authentic writing—the necessity of revealing one's own perception of truth. In each case, it is the student's person which has been dismissed and/or censored, and the content of any subsequent writing will be virtually irrelevant, since the student has been judged *a priori* incapable of portraying truth. We apprehend truth, as writers, at least as much with our bodies as with our minds—just as we hope our readers apprehend the truth in our tactile and olfactory and visual images with their bodies—yet the form or hue or movement of our bodies will suffer approbation from a community of writers much more quickly than any movement of our mind—though this approbation will almost inevitably be vehemently disguised as criticism of our work.

This situation is exacerbated in writing classes which focus on craft to the exclusion of discussion of content. Yes, sonnets and sestinas are made of lines made of words, and will be more or less successful in part because of the sound or syntax of the particular phrases, and craft is comparatively easy to discuss. But a more fundamental influence on a student's—or any writer's—success, I think, is permission to address one's personal obsessions.

Writer after writer after writer has suggested that one of the primary tasks of the student writer is to learn trust and acceptance of the self. Asked what he hopes his students receive, Marvin Bell responds, "A sense of themselves and what the possibilities are for them. . . . In maturing they begin to accept what they are and to work with what they are and to build on that" (1). Kelly Cherry says, "You have to learn your own mind. When we learn how our mind works, we begin to work with ourselves" (24). William Stafford confirms this idea: "The essential thing we're doing is we're having enough faith in our perceptions and decisions to make them paramount" (113). Wallace Stegner implicitly acknowledges this proposition when he asserts, "If you aren't a person, if you're only a copy of a person, you aren't going to write very well" (118). One of my personal goals in teaching is to encourage students to discover their passion and to embrace it. Know thyself, in other words, and the metaphors will come. That students should know themselves before they can sing of themselves might seem obvious, borne out by one of the clichés of our instruction: write about what you know about. But contextualizing this remark reveals its hazards. Listen to Adrienne Rich:

> I'd always gotten good reviews on the basis of being a dutiful daughter, doing my craft right, . . .
>
> . . . when I began to write as a woman I suddenly became "bitter," and that *was* the word that was used. . . .
>
> I wrote a lot of poems about death and that was my next book, but I sensed even then that if there's material you're not supposed to explore, it can be the most central material in the world to you but it's going to be trivialized as personal, it's going to be reduced critically, you're going to be told that you're ranting or hysterical or emotional. (191)

If someone whose talent was already confirmed at the time of this critical response can be so affected, imagine the anxiety and tentativeness of our students (or remember your own) who haven't been "certified by W. H. Auden" (193). Although many students will have been "certified" by their high school English teachers or undergraduate professors, the current instructor and current classmates are always the ones who count, just as the current poem or novel is the one which counts. For many students, their earlier education occurred with much more homogeneous classmates than the ones they find themselves among in BA or MFA programs. Many high schools are still not well integrated racially; others are segregated by sex; almost all, I would guess, address a rather narrow band of the economic spectrum. So, in the undergraduate classroom many students confront difference to a much greater extent than they have in the past, which can be very good for writing, but which also can have devastating effects both in execution and reception—to the extent that difference is threatening rather than engaging, to the extent that difference is hierarchialized and hierarchy condoned in the classroom as it is outside the classroom. Our task, then, is to create an environment in which students' distinct perceptions are able to contribute to the infinite lifetimes we long for in reading literature.

Stafford suggests that one condition of a successful writing class is that students be confident of a respectful reception (by which I do not mean uncritical—as literature is not primarily therapy, workshops are not therapy sessions; however, rejecting undue affirmation does not imply embracing negation of a student as a person): "I do it in any way I can keep them from feeling that they have to be on guard about what they write or . . . that there are unallowable things in dignified discourse . . . It's partly by creating an atmosphere of trust in the classroom" (106–107). And of course, this respect must be demonstrated across horizontal as well as vertical relationships—a teacher's respect will be insufficient if a student's classmates express ridicule—but a teacher can certainly model and guide classes toward tolerance, and this is one of the few situations in which I believe a power relationship can justifiably be exploited.

Acknowledging guardedness on the part of his own students, Alan Ziegler articulates the situation of many writing classes:

> Students sometimes hold back in their writing. There may be facts about themselves they are hesitant to expose; or they may be afraid that something they made up will be taken as factual or be analyzed as expressing the way they *really* feel "deep inside." Students may be wary of classmates' reactions—which can include teasing as well as sincere but unwanted understanding—or may worry about what the teacher will think.
>
> There is no getting around the fact that writers reveal *something* whenever they write. Any classroom questioning or analysis regarding what might be revealed can inhibit students, however, and make them overly cautious about what they write. (16)

Yes, writers reveal something, even if that something is fear of revealing something. Although the specific relationship of form and content may be influenced by one's poetics, neither the most elaborately structured nor the most arbitrarily performed piece will be devoid of the content—one of my own classmates once "wrote" a poem simply by pulling typed phrases out of a paper bag, but someone had nevertheless determined the hazardous content of that poem by placing those particular phrases in the bag.

Even if we were to acknowledge the possibility that the content of a given piece of writing could have been entirely imagined, we will nevertheless be betrayed by our choice of one invented plot or character over another. Why did my stomach lurch when a friend told a story about her son's shame, the lurch which signaled a poem, the story which became the poem, rather than on another occasion? Why did the young man in a restaurant with his red hair bushed out to his shoulders and his pitiful dialogue with the waitress trigger a piece of fiction in which a comparable character played only a very minor role? Why, when I was an undergraduate, did my work prompt a classmate to ask, "Why does the phrase 'distant relatives' occur in so many of your poems?" Our obsessions finagle their way onto the page, and good readers notice. Those of us introverts, who never rattle on *out loud* as if words are fools' gold, compound our problem because we know that things become so when we say them. "Let there be light," God had to *say* before there could be light. So the things that we keep silent custody of are never really so, but the things we give over are instantly real.

Yet, the younger a writer is, I suspect, the more overtly confined he or she is by autobiographical material. Although we may continue to write out of obsessions similar to those of our youth, our autobiographical impulse becomes increasingly layered, remaining the root of our stories but seldom their foliage (even if we think we're retaining only a leaf or berry or twig from life). We achieve this transformative capability not only through the process of reaping experiences but of grafting them together, of writing and rewriting, of the miscegenation of memory. Each time we begin a new story or poem, we've invented enough to believe it really is new; student writers often haven't yet exhausted direct experience to the extent that they're forced to invent—and often, ironically, feel guilty if they do invent or embellish. And, I think, what many traditional-age college students—not yet bored with themselves—long to do *is* to write mildly embellished autobiography. Much of the time, this is completely appropriate. Much more dangerous is a student's internal or external pressure to avoid autobiography.

For many of our students, this risk of revelation is exacerbated by their place in society. The dictum to write about what they know about means writing as a person of color in a racist culture, writing as a gay man or lesbian in a homophobic culture, writing as a woman in a sexist culture—and the culture of workshops consists of instructors and classmates who are as likely to be bigoted as anyone else in our reputed melting pot. If a writer's obsessions arise from experiences of exclusion, changing the proper nouns hardly suffices as protection when the excluder is running the workshop. (Granted, some male heterosexual Anglo-Americans also write of exclusion, but then the experience is "universal," i.e., acceptable, as we all know.) And although students who impose self-censorship may write competent, even eloquent sentences, the body of their work will lack the requisite investment and passion of the truly promising writer.

As Joanna Russ states so clearly in *How to Suppress Women's Writing,* suppression occurs in a variety of guises. Recall my earlier anecdote of an instructor who states that one type of experience has more validity—artistic and otherwise—than another. Or compare the level of acceptability of a male character's masturbation with a female character's menstruation. By virtue of the organization of that book, Russ implies that if critical traps don't snare the woman writer with one device, they'll likely succeed with another, but I believe that only those voices which never begin speaking are ultimately silenced. Writers who have realized the freedom that telling the truth entails may relinquish that freedom occasionally and for a time, but never completely or permanently. Researchers as diverse as Paulo Freire, Carol Gilligan, Mary Belenky, and Mike Rose confirm the power of a student's discovered voice. Ideally, these students will exhibit these voices in their writing classes, but even when they are internally or externally prohibited from doing so, they often, I've recently come to believe, establish another avenue.

Although the Black Student Union is a strong presence on the campus of a university where I have recently taught, black students I had in writing or literature courses were never particularly militant in class—and I believe my experience as a teacher on that campus was typical in that respect. However, mid-way through the semester, I attended a play written and produced by members of the Black Student Union. Early into the first act, I realized that as a white person, a member of the dominant racial group, I was not a member of the audience. Now, I feel marginalized all the time by virtue of my other identities, and I've occasionally felt marginalized by sophisticated black speakers who have learned to exploit their own marginalization but who have otherwise been strangers to me. And I've used my own marginalization to exclude others who might have been planning to save that experience for another time—more power than we might often assume resides at the margins of a culture, though this power cannot be actualized in the writing classroom if marginalization also occurs there. But this experience was different for me because I recognized that the power behind the voices in this play was seldom if ever demonstrated in the classroom, for the audience from which I was excluded consisted of a community which to this point does not exist in the classroom. What was crucial about that community was not merely racial identity, but the lack of a threat of punishment for racial identity. At some point, the audience and the actors became the collective speaker, and power resided in that new voice. To whatever degree possible, the writing classroom must become a community with porous boundaries, such that, regardless of the extent to which a student's audience exists outside the class, he or she can be confident that an adequate audience also exists within the class. By adequate audience, I mean individuals who are willing to attempt, if only for a time, a synoptic stance.

Unfortunately, many of the students I've been discussing are also among the students we frequently term "underprepared." Despite having met the prerequisites for our courses, some students lack sufficient basic skills to succeed—which obviously may have ramifications on their ultimate grade, but also can have ramifications on classroom dynamics. When a student turns in work which is fraught with grammatical errors, his or her classmates may express anything from empathic embarrassment to patronizing encouragement to open disdain—but the problem will seldom be ignored. Too often, in my experience, a consequence is reversion to stereotype—"He can't write Standard English because he's Black/Mexican/blue collar. . . ." More skilled, though not always more mature, students then rationalize their dismissal of what can be challenging or compelling content. Difference is again essentially silenced, even if this time it's a side effect of other students' resentment at being forced into the role of copy editor. As teachers in these situations, we have a variety of options, from providing extra tutoring to urging withdrawal from the course, but all of these choices incur the risk of re-silencing that student for a long, long time. What we cannot do, I'd argue, is merely dismiss the student to the writing center, content that such basic instruction lies outside the venue of the creative writing course.

Clearly classrooms today are places of marginalization, but equally clearly, I think, they are not inherently so. In many writing classes, at least some students do form a kind of community, though it may be adversarial to another community which has formed in the same class. Writing about what you know about often implies writing about what other members of the workshop will not know about, which is easily enough dealt with if what you know about is running a dairy farm or swimming competitively or communicating with an Australian via short-wave radio, less easily dealt with if what you know about is prostitution or incest or addiction, and much less easily handled if what you know about is anger at your exclusion from a culture by white people or by wealthy people or by men or by heterosexuals, who are all your classmates and/or your teacher.

Leading toward conclusion, I offer these brief recommendations:

1. That instructors of creative writing recognize content as an issue that will not necessarily take care of itself and that cannot simply be subsumed under discussions of craft.
2. That instructors of creative writing rely on the authority of their position to model tolerance as an appropriate response to the variety of perspectives revealed in student writing.
3. That instructors be prepared to respond intelligently and diplomatically to work which confronts their own prejudices—knowing that if they encourage students to write out of their passion, instructors *will* receive work which confronts their own prejudices.

Crucially, then, if teachers urge their students to write out of their *selves,* those teachers must transform themselves into people who find no other selves unacceptable and their classrooms into places where marginalization does not occur, from which students can emerge into mortal air, breathing and solid in their fatigue.

References

Belenky, Mary Field, et al. *Women's Ways of Knowing: The Development of Self, Voice, and Mind.* New York: Basic Books, 1986.

Bell, Marvin. Interview. Bunge 1–17.

Bellamy, Joe David, ed. *American Poetry Observed: Poets on Their Work.* Urbana: U of Illinois P, 1984.

Bunge, Nancy L. *Finding the Words: Conversations with Writers Who Teach.* Athens, Ohio: Swallow Press-Ohio UP, 1985.

Cherry, Kelly. Interview. Bunge 18–35.

Freire, Paulo. *Pedagogy of the Oppressed.* Trans. Myra Bergman Ramos. New York: The Continuum Publishing Company, 1970.

Gilligan, Carol. *In a Different Voice: Psychological Theory and Women's Development.* Cambridge, MA: Harvard UP, 1982.

Rich, Adrienne. Interview by Elly Bulkin. Bellamy 190–97.

Rose, Mike. *Lives on the Boundary: A Moving Account of the Struggles and Achievements of America's Educational Underclass.* New York: Penguin Books, 1990.

Russ, Joanna. *How to Suppress Women's Writing.* Austin: U of Texas P, 1983.

Stafford, William. Interview. Bunge 106–17.

Stegner, Wallace. Interview. Bunge 118–27.

Ziegler, Alan. *The Writing Workshop, Vol. 1.* New York: Teachers and Writers Collaborative, 1981.

4 Life in the Trenches: Perspectives from Five Writing Programs

Ann Turkle, Florida State University

Julene Bair, University of Iowa

Ruth Anderson Barnett, Grossmont Community College

Todd Pierce, University of California, Irvine

Rex West, Florida State University

What follows is an exchange among five writers who are also students in graduate writing programs and teachers. I posed several points for discussion and each of us responded, then reacted to each other's responses. Our goal was a sort of long-distance, roundtable discussion of the issues which concern those of us who have taken on this triple role: writer, teacher, student.

We began by taking a general view of our struggles to balance the roles, then addressed each role more specifically. Our student experience reflects our current enrollment in or recent graduation from programs at five institutions across the country.

—Ann Turkle

Participants

Ruth Anderson Barnett received her MFA in poetry from the Program for Writers at Warren Wilson College, Swannanoa, North Carolina, in January, 1993. She has taught at Grossmont Community College near San Diego for twenty-one years.

Julene Bair earned an MFA in fiction at the University of Iowa's Writers' Workshop and recently completed her masters in writing (MA/W) from Iowa's Nonfiction Writing Program. She finished her undergraduate degree five years ago, after having been out of school for nearly twenty years. Julene served as a graduate instructor during her tenure as a graduate student.

Todd Pierce is pursuing an MFA in fiction at the University of California at Irvine where he is a teaching assistant. He completed a Master's Degree in English literature and composition at Oregon State University where he was also a teaching assistant.

Rex West is working on his Ph.D. in creative writing (poetry) at Florida State University, where he is a teaching assistant. Like Todd, he earned his Master's Degree at Oregon State University where he was also a teaching assistant.

Ann Turkle just completed her Ph.D. in creative writing at Florida State University. Like Ruth, she was a student in the Warren Wilson program, earning her MFA in fiction there in 1988. She has been an instructor and teaching assistant at Florida State and, before that, worked as an adjunct and regular faculty member in Vermont, off and on, for eighteen years.

How have you balanced the demands of being a writer, a graduate student and a teacher?

Ruth: I'm not sure I always succeed in balancing the different demands. Since Warren Wilson's program is low-residency, I don't have to schedule classes I'm taking around ones I'm teaching. But I do spend at least twenty-five hours a week on my own writing, both poems and critical pieces, in addition to teaching a full schedule. Inevitably, one or two times a semester, I find myself facing a deadline with my supervisor in the MFA program (these come every three weeks), as well as two batches of freshman compositions and a sheaf of essay exams from my literature class. So I go to bed later. I've also cut back on the amount of writing I do on students' papers, focusing on the rhetorical issues and trying to avoid marking every error. I haven't changed textbooks since I began my program. On the face of it, it might look like I've devoted less time and energy to the teaching in order to meet the demands of the program, but I think the program has changed some of the *ways* I teach for the better.

Julene: I balance being a writer, a graduate student, a teacher and of course, a human, which is to say a person with family obligations and a beleaguered social life. I sometimes tell friends that I have several black holes to contend with. Remember that image in *Yellow Submarine* when the Beatles are making their way across the land of holes? I sometimes feel like I'm tiptoeing through just such an obstacle course. Should I allow myself to fall into any of the holes—the raising of my son, teaching, writing—I risk being lost to all the other pursuits. In both of my programs, writing and being a student are the same endeavor, and this I'm always grateful for. For me, returning to school has been a way of earning a half-time salary while spending the other half of my working time writing. Mostly, I work during those eight hours when my son is in school, so I have to be very efficient. I have to be ruthless about keeping the amount of time I devote to teaching within reasonable parameters so that there *is* time to write.

Todd: Malamud once said that nothing, not even his students, came before his writing. I keep telling myself that same thing, that my writing should come first, that I've returned to grad school to hone my craft, but in reality my students come first. For me, it is easier to lose a day's writing time than it is to disappoint my students. Like most TAs, I am a very conscientious instructor and like to be prepared, even overly prepared, for each class.

This year I am lucky. I only teach one class a term; I have only twenty students. I have whole afternoons, even whole days, that are reserved for writing and reading.

Rex: I think *balance* is a good analogy to use: I feel like a circus performer most of the time. After all, writing, teaching, and being a student—all three rings are always booming concurrently. Their saving grace is that they seem to complement each other so well. I can say the same thing to my first-year writing students that I say to myself when editing and revising a poem. And I can recycle this same "talk" again in a literature or theory class I'm taking as a graduate student. By saying "recycle" here I don't mean to imply that teaching, writing, and studenting always amount to the same old thing. In fact, quite the contrary. My point is that these three roles seem so tightly connected that I have to periodically stop and say out loud, "Okay. I'm writing a poem, not teaching one." Or, "Now I'm in a literature class, having discussion, not teaching the class or writing the poem we're talking about." Balance seems inevitable to me, given the inherent dependency of all the roles on each other. Without much effort, I find myself dividing my time and my creative energies equally among the three roles.

Ann: Different demands have risen to the top over the past four years. I was lucky in the second and third years of my assistantship to have half-time administrative duties (each semester I taught one course and served as an assistant to a departmental program for the other half of my responsibilities). Teaching is the thing I'm least able to keep in a box. Each semester I plan how to teach well *and* efficiently, but the demands of teaching well—course preparations, conference time, responding to writing—always seem to exceed the time I've allowed them. I am most acutely aware of this right now because, as an instructor, I am teaching three courses.

My student and writer selves nourish each other pretty well. I have completed my course requirements, but always found the writer/student sides of me working together. I don't know that I *do* achieve a balance. Each aspect—student, teacher, writer—necessarily waits on the other at certain points, like the students outside my office door. It is a relief that I am living on my own and don't have many family demands complicating days that are already a few hours too short.

What conflicts do you experience in trying to achieve the balance mentioned above?

Ruth: Most of the conflicts arise from guilt. I had taught for twenty years before I entered my program, and I was proud of the amount of time and energy I spent on my students. When I began cutting down on that time and energy, I felt I was cheating them. I feel that less now because I haven't witnessed any sudden plummeting of performance in my students' work. I still feel twinges, though, for instance when a student wants to make an appointment with me during a time I've scheduled for my own writing and I insist on another time. I have to stick to my original plan; otherwise, I begin thinking of myself as a teacher who writes in her spare time. This was (and still is) the major conflict. The program asks me to take myself seriously as a writer; if I schedule my writing activities *around* my teaching responsibilities, I can easily begin thinking of the writing as "less important."

Julene: This is my fifth year of teaching, so I've pretty much mastered the balance between teaching and writing. And, for the most part, school hasn't interfered with my learning. I'm being facetious, of course, but sometimes when I contemplate what it would be like to go on for a Ph.D., I realize that there is a danger of this happening. To graduate from the Workshop, I had to answer a couple of exam questions. This was a nightmare for me, because being what I like to think of as a "real" writer, I just can't bring myself to committing inanities to paper. I am invested in everything I write. I'm also in the habit of thinking in terms of publication. I hate writing anything at all that I can't envision being printed somewhere. To respond meaningfully to those exam questions, I had to do a lot of reading and research. This took two months from "my own" writing.

Todd: At one time I think I was a bit compulsive about my writing. I think most young writers are. The only thing I could do, it seemed, was write. As I get older and become more comfortable with my craft, I limit the time I write. I like to finish two pages a day, maybe three. The same with reading; I no longer have to finish three or so books a week. One or two will do. I like to keep up on the literary quarterlies—I still subscribe to about ten—and I like to read new collections and novels by authors I enjoy. But still I keep it at sixty pages a day, only two hours. I'd like to spend less time teaching, less time grading, but I have trouble limiting my class prep time. I like to have new handouts, new ideas, and these things take time. In some ways, I wish I was more like Malamud, I wish I could allow my writing to come first, but I don't think that will ever happen. I want my students to know I'm prepared, to respect me, to know I take their writing seriously, to leave the course substantially better writers. Academic vanity is, of course, time consuming.

Rex: Of course, I made my answer above sound too neat, too tidy. Rather than saying I find myself "dividing" my time equally among the writer/student/teacher roles, I should say I *tear* or *machete* my time between these roles. There just isn't enough time to be a teacher, writer, and student. But all teachers say this; this is not revelation. Somehow we cope.

Ann: You'll notice it was the conflicts that occurred to me most immediately. Perhaps I'm sensitive to issues of time right now because I'm working on a novel. To enter the world I'm creating, I need either to sustain my writing time (two hours, reliably, every day) or to have chunks of time (eight hours, a couple times a week). Either of these spaces is hard to find.

Rex: As one possible solution to the time problem, it occurred to me that English departments might allow TAs to team-teach a few courses. This would be a good way to work with all the recent theory in collaborative learning and collaborative teaching, and I imagine it would cut teaching loads significantly for TAs. I recently worked on an extensive collaborative poem with a fellow TA. It was a fantastic experience to see the creativity of two people unfold into one piece of art. Wouldn't that same kind of vibrancy show up in the classroom if that other poet and I could teach an intro to creative writing course together? Of course (and this would be the problem) the idea would require a financial commitment on the part of university administrators.

We all seemed, Ruth comments, to feel the tension between our teaching and writing selves which Todd cites in his reaction to the Malamud reference. Ruth rejects the equation that teaching well is devoting unlimited time to the task and mentions some of the strategies she's used to be responsive to her students. She says she's mentally quicker on her feet and resists "correcting" student work. She continues.

Ruth: But, it's not just my methods that have changed; it's my attitude toward what teaching is for *me.* Todd said, "I want my students to know I'm prepared, to respect me . . . Academic vanity is time-consuming." I know now that the biggest motivation for my willingness to let teaching virtually consume my time in the early days was my uncertainty about my own worth and my need to have it validated by my students. I can't believe that, in the long run, they benefited much from all my marks on their papers, even though I was always careful to note what was strong as well as what wasn't. All those scrawlings probably intimidated them, gave them too much to try to solve at once. And my "over-preparing" probably reduced my flexibility.

My point is that now my writing gives me validation, and I think finally that's better for the students; I'm more focused on what *they,* individually, need and can profit from, rather than depending on the whole endeavor to corroborate my (desired) image of myself as Super Teacher. I think we can make our writing first in priority and still not sacrifice the amount of *productive* time or the support we give our students.

Ruth goes on to describe some of the plusses of our compounded teacher-student-writer roles.

Being teaching writers gives us incredible flexibility in scheduling our time. And I sometimes think our sense that there's never enough time to do it all has its roots in an unrealistic assumption that "writing time" is just that time when words are getting down on paper. I've learned I do a lot of "writing" away from the computer: thinking about poems on the freeway, while I'm fixing dinner, when I take the dogs out for a walk. When I'm fluent, my mind is almost constantly engaged at some level in mulling over the "stuff" that will become a poem. When I'm not, no amount of free time in front of the computer will yield up a poem.

If you are a teaching assistant, did you receive any specific training in the teaching of writing?

Julene: Yes, our school has what we call PDP, the Professional Development Program. New TAs go to a week of seminars prior to the fall session, then during the first semester we meet weekly to discuss approaches. We were introduced to some theory during this course, but we really didn't have enough time to go deeply into conflicting theories and research. I was fortunate in that I had already taken, as an undergraduate, "Approaches to Teaching Writing" with James Marshall. To my mind, all TAs should be required to take such a course prior to teaching. If this were a common policy throughout colleges, then undergraduates who knew they were bound for graduate school might fit the course into their undergraduate programs.

Todd: At Oregon State University, we had a summer training session, which was followed by a teaching practicum for one quarter and later a course on contemporary composition theory. I believe Chris Anderson and other people at O.S.U. did an excellent job of preparing us to teach, making sure we had enough material for each class. We weren't required to take a theory course until we'd finished a term of teaching. During our first term, we met, once a week, for a practicum where we discussed teaching strategies and lesson plans.

This hands-on, extremely practical approach got me through my first term. It was a term of love and fear. I loved teaching, trying on this new job and altering it to make it my own, and I lived in fear that my students would discover that, at times, I really didn't know what I was doing. That practicum—those here's-some-ideas-you-might-want-to-try-next-week meetings—really gave me the confidence and information I needed.

Rex was also trained at O.S.U. and mentions Chris Anderson's influence.

Rex: Essentially Anderson argued for a naturalness in writing. As a result, I continually find myself pushing students to find their own writing voice—a comfortable voice—rather than learning to appropriate some pedantic, academic persona. Of course, this is all informed by theory. Composition theorists have long debated whether effect defines style (as Richard Lanham says) and a piece of writing must be tailored to the needs and expectations of the writer's audience (David Bartholomae), or whether writers should just plunge in and ignore considerations of audience (Peter Elbow) because style *is* the writer (E. B. White). In my experience, beginning writers are usually uninformed about these issues, so I begin most first-year writing courses by asking a theoretical question: *Who* will write your first essay?" I want students to examine their writing voices and be conscious of the personality they project. Like Lanham, I think "prose style is itself not only an object seen, but a way of seeing itself."

Ann: Because I was an experienced teacher, I didn't have to take the preparatory summer course the department requires of less-experienced TAs. There is an excellent community of teachers here with a willingness to share teaching strategies, and the yearly review of syllabi for proposed courses constitutes a sort of perpetual training. The atmosphere reinforces consistent attention to teaching. It's a hard place to get stale or cynical, and the rhetoric theory group I've participated in is partly responsible for this situation. The theory group isn't limited to rhetoric and composition majors, and our interests are really diverse (creative writing, literature, critical theory, film)—a diversity that's sometimes reflected in passionate, noisy arguments. To be honest, since I've taught writing for several years, I mainly look to composition theory to inform and support my experience. Peter Elbow and Toby Fulwiler have helped me understand how to do what I do more effectively, and their work gives me substance to support my rationale for an essentially expressivist approach. I don't mean to suggest I am inflexible. I read *College English* and other rhetoric journals to stay alive to new possibilities. For instance, I'm providing a lot more opportunities for collaboration in my writing classes. I realize rhetorical theory and issues of pedagogy are not necessarily the same thing, but I suspect that talking theory is a way for some academics to dignify a concern with pedagogy they aren't otherwise comfortable in expressing. And theory and pedagogy must, I think, overlap—so that's great.

This semester I've been mentor to four new TAs. As a result, I've paid attention to my teaching in the most practical way, and I've been reminded of what Todd describes. The immediate challenge of teaching is what goes on during the fifty minutes we have students in the classroom—how we use that time to engage them and express, reinforce, *practice* the scheme (or theory) we have for helping them to be (better) writers.

Has your life as a graduate student in a writing program given you a new perspective on the teaching of writing?

Ruth: I've learned a great deal about how to teach my poetry students by watching faculty in my program. In my own workshops, I've adopted the methods for and spirit of workshop discussion which operate at Warren Wilson. Most important, I think I've learned from my own experience with my supervisors how to help students dig deep for the real impulse in a draft, and how to articulate my intuitions about what succeeds and what doesn't in their drafts. What's surprising to me, though, is the extent to which being in a program in creative writing has changed my perspective on how to teach expository writing. Where I used to put a lot of emphasis on planning and outlines, now I have the composition students keep a journal full of freewriting, brainstorming—looser activities to help them discover what they have to say, especially in the context of examining the needs and expectations of an audience (besides me) they want to say it to. I think that as I've come to feel my own writing matters, I've found it more important to help the students imagine that theirs might too.

Julene: Well, except for a semester stint as a student teacher of Language Arts in a junior high school, the *only* teaching I've done has been as a graduate student. Many of my graduate classes were conducted as workshops. In my own teaching, I combine workshops with more guided instruction. The one major influence has come from workshop teachers who were generous with written comments. Getting extensive, written responses to my work from both teachers and fellow students was so helpful that I try to do the same for my students.

My exposure to theory has also influenced my teaching. Peter Elbow and James Britton are important and, most recently, as I've been preparing myself for the full-time teaching of composition, Toby Fulwiler. Having that diagram of James Britton's, with expressive writing at the center and transactional and poetic writing at opposite ends, crystallized my thinking quite a bit. I realized that there *is* a dichotomy between the types of thinking that go into creative and most school prose, but it rings so compellingly true that both begin at the center, in the personal experiences of the self who's doing the writing.

Peter Elbow, among so much else, gives us permission to just write, to keep the pen moving even if what we're generating seems like garbage. He gives us faith in the process, that among the garbage, we'll discover gems. And Fulwiler's insightful expansion on the writing across the curriculum premise that we write to learn is liberating for students. It's the thing they need to learn most—that writing should be a process full of surprise and leading to deeper understanding, not merely a means of showing teachers what you know.

I give the greatest credence, though, to the theories of literary writers themselves. I listen closely, for instance, when George Orwell tells us "Why I Write." The same goes for Joan Didion in her essay of the same title, and for William Stafford, Virginia Woolf, Scott Russell Sanders, and Patricia Hampl. We would not study literature, or attempt it in the first place, were it not for the wisdom of those who achieve the title. I trust capital "W" Writers most because they've proved their theories in their work.

Todd: My present graduate school experience is focused on a weekly writing workshop. At it we sit around a large table and drink wine and say things like "The biggest problem I had with your story was. . . ." Since most of the graduate students here have had many workshops before, our workshop is not a craft course—we don't listen to lectures about narrative distance or dramatic irony—we mainly just talk about each other's work, usually two or three stories or chapters a week.

I'm learning a lot in graduate school, but it is not really affecting my teaching. Right now teaching and being a student are two separate aspects of my life, for which I'm grateful. If in workshop I get a couple of metaphoric black eyes, I can usually be buoyed in the hope that my teaching is going well. Some weeks, teaching is a small piece of salvation: it can make me believe in myself.

In contrast, when I was a graduate student at Oregon State University, my classes did affect my teaching. I took craft courses and literature courses. I earned a graduate minor in college and university teaching. Those were the years in which I learned how to teach, in which I synthesized classes I took with classes I taught.

Rex: My experience as a creative writing student has given me not only a new perspective but, I think, a better perspective on the teaching of writing. As a student whose goal is to be a creative writer (rather than solely a teacher or scholar), I have naturally appropriated the methods of the creative writing workshop for the expository writing classes I teach. The large-group circle immediately creates a relationship between student and teacher that isn't found in the lecture classroom: it posits that, to quote Richard Hugo, "all writing is creative writing. . . . Discovery remains the ideal." Because I am actively writing and reading—and therefore sensitive to the difficulty and intricacy of literature and composition—I think I communicate well with my students. I try to get my students to see me as an experienced student, rather than a teacher.

I also see the theory and criticism I read influencing the classes I teach. One of the most interesting classes I took this semester was a theory course designed specifically for creative writers. The underlying notion was to bridge the gap between creative writers and critical theorists. So I tried bridging these same gaps in the classes I was teaching. I assigned an essay by Iser to my first-year writers and we talked about a phenomenological approach to reading as a way of responding to each other's essays in small groups. Regarding the notion of authorship, we talked about passages from work by Foucault and Showalter, and I was astonished at the insights these eighteen-year-olds had. Theoretical texts give students good jumping-off points at which to begin looking at their own writing process.

Ann: Absolutely. The most significant single factor is that, having studied for and written my prelim exams (my major area was the novel, my minor, American literature since 1875), I am a more confident teacher. I not only have a body of knowledge and theory at my fingertips, I'm more capable of organizing information and seeing relationships. I've also learned from observing the ways my workshop faculty teach in the workshop setting—how they use even a bad story to make a valuable observation about the way a story can work. I am better at seeing connections and better at using what my students give me by way of interests, questions, and concerns to the advantage of what I am teaching.

I'm very interested in reconciling the critical theory I've embraced with the way I teach. (In some of the literature and theory classes I've taken, there was a gap between theory and practice. Some faculty members present theory like a microscopic specimen on a slide. They'd be startled if it showed some life.) For instance, reader response theory and my own experience as a writer have changed the way I assign and evaluate reading. Rather than using quizzes or exams, I rely on reading journals, a strategy that has improved discussion and, it seems, the thoroughness of my students' reading. I can also, with a more informed rationale, encourage students to learn from all texts whether they are written by students or professionals. And by insisting that students reflect, in writing, on their reading and writing processes, I learn how to fine-tune assignments in each class I teach. Ongoing reflections on process tell me much more about what goes on in class than the most detailed course evaluation could.

My recent experience on the job market suggests one of the things that makes candidates from Ph.D. writing programs attractive to schools is that we are relatively comfortable with issues of pedagogy and critical theory.

Has your teaching given you a new slant on your writing?

Ruth: I'd been teaching for ten years before I ever tried to write a poem. I suppose teaching all those great poets in literature classes gave me something to try to emulate, some sense of voice and sensibility carried by the poem that I might not have noticed otherwise. I think there is one area in which teaching has given me a new slant on my writing. In my poetry writing course, I often find that in trying to articulate what's not working in a student's poem, and why, I realize some aesthetic principle or strategy that applies to a problem I'm struggling with in a poem of my own.

Julene: Oh, of course—always, continually. The marriage between the two is vital. Teaching functions to make you more conscious of your craft. In order to verbalize how to do something, it has to become conscious. I make new discoveries all the time. Probably the most global thing that's inspiring me currently is a deep understanding of the relationship between remembered images and imagination. I've been having my students do a series of assignments early in the term called the "Image Calendar." After we read Joan Didion's "Why I Write," I ask them to recall the "images that shimmer" the way Didion describes. They then "write up" an image from four different periods of their lives. This is all by way of collecting material for essays that they'll write later in the term. After they've collected some images, I then have them read Patricia Hampl's "Memory and Imagination." This essay is a constant source of inspiration to me. After writing a draft about her first piano lesson, she brings her "reflective self" to bear on her "narrative self," in the process discovering many inadvertent "lies" in the draft. These "lies" reveal the workings of imagination. Each time I teach that essay, I apply Hampl's reflective technique to my own writing in order to show students how the process works, and I discover something valuable about whatever piece I happen to be working on at the time.

But it's not just what I choose in advance and bring into the classroom that inspires me. My students are often very gifted. I learn from the way they do things. Good writing is really quite common. It's the opposite of what I expected going into teaching. I kind of look at the vocation the way one Japanese school of Buddhism I remember studying does at enlightenment: the potential is always there, within, but obscured, like the moon behind clouds. As teachers we sometimes get the tremendous gratification of being a beneficial wind—the agent who blows the clouds away.

Todd: I don't have a long answer for this, just the obvious answer. Yes, it has helped me to understand my writing. To teach, I need to be able to explain elements of writing and fiction to my students. I think almost every writer has an instinctual sense of, say, negative capability and narrative irony, but when I need to explain these concepts to students—when I try to find words which will shape and define these ideas—I sharpen my own understanding of their use, which, of course, helps me to write better. Writing and teaching about writing, I think, have a symbiotic relationship. I'm a good writing teacher because I write, and I'm a better writer because I teach writing. Teaching is very much a learning activity, for both students and instructors.

Rex: Yes, definitely. The link between my teaching and my own writing is the revising process. In the classes I teach—from day one—I emphasize the value of revising writing. I chant "Revise! Revise!" all semester long. I like the approach to teaching creative writing that says writing is actually the process of ordering thoughts, a way of understanding something. Each piece of creative writing is like a journey with wrong turns and dead ends, so it's necessary to find the best path to take. As a writer, I benefit from this teaching philosophy because it reminds me—every time I sit down to write—what I need to do. What's at stake here is that revision is actually the act of clarifying what we're saying: being sure we have the right words, with the punctuation in the right places, guaranteeing that my poem best says what I mean it to say. Before I started teaching, I still believed Robert Creeley, that I should *not* revise much—if at all—because I might interfere with the unconscious structure of my writing. After only three weeks in the classroom I had a new philosophy. And, not coincidentally, my own poetry began to improve.

Ann: *Everything,* not just teaching, seems to affect my writing. For instance, I've been reading fiction for two journals I've recently been associated with, and I've realized how essential strong openings are to surviving those first few minutes with an editor—and how much technically good fiction says very little. I now examine my own fiction with a more expert eye. Another significant influence is my reading of fiction but also of criticism and theory. The reading I've done, both to study for prelims and to prepare for the literature courses I've taught, has given me a whole new set of permissions and possibilities when it comes to my writing. I read Bakhtin's *The Dialogic Imagination* with relish as I prepared for prelims. What an affirmation for a novelist! As I worked on my novel, which is set on an Indian reservation, I became interested in the uses and varieties of narrative, the importance of storytelling and oral traditions. I read Robert Coles' *The Call of Stories* and J. Hillis Miller's *The Ethics of Reading.* I discovered Arnold Krupat's *Ethnocriticism* which dovetailed with my interest in Native American writing, narrative forms, Bakhtin, *and* literatures of inclusion and connection. These interests have changed the ways I discuss narrative shapes in teaching both literature and writing. A circle. Gregory Bateson, in *Mind and Nature,* talks about a "pattern which connects," and that pattern becomes increasingly apparent in my reading, writing, and teaching.

I agree strongly with Julene—that there is so much strong writing. It makes me happy I've chosen to be a writer and to groom and coach writers.

Julene: Like everyone else, one of the ways being a teacher helps me as a writer is it encourages me to practice what I preach. Rex talks about being a better reviser. I have an anecdote concerning revision. About a month ago, in delivering my standard "revision is not editing, but re-envisioning" lecture, I told my students that I was about to rewrite an academic essay that I'd written last year, and in doing so, I didn't even intend to look at the original. My students' eyes widened, as I knew they would, for the thought of that much work appalled them, which was exactly the point I wanted to drive home. Writing is work, and if you're willing to do it, you'll most likely get good results. Still, when I left the class, I had to shake my head at myself announcing it to the class. But having made the statement, I was forced, as I often am in my teaching, to evaluate my own advice. In the case of this particular essay, the advice seemed sound, so I took it. The new piece is ten times better than the original, whose main arguments I was able to summarize, from memory, in a couple of pages. The new essay advances knowledge, I like to think, rather than simply repackaging ideas. I find myself doing this type of thing all the time—following my own advice, which I may never have had access to had I not been forced to figure out how to help students make their work better.

Rex: I, too, am reading for journals and writing contests. Like Ann, I can't get over how much all this reading has helped sharpen my critical eye. I see the payoff in conferencing with students. In only a cursory reading I'm able to identify strengths and weaknesses that students can begin working with. I remember the director for my master's thesis, David Robinson, doing this with my work. In a split second after looking at a draft, he could suggest ways for honing and sharpening my writing. I'm beginning to develop this skill.

Does your program perceive or encourage a dichotomy between the teaching of expository and creative writing?

Ruth: Again, because of the sort of program it is, with no formal classes and everything accomplished through individual study, there is no explicit dichotomy between expository and creative writing. When I came into my program, I'd had a good deal of experience with both expository and creative writing; I had a Master's in literature for which I'd had to produce a thesis, and I'd been teaching freshman composition for twenty years. Working closely with my supervisors on my own critical essays, including a ninety-page discussion of voice in Randall Jarrell that was required during my third semester, taught me to loosen the academic style I'd learned in my first trip through graduate school and to approach the project using more of the tools of the creative writer. In this program, I've been encouraged, in fact pushed, to make my critical writing as much a process of discovery as my drafting of poems, as well as to involve and reveal myself more actively in the writing itself. I think most students in the program had a similar experience, so, whether intentionally or not, Warren Wilson seems to operate from the philosophy that the two kinds of writing are not completely different animals. This influence has changed how I teach expository writing in significant ways.

Julene: Not really, thank God. But I know this is rare and probably largely due to the good influence of the Workshop. Writing is perceived here as a creative act, regardless of what form or genre you happen to be working in. Lately, I've been emphasizing the value of insight in my classrooms. I tell my students that the phrase "surprising insight" is redundant. An insight, which I define as a new way of thinking about something, *is* surprising. And insight is what you're after, whether you're writing academically, in business, or attempting literature. To create implies to make something new, something surprising. Any good writing does that. Any good writing is creative.

Todd: U.C.I. separates creative and expository writing. Expository writing here seems to be concerned with analysis and structural ability. At other universities, I know expository writing (freshman composition) also focuses on self-discovery, which I feel is important in the freshman year. Writing to discover, not only your views, but also yourself.

Even here at U.C.I., I think there can be a lot of overlap between the areas of creative and expository writing. In my course, I try to smuggle as much so-called creative writing in as possible. We talk about sentence rhythms, vocal qualities of prose, periodic sentences, the shape of good paragraphs, the power of verbs, the way to use details and imagery. At the sentence level I believe there is a lot of overlap between expository and creative writing, but at the global level—the level where the paper is viewed as a whole—I don't think there is nearly as much. The aim of fiction is, by nature, different than the aim of expository writing.

Rex: It would be hard for me to imagine any dichotomy between creative and expository writing in the program I'm in. As far as my perspective on the similarities between the teaching of expository and creative writing, I feel strongly that the two courses should be taught almost identically. I think reading is a link between expository and creative writing: reading and writing are interdependent acts. William Irmscher has said we should even encourage oral reading in our classes, which I do. Somehow reading helps us develop that intuition we use as writers, what Sondra Perl (among others) calls a "felt sense." As I see it, if someone walks past my classroom and can't tell whether I'm teaching expository or creative writing, that's a good sign.

Ann: I have taught several sections of first-year writing in which I allowed the lines between fiction and nonfiction to blur. I've used a long exercise in autobiographical writing to begin both creative and expository classes, and I encourage my creative writers to do essays and my essay writers to try fiction. I can do this in a department which seems to prize good writing over genre distinctions. At the first-year level, these crossovers are easy. Oddly enough, creative nonfiction becomes a bit of a poor cousin as the course numbers go up. In our department, one is on more solid ground as a poet or fiction writer than as an essayist or memoir writer—though some faculty and students are changing this.

Julene: Todd's and my responses to this question are interestingly opposed. Todd is right, I think, in seeing the aims of traditional expository and fiction prose as entirely different. But who teaches traditional expository writing? Bernice Dicks did an interesting study (*JAC* 3:1–2, 1982) demonstrating that there is no consensus on what such a course should include. What I teach under the rubric is the personal essay, and the aim of this form is closely aligned with fiction. It operates on many of the same aesthetic principles and requires us to read interpretively. Of all the forms, it's probably the most openly involved not in self-discovery so much as self-creation, or self-*re*creation. So, rather than dividing it off from creative writing, you could argue that it is the most fundamentally creative form there is.

I was interested in what Ruth said earlier about how the instruction she's received through Warren Wilson has changed the way she teaches expository writing. Good riddance to outlines. People are thinking more and more, as a result of the work of composition theorists like James Britton and Peter Elbow, that good writing, regardless of the form, is a discovery process. E. M. Forster can't be quoted often enough: "How can I know what I think until I see what I say?" When we're done writing, we usually wind up with ideas that we didn't, in fact, think before. Writing changes us. It creates us even, I think, when we're writing exposition, trying to explain something we think we already know.

What are your most significant rewards right now?

Ruth: Publication, of course. But if I depended on that, I'd feel rewarded about twice a year. Even when something is accepted, it always surprises me how quickly my elation wears off because I'm well into new work, with new challenges and problems to solve and discoveries to make. Beyond the rewards of the writing process itself, I guess it's most rewarding to know that all over the country there are other writers, some of them fellow students but also faculty, who know my work and who support what I'm trying to do in it, people I won't lose touch with when the program awards me a degree.

Ruth also commented on the ways her MFA degree has prepared her for her future as a teacher.

The program has rejuvenated my teaching and my attitude toward it, so that I look forward to the rest of the career, unlike many of my colleagues who have been teaching as long as I but are counting the days until retirement.

Julene: Publication still rings my bell more than anything else. The thing that would make me happiest would be to sell my book to a large publisher, one where I knew it would get promoted and therefore be read. Scholarly publication doesn't pay, but I'm pretty thrilled by that prospect as well. I'm also looking forward to a full-time faculty appointment, so I won't be living at poverty level anymore.

Todd: What are my most significant rewards right now? That's easy. A simple personal satisfaction in seeing my own work improve and understanding that I can, in fact, finish a novel. Even if I never had another story or book published, I would be content knowing that I was able to write fiction that I enjoyed. Sure I'd love to be published—who wouldn't—and I hope to sell my novel and my collection, but I'm pleased with myself because I've pushed myself hard, because I've stumbled through (My God!) four years of graduate school and two graduate degrees, because I'm able to create stories that are my own, and because I believe I will stick with writing for life.

I also find satisfaction in the hope that I will find a college or university teaching position. Teaching, on most days, gives me a lot of satisfaction, knowing I can pass what I've learned on to other students.

Rex: Two things are real payoffs right now: first, publication of my writing. Seeing something of mine in print means a lot to me. Although the odds are against getting published, having my work accepted cements something inside me. Of course writers shouldn't depend on it for their inspiration or self-esteem, but I don't think any writer can deny that an acceptance letter changes the tenor of an otherwise ordinary (or miserable) day. The other reward is having a student thank me for helping him or her become a better writer. I don't mean to pull sentimental strings here, but that occasional "You really showed me something, something I'll remember" makes me stop, exhale, and remember I'm doing something worthwhile. Let's face it, teaching ain't stardom, so these moments are vital.

Ann: At the age of forty-six, it was my writing that brought me back to school. But, like Ruth, I'm surprised at how quickly my pleasure over publication fades. What keeps me writing is the satisfaction I get from the internal conversation that precedes all work, producing the work and occasionally coming close to my own standards, sharing work with friends, undertaking big projects (like the novel) which I complete. I like teaching because of the community it necessarily implies—of young people, faculty—and, at least a few of them are very invested in what they do. Over the years, I've had students who told me my course changed their lives—I like to believe them. It seems plausible because what I've studied, my life as a student, has certainly changed mine.

What other issues about your student/teacher/writer role concern you?

Julene, Ann, and Rex all saw low pay and lack of benefits as a big concern for teaching assistants, complaints we probably share with the teaching assistant universe, past, present and future. Rex associated his lack of earning power with his eagerness to feel a part of the profession.

Rex: I'm not angry because my buddy working at Sears makes twice as much as I do. But I'd like to be able to go to more national writing workshops and conferences. I'd like to join more writing organizations and subscribe to more small press journals. There's also a whole new technology available to writers. On-line INTERNET and BITNET networks give writers global access to libraries, electronic journals, ongoing discussions via E-Mail. But it's expensive to get involved with.

Ann: I like Rex's point that if we are expected to be professionally prepared, such things aren't cheap. Until we're better paid (why am I not holding my breath?), we might try some small collective efforts among graduate students to share subscriptions and technology.

II Theoretical Contexts for Creative Writing

5 Theory, Creative Writing, and the Impertinence of History

R. M. Berry
Florida State University, Tallahassee

One could persuasively argue that in America the most influential theory of literature since World War II has been Creative Writing. John Barth has estimated that by 1984 Creative Writing programs had turned out over 75,000 literary practitioners (Churchman 42), and Liam Rector, former director of Associated Writing Programs, estimated in 1990 that around 3,000 poets and fiction writers were graduating from Creative Writing programs each year.[1] (For comparison, doctoral programs in English average around 800 graduates yearly (Huber 121–2).) Although doctoral programs are the principal locus for the formal study of literary theory, the institutional home of Creative Writing is in the far more numerous colleges and universities not awarding English Ph.D.'s—places where courses in theory are rare. At present, four-fifths of all American undergraduate English programs offer courses in Creative Writing, almost half offer specializations in Creative Writing, and nearly two-thirds of all Creative Writing programs are located in English departments where no doctoral courses are available (Huber 139, 141, 173). Taken together these numbers suggest that, for the vast majority of American liberal arts students, questions like "What makes this text a poem?" are matters, not of the theory, but of Creative Writing. That is, such questions involve issues that students encounter in a locale institutionally isolated—both in its faculty and its students—from the formal study of theories of poetry.

Part of what makes this situation interesting is the likelihood that Creative Writing programs exert a more direct influence than any other part of the American academy on the nonacademic production, distribution, and consumption of literature. Most concretely, this influence makes itself felt on the public audiences for the writers' festivals, summer workshops, and readings sponsored by Creative Writing programs or faculty. Less noticeable but possibly more significant is the presence of Creative Writers on literary awards committees, editorial boards, government funding agencies, small and large presses, book reviews, magazines, and virtually all other organs of contemporary literature. Although in recent years some theory-oriented literature departments have themselves become involved in publishing poetry and fiction, responsibility within those departments for selecting or editing these works has rarely been assumed by the faculty and students most interested in theory.

During this same period, some writing programs—such as that at the University of Iowa—have recruited their faculty from trade publishers, national book reviews, and government arts agencies, thus increasing the influence of the media and government within English departments. In other words, as the academic contact with political and economic power has increased, Creative Writing has been in the thick of things while theory has remained aloof. That this development coincides with an awakened consciousness by literary critics of their political responsibilities seems ironic. Despite a generation of critical theories insisting on the historical situatedness of all literary practice, literary criticism still treats the institution for forming American writers as a world apart.

Creative Writing's Other

That Creative Writing is a theory of literature seems less peculiar when Creative Writing is compared to the literary apprenticeship it replaced. Prior to the nineteenth century the most widespread European model of the poet's education tended to de-emphasize individual creativity and to foreground the deliberate imitation of other poets (Russell 1–16; Greene, McKeon 168–71; Kennedy 116–19; Sullivan, Michael 279–82). According to this pedagogy, the apprentice poet learned to replicate and adapt various models under the supervision of someone who had established his (the gender seems historically appropriate) reputation as a master. So Horace in the *Ars poetica* cited Homer as the one whose meters should be imitated in battle scenes (1. 73), instructed the apprentice poet to thumb continually the pages of the exemplary Greek works (11. 269ff.), and implied that anyone ignorant of the established poetic conventions should not be called a poet (11. 86–87). Contrary to modern expectations, what the Greek or Roman apprentice gleaned from models was not technique only, but plots, themes, scenes, vocabulary, and even the topics of characters' speeches,[2] as though becoming a poet involved both learning a skill and acquiring a repertory of stories or lore. In this regard, literate poets in late antiquity probably remained close to the practice of earlier oral poets whose training involved learning the "epic formula" (conventional image clusters, similes, line endings, rhyme schemes, etc.) as well as the ancient stories themselves. In Book VIII of the *Odyssey* where the bard Demodocus performs a "lay" about the quarrel of Odysseus and Achilles, Odysseus (who is in the audience) endorses the poem as a trustworthy account of his personal past. He weeps to remember his sufferings, praises Demodocus for having recounted the events properly, and proclaims that the bard has spoken like a witness—Demodocus is blind—or like someone who has learned what happened from a witness. Even if we regard this scene as the epic poet's self-authorization, it points to a practice in which praiseworthy performance depends less on creativity and personal experience than on the bard's interpretation of what he has heard others say. Such an understanding of poetic creation probably bears comparison to modern performances of folk or blues music where, despite a tradition of other versions and the audience's familiarity with a song, improvisation and variation are normal features of performance. In such cases, "making it new" is roughly synonymous with learning the music. (Similar remarks could be made about rock and jazz performance where even recorded originals create no obstacle to free elaboration.) The modern tendency to regard familiarity with a model as a hindrance to originality or to equate imitation with lifeless replication may tell us more about modern anxieties—especially in an age of mechanical reproduction, print culture, and information technology—than about any conservatism inherent in repetition itself.[3] For the ancients, at any rate, an opposition between creativity and imitation did not seem to have much force. What did strike them forcefully—the Greek and Latin writers as well as their Renaissance imitators—was the sharp difference between a master's transformation of a model and a novice's copying of one. So Aristotle contrasted the discriminating poet's treatment of ancient myths to the unskillful poet's appropriation of them (*Poetics* 53a12–54a15), Horace recommended adaptations over original subjects but advised *against* word-for-word translation (11. 12–35), Demetrius distinguished Herodotus' flat quotation of poets from Thucydides' skillful integration of the poets' phrases into his own discourse (paragraphs 112–13), and Dante regarded his own imitation of Virgil (and Virgil's imitation of Homer) as signifying, not inferiority, but the restoration of poetry to its rightful greatness.[4]

The best known Renaissance version of this mimetic pedagogy is explicated in *The Courtier,* where imitation, beginning with the learning of principles and correct execution, culminates in the student's attempt to go beyond resemblance and "transform himself into his master

(Castiglione 42)." According to Castiglione's Count Ludovico, the effortlessness ("grace") of mastery can be acquired only through "labor, industry and care," and the student is encouraged not just to copy but to "steal this grace from those who seem to him to have it" (42–43). Artistic incompetence reveals itself in affectation, a condition of hypercorrectness that in Castiglione's version proceeds from too little imitation, not from too much. Genuine mastery, on the other hand, is invisible, i.e., observers cannot distinguish it from a natural facility or gift.

That such a conception of the artist's education contains a paradox is not lost on Castiglione. His text is filled with enigmatic figures and oxymorons suggesting powers of alteration beyond those customarily attributed to schooling: artificiality becomes second nature, imitation makes one spontaneous, diligence leads to artlessness, and so forth. Though exalting unconstrained action, the Count's pedagogy leaves little room for irreducible otherness, for any individuality not transformable into someone else. The only limits The Courtier acknowledges are talent, fortune, diligence, inclination—not personal uniqueness—and its images of dominance are frank and ubiquitous. And, of course, neither access to masters who "possess this grace" nor freedom to change masters is equally the privilege of all classes or both genders. At the same time, the unthinking activity of Castiglione's master closely resembles its diametrical opposite, the Creative Writer who writes from personal experience and imagination. In both cases the novice's self-conscious aping has been replaced by a naturalness apparently instinctive. However, where the difference between the Renaissance and our present institution appears sharpest is in their directly opposite remedies for affectation. Whereas Creative Writing might advise a mannered writer to find a subject, style, or voice truly her own, *The Courtier* advises further and wider-ranging imitation. Given all else in sufficient measure, Castiglione insists, imitation can make any voice, style, or subject the writer's own.

Whether such a pedagogy is more conservative or ultimately more radical, less enlightened or less self-deceived than contemporary ones seems debatable. Whether transforming oneself into one's various masters amounts to overpowering or empowering, being squelched or being liberated, probably requires a clearer notion of what such transformations can hope to achieve (and for whom) and what concrete social obstacles or interests oppose them. The Renaissance frankness about mastery may indicate hegemonic complacency. It may also indicate lucidity about the pain of fundamental change. What seems more certain is that the old pedagogy imagined no unembattled realm within which learning could occur. Education was, from the outset, a venture into occupied territory ("Steal this grace from those . . . who have it"). *The Courtier's* assumption that nothing is inviolably one's own—except one's limitations—seems the vertiginous downside of the idea that anyone can learn to become just about anything. Or as Bakhtin insists, "There are no neutral words. . . . (L)anguage is half someone else's" (*Dialogic Imagination* 293).

For Bakhtin, imitation is the inescapable condition of speaking because language is no abstract form or tool to be picked up and layed back down. Exactly what language is for Bakhtin is an interesting question: sometimes Bakhtin compares it to a geologic force or biological drive; in *Rabelais and His World* language often looks like a riot or orgy; elsewhere Bakhtin calls it "heteroglot opinion" and insists that one's idiom is always another's "ideology" or "world view." An early literary representation of Bakhtin's language is the rambling conversations found in Petronius's first-century prose narrative, the *Satyricon* (Book XV, chs. 37–38)—a kind of speech Erich Auerbach has characterized as "vulgar chatter" (Auerbach 26). The distinctive gesture of such chatter seems to be its readiness to repeat another's words on scant authority ("I don't know myself, I've heard it—but they say . . ."[5]), and its modern instance is surely Sterne's *Tristram Shandy* with all its delight in being led astray. So call Bakhtinian language "rumor" or "gossip," but learning it certainly involves more than communicative competence. It usually involves getting embroiled in a fight—someone else's—over questions one only partially understands, a squabble which predisposes speakers—perhaps through no fault of their own—to certain blindnesses or brutalities or places upon them burdens they never undertook. (What has it meant to learn the language of De Man and Heidegger?) Consequently, the earlier distinction between imitation and copying—Castiglione's distinction between mastery and doing things correctly—becomes, within the horizon of Bakhtin's poetics, the difference between merely repeating another's words and actually becoming answerable for them. As it turns out, this last can be a hard trick to pull off.

One Bakhtinian example of answerability involves the quotation of scholarly authorities (*Dostoevsky* 188f., *Dialogic Imagination* 338–43). In citing an author's words for purposes of confirmation or disagreement, a writer accrues risks as well as—sometimes instead of—power. She may get the quote wrong, misunderstand it, assimilate an alien voice too blithely. Angry partisans can repudiate her claim to these words. Or compare the opposite case: she becomes liable for the failings of the cited author, must defend her own text from accusations directed at another. In both cases, the writer must answer for more than just copying, i.e., quoting. At the same time, this "more" may not be a matter of her own creation. In fact, Bakhtin speaks often of the rebelliousness of one's own utterances, their refusal of one's intentions or their propensity to place themselves into quotation marks against a speaker's will (*Dialogic Imagination* 294). For Castiglione, such inadvertent quotation might signify (mere) correctness, mark the tyro or—in the classical pedagogy—expose the undiscriminating hack, but for Bakhtin it discloses speaking's natural state. The Bakhtinian corrective to an unauthorized quotation, then, would not be the author's own word but the skillfully fabricated account of what another "would say" or "might have said," an account for which answerability can become complex. Who is answerable for an ancient historian's version of what a leader was expected to say on a solemn occasion or for a nineteenth-century realist's construction of a typical or representative idiom? In such cases, composing speeches and listening to them, understanding how to speak and what has been said, making up and making over, become deeply intertwined. For Bakhtin, the risk of refusing to speak in the voice of another is silence.

If such an imitative practice or pedagogy amounts to a theory of literature, then exactly what theory is it? We come closer to answering this question if we treat it as a practical question about poetry's grounds. That is, in the following three questions literary theory and literary pedagogy are not distinct: Upon what does poetry base its work? What bodies of lore or practical knowledge or insight test what poets say? Where ought poetry to turn for its genuine subject matter (as opposed, say, to some spurious subject matter foisted on poets by patriarchy or by media executives or by an academic institution like Creative Writing)? Creative Writing readily acknowledges two grounds of literary practice: the writer's 1) imagination, and 2) experience. The writer's audience might constitute another ground (3), but to the extent that Creative Writing's audience is abstract—"the average reader"—it remains indistinguishable from 1) and 2). To the extent that Creative Writing's audience is concrete, it is either the other students in the writing workshop (whose synecdochic representation of the diversity of real readers seems problematic (see Morton and Zavarzadeh)) or the "literary marketplace" comprised of press editors, arts endowments, and other Creative Writing programs (whose synecdochic representation of the diversity of real readers also seems problematic). As the following will show, Creative Writing established itself in the academy during the 1930's by claiming 4) universal grounds for its practice, e.g., artistic form, the constants of taste, the principles of good writing, poetic technique, humanist values, etc.—but the erosion of such claims after World War II has transformed them today into authorizations of 1) and 2) or of "the literary marketplace."

The old pedagogy assumed grounds sharply different from these. For ancient and Renaissance poets, literary practice was grounded on the encounter with other voices. Learning to write about a subject, character, desire, conflict, pain meant struggling to hear and be heard in a language always already speaking about these things. Such a view of poetry is probably rhetorical in a very old sense of rhetoric,[6] though I would be more inclined to call it hermeneutic. Its fundamental urgency was not to create but to give voice to what persisted in the present as garbled noise, the dead letter, or a stubborn trace. In addition to the literary activities of expressing, representing, or aesthetically forming, this poetic practice sought to open the present to its abolished other, to "deal with the . . . problem of anachronism" (Greene 2) or to acknowledge "the tradition in which (the poet) was bred" (Russell 1).[7] Although inseparable from imagination and experience, it was absolutely incompatible with Creative Writing. Creative Writing's differentiation of itself from literary study appears—to an imitative poetics—as the severing of practice from its ground in the real life of language, the history of saying. The distinctive pedagogical innovation of Creative Writing—viz., the workshop—is a forum oriented exclusively to the present.

Poets as Professionals

According to D. G. Myers, whose dissertation on Creative Writing is the most complete source of information about the institution's past, the origins of Creative Writing are found in the early composition pedagogy (especially as developed in the freshman writing courses at Harvard in the late nineteenth century) and the creative expressionist wing of the progressive education movement. Myers regards Creative Writing as primarily a classroom phenomenon and claims that its pedagogical practices were well known among American educators a decade before their first incorporation into a university degree program in the thirties. To the extent that Creative Writing had roots outside the schools, those roots were found in New England transcendentalism and popular journalism. Stephen Wilbers, in his history of America's first graduate Creative Writing program (the University of Iowa's Writers' Workshop), makes no mention of the new composition pedagogy or progressive education but stresses instead the role of a vigorous midwestern regionalism that focused interest on the work of apprentice writers. According to this view, the Writers' Workshop at Iowa developed out of the (non-academic) literary activity of local communities and the writers' clubs that organized this activity. Whereas Myers sees Creative Writing as part of a nationwide emphasis on individual-based instruction and professionally useful education, Wilbers argues that writing at Iowa arose as a protest against a homogeneous national culture, especially one dominated by the East.

Both Wilbers and Myers agree, however, that the architect of Creative Writing within the academy was Norman Foerster, a former student of Irving Babbitt at Harvard and a proponent (along with Babbitt and Paul Elmer More) of the "New Humanism" (see Grattan). Foerster—who became director of the School of Letters at Iowa in 1930—was an outspoken literary theorist whose several books on American culture and the history of criticism attempted to establish a coherent foundation for an evaluative critical practice. His desideratum was a unified notion of literary study and practice that he called "scholarship." His enemy was "research." As Gerald Graff has explained in *Professing Literature*, during the early decades of the twentieth century a struggle was under way between institutional forces waving the banner of professional expertise—the "researchers"—and other deeply divided forces that during the twenties and thirties would finally make common cause under the banner of "criticism" (Graff 121–44). The researchers spoke often of the admirable rigor of the natural sciences and viewed with embarrassment the prevalence of "impressionism," "dilettantism," "subjectivity" among their colleagues. The high-water mark of their power was probably the 1927 change in the statement of purpose of the MLA constitution. Originally it read: "the advancement of the *study* of the Modern Languages and their literatures." In 1927 it was altered to read: "the advancement of *research* in the Modern Languages and literatures."

Foerster's voice was one among many that deprecated the humanities drift toward science.[8] The critics attacked the researchers on several fronts: research involved the accidentals of literature but ignored "literature itself"; it substituted mechanical method for "living thought"; it prepared students for academic vocations but didn't educate them; it substituted pedantry for learning; and so forth. Many of these arguments were based on "genteel" assumptions that imagined a natural alliance between Christianity, liberal democracy, and Aristotle, and they invariably presupposed a universe the size of white middle-class males. Foerster's arguments were not exceptional, but central to them was a polemic that invited less respectable persons to make common cause with him. Simply said, it was that a necessary part of literary scholarship was the study of its own grounds. A methodology of research without a theory of literature was just runaway technique.

In Foerster's "letters curriculum"—viz., linguistics, literary history, criticism, and Creative Writing—criticism was to be the organizing center. Its centrality arose from Foerster's conviction—shared by many other opponents of research—that criticism disclosed the universal principles of literariness[9] and, therefore, comprised both a distinct object of study and a basis for all other professional activities. One far-reaching consequence of this idea was that it replaced romantic distinctions, e.g., science/imagination, with modernist ones, e.g., theory/practice. That is, Foerster's concept of literary study imagined two interdependent activities within a unified field of knowledge instead of two epistemologically distinct realms or antagonistic psychological faculties. A single individual not only could be a writer and a critic, but she could hardly avoid it. Although the relations of the New Humanists with the New Critics, neo-Aristotelians, and Marxists[10] were not always harmonious, on the idea of a unified criticism and practice there was widespread agreement among the camps, especially among those partisans who, like Robert Penn Warren, Allen Tate, R. P. Blackmur, Yvor Winters, or John Crowe Ransom, were themselves practicing poets. In Foerster's program of letters, criticism was what all "scholars" knew, and writing—articles, poetry, treatises, journalism, histories, fiction, reviews, commentaries—was what all "scholars" did.

Creative Writing, then, entered the academy through this argument for criticism.[11] Precisely because literary criticism made the grounds of professional practice explicit ("a new expertness in the analysis of poetic patterns" ["Esthetic Judgment . . ." 71]), the academy could play a role in present culture—educating and supporting writers—without compromising its integrity or reverting to amateurishness. Criticism would be the institutional guardian of scholarship's integrity. Moreover, because criticism studied the fundamental principles of literariness, non-academic cultural practitioners—poets, publishers, magazine editors, book reviewers, arts agencies, librarians—needed what the academy had to teach. Finally, because criticism abstracted the universal essence (i.e., "those constants . . . in which reside the standards that defy the varying provincialisms of the ages of history" [*American Scholar* 33]) from the accidents of historical change and cultural difference, it made the literary past immediately relevant for present practice. Writers did not have to become pedants to learn from tradition. What Creative Writing offered in exchange for this theoretical grounding was public influence. That is, writers in the academy promised scholars increased contact with economic and political power, a greater role for "humanist values" in decisions made by the media, and a wider range of jobs for graduates of university literature programs. If criticism was the theoretical center of Foerster's curriculum, Creative Writing was its social and practical arm.

In order to put his plan into practice, Foerster had to persuade the research-oriented faculty of the language departments at Iowa that "creative" work could be systematically evaluated, had to explain procedures to an administration disposed to encourage the arts but uncertain just how far, and most difficult of all, had to convince a national professional audience that giving a Ph.D. for "creative theses" was not soft-headed (Wilbers 43–59). He devised a curriculum of literary study in which writing would form a sub-specialty (roughly equivalent to an advanced graduate student's specialization in a period or genre). The exclusive concentration on this sub-specialty would wait until a student's final year(s) after his or her completion of the Ph.D. comprehensive exam. (Foerster opposed the study of Creative Writing at the undergraduate level.)[12] Until that time, all students (including poets and fiction writers) would follow more or less the same general plan of study. This involved courses in criticism, literary history, linguistics, and "Imaginative Writing" (Foerster's now forgotten name for Iowa's writing pedagogy). During the thirties and forties Foerster made this curriculum and its rationale the basis for a number of essays on the subject of literary scholarship, and in 1931 he hosted a national conference on Imaginative Writing at Iowa for the purpose of introducing his pedagogical innovation to a professional audience.

Reading about Foerster's curriculum is a little astonishing today, since it bears so little resemblance to existing Creative Writing programs. Today's writing program is less likely to consider itself a sub-specialty of literary scholarship than to define itself in contrast to literary scholarship. Specialization in writing usually begins with the first year of graduate study or, in an increasing number of colleges and universities, at the undergraduate level. The Creative Writing curriculum is constructed by analogy with the literature curriculum with workshops functioning as the credit equivalents of period courses, and its degrees replicate the familiar liberal arts sequence—B.A., M.A./M.F.A., Ph.D. Creative Writing now has its own professional organization, its own job-list, its own professional newsletters (*AWP Chronicle, Poets and Writers*), and its own network of journals that function within the academy in a manner parallel to scholarly journals (i.e., publication is the professionally sanctioned route to jobs, raises, tenure, promotions). Though virtually all Creative Writing programs require some study of literature, few require—still fewer actually provide—any systematic study of criticism or of the relation of literary theory to literary practice. Criticism within the academy has become its own specialization. Creative writing, on the other hand, takes its direction from imagination and the practical experience of "published writers"—its version of a professional elite. In a series of recent articles Marjorie Perloff, Peter Stitt, Reginald Gibbons, Donald Morton, and Maslud Zavarzadeh have all indicated that the widest division in contemporary literature departments is that between Creative Writing and critical theory and have offered various reasons for this: the premodernist assumptions of Creative Writing and the postmodernist assumptions of theory; two diametrically opposed views of textual production; different power bases within the university bureaucracy, and so forth. But whatever reason is offered, few persons would argue that Creative Writing has become either the unifying force within the academy or the enlightened influence outside it that Foerster envisioned.

There are ironies here, perhaps more than the obvious ones. In order to enter American universities, practicing fiction writers and poets identified themselves with a theory of literature that, once Creative Writing was established, they seem to have abandoned. In 1944 when Foerster left Iowa in protest over administration attempts to dismantle his humanist curriculum, both the present and past directors of the writing program—though expressing personal respect for Foerster—acknowledged that they saw no essential connection between their program and Foerster's curriculum. Creative Writing's historical trajectory since 1930 has not paralleled changes in literary criticism but has followed more closely the steps taken by Americans professions such as law and medicine during the late nineteenth and early twentieth centuries in their attempts to establish and control their vocational practices.[14] That is, within the university, Creative Writing's energy has gone toward establishing its professional autonomy, not its intellectual affinity with humanists or with any other group. The commonplace explanation for Creative Writing's divergence from criticism, i.e., that the interest of writers in the university was from the outset more economic than intellectual[15]—probably obscures what is genuinely odd in this history. If writers recognized that the cultural institutions of the media and government were failing to support them, why did Creative Writing, once in the university, not become a source for critique of these failing institutions? Why did university Creative Writing programs, on the contrary, work to solidify their relations with press editors and literary agents while defining their academic practice more and more in opposition, not only to a particular theory of criticism (i.e., New Humanism), but to criticism as such? Compared with the heteroglot practices and tastes found in literary history and studied in English departments, the media's notion of a predictable mainstream readership must have looked—at least to some writers—artificial and boring. Why, then, did practicing writers not use their new institutional support to free themselves from the media's domination and establish literary practice on other grounds?

The answers to these questions explicate the theory of literature that Creative Writing is. Though not absolutely preventing any critique of the publishing industry, Foerster's rationale for his writing program provided no practical basis for such a critique and probably could not have established Creative Writing if it had. Far better than his scholarly contemporaries, Foerster glimpsed the potential of American literature's mediating position between the academy and the public. Much of his plan's attractiveness was its attempt to make this position explicit. If criticism knew what writers practiced, then publishers, newspaper editors, literary agents, booksellers, librarians, all needed what scholars taught. The blind spot in this vision, however, was how badly it underestimated the conflict between the past (especially as interpreted, attacked, and reshaped on university campuses) and the needs of American corporations for identifiable, marketable commodities. Whether or not this blind spot resulted from Foerster's own blindness seems debatable. It may have been strategic. Had Foerster's theory emphasized the incompatibility of humanist values with mass marketing, his plan to train writers to work for trade publishers might have appeared far more controversial and partisan than the academy would have tolerated (Allen Tate in 1941: "[Matthew] Arnold is still the great critical influence in the universities" [929]). A deeper explanation may be that Foerster's theoretical blind spot was just his humanist vision of history. Foerster was certainly not blind to the dehumanizing effects of consumer capitalism (Foerster once characterized Babbitt as believing "nearly everything (is) wrong with modern civilization" and compared this judgment to "the socialists" ["Esthetic Judgment . . ." 78]), and he tended to denigrate the books currently being published. His lack of emphasis on the conflict between literary tradition and the media probably amounted to a faith that, in an open confrontation with consumerism and mindless productivity, tradition would hold its own. What Foerster himself may have underestimated was not the differences between economic realities and humanist values, but the aggressive resistance of the former.

But however one explains the absence of a practical media critique in Foerster's program, the problems this lacuna presented for Creative Writing were less obvious in 1931 than they would be a few decades later. From the time that Foerster hosted his national Imaginative Writing conference in 1931 until the 1980's, the costs of commercial book production and the attendant financial risks to large trade publishers increased dramatically. In 1931 a press like Scribners could pay for production costs of a book with a sale of about 1,500 copies. By the early sixties the "break even" number for a comparable press had reached only about 3,000. Today the figure for most trade presses is over 6,000 and can be as high as 15,000 copies, usually at a(n inflation-adjusted) cover price considerably higher than the 1931 volume. Even more significant, where Scribners could survive financially on a strong backlist of books that recouped initial investments over a period of several years, trade publishers today survive on fluid capital and changing inventories. A book that cannot recoup its publication costs within two to three years is, in today's market, a loss. The increased mobility of authors has undermined the economic rationale for taking a chance on an unprofitable work in order to publish a later profitable one by the same author. The later work will probably go to another publisher. This same historical period has seen the rise to autonomous power of literary agents, whose advocacy on behalf of authors has greatly increased the discrepancy in the literary world between the haves and have-nots and added to the amount of duplicated activity and middle-level personnel within publishing houses. The number of books published has increased between five- and tenfold, while the processes of agglomeration have meant a simultaneous decrease in the diversity of economic interests publishing them. According to Newman (152), ten American publishers in 1982 could account for approximately 85 percent of all mass market books. Very few of the books from the twenties and thirties still being taught in English departments today sold well enough to survive these post-sixties market pressures. By today's standards, even *The Great Gatsby* would have been a loss.[16] To the white men who dominated both English departments and publishing companies in the thirties and to those students (like Flannery O'Connor) whose professors helped them secure publishing contracts, Foerster's account of the shared interests of universities and publishers probably seemed enlightened. Much of the prestige of a publisher like Scribners derived from just such a non-businesslike depiction of its activities, a depiction that in 1931 was not altogether misleading. But Foerster's harmonious account of universities and the media, which in 1931 involved only a blind spot, after the early sixties required either a myopia more pervasive or a concept of literary tradition sharply different from the New Humanist one. Foerster's intention was never to encourage either of these developments.

On the contrary, his aim—like that of Babbitt and Paul Elmer More—was to increase the power of intellectual leadership within a society he believed badly needed it. That his polemics worked best against his intention, that they convinced the academy of the media's tractability while failing to impress upon the media its need for criticism—humanist or otherwise—may indicate a dividedness within the New Humanism itself.

The nature of this dividedness becomes clearer if Foerster's uncritical treatment of the media is juxtaposed with his account of literary authority. For the New Humanism, authority was closely associated with duration. As Foerster explained it, cultural tradition inscribed certain fundamental human "values"—aesthetic, ethical, philosophical, religious—in the literary monuments of the past, especially from the Greeks through the eighteenth century: "a fairly consistent scale of values in the tradition of humane letters, stretching all the way from Homer to Goethe" ("Study of Letters" 25). The philologist, historian, critic, and poet all depended on these values for the coherence and validity of their practice. This was the thrust of Foerster's case against the researchers. However, the exact relationship of the practicing critic to the practicing poet in this theory remained unclear. At some turns in his writing Foerster emphasized their fundamental equivalence to the extent of classifying works like Arnold's *Culture and Anarchy* as "imaginative literature" ("Study of Letters" 24, note 18). Other times he insisted only that the "constants" of literature were equivalent to criticism (*American Scholar* 33) or that the poet possessed the same knowledge as the critic but in less systematic fashion ("Esthetic Judgment . . .' 83–4). Elsewhere the poet's knowledge was taken to be narrower—i.e., literary aesthetics only—than that of the critic whose expertise included the fundamental values of all culture ("Esthetic Judgment . . ." 714). But the institutional problem of these formulations was that they authorized critics to teach poets better than they authorized poets to teach poets. If the values authorizing poetic practice were located in the monuments of the past, then the teachers of poetry—theory, history, practice—should be those who studied the monuments.

Or, said another way, Foerster's humanism made more sense as a rationale for the authority of poetry than for the professional accreditation of poets. The difficulty seems to have been that, although Foerster had a coherent philosophy of value—aesthetics and ethics—he had no theory of interpretation, no hermeneutics. As a result, his idea of tradition tended to behave erratically when confronting the present. For example, what did literary criticism, in its attempt to "escape from the ideological prejudices and limitations of (its) own time," have to learn from present literary practice? In "The Study of Letters" (a 1941 apologia for his Iowa curriculum) Foerster argued that literary scholars, including critics, could better learn to understand literary works by trying to write them: "Pen, paper, and waste basket are the apparatus of a laboratory second only in importance to the central laboratory of the literary scholar—the library" (26). In this view, the practice of writing poetry, though "second . . . in importance" to reading it, has the relative value of *testing* ("a laboratory") what the poet-critic learns from reading, which is itself conceived both as a test (laboratory) and as a collection of texts (library). But writing has no positive knowledge of its own. What literary practice teaches are the limits of what the practitioner always already knows, not the tenets of an autonomous discipline.

All of which makes unintelligible Foerster's statement in the next paragraph of the same essay that "the standard" for evaluating imaginative work in the academy should be "equivalence to the quality of the books issued by the best *American publishers*" (27). Foerster was not under the mistaken impression that the editors at Random House studied Longinus. He may have believed that the durability of humanist values made unavoidable a continuity between present literary judgment—at least, at its "best"—and the monuments of the past, although one would be hard pressed in that case to explain why he felt so strongly that writers (and editors) needed educating. In an essay in the same volume, Wilbur Schramm (first director of Iowa's writing program and, later, an influential television and mass media theorist) elaborated a view of literary practice grounded not on the study of the past, but on a Cassirer-like symbolic order of language, and perhaps Foerster assumed a similar linguistic theory without appreciating its nonhumanist consequences. But whatever the explanation, Foerster's humanist past simply vanished when confronted with its first critical task. The systematic study of the "constants" of literature not only entered into dialogue with the judgments of media executives; it deferred to them absolutely. Small wonder many Iowa writing students considered Foerster's critical theory of "academic" interest only.[17]

Foerster's volte-face becomes less bewildering the more one senses how little reality the past actually had for the New Humanists. Whether constituted as a body of texts, a scale of values, a philosophy or a critical practice, the great humanist tradition could repudiate the present ("there is nearly everything wrong with modern civilization") or turn into it ("equivalence to . . . the best American publishers") but it had great difficulty sustaining a productive quarrel with existing institutions or conditions. Tradition made contact with present practice only by erasing its own otherness and becoming indistinguishable from the New Humanist project of cultural reform. Faced with a situation in which the past could not sensibly do this—e.g., the accreditation of practicing writers as humanist scholars—literary tradition ceased to count. A coherent case for the relative or contingent validity of publishers' judgments might have been made—especially if the media's interests and economic exigencies had been better understood—but such a case would have meant placing the past and present into relations of answerability and mutual questioning, not into virtual identity. As a result, Foerster's rapprochement of tradition and the media meant that, wherever institutions followed the Iowa model, the study of the past would remain extraneous ("academic") to the study of writing. If judgments of the "best" publishers already replicated the "scale of humane values . . . from Homer to Goethe," then the "constants" of literature must result from familiar human capacities (e.g., imagination, native judgment) or from practical experience, but not from any study of literature and criticism. Tradition amounted to a high-sounding abstraction, and, in Morton and Zavarzadeh's phrase, the "voice" of the Creative Writer turned into "the 'voice' of the entrepreneur" (172–73).

Conclusion

Creative Writing today is the New Humanist theory of literature without the impertinence of history. The institutional divergence of writing programs from literature programs during recent decades reflects the conflict of universalist theories with explicitly historical ones. While Creative Writing attends to what is always present to it, literary criticism contends with writings it inherits. Creative Writing's divergence from Foerster's own theory reflects the New Humanism's conflict with itself, its tendency to erase the past on which its authority and practice were based. Foerster's deference to the media institutionalized these divisions, and, despite its success occupying the gap between English departments and the public, Foerster's innovative program has never become a force for change as he envisioned. Treating the writer's language as unoccupied territory, Creative Writing from the start suppressed its own otherness. As Thomas Greene has argued, a fundamental impulse of Renaissance imitation may have been to confront similar estrangements, ones in which amnesia, anachronism, and linguistic transience threatened to render poetry unrecognizable to itself. An early poet confident of the tradition and community he inhabited may not have felt particularly self-conscious about imitating, but for poets—both in the Renaissance and today—whose relation to tradition is what modernity has rendered problematic, making one's writing answerable to and for some past may be precisely what's needed for that writing to count. This task can seem overwhelming, for it demands nothing less than the full acknowledgment of the nightmare that history threatens to become. To the extent that Creative Writing protects present poets from this nightmare, it obscures obstacles to practice and lulls poetry into continued sleeping. A political task of literary study today, of its theory and practice, its creation and criticism, its teaching and writing, is to wake up.

Notes

1. From the author's telephone interview with Rector, June 4, 1990. The number of graduates cited by Rector is probably much too low, as is Barth's calculation. Writing in *1984,* Churchman already considers 3,000 to be an underestimate.

2. According to Thomas Greene, the Ancient and Renaissance concept of imitation involved far more than just a series of classroom exercises. "*Imitatio* was a literary technique that was also a pedagogic method and a critical battleground; it contained implications for the theory of style, the philosophy of history, and for conceptions of the self" (Greene 2).

3. Dale Sullivan argues that the eclipse of imitative pedagogies is a direct result of widespread (dubious) assumptions within modern culture ("Attitudes Toward Imitation," 15–19). For a positive treatment of repetition by a modern thinker, see Gertrude Stein, 261–280.

4. According to the *Inferno* (Canto I, 11. 82–87) Dante's claim to importance as a poet is based, not on his originality, but on his imitation of Virgil. On Dante's attitude toward imitation, see Greene (especially chapters 2–3).

5. Petronius 58.

6. For an account of the old rhetoric and its relationship to hermeneutics, see Bruns's "Introduction" and "Systems versus Tongues."

7. For a recent instance of the relation of literary practice to its past, see Henderson.

8. For an attack on positivism that closely parallels Foerster's, see Tate, "Literature as Knowledge."

9. In *The American Scholar* Foerster characterized the subject matter of literary criticism as "the 'laws' of literature" which he compared in their exactness and constancy to "the 'laws' of nature" (34). For an aestheticist version of Foerster's faith in universal principles, see J. C. Ransom's comparison of poetic structure to musical structure (which manifests "the structural principles of the world") and the latter to "pure mathematics" (888).

10. For Foerster on Marxist criticism, see his remarks on "General History" in *American Scholar* (21–24) and "the socialists" in "The Esthetic Judg-

ment . . ." (78). For a contemporary Marxist critique of the New Humanists, see Edmund Wilson "Notes on Babbitt and Morel" in Grattan (39–60).

11. For example, see "Study of Letters" 12.

12. A major problem with modern culture for the New Humanists was the tendency toward specialization. For someone like Babbitt, the compartmentalization of knowledge into distinct fields and each field's separation from the discussion of human values (e.g., morality and aesthetics) tended to make science dangerous, disciplines incoherent, and criticism uninformed. This was especially problematic in areas of practice such as technology or the arts where knowing how to do something was often dependent on understanding what was worth doing. In an important sense, the New Humanism was fundamentally hostile to specialization, and Foerster's program was carefully designed to place primary emphasis on general humanist culture over professional specialties.

13. According to Myers, Foerster was reticent to specify a required curriculum for poets and fiction writers at Iowa, and this seems to have been a point of incoherence in his theory from the outset (197–202).

14. James L. W. West has an illuminating discussion of the difficulties of professionalizing writers but does not consider the relation of writers to the academy (7–21).

15. On the university as a patron for writers, see Blackmur (especially 279–88).

16. For the sources of publishing data see, West, Noble, Newman.

17. According to one Iowa student, "in the group meetings of the Workshop, the students read and 'tore apart' each other's writings. . . . Literary criticism *in the academic sense* was left to Norman Foerster's required course in the subject" (Wilbers 65). For Schramm's affectionate but similarly condescending remarks about Foerster's New Humanism, see Wilbers 73–4.

References

Aristotle. *Aristotle's Poetics: A Translation and Commentary for Students of Literature.* Trans. Leon Golden. Commentary by O. B. Hardison, Jr. Tallahassee: University Presses of Florida, 1981.

Auerbach, Erich. *Mimesis: The Representation of Reality in Western Literature.* Trans. Willard R. Trask. Princeton: Princeton UP, 1953.

Bakhtin, M. M. *The Dialogic Imagination: Four Essays.* Ed. Michael Holquist. Trans. Caryl Emerson and Michael Holquist. Austin: U of Texas P, 1981.

———. *Problems of Dostoevsky's Poetics.* Ed. and trans. Caryl Emerson. Minneapolis: U of Minnesota P, 1984.

Blackmur, R. P. "A Featherbed for Critics." *The Expense of Greatness.* Gloucester, MA: Peter Smith, 1958. 277–305.

Bruns, Gerald L. "Introduction: Criticism as Invention." *Inventions: Writing, Textuality, and Understanding in Literary History.* New Haven: Yale UP, 1982. 1–13.

———. "Systems versus Tongues: Or, the New Rhetoric versus the Old." *Inventions: Writing, Textuality, and Understanding in Literary History.* New Haven: Yale UP, 1982. 88–107.

Castiglione, Baldesar. *The Book of the Courtier.* Trans. Charles Singleton. Garden City, NY: Doubleday, 1959.

Churchman, Deborah. "Fertile Time for Creative Writing: More College Courses Every Year." *New York Times: Education Winter Survey* 8 Jan. 1984: XII/42+.

Demetrius. "From On Style." Trans. G. M. A. Grube. *Classical and Medieval Literary Criticism: Translations and Interpretations.* Ed. Alex Preminger et al. New York: Ungar, 1983. 141–54.

Foerster, Norman. *The American Scholar.* Chapel Hill: U of North Carolina P, 1929.

———. "The Esthetic Judgment and the Ethical Judgment." *The Intent of the Critic.* Ed. Donald A. Stauffer. Princeton: Princeton UP, 1941. 63–88.

———. "The Study of Letters." *Literary Scholarship: Its Aims and Methods.* Chapel Hill: U of North Carolina P, 1941. 1–32.

Gibbons, Reginald. "Academic Criticism and Contemporary Literature." *Criticism in the University.* Ed. Gerald Graff and Reginald Gibbons. Evanston: Northwestern UP, 1985. 15–34.

Graff, Gerald. *Professing Literature: An Institutional History.* Chicago: U of Chicago P, 1987.

Grattan, C. Hartley, ed. *The Critique of Humanism: A Symposium* (reprint). Freeport, NY: Books for Libraries Press, 1968.

Greene, Thomas M. *The Light in Troy: Imitation and Discovery in Renaissance Poetry.* New Haven: Yale UP, 1982.

Henderson, Mae Gwendolyn. "Speaking in Tongues: Dialogics, Dialectics, and the Black Woman Writer's Literary Tradition." *Changing Our Own Words: Essays on Criticism, Theory, and Writing by Black Women.* Ed. Cheryl A. Wall. New Brunswick, NJ: Rutgers UP, 1989.

Horace. "Ars Poetica." Trans. Norman Dewitt. *Classical and Medieval Literary Criticism.* Ed. Alex Preminger et al. New York: Ungar, 1983. 158–69.

Huber, Bettina. "Appendix: A Report on the 1986 Survey of English Doctoral Programs in Writing and Literature." *The Future of Doctoral Studies in English.* Ed. Andrea Lunsford, Helene Moglen, James F. Slevin. New York: MLA, 1989. 121–76.

Kennedy, George A. *Classical Rhetoric and Its Christian and Secular Tradition from Ancient to Modern Times.* Chapel Hill: U of North Carolina P, 1980.

McKeon, Richard. "Literary Criticism and the Concept of Imitation in Antiquity." *Critics and Criticism: Ancient and Modern.* Ed. R. S. Crane et al. Chicago: U of Chicago P, 1952.

Michael, Ian. *The Teaching of English: From the Sixteenth Century to 1870.* Cambridge: Cambridge UP, 1987.

Morton, Donald, and Mas'ud Zavarzadeh. "The Cultural Politics of the Fiction Workshop." *Cultural Critique* 11 (1988–89): 155–73.

Myers, D. G. "Educating Writers: The Beginnings of 'Creative Writing' in the American University." Diss. Northwestern U, 1989.

Noble, J. Kendrick, Jr. "Book Publishing." *Who Owns the Media? Concentration of Ownership in the Mass Communications Industry.* Ed. Benjamin M. Compaine. White Plains, NY: Knowledge Industry Publications, 1982. 95–141.

Perloff, Marjorie. " 'Theory' and/in the Creative Writing Classroom." *AWP Newsletter* (November/December 1987): I+.

————. " 'Homeward Ho!' Silicon Valley Pushkin." *American Poetry Review* (November/December 1986): 45+.

Petronius. *Satiricon.* Trans. J. P. Sullivan. New York: Viking Penguin, 1976.

Russell, D. A. "De imitatione." *Creative Imitation and Latin Literature.* Ed. David West and Tony Woodman. Cambridge: Cambridge UP, 1979. 1–16.

Stein, Gertrude. "The Making of Americans (Selected Passages)." *Selected Writings of Gertrude Stein.* Ed. Carl Van Vechten. New York: Vintage, 1972. 259–326.

Stitt, Peter. "Writers, Theorists, and the Department of English." *AWP Newsletter* (September/October 1987): I+.

Sullivan, Dale L. "Attitudes Toward Imitation: Classical Culture and the Modern Temper." *Rhetoric Review* 1 (1989): 5–21.

Tate, Allen. "Literature as Knowledge." *Critical Theory Since Plato.* Ed. Hazard Adams. New York: Harcourt Brace Jovanovich, 1971. 928–41.

West, James L. W., III. *American Authors and the Literary Marketplace since 1900.* Philadelphia: U of Penn P, 1988.

Wilbers, Stephen. *The Iowa Writers' Workshop: Origins, Emergence, and Growth.* Iowa City: U of Iowa P, 1980.

6 Teaching Creative Writing if the Shoe Fits

Katharine Haake
California State University, Northridge

I started out my professional life as a teacher knowing exactly what to do. I was absolutely confident I would be good at it; in fact, I believed, I already was. My-better-than-ever-expected job offer in a tenure-track position teaching creative writing at a large state university proved that. Or did it? For of course the other side of my conviction that I had at last finally succeeded was my continuing suspicion I was about to be discovered as an impostor. How was I to reconcile this all too familiar ambivalence?

In retrospect it interests me that my concerns were almost overwhelmingly egocentric. I certainly wasn't thinking about the vast amount of untried time in the classroom I was facing. Nor do I think I was thinking very clearly about students, having at some point implicitly embraced (though of course I would have strongly denied this) the prevailing attitude that students were, well, bone-headed and, to some extent, an inconvenience and a bother. All those student stories, abominably written, to read. What would happen to my own creative/writing time?[1]

In any event, teaching itself was simple. I had seen that. What could it take, after all, to sit around in a circle and explain to my students how to make their stories better? I knew how to make their stories better. If my own early workshops had been painful and discouraging and my latter ones vaguely disappointing—apexes for the most gifted writers, nadirs for everyone else—I would add a critical framework and vocabulary: I would teach them how to talk about texts.

Basically, what I did was to try to condense into three or four classes the essential principles of narratology as I conceived them to be useful for writers. I introduced concepts of story and discourse, sequential ordering, temporality, focalization, structure itself. I talked about the narratee, narrative strategy, narrative stance. I taught that writing proceeds from language, which is itself a system of signs, governed by rules and conventions, and not a transparent medium through which we reflect on the world. And I quoted Richard Hugo: "If you want to communicate, use the telephone" (5). What I wanted was that my students would somehow come to view their texts as autonomous literary artifacts, separate from their real selves and subject to analysis. What I told them was my goal as a teacher was to "disorient them sufficiently so as to force them into a new space for writing."[2] I thought this sounded pretty good, don't you? So I started out with them, as François Camoin once started out with me: if you want to build a funhouse, a set of working blueprints would prove useful.

Now every time I sit down to begin this essay I don't quite know how. In part, I am worried that having long since abandoned the idea that it is appropriate or useful to tell students how to "make their stories better,"[3] I may inadvertently find myself being prescriptive here. But the problem is also one of writing: which of the various stances and voices available to me—academic, personal, teacherly, writerly, to name a few—do I want to assume? Where can I insert myself into the space formed by the coalescing of these words? How will the decision I eventually make affect your encounter with this text? In what manner do these words come to you? By what authority?

In part because of such questions of modes of existence, circulation, and subject function (I will return to this later), things seem more complicated than I once would have imagined, and I get up, eat some potato chips and ice, do a little wandering, and wonder: do your students struggle to analyze their own textuality? What does it mean if they do?

This is what happened: among the students enrolled in the workshops I was teaching then, which naturally were fiercely demanding (students will rise to your expectations), a small percentage was writing very well, much better than I had been led to expect in my large multicultural suburban institution. The literary magazine was flourishing. Graduates were going off to prestigious MFA programs. Some began to publish. Many became personal friends. And, I must confess, I loved the adoration. Isn't that what writers want? Well, I don't really know about that, but I do know from experience that if you become a successful mentor to your students, they will in fact adore you and they will want, oh they will want, to be like you.

But another small percentage of the students in my classes was floundering, and the vast majority was clearly disinterested in the critical framework I'd provided. Half were in the class because they wanted to "express themselves"; another half were there for easy credit. At first I just tried to ignore them, convinced that since I was the teacher my own goals and objectives for the course were to be preferred to theirs. But after a few years of that, I started thinking about all the college credit that was being awarded—for what? Writing was my life, and had been for fifteen years before I ever had a classroom of my own to stand in front of. Now minds were passing, barely present, through those classrooms, and in time I had to recognize my own complicity in their inertia.

The first graduate degree in creative writing was conferred at the University of Iowa in 1931. Since then, the discipline has flourished, and today it remains one of the healthiest and fastest-growing branches in the whole constellation of English studies. For thirty years, new creative writing programs have continued to develop. Associated Writing Programs, an academic organization founded in the 1960s to coordinate and provide professional services for creative writing programs and their graduates, now lists several hundred members. Degrees conferred by such programs include the MA, the MFA, the DA, and the Ph.D. with a creative dissertation, and number more than a thousand annually. From the beginning, the goal of creative writing programs has been to produce writers who publish. Secondarily, these writers have been expected to make their living as teachers. Inevitably, the initial explosion of graduate creative writing programs has been closely followed by a parallel explosion in undergraduate programs: creative writing teachers need students to teach.

This is clearly not an exponential expansion that can continue unchecked, and currently a public debate has polarized around the resulting profusion of university-trained writers. Advocates on the one side lament the proliferation of competent, useless "McPoems," and, on the other, champion the need for at least a "million poets." However diverting these exchanges may be, they cannot mask the depth of the unease that has, on the whole, affected the discipline. All the evidence—from contemporary critical theory to our own plain common sense—indicates that we cannot continue on as we have been, but many among us would prefer not to face the implications or consequences of such a reality. I would argue that recognizing the necessity for change does not represent the end of creative writing studies, but rather the opportunity to reconceive the traditional goal of such studies—publishing and teaching—as only one of many we can imagine for our students.

Before I can suggest alternative academic goals for creative writers, I must review the pedagogical framework that has provided order and stability throughout the discipline. Since the first classes were developed at Iowa, teaching creative writing in America has largely conformed to the model of a text-centered workshop where apprentice writers come together to craft poetry, prose, and drama and offer it for criticism to peers and the master writer. As it is now conceived in the familiar institutional context of our post-secondary academic system, creative writing has become so closely affiliated with this view of the "workshop" as to seem very nearly indistinguishable from it. While much of the current debate about creative writing teaching centers on the function and value of the workshop, support for its fundamental assumptions remains strong.

We assume, for example, that such workshops will be composed of homogeneous groups of talented students with strong vocational commitments to writing. We agree that the appropriate product of the class will be a publishable literary text in a conventional genre. We assess "publishability" in terms of poorly articulated, but nonetheless prevalent, standards of "good writing." We promote the idea that these standards reflect universal and enduring aesthetic values that exist somehow outside of their cultural construction. We regard publishing in more elevated terms than other forms of writing achievement. We proceed as if writing is somehow a "natural" activity, firmly rooted in talent, which cannot really be taught, but only nurtured. We assure the credibility of writer as "inspired," often tormented, genius, who somehow presents a special case in the academy. Perhaps most troubling to me, we foster false expectations on the part of our students—that the "best" writers will eventually emerge, go on to publish, secure teaching jobs, and so on. These are problematic assumptions at the graduate level. At the undergraduate level, they are much more seriously flawed.

In "Claiming Our Own Authority," I argued against the familiar mentor-model of instruction that dominates the traditional creative writing workshop, citing especially the dissonance that exists between the traditional male "mentor" and his often female students. Since then I have begun to see that the ideology embedded in the very way we conduct ourselves as a discipline is alienating and problematic for male students as well. For we only have to look at the constitution of our classes, where issues of race, class, and gender are increasingly foregrounded, to know that each of the assumptions I've cited above is potentially damaging to students whose experience of life and view of what writing is, as well as what they may desire or expect from it, can differ profoundly from our own.

Perhaps it is time for us now to ask ourselves explicitly what we mean by creative writing teaching. If the workshop is of questionable, or limited, value, what alternative methodologies can we conceive for our pedagogy? What might be appropriate goals for our classes? How might we learn from current composition theory to shift our emphasis away from the product to the process of writing? What might constitute an effective creative writing curriculum at the undergraduate and graduate level? How can creative writing be most productively situated within English studies? What are the ideological assumptions of our enterprise? How can critical, cultural, and composition theories inform and enrich our discipline? Finally, what is it we want our students to learn?

I don't propose to have the answers to these questions—or even all the questions—at this point. However, one thing puzzles me. These have been tumultuous times for English studies in general. Whole new disciplines have emerged simultaneously, often in competition with each other for status and support. Once focused mainly on the study of literature, English departments now include such related but disparate fields as composition and rhetoric, critical theory and textual studies, professional writing, teacher preparation, and so on. Given this marked evolution, and the attendant painful task of self-reassessment, it seems curious that many creative writers have tended to remain atheoretical, even antitheoretical. Largely unaware of our own institutional history and of the ideological implications of our own teaching and writing practices, we continue to nurture romantic myths about ourselves that critical developments around us have long since exposed as false. I believe that if we are to take seriously the questions I've asked above, we must become more informed about the work of our colleagues. A spirit of intradisciplinary curiosity will help us reconstruct our own project in such a way as to respond not only to the needs of all our students, but also to our own.[4] For if, as I believe we must, we reject as our purpose the unexamined, single-minded pursuit of the literary artifact, surely we must then ask how we might begin to re-envision and transform not just our expectations of our students and their work, but those also of ourselves and our own work, at least within the context of our discipline. To the extent that theory helps us explore such possibilities, it belongs in our classrooms, on our own terms and for our own purposes.

But yet we continue to resist it, and to echo Ostrom in the introduction to this volume: are we afraid, what are we afraid of?

Once I believed our suspicion (which is met, incidentally, in equal part by many of our colleagues in theory, who, I'll admit, tend to view living writers as, yes, inconveniences and bothers) was grounded not in fear so much as in misunderstanding. Are we wrong to crave appreciation, love? What is wrong with wanting to be appreciated, loved? Now, less ingenuously, I suspect our mistrust directly proceeds from questions of power—who has it, who doesn't, how and why we try to keep the appropriation and distribution of it throughout the discipline, both at large and in its particular instances, roughly as it is.[5] That it took me more than twenty years of formal education and several in a tenure-track position to begin to ask these questions suggests how closely power is guarded in our institutions.

For a variety of reasons, and to varying degrees, theorists have the power now in our departments, and creative writers, on the whole, tend not to like this. We write the texts. We outnumber them.[6] They should come to us, ask us about us. We're going on right under their noses.

And yet, despite such impeccable logic, theorists persist in refusing to recognize us as being central to their study. In fact, don't they say there's no center at all?

Derrida claims he never said there was no center; he said the center was a function. So we might ask, what is our function? I can't tell: are we miffed, or jealous?

Maybe this debate is beginning to seem worn out or dated. It has been five years, after all, since Peter Stitt and Marjorie Perloff laid out the basic tenets of the anti- and pro-theory camps in what was then called the *AWP Newsletter.*[7] In their exchange, Stitt wonders why we can't just be civilized about literature and writing anymore, and Perloff responds that what Stitt construes as "civilized" is merely an ideological product of the dominant culture. This is, by now, familiar rhetoric.

But in the end both miss a vital point creative writers should find well worth considering. "Theorists," Stitt argues, "are not special people possessed of a special and difficult body of knowledge. They are people who read weird texts while riding on hobby horses of their own devising" (1). And Perloff responds, "Yes . . . and they also *write* weird texts of their own devising" (3). True enough, but one might as well argue that neither are "creative" writers special people, possessed of a special and difficult talent. Stitt says, "Pull [the theorists] down, muss their haberdashery." Why not muss our own worn jeans and Guatemalan t-shirts? By maintaining a sense of irony, humor, and perspective about our own activities, we may gain a new and more playful access not only to theory, but to writing itself.

Having said that, I would caution that play can be as threatening as the other, more "serious" side of theoretical discourse. It is all part of the same will to power, authority, and mastery that drives the most zealous among us. And I don't know. I guess that if forced to choose between one extreme and the other, I might (or might not)[8] find myself siding with those creative writing teachers who, fiercely protective of their students, would guard them against the "infection" of theory. Let them, they argue, just write. But of course it is our stubborn insistence on polemics like this that maintains creative writing as the most under-theorized, and in that respect the most anachronistic, area in the entire constellation of English studies.

The either/or logic of paradoxical thinking impoverishes our discipline if it shuts us off from the complex and ambiguous insights theory affords us. Since those insights profoundly challenge many of the ways we have conducted ourselves in the past, it stands to reason that those who will resist them most strongly are those who have benefited most from the way things are. In fact, I have noticed that as this debate begins to trickle down from the top ranks of our institution a shift is occurring that demarcates itself along gender lines and other lines of marginalization. I suspect that as we learn, tentatively, to articulate ourselves and the effect of our positions on our writing in our own terms, we undermine the very structure of power that has inscribed us as being peripheral. I believe that this is information that belongs in the hands of the least powerful among us, our students (including undergraduates), whose critical life-decisions should be based on something more substantive and "reality"-based than the compelling urge to "express" themselves. Finally, I am convinced that such knowledge can empower students to become better, more creative, more interesting writers, and that this self-awareness alone is what may ultimately sustain their writing.

But here's the apology I wear like a convention badge: I'm no theorist, not, I swear it, by a long shot. What do I know about theory, I say. After all, I'm just a writer, a *creative* writer.

In his "The Writer in the University," Scott Russell Sanders covers much of the most familiar head-in-the-sand territory, arguing against what he perceives as the elevation of either theorist or reader (take your pick) over the author, whose death he continues to lament. According to Sanders, theory turns artists into puppets whose "strings are jerked by some higher power—by ideology or the unconscious, by genetics, by ethnic allegiance, by sexual proclivities, by gender, by language itself" (11). Language, he argues to the contrary, "is not a prison house, . . . [but] the means of our freedom" (13), and, since we can't change race, class, or gender, we should concentrate on "artistic criteria"—the one thing over which we have any control.

Look, I'm not trying to be contrary, or "eat anyone alive,"[9] but language is a tricky thing, and only those who have not experienced its treacheries can be complacent about the freedom it allows us. As Xaviere Gauthier has argued, "As long as women remain silent, they will be outside of the historical process. But if they begin to speak and write *as men do,* they will enter history subdued and alienated; it is a history that, logically speaking, their speech should disrupt" (*NFF,* 162–63).

What?

Here's a little story for you, maybe—to follow Sanders's analogy of narrative as "food, not fodder" (12)—not a full meal, but a handful of tortilla chips, with dip: I did not speak in college. (Shh. Foucault asks, "What does it matter who is speaking?") For four long years I did not speak, though I was a good girl/student. Many of my course evaluations read like the one Page Stegner wrote for me: "Very quiet in class; very talented on the page." (Shh. Does it matter? What does it matter?) I was completely mute. Of course I was shy, and female, and a small-town girl to boot, so naturally I believed my silence was somehow in me. *Moby Dick* had taught me I could never be a writer. Who, or what, had taught me I must not dare to speak? Then, five years after Melville and almost out of college, an odd and, in retrospect, revealing thing happened. I met two young men who did not seem to suffer from the same degree of doubt about their talent or intelligence or right to be a writer, and though it was difficult, I decided that if they could take creative writing classes, maybe I could too, and I did.

Even so, it would be another ten years before I learned to question what had once seemed "natural" about who speaks and writes, and who, in effect, does not. That was in a graduate seminar on feminist theory when the professor, Karen Lawrence, casually mentioned, almost as if in passing, that a person never simply "speaks," that there has to be a context in which that person feels privileged to speak. How had this basic fact escaped me? At the time, I looked back over all those years of struggle to find a voice, any voice, and I wanted to weep. But even with the privilege, Lawrence was going on, you have to beat them at their own game, out-use the terms of their discourse.

"Readers," Sanders assures us, "are not merely playing among signs but are taking in and comparing visions of what it means to be human" (12). If you could cup it in your hands, this being-human thing, and hold it out to your reader, would you assume your reader would recognize your offering? Even at sixteen, reading *Moby Dick,* I had enough sense to recognize the authorized version of this human thing, and to know I wasn't any part of it.

Last April, when Los Angeles was burning, a handful of my students were unable to go home. I thought about them during the several hours that I was stuck in traffic on the affluent west side, trying to get to my own quiet home, from which we would see smoke now for days, but no actual flames. Much of the gridlock was caused by people like me, going home, but some of it was also caused by people taking little "vacations," going north to Santa Barbara, or south to San Diego, anywhere else to wait out the conflict. We studied each other in our bought-new automobiles, and I thought about my students whose communities, where I had never been, were burning down and frightening the rest of us.

I've been told since I was a child that I have a very good imagination, but I'm not laying any claim to knowing what it "means to be human" in such a moment as my students faced that day. What I can recognize are the dynamics of dominance, enforced silence, and sudden eruption, a claim to articulate the self in terms the master cannot begin to fathom. Thus, when Sanders urges us to concentrate on "artistic criteria" as the only aspect of writing over which we have any "control," I would have to ask whose criteria are these? Where did they come from? What version of the "human-thing" do they uphold?

These questions are, of course, similar to those proposed by Michel Foucault's analysis of the complex institutional processes by which, in our culture, an author is constructed, "What is an Author?" Here, Foucault argues that while we are accustomed to conceiving of such a figure as an inspired genius in whom creativity abounds and from whom an "inexhaustible world of significations" flows, the opposite is, in fact, the case. Instead, the author is the ideological product by which our culture "limits, excludes, and chooses, . . . (impeding) the free circulation . . . of fiction, . . . and (marking) the manner in which we fear the proliferation of meaning" (159). Thus, Foucault concludes, it is time to stop asking the familiar questions about who really spoke, with what authenticity and originality, expressing which deep part of the self, and begin to ask instead, as I noted above, about the modes of existence of a discourse, where and how it might be used, and who might use it.[10]

In the context of such logic, one must reassess Sanders's argument that the death of the author is hardly a slogan to please a living one, or that we would prefer not to think of ourselves as puppets. For of course when the "living author" has no free (or any) access to the discourse, it becomes a different matter to see just how the puppet strings work.

And, as I argued in "Claiming Our Own Authority," this is something students have an uncanny instinct for. They know at once this discourse isn't theirs, that it works to silence them, that they are "women" too in this context. Among our colleagues there are still plenty who hold with Stephen Dedalus the burning commitment to "forge within the smithy of [their] soul[s] the uncreated conscience of [our] race." For the rest of us, I don't know, I'm content to let my "race" speak for itself. It's pleasure enough to speak for myself after half a lifetime of self-conscious silence.

Theory helps us recognize the puppet strings. It helps us analyze not *what* texts mean, but *how* they mean, not who we are, but how we are what we believe we are at any given moment, and how, as well, that changes, as it does. This is useful knowledge for writers who, while they're occupied with their analysis, might want to clip a string or two, for play or emphasis, or out of curiosity or the tradition of rebellion. No, I'm not saying it's not possible to be a rebel (or not) anymore, just that it's wise to have some sense of what we're doing when we are.

Even so, I have learned to call theory the master discourse, and am not oblivious to the irony of my affiliation to a discipline that is itself so strictly regulated as to seem, at times, impenetrable. Indeed, I remember my stunned feeling after very nearly failing my Ph.D. prelims in theory because I couldn't get my mouth around its words—post-Derrida, the one remaining privileged object was phallocentric discourse. This was no more ingenuous at the time than it is now, nearly ten years later: who has access to theoretical discourse remains a highly charged issue, with its primary texts as closely guarded as the New Critics once guarded their Great Works of Literature.

You could call theory jargon-laden, or you could call it plain bad writing (which is what people often do when they're fed up), but I think the functional principle that sustains the stylistic eccentricities of theory is, again, one of power. Theoretical texts, more often than not, work to position the reader as submissive to the will of the master theorist/writer. Especially, uninitiated readers are very often frustrated and stymied. Like me, in the reading I did for my prelims (for I never had a class in theory and was so intimidated by the theorists in my department I could not go to them for any help), the uninitiated may feel like knocking their heads against a wall. For six or seven years I felt like that. Then, I don't know, I began to think about the "modes of existence of the discourse" and where there were places in it for possible subjects. From there to rejecting the terms of the master is only a sigh of relief, in the aftermath of which writing can really begin, though not without a new set of problems.[11] Theory students at Irvine, for instance, were abuzz with my effrontery when I playfully/(obtusely) mis/read Foucault in the *AWP Chronicle.* And even my good friends in theory can't stop themselves from asking how I can teach Derrida without teaching Plato and Aristotle first?

One answer, of course, is that I don't. I teach, instead, borrowed (well, all right, stolen—appropriated?) metaphors for writing like "coherence in contradiction expresses the force of a desire" (Derrida 109), like "writing is the destruction of every voice, of every point of origin" (Barthes 168), like "the difference between what we say and what we mean may constitute the only depth in us" (where, oh where, did I read this?), like

> At the moment of speaking, I would like to have perceived a nameless voice, long preceding me, leaving me merely to enmesh myself in it, taking up its cadence, and to lodge myself, when no one was looking, in its interstices, as if it had paused an instant, in suspense, to beckon to me. There would have been no beginnings: instead, speech would proceed from me, while I stood in its path—a slender gap—the point of its possible disappearance. (Foucault, "Discourse" 215)

Another answer would be: what does it matter?

In "Understanding Criticism," Geoffrey Hartman says that the difference "reading makes is, most generally, writing" (19). What difference, we might ask in turn, most generally, does writing make? It is a good but explosive question,[12] for certainly at least some part of the distrust between creative writers and theorists can be located in definitions, perceptions, and constructions of writing. We could be a long time debating, for example, such a question as whether we write the writing, or the writing writes us. But whatever value this discussion may have for us as writers, and I would argue that it is high indeed, as teachers a much more urgent question should be what difference writing makes for our students. Even to teach them to ask can be perceived as a radical move.

When I almost failed my theory prelims, my adviser—himself a creative writer, who had somehow "got me by"—suggested that I discreetly just not present myself on the job market as a person capable of teaching theory. Nonetheless that's exactly what I ended up teaching, since at my school we have a required senior-level theory course for writers, one in poetry and one in narrative, and someone had to teach it.

In a way, it is true, I backed my way in. Theory *had* been important for me in graduate school. It taught me how to conceptualize and talk about my work within the workshop, and consequently authorized certain experimental narrative strategies I was trying out. Without the ability to articulate exactly what interested me in these strategies, the inevitable workshop approbation would have muted, perhaps even effaced them. But as Eugene Garber suggests in his correspondence with Jan Ramjerdi elsewhere in this volume, theory has changed workshops differentially—some have it, others don't. In my own graduate school workshops, those which had it made infinitely better sense to me than those which didn't, and as I began to better understand what I was doing and why, my work became more tenable for me.

I know many writers find theory dry and hard, but this, I swear, was exciting. Not that I ever really felt I *understood* theory the way I was supposed to. But in private it was such a great relief to know I didn't *have* to be an author. It was truly liberating to begin to understand what it might mean that writing proceeds from language, not me. And it was importantly validating to recognize that stories are constructed, convention-driven, and ideologically charged, as indeed we are ourselves.

Our students come to us very much the same way as I came to writing twenty years ago. They have internalized vague notions about what stories are, derived largely from their experience with either non-written narrative texts (what they absorb from the culture) or pre-modern and modern high literary texts (what they are taught in school). They think of writing as an ordeal through which they struggle to find the "right words" to "express" an idea that exists somehow outside language in their heads—what I call "writing backwards." They think writers are people who write, authors are people who publish, and that being the one or the other is simply a matter of accomplishment, talent, and maybe a little bit of luck. They view this whole mesh of effects as both natural and right. Depending on their past experience, they see themselves as either "good" or "bad" writers.

For our part, we do little to persuade them otherwise. We tell them "write three stories," without ever asking "what's a story?" We judge their success or failure by how "good" their work is, without adequately defining what's "good." We proceed as if these are indeed "natural" concepts, without tracing how and why they came into our culture. Very often we assume that our students want to be writers, without distinguishing between writing itself and the life of a writer as we know it to be. We encourage them to publish, without acknowledging the institutional pressures publishing exerts on those who aspire to it.

Lacking this kind of knowledge, our students are as ill-prepared to become professional writers—never mind the whole host of *other* reasons they might choose to write—as we once were. Because we were among the lucky few to figure things out does not mean our students will benefit from the same painful initiation.

Some years ago, at an Associated Writing Programs annual meeting, an exchange occurred between a visiting theorist and a well-intentioned male writer who worried about the tenability of his continued teaching if he were unable to "nurture" his students on the same "great writers" who had nurtured him in his own development as a writer. The exchange made many of us uneasy, for in it we were forced to recognize that between our egalitarian belief in the rights of each of us to speak and our passionate conviction in the meritocracy by which "great" writing is recognized and appropriately valued, there is no easy middle ground. The visiting theorist assured us that Foucault's intentions were profoundly humane and liberating, but of course liberation is only desirable to those who are not free. To the extent that the dominant literary culture in this country is largely white, middle-class, and male, access to that culture will be determined by how one accommodates oneself to the strategies and values of that culture.

Much is currently being made of the opportunities now opening out for a widening range of American voices. These opportunities are the direct result of resistance to the historical distribution of power within our institutions of literary culture. Resistance depends upon analysis, which marginalized groups acquire by experience, and is almost always accompanied by some form of backlash. Often, it has seemed to me that creative writers are more reluctant than our other English-studies colleagues to give up the idea of the author and the meritocracy attendant upon it. This is part of the backlash. As much as we may celebrate the diversity of emerging literary voices, we are suspicious of them. They are not familiar. By what standards can they be judged? How do we know they will endure?

Such questions aside, I suspect that a quick review of the New York publishing lists or the tables of contents of major literary journals will reveal the celebration is as much a liberal construction driven by guilt and politically correct thinking, or by a cynical market determination that multiculturalism "sells," as it is an actual change in the way things are. Except in the most limited sense, publishing venues are not becoming more accessible to marginal writers so much as marginal writers are demonstrating resistance by creating their own publishing venues. Is this diversification or fragmentation, and how is it reflected in our classrooms?

Those of us who came to writing aspiring to express our deepest selves may well desire to maintain the modernist view of the author as inspired artist. And I don't know. Sometimes it seems that we, almost all of us, must start out this way—we are the products of our education and reading. But those of us who have also had difficulty recognizing ourselves as reflected in that education and reading will adapt more readily to the idea that the self we aspire to express is not natural, singular, and constant, but rather constructed, multiple, and fluid. Assume, for a moment, the latter. Assume that the self—one of many—is constructed in the act of writing, moment by moment, by our entry into language, not our mastery over it. Assume as well that the same may be true when we enter the classroom, that instruction—meaning—is achieved there in the play of signification that occurs *between* teacher and students. Between these assumptions and the ones described above as implicit in the workshop lie two pedagogical stances. One might say, then, that the workshop is the teaching model by which we mark the manner in which we fear the proliferation of meaning.

The first few times I taught my theory course I was so intimidated by what I was doing (for how could I not relive my prelims every time I entered the class?) I wrote pages and pages of notes from texts and read assiduously from them. Little by little I got used to the words and ideas I was using. In my own voice they didn't sound so foreign. After awhile I stopped worrying so much about who properly owned these words and what they might have me do with them (interpret literature, for instance, there's still that), and started playing with them instead as a strategy for, yes, (creative) writing. Students were responsive. The catalogue's straight "theory" course became a hybrid theory/writing course as, in it, we began to explore what might happen to our writing when we held it out at different angles and tried thinking about it in new ways.

Even so, I cannot stop myself from apologizing to anyone who "really" teaches theory that, of course, I don't "really" know anything about it. Last spring a newly hired colleague, something of a semiotician I think, narrowed his eyes at me, not quite suspiciously, and said, "Oh, but I think you do." Then, just before walking away, almost as an afterthought, he added, "I can always tell a Haake product." Like many, he is curious about what I "really" do in that class.

Out of the great mass of theory, I routinely introduce Saussure, Barthes, Derrida, Foucault, some feminist theory, and a good bit of structuralism. And here's why: As self-evident as it may seem to us now, it no doubt was not evident once, and students must be taught that language does not point outside itself to something else, but signifies according to (arbitrary) relations of similarity, opposition, and placement. Perhaps Sanders is right, that when we are reading we are "not merely playing among signs" (12), I don't know, but if we continue to behave as if when we are writing meaning is somehow independent of such play, we are not teaching writing but something very different, whatever we may choose to call it. Once students learn how to conceptualize language in more descriptive ways, it makes more sense to them that they must learn to work it as a material itself, and not merely a recalcitrant means of communication.

Thus, it becomes possible to talk about Derrida's logic of "supplementarity," described in "Structure, Sign, and Play," as a logic of writing. Because of the focus on finished product throughout the educational system, writing often seems somehow static to students, as if it exists in an idealized form prior to the actual writing. Like Derrida's concept of the "center," this idealized writing does not exist, and to recognize this absence is to make play possible for student writers. In describing the movement of "supplementarity," Derrida writes: "One cannot determine the center and exhaust totalization because the sign which replaces the center, which supplements it, taking the center's place in its absence—this sign is added, occurs as a surplus, as a *supplement*. The movement of signification adds something, which results in the fact that there is always more . . ." (119). Writing, I teach students in conjunction with this reading, is a process of "burrowing," of learning to pay attention to the "always more," and to respond to its imperative with, inevitably, more writing.

This is, of course, simply one way of talking about—of "supplementing"—what I have always tried to teach about how writing proceeds from language. But in the past, students have often misconstrued the concept as something they like to call "stream of consciousness," just letting the writing "flow." Certainly "flow" is part of it, but as "flow" responds to and is determined by language itself—the always more of it—not to what the writer may be "thinking." Learning to theorize, even in very simple ways, the "supplementary" nature of language and writing gives students a framework within which to break old bad writing habits, and it doesn't take high post-structuralist scholarship to teach them this.

Without attempting to summarize the whole semester, I would just add that Foucault's critique of authorship not only allows students to see a place for themselves in writing they might have never seen before, but also motivates them to ask questions about the distribution of power within and across discourse boundaries. I find feminist theory[13] particularly useful in providing for an ideological critique of language, form, and structure, as well as for challenging students to engage in explicitly experimental modes of writing. The point of such a challenge is not to valorize experimental writing, but rather to encourage students to explore different aspects of language and form than they might "naturally" try on their own. And yes, I still teach what my theorist colleague calls "that old dinosaur, structuralism,"[14] because, more critically than readers, perhaps, writers need a descriptive terminology for their product and activity.

To the extent that theory illuminates in some part what we do, it may also transform our thinking about it, what it is we are doing when we write, and generate, in an important sense, new writing. As an example of how such questions can inform a specific class activity, I might take that "little triangle for the short story." Students know this little triangle, whether or not they have been taught to call it by its standard terminology. They understand the concept of rising action, climax, denouement. They accept it as the way a story is, and struggle, as I once did myself, to write it right. Inevitably, the struggle to master a form precludes important questions about the origins and ideological function of the form. Reading Barthes, we may come to understand that stories *are* this way because they share certain affinities with male sexual pleasure. Making this an explicit part of any classroom discussion about narrative structure gives students options they might not have in the absence of such knowledge. A male student might more passionately embrace the form, and work it more effectively. A female student might more clearly understand her own alienation from it, and begin to explore other formal structures. What might the form of a story based on female sexual pleasure look like? How might an exploration of language guide her to it?[15]

Does this make them better writers? It makes them more aware writers, more self-conscious—more, in some sense, in control of their work. For of course if ideology is powerful largely to the extent that it remains invisible, students can learn to be powerful too, largely to the extent they are taught to "see." In our classrooms, this includes acknowledging, at the very least, that language and literary convention are not ideologically pure but are instead highly encoded systems by which we are constructed and through which we come to know the world. Such an acknowledgement does not mean there is no world to know; it means we are responsible for knowing, and teaching, how we come to know it, and, by extension, how we represent it.

Beyond that, students are on their own, and it seems to me more and more that our real obligation as teachers is to provide them with a critical framework and vocabulary within which to frame their own guiding questions for writing. What, I ask, is *interesting* to you? What will *sustain* your interest over the years? As I look back and consider the many writers I have known who have stopped writing—often women, often discouraged about publishing, often in response to years of public rejection and the personal disinterest of people they love—it seems to me that writing ended for them because they were taught to ask the wrong questions. Clearly our first goal as teachers should be that writing not end for our students. And if we are honest about this, we must also embrace the possibility that student writing concerns may differ vastly from our own. Doing so might well change the way our discipline conducts itself and lead to a true diversity of voices within it. What might the future of creative writing studies look like then?

The final assignment in my theory/writing course has evolved into a project that combines critical and creative discourse in such a way that the two somehow illuminate each other. I encourage collaboration, multi-media experimentation, and play. Last semester, projects included a video tape in which, at the end, student/characters killed off their own author using cardboard signs labeled *gun, author, death;* two narratological board games; origami-bound scrolls inscribed with a personal fragmented narrative on cross-cultural conflict; performance art; a computer program designed to randomly generate narrative; and a pair of white tennis shoes with the following story written on them, accompanied by this set of instructions:

> *This project comes with instructions: You'll notice that there is a story written on the sneakers that are enclosed. Please put the sneakers on before reading them. Wear them for a day. I realize that it is difficult to read something written on a pair of shoes if you are wearing them so I have copied the story on these pages to make everything easier. Please read the following while wearing the sneakers:*
>
> Here you are walking down the street in a pair of new shoes. At first it was exciting to receive the strange package but now you are remembering the Indian proverb about shoes and you wonder what you are in for. They fit OK. Almost perfect. While you are waiting for the light to change you move your toes around inside of your sneakers. They are a little rough around your heels but you know they'll break in given time. The early afternoon air is cold so you pull your coat tight around your body.
>
> You turn into Bobbie's cafe to get some coffee. Bobbie waves "hello" from behind the counter and pours you a cappuccino. You place your hands around your drink and let the heat fill your body through your fingers. On her way back from one of her tables Bobbie notices your shoes. You tell her that one of your students gave them to you as part of a project and you have been

> walking around in them all day. You stay in the cafe out of the cold for about an hour talking to Bobbie. You talk about feminist literature, the riots and Bobbie's new espresso machine. After promising to come by again next week you make your way down the street.
>
> At the corner by the bus stop you see a man who looks like a professor that you had in college. You remember arguing with him about voice and a female language. You try to picture how your teacher would look now after all this time. You decide that this man does not look like your teacher at all and keep walking by. This man, teacher or not, has brought college back to you and you remember a day as cold as this one wandering around taking a break from studying for finals. You remember feeling lost and scared and unsure of yourself. You think about the student who gave you the sneakers and you wonder if she ever feels lost and doubtful.
>
> You decide that you had enough with this project and that you are going home. You had left your husband in charge of the kids and you know you have to get back before they wreck the place. Besides there are all those other projects to grade. You stop at a grocery to pick up some fresh fruit for home. A fat lady near the dairy section is staring at your shoes. For a moment you see yourself as if you were someone else. The thought makes you giggle. You tell yourself that they just don't appreciate participatory literature. Hyperfiction—the wave of the future. You've selected and paid for your items and now you are heading home. One more hill and you are there. You think about the story on your shoes and wonder what it would have been like if someone else had been wearing them.

The student who wrote this was an "average" student. At the end of the paper she added this postscript: "I decided not to write my comments on feminist literature on paper because that is how men write. Instead I chose to write it on the tongues. It seemed appropriate." On one tongue, in red ink, she had written, "Welcome to the Wild Zone. My Wild Zone is my tongue. I will follow you down until you are haunted by the sound of my voice." On the other, "I'm female so I don't have to explain this: Read between the spaces." On the sole of each shoe, in bold black capital letters, was the single word: AUTHOR.

My only other question is: What size shoe do you wear?

Appendix—Directed Writing Exercise

Reading

"Creations." *New French Feminisms: An Anthology.* Eds. Elaine Marks and Isabelle de Courtivron. New York: Schocken Books, 1981. 159–86.

Jones, Ann Rosalind. "Inscribing Femininity: French Theories of the Feminine." *Making a Difference: Feminist Literary Criticism.* Eds. Gayle Green and Coppelia Kahn. New York: Methuen, 1985. 80–112.

For Julia Kristeva, writing is located somewhere within a pre-linguistic erotic energy—what she calls the "semiotic"—that derives from the polymorphous bodily pleasures and rhythm play of the infant-mother communication, a communication that is harshly censored by paternal—or social—discourse. This semiotic can set the "bodily rhythms of poetry against the linear structures of and codified representations of the Symbolic" (Jones 86), and thereby explode them. Maternity, too, challenges this discourse, for maternity breaks down the boundaries between self and other, subject and object, inside and outside, and in so doing resists, or should resist, the symbolic. Thus, for Kristeva, a feminist praxis can only be "negative, at odds with what already exists so that we may say 'that's not it' and 'that's still not it' " (*NFF* 137).

For Luce Irigaray, to speak as a woman is to "reproduce the doubleness, contiguity and fluidity of women's sexual morphology and the multi-centered libidinal energy that arises from them" (Jones 86). As Jane Gallop describes it in *The Daughter's Seduction:*

> The difference (between male and female sexuality) is that desire is metonymical impatience, anticipation pressing ever forward along the line of discourse so as to close signification, whereas feminine sexuality is a "*jouissance* enveloped in its own contiguity." Such *jouissance* would be sparks of pleasure ignited by *contact* at any point, any moment along the line, not waiting for a closure, but enjoying the touching. As a result of such sparks, the impatient economy aimed at finished meaning products (theses, conclusions, definitive statements) might just go up in smoke. (30–31)

Hence, Irigaray's sense of formal and stylistic tendencies in female writing, such as double or multiple voices, broken syntax, repetitive or cumulative rather than linear structures, open endings, etc.

Whereas Helene Cixous is interested in an "erotics of writing" that derives from the female body as a positive source, a plenitude that can lead us out of the inscription of language and into liberatory texts. For her, women's openness to others can be articulated in texts by the breaking down of contradictions through the juxtapositions of such things as "meditation and narrative, literal and fantastic images, past and present, concrete detail and incantatory flow" (Jones 89).

As we have seen from Rhys, Paley, and Bowles, such writing need not be experimental or avant-garde, although certainly it can be. Explore in a piece of "imaginative writing" how such ideas might be expressed in and transformed by your own work. Five pages. Remember the concept of liberatory text—i.e., don't fight this, it's a process, have fun.

Notes

1. In his recent article, "The Writer in the University," published as part of an *AWP Chronicle* symposium on "Tradition and the Institutionalized

Talent," Scott Russell Sanders quotes Donald Hall, Frank O'Connor, Elizabeth Bishop, and Theodore Roethke on the drudgeries of reading student work. From Hall: "The poet may prolong adolescence into retirement by dealing only with the products of infant brains." From Roethke: "Lord, I'm plumb tuckered out lugging these hunks of pork up the lower slopes of Parnassus. . . ." And so on. Sanders himself goes on to find it odd that such writers, in their ". . . prime, should have to earn a living by coaching beginners instead of by writing." (10) For myself, I find it odd that people who deplore the task of teaching should nonetheless call themselves "teachers." I also find odd Sanders's attitude that artists should somehow be exempt from the concerns of daily life we all share, like earning our living, like common labor. I am reminded of a writing teacher who once advised me what it really took to be a writer was that you should sit at your desk four hours a day. Even if you didn't write anything right off, he assured me,you'd soon be bored enough to get to work. Then he added, "And be sure to let your wife know not to disturb you."

2. It would be many years before a composition colleague would suggest that there are, in fact, productive and nonproductive forms of disorientation.

3. My objections to conceiving of the role of a teacher as that of "better-maker" developed over time and in response to my growing realization that what had once seemed so self-evident about "good writing" was becoming increasingly unclear. What was I to do with all those stories that came from students whose lives were not at all like mine, and whose work did not reflect the value I placed on high literary form? For years what I did was try to impose my values on that work. I listened to myself preface comments in workshop with phrases like these: "What this story wants to be . . ." "What it needs . . ." "What if you . . ." Even after I began to recognize these incursions into other peoples' texts/stories/lives as colonizations, I kept it up, not knowing what to replace it with. Over time, I began to realize that what students need to know is not how to "fix" any given story, but how to read, instead, the conventions of the discourse—in general, any discourse, and in particular, a fictional literary narrative text. Where a writer decides to locate herself and her work within the context of these conventions is a decision that should not involve the teacher. I am not saying not to "advise" students; I am saying to respect who they are, and also to trust their decisions. Additionally, reading a discourse is a skill that can be transferred, from story to story, context to context, time to time in a person's life.

4. This is not an activity that should be naively undertaken. As Barthes reminds us in "From Work to Text," "Inter(tra)disciplinary activity is not a peaceful operation: it begins *effectively* when the solidarity of the old disciplines breaks down—a process made more violent, perhaps, by the jolts of fashion—to the benefit of a new object and a new language, neither of which is in the domain of those branches of knowledge that one calmly sought to confront" (73). To the extent that we are willing to *effectively* engage our sister disciplines in English, we must be willing also to find ourselves transformed.

5. As Geoffrey Hartman writes in "Literary Commentary as Literature," "Today our problem is more with the critics of critics: with those that bite or bark at their own kind, not only in their 'rage to get things right' but also in order to idealize creative genius or to separate out, bureaucratically, the functions of the critic and the artist" (211).

6. At my school, undergraduate creative writing students represent nearly half of an English major (750 students) that also includes a literature and a credential option; there are five full-time faculty in creative writing, one in literary theory. Nationally, more than two of schools offer advanced degrees in creative writing; one can only assume that considerably fewer offer them in theory.

7. Shortly thereafter, Associated Writing Programs changed the name of their publication from "Newsletter" to "Chronicle." It is interesting, in this context, to speculate about the role the will to power and authority played in this name change.

8. Is this "waffling"? One way of defining "waffling," of course, is not the inability to choose, but rather the important ability to hold contradictory tenets to be simultaneously true, thereby allowing for complexity and ambiguity.

9. Please see the opening paragraph of Eric Torgersen's "Liberation, Bureaucracy, & Silence," elsewhere in the same *AWP Chronicle* (September 1992). In it, Torgersen describes a 4:00 a.m. conversation with a "good, serious, male poet and critic" in which Torgersen suggests that he write an essay that "would try to say... something like, 'what I really think about feminism.' " Although Torgersen is unable to remember the male poet/critic's exact response, the gist of it was, "You're crazy, they'd eat you alive" (17). I have been thinking about this for some time now. I have been thinking of it in terms of what I have noticed as a growing rift at annual meetings of AWP between women-identified and men-identified participants. I have been thinking about the source of this rift as both fear and loathing, and I am trying very hard to understand it.

10. The questions themselves, as Foucault articulates them, are: "What are the modes of existence of this discourse? Where has it been used, how can it circulate, and who can appropriate it for himself [sic]? What are the places in it where there is room for possible subjects? Who can assume these various subject-functions?" (160). These make excellent classroom questions, and you will be amazed at how clearly students see their implications and importance.

11. Recent research on women suggests that even the most high-achieving among us dread being found out as impostors. This does not mean women are frauds. What it means is that the way the iconography of power works is directly proportional to the ease with which you can project yourself on it. This is a complicated problem, but what I'm trying to suggest is that if you think, as a woman (or a creative writer doing "theory"), you have problems occupying positions of authority, imagine how tricky things get when you begin explicitly to challenge those positions themselves.

12. At least part of the explosiveness of questions like this is directly tied to the problem of ownership. Who'd have thought when I first started out just wanting to "express myself" (for I'm sure I did once, didn't you?) I'd be wondering, all these years later, who owns writing?

13. I especially find French feminism provocative, in part because they so radically revise student views of the world, and I almost always use the "Creations" section from *New French Feminisms.* But in any given term I might also teach Elaine Showalter, Nancy Chodorow, Jane Gallop, Ursula Le Guin, Rachel Blau du Plessis, Toril Moi, Joanna Russ, and so on. The point

in selecting theoretical readings for creative writers is not to cover any particular body of knowledge so much as it is to suggest challenging questions. In this respect, my reading list is always fluid and often reflects the last thing I read that excited me. Because of past training and practice, students may experience this material as difficult, and so it is important to be able to share your enthusiasm with them. I also think it is important not to claim mastery myself, or to promote it as an ideology of reading. Rather, I try to struggle through perplexing passages with my students as a model for a strategy of reading that actively engages textual difficulties. First I want students to think about their writing practices, and then to rethink and rethink them. For writers, theory—feminist, or otherwise—provides a useful tool for such reconceputalization, and is only truly alienating when presented as an end in itself.

14. Some suggestions: Mieke Bal, *Narratology: Introduction to the Theory of Narrative;* Seymour Chatman, *Story and Discourse: Narrative Structure in Fiction and Film;* Gerard Genette, *Narrative Discourse;* Steven Cohan and Linda M. Shires, *Telling Stories: A Theoretical Analysis of Narrative Fiction.*

15. In terms of guiding students to things, I have come to rely heavily on directed writing exercises, especially as a means of encouraging students to try writing, as William Gass says, "against the little grain they've got" (quoted in Moxley, *xv*). The exercises themselves attempt to translate theoretical issue into practical suggestions or instructions for writing. They are designed to be both open-ended and strictly circumscribed, and at least part of their value rests in the individual struggle to "figure them out." For an example of one such exercise, please see Appendix.

References

Bal, Mieke. *Narratology: Introduction to the Theory of Narrative.* Toronto: U of Toronto P, 1985.

Barthes, Roland. "The Death of the Author." *Image, Music, Text.* Trans. Stephen Heath. New York: Hill & Wang, 1977. 142–48.

————. "From Work to Text." *Textual Strategies: Perspectives in Post-Structuralist Criticism.* Ed. Josue V. Harari. Ithaca: Cornell UP, 1979. 73–81.

Chatman, Seymour. *Story and Discourse: Narrative Structure in Fiction and Film.* Ithaca: Cornell UP, 1978.

Cohan, Steven, and Linda M. Shires. *Telling Stories: A Theoretical Analysis of Narrative Fiction.* New York: Routledge, 1988.

Derrida, Jaques. "Structure, Sign & Play in the Discourse of the Human Sciences. *Modern Criticism and Theory: A Reader.* Ed. David Lodge. New York: Longman, 1988. 107–23.

Foucault, Michel. "The Discourse on Language." *The Archaelogy of Knowlege and The Discourse on Language.* Trans. Rupert Swyer. New York, Pantheon Books, 1982. 215–37.

————. "What is an Author?" *Textual Strategies: Perspectives in Post-Structuralist Criticism.* Ed. Josue V. Harrari. Ithaca: Cornell UP, 1979. 49–50.

Gauthier, Xaviere. "Creations." *New French Feminisms: An Anthology.* Ed. Elaine Marks and Isabelle de Courtivron. New York: Schocken Books, 1981. 160–64.

Haake, Katharine. "Claiming Our Own Authority." *AWP Chronicle* 22.2 (October/November 1989): 1–3.

Hartman, Geoffrey. *Criticism in the Wilderness: The Study of Literature Today.* New Haven: Yale UP, 1980.

Hugo, Richard. *The Triggering Town: Lectures and Essays on Poetry and Writing.* New York: Norton, 1979.

Jones, Ann Rosalind. "Inscribing Femininity: French Theories of the Feminine." In *Making a Difference: Feminist Literary Criticism.* Ed. Gayle Greene and Coppelia Kahn. New York: Methuen, 1985. 80–112.

Jorgersen, Barry. "Liberation, Bureaucracy, & Silence." *AWP Chronicle* 25.1 (September 1992): 17–19.

Moxley, Joseph. "Introduction." *Creative Writing in America: Theory and Pedagogy.* Urbana, IL: National Council of Teachers of English, 1989. *xi–xxii.*

Perloff, Marjorie. "Theory and/in the Creative Writing Classroom." *AWP Newsletter* (November/December 1987). 1–4.

Rimmon-Kenan, Shlomith. *Narrative Fiction: Contemporary Poetics.* New York: Methuen, 1983.

Sanders, Scott Russell. "The Writer in the University." *AWP Chronicle* 25.1 (September 1992): 1, 9–13.

Stitt, Peter. "Writers, Theorists, and the Department of English." *AWP Newsletter* (September/October 1987). 1–3.

7 Pedagogy in Penumbra: Teaching, Writing, and Feminism in the Fiction Workshop

Gayle Elliott
University of Wisconsin, Milwaukee

Words are my way of being
human, woman, me.

Ursula K. Le Guin
"The Writer On, And At, Her Work"

Virginia Woolf's Angel in the House has re-embodied within the attics of academe. No longer the idealized version of the genteel Victorian lady, she is, instead, the personification of the creative writer in the academy, gender-coded as "other," critical theory's underprivileged partner on the distaff side of English studies. If one is to follow Woolf's advice and hurl the inkpot—or, to update the image, the computer mouse—at this phantom which still stubbornly haunts university stairwells and halls, it might be best to know where she has come from and how she is figured. Who has summoned her here, and when will she be sent on her way?

In an age in which we've been adjured, prematurely, to mourn the death of the author—preceded to the grave, according to Louis Dudek, by the death of "God, the Father"—art, "enduring and timeless," was "the one thing we could truly depend on" ("The Idea of Art" 50). Dudek describes art as the "vehicle" that "carried and contained" a multitude of former glories: "permanent beauty, the wisdom and curative power of nature, the truth of human feelings, the virtue of distilled religion, the highest truths about our earthly existence" (51). This rarefied ideal of art sounds not a little like the Victorian notion of woman. Woolf rose up and killed her "Angel," although, admittedly, "She died hard" ("Professions for Women" 60). The Angel in the Academy may be equally difficult to dispatch; as Woolf confesses, "It is far harder to kill a phantom than a reality." Woolf contended that killing the Angel in the House is "part of the occupation of a woman writer." Having internalized the patriarchal view of the nurturant, self-sacrificing woman, Woolf was forced to take exceptional measures to free herself from culturally imposed limitations.

Academic creative writers might be well-advised to take Woolf's story of interior conflict as a cautionary tale. "Had I not killed her she would have killed me." Woolf justifies the metaphorical murder as an act of self-defense: "She [the Angel] would have plucked the heart out of my writing" (59). Woolf violently refuses to abide the Angel in her House; poets and fiction writers should refuse with equal fervor to tolerate the Angel in Academe.

To construct woman as essence and creative writing as essentially "feminine"—as opposed to the more "masculine" disciplines of criticism and (empirical) theory—is to perpetuate binary oppositions that serve none of us well. In this essay, I interweave voices which represent a variety of literary and critical perspectives, hoping to define areas of agreement, seeking also to resolve contraries within both feminism and the discipline of English studies. Rather than privileging any single voice, I illustrate the ways in which different viewpoints—engaged in ongoing discussion, collaboration, and critique—complement and enhance one another.

R. G. Collingwood defines art as "expression of emotion" and as "imagination" (*The Principles of Art* 6). While art is, arguably, much more than that, it's interesting to note that these are the very attributes traditionally poised in opposition to rationality and reason. The public/private, masculine/feminine split theorized by feminists (Jaggar, Whitbeck, Grumet) is mirrored within most English departments, where creative writing is positioned lower within the hierarchy than its "opposite," critical theory. "Within the western philosophical tradition, emotions usually have been considered as potentially or actually subversive of knowledge" (Jaggar 129). Poetry and fiction—as creative arts—are thus considered intellectually suspect and, if only because of their subversive nature (Whose knowledge is being subverted, if not that of the patriarchal majority?), their practitioners should certainly be supported by feminist colleagues. As Bell Hooks writes, "[C]oming to voice is an act of resistance" (*Talking Back* 12).

> [T]he view that the masculine and feminine are opposite principles that symbolize other major oppositions, especially an opposition of self and other . . . is central to masculist ontology. (Whitbeck, "A Different Reality: Feminist Ontology" 54)

From a neoclassical perspective, woman is viewed as an incomplete man; if this logic is extended, the creative writer—whose realm of the imaginary is "opposite" that of reason—is merely an incomplete (inadequate) theoretician! In sharing the need to reconceptualize these dualistic configurations, feminists and creative writers meet on common ground. Madeleine Grumet asserts that "Feminine ways of knowing are rooted in relatedness, in attempts to integrate the parts of their experience that the politics of gender, family, school, and science have separated" (*Bitter Milk* 17). In the same way that the fields of creative writing and composition studies occupy certain positions of relationality, so, too, do feminist theorists and creative writers.

Garry and Pearsall note, "Feminist thinkers are challenging the dualism that underlies and pervades much traditional ontological (metaphysical) theory. Feminist philosophers are carefully scrutinizing the dichotomies of self-other, spirit-matter, mind-body, and active-passive, for these dichotomies reflect the fundamental oppositions between dominant-subordinate, and valued-devalued beings" (*Women, Knowledge, and Reality* 48). In her studies "Woman and Nature" and "Pornography and Silence," Susan Griffin draws a correlation between the masculist need to control nature and the desire to dominate women. The chauvinist mind, according to Griffin, has convinced itself that culture is more powerful than nature and will go to great lengths to eschew evidence to the contrary (*Made From This Earth* 148). Yet, ironically, the denial of any power external to his own becomes, in effect, an investment of belief in the same: ultimately, man fears that which he seeks to rule. What might be said, then, of the dominance within English of critical theory?

Perhaps Griffin provides a key: whereas critical thought is abstract, disembodied, writing a poem is "a very concrete art, and very precisely sensual" (243). Social/political ideologies often assume rhetorical forms which attempt to separate and hold themselves aloof from matter entirely, repudiating the body as if it exists as a thing apart from intellect. On the other hand, "Poetry," as Griffin observes, "is musical," and moves directly through the body, "resonating with the physical heart and the metaphorical heart at once" (243). Woman, then—and the masculist projection of the "feminine"—is representative of the life and rhythms of the body, of feeling (both sensual and emotional), of love, of Eros, and, concomitantly, of loss of control. To know woman completely (the Biblical euphemism for sex)—to complete the sexual act, to achieve orgasm—man must relinquish control. Griffin sees a correlation with poetry: "the use of poetry can only be had by surrender" (243).

Poetry, Griffin believes, speaks not only in the familiar, well-modulated voice of the conscious mind, but in the language of the unconscious as well: "The fear of poetry is the fear of sexual knowledge is the fear of the knowledge of the body, of darkness" (244). Perhaps poetry reminds the critic that, in spite of his elegantly contrived cultural/literary theories, even he faces still unanswered questions and the ultimate indignity of confronting his own (untheorizable) death. To protect itself from the knowledge of its own eventual demise, the divided mind suppresses whatever it most fears.

> This is a world view in which the self is irrevocably split so that it does not recognize its other half, and in which all phenomena, experience, and human qualities are also split into the superior and inferior, the righteous and the evil, the above and the below. (163)

On this point feminists find support from what may seem an unlikely source, for Berkeley physicist Fritjof Capra also addresses the dilemma of the divided self, referring to it as the "crisis in perception" which pervades Western thought. Capra maintains that such bifurcatory models have now become outmoded. While critical theory purports to adhere to "scientific" research methodologies and habits of analysis, the scientific community itself has moved beyond the mechanistic Cartesian paradigm which has for so long informed scientific thought. Modern physics no longer conceives of the universe as a huge machine consisting of separately functioning parts; this paradigm has given over, instead, to a view of a living universe in continual evolution, a single, organic whole "whose parts are essentially interrelated and can be understood only as patterns of a cosmic process" (78). This fundamental conceptual change, as Capra points out, must eventually be accompanied by a philosophical change as well.

Significant shifts in scientific constructs of the universe have, historically, transformed the cultures which have conceived them. Capra's systems view—which focuses upon the interrelatedness of living systems—foresees a far-reaching change in thinking that can occur if we consider ourselves not in competition with, but interdependent to, other living things. Writes Carolyn Merchant, science historian at the University of California, Berkeley:

> [W]e must re-examine the formation of a world-view and a science which, by reconceptualizing reality as a machine rather than a living organism, sanctioned the domination of both nature and women. (41)

Capra agrees: "Exploitation of nature has gone hand in hand with that of women. . . ." (40).

Capra addresses this (nature/woman as "other") and other culturally imposed divisions by questioning our very concept of duality, stating emphatically that nowhere in the universe do opposite poles remain statically apart, for always there is a dynamic exchange of energy between the one and the other. He draws upon Taoist philosophy—which preceded twentieth-century physics by several centuries—to make his point: "Ancient Chinese philosophers believed that all manifestations of reality are generated by the dynamic interplay between two polar forces which they called the yin and the yang" (28). Westerners tend to oversimplify the concept of the *yin*—traditionally associated with the feminine—as passive, in turn determining the *yang*—the masculine—to be active. The Chinese, however, conceived of reality as a cyclical process of movement, one of constant flux and change; there are two kinds of activity in the universe then: that which is in harmony with, and that which works against, the natural flow of things. Yin action is responsive and cooperative; yang is aggressive and competitive (38). (Capra's explanation of the yin and the yang is, naturally, more complex than I'm able to render here and should be read in its entirety for greater clarity.) Though its difficult for Western minds to grasp, the opposites described by Capra exist not in separate categories but as extreme poles within a unified whole:

> Nothing is only yin or yang. All natural phenomena are manifestations of a continuous oscillation between the two poles, all transitions taking place gradually and in unbroken progression. The natural order is one of dynamic balance between yin and yang. (35)

Lest we forget, Capra's interest is, first and foremost, that of the physicist. The interplay between yin and yang is reflected even within the subatomic particles of which matter is composed. So, as Capra explains, quantum theory holds that nothing exists in isolation, and nothing remains unaffected by the other systems of which its a part. (William Blake was right, after all, when he wrote: "Everything that lives / Lives not alone nor for itself.") We are—as are the atoms of which we're composed—dual in nature; we seek to maintain our own, individual sense of integrity even as we are constantly affected by those systems around us. Our very brain structure reveals a similar dynamic. The two complementary modes so essential to the understanding of the nature of living systems are reflected also in the divided hemispheres of our brains: as we now know, the left hemisphere is associated with analytical, linear thought and the sequential processing of information; the right functions more holistically and is associated with creativity and synthesis. The deep-rooted preference for left-brain activities may itself "be related to the patriarchal value system," (294) for "In the past, brain researchers often referred to the left hemisphere [*right* side of body] as the major, and to the right [*left* side of body] as the minor hemisphere, thus expressing our culture's Cartesian bias in favor of rational thought, quantification, and analysis" (293).

It is now recognized that one can increase one's mental abilities (both creative and analytical) by integrating the two complementary modes of the left and right hemispheres. Capra suggests that this interplay between two supposed opposites might also be the way to achieve individual and cultural balance. Perhaps the model he proposes—which recognizes as fundamental to full functioning the interaction of seemingly opposed extremes—would serve equally well to breach divisions within the discipline of English studies. For even as scientific methods evolve, so too must the means by which we structure our thoughts and our words; the modes of research and analysis upon which we've sought to professionalize our discipline have, themselves, changed.

Nature is composed not of the solid little building blocks previously imagined (the basis of "hard" science), but of subatomic particles constantly in motion; nature, is—*by* nature—forever altering its revelation of itself: "An electron is neither a particle nor a wave, but it may show particle-like aspects in some situations and wave-like aspects in others. While it acts like a particle, it is capable of developing its wave nature at the expense of its particle nature, and vice versa, thus undergoing continual transformations from particle to wave and from wave to particle" (79). The binary splits underlying Western culture are based, erroneously, upon a paradigm which exists nowhere in the material universe, a conceptual model in which opposites maintain an obstinate and noninteractive positionality at two ends of an imaginary pole. But, as Capra demonstrates, this is hardly the nature of reality, and certainly not the nature of male and female. The psyche of each man and each woman is not predetermined and static, but consists, instead, of "a dynamic phenomenon resulting from the interplay between feminine and masculine elements" (36). A similar notion occurred to Virginia Woolf, who suggests that within each human soul there exist two sexes, the mind by nature androgynous, consisting of both masculine and feminine parts: the "man-womanly" and the "woman-manly." If there is intercourse between the two, creativity becomes possible (102). (Woolf's model comes remarkably close to the right brain/left brain function later described by science.) Both Woolf and Capra would likely agree that art is the result of a harmonious union between these "male" and "female" selves. The same dynamic within the culture as a whole would, according to Capra, initiate a period of high attainment, producing integration and balance in the arts and sciences while enhancing the intellectual and esthetic development of each. Capra provides several historical examples to illustrate his point, the Renaissance the most obvious.

Since reality is composed of interconnecting systems, we cannot consider the study of the natural world or of physics (the ecosystem, the nature of reality) apart from the systems to which they are related (whether of human or more "natural" construct). Capra describes our current "multifaceted cultural crisis," then, within the broader "context of human cultural evolution," which he sees not in terms of a society-in-stasis, but as a social order which is at this moment experiencing a series of on-going "dynamic patterns of change" (26). (The same might be said about social institutions; certainly, if we consider the forces for change exerted from both within and outside the academy, we see, on a lesser scale, the same dynamic at work.) We are, therefore, in an unprecedented moment of transition which must—if we are to survive—transform the nature of our culture and, indeed, the very foundations of our thinking. We must cease seeing the world in terms of conflict and division. Capra—along with feminist scholars and many women writers—describes this obsolete value system as masculist, perpetuated by political, academic, and economic institutions. Here Capra acknowledges similarities between "the Marxist view of cultural dynamics"—with its dialectical interplay between opposites—and the Chinese notion of yin and yang; yet, ultimately he disagrees with the Marxist view that class struggle and eventual revolution are an essential aspect of social change. Taking exception to the Darwinian notion that life consists of continuous competition and struggle for survival, Capra suggests instead that "all struggle in nature takes place within a wider context of cooperation" (34).

Capra believes the societal transformation he outlines is positive and needed within a broad historical and global context, in spite of the psychic discomfort any major philosophical shift incurs. The acknowledgment and resolution of contraries, seen by the feminist movement as an essential aspect of political change, has become a powerful force for cultural evolution. As feminists point out, superior/inferior, dominant/submissive—along with other dualistic figurations, whether social or scientific—must be considered obsolete, unworkable paradigms. Yet even amidst such divisions, we might also seek opportunity:

> So often in the history of thought a paradox has led to the discovery of a larger and more fundamental truth, even a new

> paradigm, in the attempt to reconcile two apparently contradictory phenomena. (Griffin 178)

It is, perhaps, the artist in Griffin that sustains such wholeness of vision. Rather than inscribing binary splits such as reason/emotion, rationality/imagination, poets and fiction writers attempt in their work to reveal *connections,* gathering together the tenuous strands they see threaded throughout our complex and varied lives. Woolf put it this way:

> The method, if triumphant, should make us feel ourselves seated at the centre of another mind, and, according to the artistic gift of the writer, we should perceive in the helter-skelter of flying fragments some unity, significance, or design. ("Introduction," *Women and Writing* 29)

Surely, then, oppositionality is in the eye of the beholder; at every point of *opposition* is a point—an opportunity—of *intersection.* Women who write theory and women who write fiction have writing in common; reading one *another's* work can but enhance our *own.* Observes Carolyn Forche, "Philosophy has always been interested in poetry; poetry has always been interested in philosophy." Yet the twentieth-century mind is a mind in conflict. Thus, Caroline Whitbeck, in outlining a feminist ontology, argues for a reconceptualization of the "self-other *opposition*" in which our thoughts have been cast. She proposes, in its place, a "self-other *relation* . . . assumed to be a relation between beings who are in some respects analogous" (62). Certainly, this approach is more compatible with Capra's holistic systems view of life: The conception of the universe as an interconnected web of relations is one of two major themes that occur throughout modern physics (Capra 87).

Recognizing that as academics we can, paradoxically, maintain the integrity of individual positionalities even as we distinguish various points of relation, we can begin to resolve divisions in our own discipline and, at the same time, address similar divisions within society. Many interdepartmental conflicts—which often pit one concentration of study against another—replicate the "self-other opposition" to which Whitbeck refers. She rejects such "dualistic ontologies," suggesting that we abandon the attack-and-defend approach in the arena of ideas. Rather than positing the personal/political or imaginative/theoretical as somehow adversarial, we might better choose, instead, to initiate dialogue between them. Capra would concur: What is good is not yin or yang but the dynamic balance between the two; what is bad or harmful is imbalance (36). The feminist ontology Whitbeck espouses "is based on a conception of the relation of self and other(s) that is neither oppositional nor dyadic" (51). Our experience as feminists—whether as theorists or as poets or fiction writers—provides us with many points of analogy.

In remarks prefacing *The Daughter's Seduction,* Jane Gallop admits her intention to establish "an opposition between two thinkers or terms" with the express purpose of then moving "beyond the belligerence of opposition to an exchange between the terms" (*x*). Perhaps such an exchange between feminist theorists and creative writers can begin a dialectic that also addresses the larger conflict between the "feminized" discipline of creative writing and the more "masculized" field of critical theory. As Gallop notes, "The most stubborn opposition is the continual constitution of 'opposite sexes' which blocks the possibility of a relation between them" (*xi–xii*). A more inclusive discourse will inevitably lead to greater understanding between feminist theorists and creative writers, strengthening the voice of feminism and sparking needed change.

As we, as feminist writers, articulate to one another across barriers of difference the points of relation that intersect our work, we collaborate—each as speaking subjects—to redefine and rewrite our worlds, creating, in the process, an intellectual kinship which overreaches individual and cultural bounds. Political change is a cooperative venture. "Thus are we all involved in a grand collective effort: familial: sometimes rivalrous. But collective" (Joyce Carol Oates, *The Georgia Review* 121).

> At this particular stage of feminist movement in the United States, feminist scholars must pause to reconsider the approach we take to our work within the university. (Hooks 40)

Feminist scholars, as theoreticians, are in a curiously contradictory position: as women, they are signified as "other," often marked as outsiders within their own departments; however, as theorists, they find themselves privileged above other women with whom—as feminists—they might otherwise be aligned. The feminist self, not surprisingly, mirrors the cultural divisions it critiques. Still, the polarization that exists between those who profess critical theory/literature and those who teach composition/creative writing need not be replicated by feminists, who are, after all, represented throughout the university in departments across the disciplines. How, then, might feminism and creative writing complement one another? How might our efforts to reconcile dualities help us, eventually, to create a more unified vision? Instead of positioning ourselves dyadically, we might consider, instead, the ways in which our disciplines inform and enhance one another, locating those points of relation which Whitbeck defines as comprising a feminist ontology.

Women writers—and feminist theorists—have deplored the male-centredness with which our history and literatures have been shaped. [And here I acknowledge that any split in this discussion *between* feminist critics and creative writers is itself misleading, done within this context merely for convenience. As writers and thinkers, we are not so easily divided into tidy binary packages.] Both feminist theorists and women writers experience coming to voice as self-liberatory; both feminist classrooms and writing workshops seek a sense of intellectual community. The creative writing workshop has served as a point of departure from traditionally hierarchical classroom power structures and has evolved its own pedagogy; feminist theory seeks also to delineate new pedagogical approaches and to critically engage the old.

Women's literature has helped make feminist concerns tangible in an accessible voice to a wide and varied audience; feminism has broadened publication opportunities for women and has provided the works of poets and fiction writers with an animated and challenging feminist critique. The feminist imperative of reclaiming one's own history, writing from within the resonance of personal experience, is shared by both academic and creative writers. Griffin notes the effect: "Because each time I write, each time the authentic words break through, I am changed. The older order that I was collapses and dies" (232).

Feminist theorists strive "to transform the production and dissemination of knowledge" (Lather 50); creative writers seek to discover through language a deeper sense of who we are. Both can be seen as counter-hegemonic forces; however, while this is the *intention* of feminist theory, it is often but a *by-product* of creative writing. But art is a great force for change, nonetheless, is, in fact, *transformative,* in both the personal and political sense. As Griffin affirms, "[P]oetry is a powerful way of knowledge" (16).

> Which is why all art is political, despite the effort of some artists to deny the fact. But its "political" quality may simply be the fact of its obdurate existence: *I stand here,* the artist declares; *the State stands there.* In any case, art is not an escape from experience, still less from reality: it is experience, it is reality, in its own inviolable terms. (Joyce Carol Oates 121)

Feminist theorists and women poets and fiction writers share the struggle to transcend the restraints and limitations of everyday experience imposed upon them by familial, cultural, and educational institutions. Academic women who write—whether positioned as "artists" or "theorists"—must overcome many of the same time constraints imposed by conflictive gender roles and must also confront class/

economic/racist/sexist/heterosexist biases as they attempt to storm the walls of an astonishingly well-defended male academy. Yet these very struggles—and the resulting gains made as they are articulated within women's writing—are what bind us together, spiritually, as analogous actors on the stage of cultural change.

> [E]ach effort of writing represents that codified metaphorical definition of the self-in-progress; the heart's measurement of a certain irretrievable chunk of time. (Oates 121)

Our culture—and perhaps the feminist movement—are in moments of crisis. But Capra points out that the Chinese term for crisis—*wei-ji*—is composed of the characters for 'danger' and 'opportunity' (248). The danger is that feminists will replicate the same bifurcatory thinking as the patriarchal institutions they endeavor to transform; the opportunity is for greater cooperation and community between women seeking change. If we seem to be approaching one another from greatly divergent viewpoints, so much the better. For even in addressing contradictions we engage in mutual exchange; it is perhaps the clash between extremes that in the end proves so illuminating.

Feminist theorists and women writers need each other. We both write and teach while working from within educational institutions to transform the culture that produced them. We have often found ourselves in concert: we've worked most closely when transforming the canon to include women's voices, women's work; articulating class differences; opposing the privileging of texts according to gender, race, or class; asserting control over course content. Telling our stories—whether in critical narratives, poetic, or fictional terms—is no less than a revolutionary act.

> The pursuit of art, then, by artist or audience,
> is the pursuit of liberty.
> Ursula K. Le Guin (*The Language of the Night* 150)

> An artist makes the world her world.
> An artist makes her world the world.
> Ursula K. Le Guin
> ("World-Making," *Dancing at the Edge of the World* 47)

Because the eye through which I view the world is a writer's eye, the voice through which I speak the narrative "I," it makes sense that any discussion of feminism, creative writing, and pedagogy, must sooner or later shift to first-person. As a writer, I am my own subject: I write from the self and in this I have no choice. Fiction writers and poets must draw from their own experience; for the creative writer, then, there can be no public/private split. I am a feminist; I am also a writer and a teacher of writing. I cannot separate these various selves, but insist they live together.

Writes Le Guin:

> The writer at her work
> is odd, is peculiar, is particular,
> certainly, but not, I think,
> singular.
> She tends to be plural.
> I for example am Ursula; Miss
> Ursula Kroeber;
> Mrs. then Ms. Le Guin;
> Ursula K. Le Guin; this latter is
> "the writer," but who were,
> who are, the others?
> She is the writer
> at their work
> (The Writer On, And At, Her Work 216–17).

As a fiction writer, I work toward *integration,* connectedness, allowing all the intricacies of the story to come together to make a whole. As Le Guin writes, "There is a relationship, a reciprocity, between the words and the images, ideas, and emotions evoked by those words: the stronger that relationship, the stronger the work" (*Dancing* 196). Perhaps it is this need in my work to recognize patterns, to see the way things fit together, that informs my approach to both teaching and feminist theory. Perhaps, too, it is a need for unity and completion that drives me now to resolve one self (one identity) with the other. Whitbeck's feminist ontology—which proposes that relationships, not oppositions, are constitutive of self—allows room for all the human complexities of which life (and literature) are made:

> Since the relations of self to others are relations among analogous beings, and the scope and limits of that analogy are to be discovered or, if the other is another person, to be mutually created and transformed, relationships between people are understood as developing through identification and differentiation, through listening and speaking, with each other, rather than through struggles to dominate or annihilate the other. (Whitbeck 63)

Whitbeck's description *could* apply to the dynamics within a short story itself or, in fact, to the relationships created by teachers amongst student writers in workshops. As a creative writer, far from seeing the world in binary opposition, it is the dynamic interplay of energies *between* polarities, sometimes termed conflict in a story, but actually more complex, that intrigues me. Le Guin denounces previous assumptions about conflict as an element essential to good fiction:

> Existence as struggle, life as a battle, everything in terms of defeat and victory: Man versus Nature, Black versus White, Good versus Evil, God versus Devil—a sort of apartheid view of existence, and of literature. What a pitiful impoverishment of the complexity of both! (Dancing 190)

Le Guin dubs this perennial focus upon conflict as the "gladiatorial view of fiction." The creative writer must reject Idea as *domination*—the analytical mind opposing the intuitive—for to create, a writer's faculties must function in *cooperation.* Cornelia Nixon confides: "In grad school I learned to hunt down an idea and kill it. As a novelist, my relationship to my work is different. I must woo my words onto the page" (MLA Convention, 1991). In *Talking Back,* Bell Hooks, too, rejects "the notion that the self exists in opposition to an other," saying of black women:

> We learned that the self existed in relation, was dependent for its very being on the lives and experiences of everyone, the self not as signifier of one "I" but the coming together of many "I"s, the self as embodying collective reality past and present, family and community. (31)

We are not one self only, but a congeries of viewpoints, intersecting, contradicting, meeting then diverging, yet—perhaps—radiating, nonetheless, from a single luminous center. It is within this center that feminist theorists and creative writers meet. For "feminisms," too, are representative of a host of different viewpoints, and the feminist movement also "embod[ies] a collective reality" still in evolution. Elizabeth Minnich observes that the word "feminist" is itself a term in process—a concept familiar to writers, whose work is also defined as *process.* She characterizes "feminist" work in this way:

> On the most basic level, I think that feminism has to do with a cast of mind; a way of thinking, and a movement of heart and spirit; a way of being and acting with and for others. The cast of mind is fundamentally one of critique; the movement of the heart is toward friendship. (317)

If we can define this "movement of the heart . . . toward friendship" as moving toward mutuality and reciprocity, then we find ourselves meeting in a common personal/professional/political sphere, where we exist not as self and other—diametric opposites—but as analogous beings who have in common vital interests. Marilyn Sewell, in her preface to *Cries of the Spirit,* a collection of women's poetry, describes both women's art and spirituality as "*That which moves toward wholeness*" (3). This movement of the heart and spirit toward wholeness must ultimately be based upon a regard not only for one another, but also for the communities—both intellectual and cultural—in which we live. As Freire wrote, "Dialogue cannot exist . . . in the absence of a profound love for the world and for men [sic]. The naming of the world, which is an act of creation and re-creation, is not possible if it is not infused with love. Love is at the same time the foundation of dialogue and dialogue itself" (77). Feminism, composed of a host of varied viewpoints, will probably never speak in a single, monolithic voice. But it is the recognition of the *process*—the "moving toward" understanding—that gives the movement its power and light.

> [W]riting has changed me. And there is the powerful need we all have to tell a story, each of us with a piece of the whole pattern to complete. Linda Hogan ("Hearing Voices," *The Writer on Her Work* 80)

Creative writing, as a discipline, comes late to the discussion of pedagogy. Perhaps this is because creative writing is not about the production of knowledge but the rendering of experience, the creation of art. And art and theory find themselves often at odds, the critic convinced literature exists to be deconstructed, the writer regarding the theorist with all the suspicion of a live specimen who's about to be dissected. Yet it was within the writing workshop that the shape of the classroom literally changed: once-regimented rows of desks rearranged into a single, inclusive circle, the power dynamic between teacher and student altered accordingly.

The writing workshop is the antithesis of the traditional lecture course where all that is demanded of the students is that they passively absorb whatever gospel is professed. The aspiring writer cannot simply sit and wait for the transfer of knowledge from teacher to student—Moses handing down tablets where the truth is etched in stone—because the student's charge is to discover her own words, her own story, and truth is continually in the making. The workshop, then, as a vehicle for the creative process, exemplifies the cooperative, dialectical relationship defined by Freire as essential to liberation:

> Through dialogue, the teacher-of-the-students and the students-of-the-teacher cease to exist and a new term emerges: *teacher-student with students-teachers.* The teacher is no longer merely the one-who-teaches, but one who is himself taught in dialogue with the students, who in turn while being taught also teach. They become jointly responsible for a process in which all grow. ([emphasis added] Freire 67)

Students in a writing workshop offer their work for critique in the spirit of cooperation and mutual responsibility; thus, everyone has contributed something to the story's final telling. So, learning in a workshop is a communal effort; the writers generate the "texts" for the course and they also engender the tenor and scope of the criticism. Member writers base their trust in one another on *mutuality;* each—including the professor—will alternately be in the position of writer, each of critic; roles interchange session by session. The dynamic of the workshop revolves not around any single "knower," but around the interchange within the circle itself. And while it would be false to claim there is no competition amongst writers, competition is not the ethic or motive force of the workshop: the work creative writers do is not oppositional by nature. One story is not poised, as one theory supposes, against another—not pitted against, threatening or displacing—the next. Art is not combative, nor is it linear nor hierarchical: that one story is "true" (rings true or reveals a human truth) does not make another false. One need never "defend" one story against the next; fiction establishes its own aesthetic and moral universe and must stand on its own merits. Most importantly, although books are—if a writer is lucky—eventually bought and sold, art is not in its inception a *product,* so is not, in the workshop, handled proprietarily.

> The artist appeals to that part of our being . . . which is a gift and not an acquisition—and, therefore, more permanently enduring. (Joseph Conrad, *The Gift xi*)

"It would seem, then," observes Barbara Johnson, "that as soon as there is more than one effective source of authority in a pedagogical system, it is impossible for the teacher-critic to remain masterful, objective, and external to the object of his criticism" ("Teaching Ignorance: L'Ecole des Femmes" 167). Thus, poets and fiction writers encounter a different set of teaching challenges than do their colleagues in literary studies or theory. The "banking" paradigm decried by Freire was *never* a workable model for the writing workshop: even the most accomplished author cannot hope to "deposit" into the hopeful student the substance of what she, herself, "knows" about craft. Each writer draws from her own lived experience and develops her own unique way of transmuting her vision into art; *she* is the source—the epistemological center—of her fiction or poetry. The more mature writer—the teacher-author—may have discovered how to tap into the reservoirs of her *own* creativity, but she also knows that her experience—her knowledge, her perspective and personal history, her characters, her voice—are hers alone and can belong to no one else; they would, in fact, be unusable in any other context. Every writer must learn to draw from her own well.

This, then, is one of the difficulties with articulating a pedagogy of the workshop. How does one put into theoretical terms the processes of art? How does one reduce to a science what is part craft and part (the very word seems fraught with risk in an age of scientific proof) *inspiration?* The suspicion has always been that writing cannot be taught. Yet those of us who write know that the crafting of fiction or poetry is an exacting and taxing discipline. As Ron Tanner points out,

> [L]iterary study seems rigorous because it demands scrutiny of a containable subject—the 'great books' themselves—about which professors may lecture and students may be examined. Unlike much literary study and most traditional courses in the academy, creative writing isn't informational and can't be made so. (10)

Of course, students *are* tested on the complex and varied elements of their craft—structure, syntax, imagery, form, style, metre—every time they submit a story or poem to the workshop. And literary critics examine the work of poets and fiction writers scrupulously. Still, teaching creative writing presents its own particular challenges; because the work of the writer is not easily quantifiable, artists within the academy have been regarded with some skepticism: the process by which art is made—unlike the constructing of scientific or critical theory—is impossible to track empirically from inception to completion. Nevertheless, many of the problems faced by teachers of writing are common to the profession in general.

Shoshana Felman notes, "Socrates, that extraordinary teacher who taught humanity what pedagogy is, and whose name personifies the birth of pedagogies as a science, inaugurates his teaching practice, paradoxically enough, by asserting not just his own ignorance, but the radical impossibility of teaching" ("Psychoanalysis and Education: Teaching Terminable and Interminable" 21). Freud, though viewed by Felman as an "extraordinarily effective pedagogue," appears to have shared the same conviction, deeming education one of the "three impossible professions" (21).

Small wonder that creative writing teachers have been reluctant to articulate a pedagogy for the workshop. First of all, like art itself, the teaching of fiction or poetry varies from writer to writer; each workshop, like the work that emerges from it, has its own original stamp. The course material changes as the writers themselves change from one semester to the next; the course, then, is—again, like its writers and their writing—always in evolution. There is no tangible subject matter over which the student, finally, prevails; while a theory can be *mastered,* a story must be *evoked.* The teacher, then, participates in a process of discovery—praising, provoking, guiding, and refining.

Secondly—and more persuasively perhaps—creative writers are reluctant to divert themselves from the task to which they've committed themselves professionally; writers within the academy are not given promotion or tenure by publishing critical articles, but their own poetry or fiction: they must, therefore, concentrate upon writing *itself.* Ideally, creative writers help shape the literature their colleagues critique. Even so, as colleagues we can only gain from further consideration of the student-teacher relationship, the classroom dynamic, and the philosophy of the workshop.

Those who founded Iowa's program believed, as Wendy Bishop reports:

> [T]hat "no university could undertake to turn out writers as it produces physicians, lawyers, chemists, and teachers." He [Wilber Schramm, first director of the Writers' Workshop] observed that a man [sic] cannot be taught "to write, or for that matter, to practice any profession," but that "the teacher directs, aids, encourages; the student learns by his own effort." The necessary program for the university, then, was simply to "open the riches of the university to the young writer. . . ." (8)

Bishop comments: "This description reflects an essentially romantic, subjective view of literary creation and writing instruction; writers can be nurtured but not really taught" (9). Bishop is right to demystify the creative act and to insist that writing instructors assume responsibility for their own pedagogical practices. Those of us who write and teach should be willing to account for ourselves professionally. I suspect, though, that creative writers have been hesitant to theorize about their classrooms, in part because some of the terms with which they would have to do so would prove problematic in "academic" discourse. (Indeed, Bishop refers to the assumption that writers can be "nurtured" but not "taught" as if here she senses weakness, as if it is *here* we must take a stand and *prove* our analytical prowess. And certainly creative writers have often found themselves defending what seems to critics to be a "softer," less rigorous discipline. But must we accept without debate the underlying premise here—that these two concepts are mutually exclusive, that one *either* teaches *or* nurtures, never both—and that we, as creative writers, must anticipate at the outset being accused of *indulging talent* at the expense of *instilling discipline?* Must we begin our discussion of pedagogy by accepting rules laid out for us on another playing field and in the service of a different cause?)

Certainly, we can *describe* what goes on in the workshop and also talk about writing-as-product once it's on the page. An essential tenet, for instance, is—as Tanner attests—that the workshop is "intensely process-oriented" (10). Students practice the art of writing as well as that of analysis, articulating their approach to criticism and to craft before an audience of peers. It is taken for granted that, as Lewis Hyde observes, "All artists work to acquire and perfect the tools of their craft, and all art involves evaluation, clarification, and revision" (*The Gift: Imagination and the Erotic Life of Property* 145). But Hyde also points out that "the imagination does not barter its 'engendering images' ":

> In the beginning we have no choice but to accept what has come to us, hoping that the cinders some forest spirit saw fit to bestow may turn to gold when we have carried them back to the hearth. (145)

It's the "creative" part of creative writing that its teachers may prefer not to address in any formal, theoretical way. There is, as Hyde suggests, a lingering suspicion "that the gift [will be] lost in self-consciousness" (152), that the Muse is, by nature, shy, and can be frightened off by excess speculation. How, exactly, are we to account for the nuts-and-bolts of the workshop and at the same time admit aloud that there are aspects of the creative process that are difficult to quantify and convey?

The challenge of the workshop has been to ascertain what elements of writing can be taught, which simply encouraged. In what terms do writers speak about those creative forces which even they can't fully apprehend? And who wants to tamper with the artist's often *cultivated* (and perhaps too easily tolerated) Mystique, which abounds with elevated myths referring, reverentially, to the "act of Creation," "the nature of Genius"? Surely not the practicing poet, more prone to write, as Ginsberg does, of the necessity of *abandoning* grand notions about "expressing yourself to the nations of the world" and urging, instead, hard and honest labor—"Abandoning the idea of being a prophet with honor and dignity, and abandoning the glory of poetry and just settling down in the muck of your own mind" (145).

No working writer is apt to want to embarrass herself by professing in a treatise about pedagogy to know the truth about Great Art—considered by Marxist theorists, after all, as a tool of elitist oppression. (I myself find even the definition of the short story to be in continual evolution.) But those whose work I most respect, and whose writing indicates, beyond doubt, that they have some modest discernment of what constitutes true art, often agree, as Le Guin observes, that "The great writers share their souls with us—'literally' " (*Dancing* 197):

> Imagery takes place in "the imagination," which I take to be the meeting place of the thinking mind with the sensing body. What is imagined isn't physically real, but it *feels as if it were*. . . . This illusion is a special gift of narrative. . . . (196).

But how do we accommodate art as *imagining,* narration as *gift,* in a culture based upon conspicuous consumption and the *material* labors of its people? How do we enunciate a pedagogy about poetry and fiction as *arts,* when existing academic discourses demand, by virtue of their very terminology, that our thoughts all be recast? Once again we're faced with the contradictions of the public/private split, a division which must be accounted for in any discussion of creative writing and pedagogy.

Grumet confides her dismay upon first discovering that curriculum theory focused solely upon the lives of *men* as primary sources of study. Male action and labor within the public world became the locus of Marxist analysis and the critical pedagogy emerging from it; the experience of *women* within the family, as those who bear and nurture children, was missing completely. Despite a stated goal of achieving social justice, what resulted was a one-sided discourse from which women were omitted.

A similar omission occurs when creative writing—a "feminized" discipline—attempts to enter a conversation-in-progress in terms that fail to meet its needs. Creative writers will be unable to delineate their teaching practices until the binary oppositions within English departments begin to be resolved; the very terms of our discussion—"creativity," "self-expression," the "nurturance" of talent, the writer's "craft"—relegate us to a "lesser" intellectual sphere. (Compare the accompanying valuations that distinguish the poets "craft" from the critic's theory, or "creativity" from "productivity," and perhaps you'll see my point.) Grumet and other feminist theorists, concerned that the contributions of women have been left out of assessments of the labor force, are attempting to redress this omission by theorizing the domestic, nurturing roles of women. Paramount to their success will be the revision of previous distinctions between men's and women's labor. Educational theorists have appropriated the terminology of *reproduction*—referring, for instance, to the "reproduction of society"—until its original meaning has been obscured. Grumet suggests we interpret the expression literally, urging women to take back the language of political transformation and redefine its terms (4). For not until the labor of women is accounted for (and this includes, but is not limited to, the labor of giving birth) will the contributions of women be fully apprehended.

Theory which focuses exclusively upon economic productivity and the worker-as-male denies women's reproductive labor and perpetuates male hegemony. A similar ethos is at work within the academy, which views the *production* of theory differently than it views the *creation* of art: theory is coded as masculine (productive, essential), and art as feminine (procreative, elective, supplementary); the first is the work of the world (thus subject to either privilege or oppression), the second, the work of a strictly domestic sphere (thus—like motherhood—"voluntary," self-fulfilling, and, as such, intrinsically but not monetarily rewarding, and consequently more easily dismissed). Just as feminists now insist that woman's reproductive role as bearer and nurturer of children must be theorized in terms of our roles as teachers within a patriarchal academy, so too must artists/creative writers resist, critically, the figuring of their discipline as an undervalued helpmeet to the more essential work of theory. (Here we might follow the lead of feminist theorists and insist upon reappropriating words that have been lost to us, redefining productivity not simply in economic terms, but in its creative sense, as well.)

We need not accept divisions bequeathed us from critical theory, assuming, for instance, that "nurturance" is anti-intellectual and antithetical to reason. Why perpetuate the binary splits that Whitbeck so deplores? Must we agree so readily with a dominant critical view that disparages "nurturance" (of talent, of ability) out of hand, immediately consigning this aspect of our labor to a lower, "feminine" realm? Why not, as an alternative, discuss our discipline from our own perspective and on our own terms? Why not scrutinize for ourselves the process by which we attempt to assist less experienced writers—dismissed by some as "nurturance"—and admit that such encouragement comes in a number of forms, that it is as honorable an aspect of our pedagogy as is designing a course in narrative strategies or poetic craft and theory? Why not consider the ways in which the instilling of discipline and the nurturance of talent *complement* one another, admitting that as instructors we provide not only structure and rigorous critique, but also a context and climate within which a natural gift—and a community of writers—can flourish?

I propose the retheorization of nurturance *because* the suggestion of "caretaking" in an academic context seems so fraught with peril. Feminism, understandably, has resisted the casting of teachers as "nurturers" because nurturance is too readily dismissed by an essentialist mind as a strictly "feminine" trait (women should be teachers because they have an affinity toward nurturing; writing teachers nurture because theirs is a "soft" discipline concerned merely with self-expression). But if we recall Capra's insistence upon a dynamic interplay between complementary modes of perception, we cant afford to surrender so vital an aspect of cognition—either in our writing or our teaching.

Few of us would dispute the need to nurture inborn ability (indeed, many of the pedagogy papers submitted to the 1992 AWP convention—by male and female colleagues alike—showed a good deal of concern not only for the nurturance of students, but also for extending this nurturance beyond the classroom and into a broader community of writers). But this kind of labor—like the labor of women in the home—has in the past gone untheorized, thus unacknowledged. Rather than ignore or deny this aspect of our work, devaluing it because it seems to replicate woman's nurturing role within the patriarchal family structure, we might instead take the lead of feminist theorists and *elevate* it by discussing its pedagogical value in theoretical terms. Until all aspects of art—similar to the domestic contributions of women—are recognized as *labor,* equal in value to that accomplished by critical theory, creative writers will never achieve the academic status of our more privileged colleagues.

> It's silly to suggest the writing of poetry as something ethereal, a sort of soul-crashing emotional experience that wrings you. I have no fancy ideas about poetry. It doesn't come to you on the wings of a dove. It's something you work hard at. (Louise Bogan 84)

Acknowledging fiction and poetry as bonafide intellectual labor is to acknowledge, also, its power in the world. In fact, writing may be the ideal bridge between the public and private spheres, the personal voice political in its uncompromising declaration of itself. Critical theorists and pedagogues believe in the transformative potential of education and praxis; the creative writer believes in the transformative power of language. If there is a point of intersection, it is that both theory and art conspire to help developing intellects become conscious of themselves. Affirms Grumet, "We work to remember, imagine, and realize ways of knowing and being that can span the chasm presently separating our public and private worlds" (*xv*). Forche, too, attests to the transformative power of writing, remarking that "Creative writing programs have helped democratize literature." The voice of the poet or fiction writer is often the first to break free of oppression, for writing is itself a socially emancipatory act:

> Our writing, our talking, our living, our images have created another world than the man-made one we were born to, and continuously in this weaving we move, at one and the same time,

> towards each other, and outward, expanding the limits of the possible. (Griffin 220)

This continual interplay between the individual and communal sense of self—the assumption that each profoundly affects the other—is an eloquent articulation of Capra's "systems view" of life (The particle is at once both a particle and a wave; the individual is at once both an individual and part of a community). Only when we recognize the interrelatedness of our efforts—that we are creators in both the individual and collective sense—can we initiate responsive dialogue that at once comprehends and transforms:

> Then all the stories would have to be told differently, the future would be incalculable, the historical forces would, will, change hands, bodies, another thinking as yet not thinkable, will transform the functioning of all society. (Cixous, *Cries of the Spirit* 16)

> The very institutions I repudiate for their perpetuation of patriarchal privilege are the ones within which I have found the voice that tries to sing the tune of two worlds. (Grumet 29)

A mutual impulse toward liberation unites women writers and feminist theorists and has contributed to current interrogations of pedagogy. As creative writing programs flourished in the sixties and seventies, graduates with MFAs sought to create spaces for themselves within the academy by teaching undergraduate writing workshops; many also found themselves teaching composition courses, the practices of the workshop readily translating into the composition classroom. Instructors in these courses found they were teaching the same undergraduates; they discovered, too, that their pedagogical approaches had much in common. Both teachers of composition and creative writing shared an ethic of non-hierarchical teaching and learning; both also believed in writing as an impetus for personal and social change. And both were positioned—as previously noted—as "other" within their home disciplines, fundamentally opposite criticism and theory.

> In its most idealistic manifestation—power to the writer as well as to the people—writing instruction was revisualized; it should serve students and no longer be utilized as a way to discriminate against students. (Bishop 10)

This liberating approach to the teaching of writing—borrowed from Freire's dialectical pedagogy—focused upon the relationship of power to knowledge. Teaching practices emerged from the lives of students themselves, authenticating the *student's* perceptions of personal and social realities. Instructors in writing classes sought to validate "non-traditional," "non-academic" forms of expression and styles of language which arose from specific cultural and economic contexts, whether race, class, or gender-related. Such acknowledgment proved especially vital to the beginning writer, particularly in the cases of minorities and women traditionally silenced in the culture and the canon.

Admittedly, the writing workshop is not wholly free from the prejudices of the outside world or even of the academy. Even as educational institutions reproduce social classes, cultural structures, and "labor/management relations," so too can literature replicate existing cultural values. But by acknowledging the political power of writing—and potential limitations and prejudices within the classical canon—composition and creative writing teachers helped initiate what is now a system-wide dialogue about multiculturalism and artistic diversity. And certainly contributions made by women writers—from Virginia Woolf to Tillie Olsen to Ursula K. Le Guin—have helped those of us in English studies recognize that a variety of literary voices enriches both our own discipline and the culture as a whole.

For a diversity of voices to resonate within our literature—and for all the disciplines within the academy to make themselves heard—we must resolve the public/domestic split. Just as some theorists are working to valorize the contributions of the domestic sphere as a source of educational theory, I propose a reconsideration of the "domestic" side of English studies and particularly of creative writing, attempting to heal the divisions within our own departments. For it is by claiming our own transformative language and entering theoretical discourse on our own unnegotiated terms that we, as creative writers and teachers, can better know ourselves. Virginia Woolf writes in *Three Guineas:* ". . . the public and the private worlds are inseparably connected; . . . the tyrannies and servilities of the one are the tyrannies and servilities of the other."

The public/private split is based upon a critical pedagogy which figures labor as the exclusive province of men. Marxist theorists construct a world based upon—albeit in critique of—a capitalist economy; even creativity is defined materially in terms of productivity and as a tool for political change. In contrast, Lewis Hyde, like Le Guin, perceives the nature of narrative as gift. A poet himself, Hyde, in his own efforts to theorize about the artist struggling to survive within a market economy, attempts to find a language and ethic to account for current assumptions and practices regarding the creation of art. These separate strains of thought—"the idea of art as a gift and the problem of the market" (138)—intersected when Hyde perused research in the field of anthropology. As Hyde discovered, other disciplines and professions—law, ethics, medicine, and public policy among them—have also taken up anthropology's examination of gift exchange. (Medical sociologists, for instance, have researched the ethos of the gift in relation to medical questions such as the transfusion of human blood and the transplanting of human organs, deemed as "sacred properties" [*xvi*].) Interestingly, the British medical economy categorizes blood as a gift, whereas the American system treats it most often as a commodity.]

Hyde distinguishes an ethic of *exchange* from an ethic of *barter,* the former a mutual giving and receiving, the latter mere commerce. Hyde asserts that "a work of art is a gift, not a commodity. . . . that works of art exist simultaneously in two 'economies,' a market economy and a gift economy" (*xi*). In defining art—the story or poem—as a "gift," Hyde seeks not to romanticize or idealize it, but rather to separate and critically analyze the separate processes of creativity. He acknowledges that any writing, including everything from schlocky romance novels to recognizably great works of art, can be bartered in the marketplace; in invoking art as "gift," he does not mean, necessarily, that it will never become "an item of commerce" (*xii*). He does draw distinctions, however, between the gift in two different forms: the first, as talent, as that essential spark which has, by mysterious means, "been bestowed upon us" freely; the second, as inspiration, as the initial impulse to create. Hyde attempts, then, "to write an economy of the creative spirit; to speak of the inner gift that we accept as the object of our labor, and the outer gift that has become a vehicle of culture" (*xvii*). The former is extremely difficult to discuss because, in doing so, we encounter art at its inception, "the inner life of art." The latter regards its external life after "it has left its maker's hands" (*xii*) and then becomes a "property." But Hyde emphasizes that one thing is essential: "[A] work of art can survive without the market, but where there is no gift there is no art" (*xi*).

When applied to the writing workshop, Hyde's notion of gift exchange makes a great deal of sense. The story or poem, after all, is regarded by the group not as a product or commodity, but instead, as a gift in the sense that Hyde has defined it; the group readily accepts that the workshop piece, or "gift," will circulate—passed along in manuscript and conversation from person to person around the circle till it returns, eventually, to the writer who sends it forth. Each writer/critic gains through this interchange: the writer receives critical insight into her own work; the critic formalizes a critical approach which benefits both her own—and the other students'—writing. So every participant—as part student, part pedagogue—is empowered in two complementary ways. Vital to the writing workshop is a sense of community amongst its writers, and as Hyde points out, "... when gifts circulate within a group, their commerce leaves a series of interconnected relationships in its wake, and a kind of decentralized cohesiveness emerges" (*xiv*). Writers develop a sense within the workshop not only of their own individual writing aesthetic, but also of the relationship of their work to the wider community of writers of which they're a part. "Between a writer and her work, between her work and the world, lies the territory of reciprocity" (Janet Sternberg, *The Writer On Her Work* 17).

This spirit of exchange is basic to the pedagogy of the workshop, and—in encouraging interconnectedness—I think it also exemplifies the reciprocity and mutuality which characterizes Whitbeck's feminist ontology. Hyde suggests that "gift economies tend to be marked by three related obligations: the obligation to give, the obligation to accept, and the obligation to reciprocate" (*xv*). Hyde's paradigm proposes the resolution of contraries, for he views "gift exchange as an 'erotic' commerce between *eros* (the principle of attraction, union, involvement which binds together) and *logos* (reason and logic in general, the principle of differentiation in particular). Capra, of course, refers to the same dynamic of which Hyde speaks—eros/logos—as the yin and the yang. (Hyde contends that "[a] market economy is an emanation of *logos*" (*xiv*).

Just as the human mind is an integrated whole consisting of interdependent, interrelated patterns, so too does the best of human thought synthesize seeming opposites to create unity of vision. The interplay within each writer—and within the workshop as a whole—between the complementary functions of student/teacher, writer/critic, and author/audience create the synthesis of which art, and knowledge, are made.

In resolving the binary splits generally inscribed within theoretical discourses and traditional classrooms, the writing workshop presents an alternative model for teaching that can be effective across the disciplines. An economy of exchange amongst students provides an excellent alternative to authoritarian, "banking" pedagogies and is based not upon ideas in opposition, but rather on the shared assumption that, as Polish poet Czaslaw Milosz puts it: "a shining point exists where all lines intersect."

> Her work, I really think her work
> is finding what her real work is
> and doing it,
> her work, her own work,
> her being human,

her being in the world.

So, if I am
a writer, my work
is words. . . .

(Le Guin, *The Writer On Her Work* 213)

References

Aronowitz, Stanley, and Henry Giroux. *Education under Siege: The Conservative, Liberal, and Radical Debate over Schooling.* South Hadley, Massachusetts: Bergin and Garvey, 1985.

Bishop, Wendy. "On Being in the Same Boat: A History of Creative Writing & Composition Writing in American Universities." *AWP Chronicle* March/April 1992.

Bogan, Louise. *The Writer's Quotation Book: A Literary Companion.* Ed. James Charlton. New York: Penguin, 1986.

Capra, Fritjof. *The Turning Point: Science, Society, and the Rising Culture.* Bantam: Toronto, 1983.

Cixous, Helene. *Cries of the Spirit: A Celebration of Women's Spirituality.* Ed. Marilyn Sewell. Boston: Beacon Press, 1991.

Collingwood, R. G. *The Principles of Art.* Oxford: Clarendon Press, 1938, 6.

Dudek, Louis. "The Idea of Art." *Canadian Literature* 125. Vancouver: U of BCP. Autumn 1990. 126:50–64.

Felman, Shoshana. "Psychoanalysis and Education: Teaching Terminable and Interminable." *The Pedagogical Imperative: Teaching as a Literary Genre.* Ed. Barbara Johnson. New Haven: Yale UP, 1982. 21–44.

Forche, Carolyn. Keynote Address, *AWP Conference,* Minneapolis, April 4, 1992.

Freire, Paulo. *Pedagogy of the Oppressed.* Trans. Myra Bergman Ramos. New York: Continuum, 1990.

Gallop, Jane. *The Daughter's Seduction: Feminism and Psychoanalysis.* Ithaca, New York: Cornell UP, 1982.

Garry, Ann, and Marilyn Pearsall, eds. *Women, Knowledge, and Reality: Explorations in Feminist Philosophy.* Boston: Unwin Hyman, 1989.

Griffin, Susan. *Made From This Earth: An Anthology of Writings.* New York: Harper and Row, 1983.

Grumet, Madeleine R. *Bitter Milk: Women and Teaching.* Amherst: U of Massachusetts P, 1988.

hooks, bell. *Talking Back: Thinking Feminist, Thinking Black.* Boston: South End Press, 1988.

Hyde, Lewis. *The Gift: Imagination and the Erotic Life of Property.* New York: Vintage, 1983.

Jaggar, Alison M. "Love and Knowledge: Emotion in Feminist Epistemology." *Women, Knowledge, and Reality: Explorations in Feminist Philosophy.* Ed. Ann Garry and Marilyn Pearsall. Boston: Unwin Hyman, 1989. 129–55.

Johnson, Barbara. "Teaching Ignorance: L'Ecole des Femmes." *A World of Difference.* Baltimore: Johns Hopkins UP, 1987.

Lather, Patti. "Critical Theory, Curricular Transformation and Feminist Mainstreaming." *Journal of Education* 166.1 (1984): 49–63.

Le Guin, Ursula K. *Buffalo Gals and Other Animal Presences.* New York: Plume, 1987.

———. *The Language of the Night: Essays on Fantasy and Science Fiction.* New York: Berkeley, 1985.

———. "Prospects for Women in Writing." *Dancing at the Edge of the World: Thoughts on Words, Women, Places.* New York: Harper and Row, 1990. 176–78.

———. *Searoad: Chronicles of Klatsand.* New York: HarperCollins, 1991.

———. "The Writer On, And At, Her Work." *The Writer On Her Work, Vol. II.* Ed. Janet Sternburg. New York: W.W. Norton, 1991. 210–22.

Minnich, Elizabeth Kamarck. "Friends and Critics: The Feminist Academy." *Learning Our Way: Essays in Feminist Education.* Bunch, Charlotte, and Sandra Pollack, eds. Trumansburg, New York: Crossing Press, 1983. 317–29.

Nixon, Cornelia. "Creative Writing: The Afterlife of Literature." *MLA Convention,* Dec. 1991.

Sewell, Marilyn, ed. *Cries of the Spirit: A Celebration of Women's Spirituality.* Boston: Beacon Press, 1991.

Sternberg, Janet, ed. *The Writer On Her Work, Vol. II.* New York: W.W. Norton, 1991.

Tanner, Ron. "How to Be an Artist in the Anthill of Academe." *AWP Chronicle* Apr. 1991: 1–11.

Whitbeck, Caroline. "A Different Reality: Feminist Ontology." *Women, Knowledge and Reality: Explorations in Feminist Philosophy.* Ed. Ann Garry and Marilyn Pearsall. Boston: Unwin Hyman, 1989, 51–76.

Woolf, Virginia. "Professions for Women." *Virginia Woolf: Women and Writing.* Ed. Michele Barrett. New York and London: Harcourt Brace Jovanovich, 1904. 57–63.

———. *A Room of One's Own.* New York: Harcourt Brace Jovanovich, 1927.

———. *Three Guineas.* New York: Harcourt Brace Jovanovich, 1966.

8 Literary Theory and the Writer

Jay Parini
Middleberry College

A major problem exists in American intellectual and cultural life today, especially on campuses. Theory and practice have been torn apart. More specifically, the "creative" writers—poets and writers of fiction—don't speak to the critics of literature, many of whom practice what is now called "theory." In some cases there is open warfare, with the writers disdainful of the jargon-ridden prose and outright philistinism of theory; for their part, the critics have less than no interest in the "texts" being woven right under their very noses. To them, the only good poet is a dead poet.

Once upon a time, of course, the major "creative" writers were also the major critics. Ben Jonson, John Dryden, Samuel Johnson, Wordsworth and Coleridge, Matthew Arnold, T. S. Eliot—all defined the terms in which their works might be understood and judged. The critical and creative aspects of their writing co-existed happily in the same imagination. The problem, which I take to be a large one that has ramifications well beyond literature faculties, began when criticism turned "professional." F. R. Leavis and Cleanth Brooks, two influential critics in the professional mode, were among the first important writers about poetry who were not themselves poets. A gap opened between imaginative and critical writing which has only widened.

The New Critics, "professional" though they were, at least pretended to welcome writers on campus. Robert Penn Warren, John Crowe Ransom, Theodore Roethke, and Richard Wilbur all flourished in the genteel atmosphere of *Understanding Poetry.* Indeed, the New Critics were all Sons of Tom (Eliot) and tried to write as well as he did, crafting their sentences in shapely and lucid ways that still make for good reading. (I recently plucked a crumbling paperback of *The Well-Wrought Urn* from my bookshelf and gasped: Professor Brooks wrote like an Anglican angel!)

The problem with the New Criticism, of course, was its pretense to being apolitical. As Lionel Trilling wrote in *Beyond Culture* in 1968, "We all want politics not to exist." The supposed purpose of high art is to go beyond politics, to rise above the taint of ideology, to loft us thither into the ozone layer of aesthetic bliss, a place where all ironies and paradoxical motions of a given text are, at last, harmonized. This approach to literature led to what Mikhail Bakhtin, as early as 1926, referred to as "the fetishization of the artistic work artifact," a formalist heresy that continued right up through the end of the New Criticism and continues today in neoconservative circles. (Joseph Epstein, for instance, complained in a recent issue of *The New Criterion* that "the intrusion of politics into culture" is "one of the major motifs" of the last twenty-five years.)

It was hard for the New Critics to worship art and simultaneously kick poets in the teeth, so they hired their token poets and novelists, assigning them courses in "creative writing." Terminology had no room in its optative future for writers. The poststructural boom of the late seventies and eighties, which followed as the night the day from the professionalism of the fifties and sixties, marked the end of any pretense of cooperation. The writers would hereafter be banished to creative writing and MFA programs, which were often housed in buildings on another part of campus, somewhere quiet where the writers could have green thoughts in their green glades. The critics, meanwhile, would go their querulous ways together.

The loss of contact between theory and practice has, however, been destructive for both sides. The relative ignorance of most poets and novelists with regard to theory has damaged the quality of their poems, stories, and novels. In the realm of fiction, for instance, even our best writers in America seem hopelessly convention-bound, repeating either the empty formal experiments of yesteryear in France or naively reproducing realistic novels that neither challenge the assumptions of the society at large nor push—even tug slightly at—the limits of discursivity.

Let me take a prominent and obvious example, John Updike. I love Updike's writing: the shimmering prose, every sentence an act of complete attention. But if Updike had been reading, really reading, the works of feminists like Carol Gilligan, Annette Kolodny, and Elaine Showalter, I suspect he would have avoided the kind of embarrassing sexism that mars a recent novel such as S., which is supposed to be spoken by a woman. From *The Poorhouse Fair* through *Couples* and *Rabbit at Rest,* Updike writes about male/female relations with blissful but ruinous ignorance of the politics of sexual roles (or politics generally). He is a brilliant boy-man with a pen, writing himself into a gloriously echoing but solipsistic hole.

On the other side, the critics—in particular those with a theoretical bent—have been largely out-of-conversation with the culture of poets and fiction writers, who have come to depend on each other for criticism. (Note, for instance, that novels and poetry collections are almost exclusively reviewed by novelists and poets in such places as *The New York Times Book Review* or in the literary quarterlies. The critics who used to write those reviews have long since died in tenured positions.) This was not the case in the Bohemian culture of the twenties, for instance, when clusters of poets, novelists, critics, and thinkers of all stripes gathered in the street cafes of Paris, Greenwich Village, Prague, Berlin, Frankfurt, and Vienna. The modern university, by contrast, has been vitiated by the mania for specialization that seems necessarily to follow from the drive toward professionalism.

One of the many negative consequences of the isolation of theory from practice has been the development of a baroque and technocratic language cut off from a wider sense of audience. One doesn't have to look far for examples. Here is a passage randomly taken from *The Tain of the Mirror* by Rodolphe Gasché: "Because consciousness is thus interpreted in terms of spatiality, making self-relation a function of a prior dichotomy of subject and object (the subject as object), it is logically impossible to avoid *regressus ad libitum.*" (When, *please,* will people in English epartments stop using the word "privilege" as a verb?)

I would not want to minimize what might be thought of as "real fears" on either side. In "What Is an Author?" Michel Foucault describes an author as nothing more than "a certain functional principle by which, in our culture, one limits, excludes, and chooses." His notion of author-function is, in fact, complex and exhilarating, but it's definitely not what Shelley had in mind for his merry band of "unacknowledged legislators." The author as "functional principle" does nothing to enhance the writer's self-image, however suggestive it might be as a description. Furthermore, there was nothing heartening for writers in the Derridean emphasis on the "undecidability" of a text, which is reduced to a "play of signifiers" that seems to whither away under all scrutiny, leaving behind nothing but "traces."

It is mostly ignorance of the rich folds of nuance and the witty overtones of a particular mode of overstatement favored by poststructuralists that frightens the "creative" writers. But I can't blame them. Sitting down to spend an evening with Jurgen Habermas on the concept of universal pragmatics sometimes just doesn't seem worth the oil in the lamp. Yet there is an immense amount to be gained through familiarity with Elaine Showalter, Edward Said, Terry Eagleton, Catharine R. Stimpson, and many others.

Looking at theory from the outside, as most writers do, one sees a war of methodologies and sectarian cultural interests. But there is a kind of glue holding these various theoretical schools together. Something like a general discourse theory has emerged since the late seventies, one that cuts across disciplines and has much in common with classical rhetoric. As Terry Eagleton notes in *Literary Theory:*

> Rhetoric . . . shares with Formalism, structuralism and semiotics an interest in the formal devices of language, but like reception theory is also concerned with how these devices are actually effective at the point of 'consumption'; its preoccupation with discourse as a form of power and desire can learn much from deconstruction and psychoanalytical theory, and its belief that discourse can be a humanly transformative affair shares a good deal with liberal humanism.

It is, I think, at this junction—rhetoric—where literary theory and creative writing should and can meet. Why did people study rhetoric in the first place? Not simply because, like Mount Everest, it was there. They worked for a particular kind of knowledge: knowledge of the most productive ways of "making" language, of creating meaning and eliciting responses within the bounds of predictability. Likewise, critics today labor in the vineyard of theory to find out what is there, to "deconstruct" how it works or works against itself to complicate meaning, to see how meaning itself is produced, to gauge the effects (as well as the affects) of this meaning on the reader.

A good critical essay—like a poem or story—is an attempt, an *essai,* a journey toward an end perhaps only dimly sensed at the outset. "Creative" writers join with critics here in seeking what Wallace Stevens has called "The poem of the mind in the act of finding / What will suffice" (935). Writers can only benefit from an enhanced understanding of rhetorical issues, which nestle at the living center of their craft. And critics alert to the demands of narrative (a critical essay is, after all, nothing more than the "story" of a reading) will find themselves once again in possession of that amazing thing: a real audience.

References

Eagleton, Terry. *Literary Theory: An Introduction.* Minneapolis: U of Minnesota P, 1983.

Stevens, Wallace. *The Norton Anthology of Poetry.* Ed. Alexander W. Allison et al. 3rd ed. New York: Norton, 1983.

III Creative Writing and Pedagogy

9 Creativity Research and Classroom Practice

Linda Sarbo and Joseph M. Moxley
University of South Florida

As writing instructors we recognize creativity in the fresh perspective of a student's short story, in its novel amalgam of familiar elements, and, with a polite allowance for personal taste, we can be reasonably sure that others will respond in the same way. Creativity operates successfully as a shared concept, and we're pleased to encounter it in our classroom. Yet, when we turn to researchers for innovative ideas about how to foster our students' imagination and creative abilities, we may be inclined to conclude along with Richard Woodman and Lyle Shoenfeldt that "Creativity seems to be one of those concepts understood by everyone in the world except behavioral scientists" (77).

In order to investigate creativity, researchers must look behind the product and somehow organize the unseen process into a theoretical construct. In a sense, the models they construct are concrete metaphors that seek to explain creativity in the same way that the double helix solved the mystery of DNA. But the creative potential of the human mind and the variables which influence it are infinitely more complex than the physical and chemical laws which govern molecular biology.

In addition to the problems of inaccessibility and complexity, creativity research must also contend with a more fundamental obstacle: creativity's imprecise and ambiguous definition. The complex process of social judgments by which our society defines a creative work is fraught with subjective and irrelevant influences, and even experts in a particular field—music critics, art historians, scholars, and scientists—often disagree on the creative value of a work. Then, too, creativity must be defined in behavioral terms that can accommodate products as diverse as a preschooler's drawing and Einstein's theory of relativity. This is a tall order, and, not surprisingly, one that creativity theory has been unable to fill.

There is agreement that a creative act must be original or novel, that it must be seen as valuable or interesting, and that it cannot be accidental. These qualitative conditions define creative products but do not provide operational signposts by which researchers may chart their journey into theory. Consequently, creativity researchers are free to construct their theories in terms unique to their discipline, and clinical, cognitive, and personality theorists have contributed materially to the construction of a creativity paradigm. No one theory has emerged that fully accounts for the complexity of creative behavior, and all are of limited use in its precise measurement or prediction. But since our primary concern in the classroom is with fostering creativity, each of these competing theories can usefully inform our teaching practices.

Creativity as an Unconscious Process

Influenced by then-dominant Freudian psychoanalytic theory, early twentieth-century philosophers such as Henri Poincaré and Karl Popper viewed creativity as an *unconscious process.* By examining their own creative experiences and the biographic accounts of eminently creative people, Poincaré and Popper, working independently, developed an influential theory. In *The Courage to Create,* Rollo May eloquently articulates the essential elements of this theory. May asserts that a creative act occurs when an artist becomes intensely engaged in an encounter with his or her world. In this state of total absorption, the artist experiences a heightened awareness in which the conscious, subconscious, and the unconscious converge in a *suprarational process* to produce a creative insight. This sudden illumination occurs at the moment of transition between prolonged conscious effort and relaxation and is characteristically concise, elegantly simple, contrary to prior rational thought, and accompanied by a sense of immediate certainty.

Because May traces the origins of creativity to the unconscious, he assumes that creative acts cannot be voluntarily or involuntarily induced. On the other hand, a logical corollary of this theory offers teachers an indirect means for engendering creativity in their students. Since creative acts are dependent upon the intensity of the artist's *commitment* to the encounter, we can help preserve our students' creative opportunities by facilitating their engagement in the writing process. Elizabeth Hardwick describes the experience this way:

> There is, I'm sure, something strange about imaginative concentration. The brain slowly begins to function in a different way, to make mysterious connections. Say, it is Monday, and you write

> a very bad draft, but if you keep trying, on Friday, words, phrases, appear almost unexpectedly. I don't know why you can't do it on Monday, or why I can't. I'm the same person, no smarter, I have nothing more at hand. . . . It's one of the things writing students don't understand. (quoted in Plimpton 130)

When we define our primary responsibility in terms of our students' engagement, we limit our role in their process and tacitly insist that they take charge of their writing and find for themselves "the secret room where dreams prowl" (Gardner, *On Becoming a Novelist* 120).

The perception of creativity as an unconscious act supports the "romantic" compositionist's ideal of the teacher as facilitator, focuses our attention on process rather than product, and forces an examination of how we can foster our students' engagement in the creative writing process. Perhaps, for example, teacher-assigned topics, forms, and genres are less likely to offer opportunities for student engagement than student-sponsored writing. We need to question whether an orderly syllabus and the advantages of evaluating similar writing products serve our convenience rather than our students' creative process.

Formal exercises and assigned writing need not be abandoned altogether, but they will be more valuable when they respond to problems students are encountering in writing. Admittedly, student writers need experience with a variety of forms and genres, but we can design course requirements in a portfolio format that gives students more control over the shape of their writing. We cannot, for example, expect students to take seriously our admonition to discover the form inherent in their poems when our syllabus reflects the attitude that "If today is Tuesday, it must be sonnets."

Creativity as a Cognitive Process

Thanks to the influx of federal dollars to fund quantitative research, since the 1950s researchers have struggled to arrive at a more "scientific" understanding of creativity than the psychoanalytic, humanistic view represented by May. Perhaps encouraged by the success of intelligence tests developed by Binet and Thurstone, cognitive psychologists theorized that creativity, like general intelligence, is a cognitive process, a special way of thinking and solving problems. In his presidential address to the American Psychological Association, J. P. Guilford, a distinguished cognitive theorist, presented his problem-solving model of creativity. His model dominated creativity research for the next twenty-five years and is the foundation for much contemporary research.

Guilford hypothesized that at least eight primary mental abilities, which he collectively labeled *divergent thinking,* underlie creativity: sensitivity to problems, fluency, flexibility, originality, synthesis, analysis, elaboration, and evaluation. On the basis of Guilford's model, researchers constructed tests which could reliably measure and predict divergent thinking.

As early as 1971, disillusionment set in as it became apparent that these cognitive functions are necessary, but not sufficient, determinants of creative behavior. That is, while divergent thinking is associated with creativity, it is not equivalent to it. In retrospect Guilford seems to have committed the error about which Sherlock Holmes warned Doctor Watson: "It is a capital mistake to theorize before one has data. Insensibly, one begins to twist facts to suit theories, instead of theories to suit facts" (quoted in Brown 18).

While some theoretical orientation is necessary for scientific data gathering, cognitive researchers failed to anchor their measures of divergent thinking to real-life creative behavior. Unlike intelligence tests, which can be validated by subsequent academic performance, measures of divergent thinking were not tied to creative works.

Guilford's quixotic tilt at the windmill of creativity failed to establish a comprehensive model of creative behavior. We know now that creativity involves more than a narrowly defined set of problem-solving abilities. In spite of its theoretical flaws, Guilford's model enlarged our understanding of the cognitive aspects of creativity and significantly influenced the way we think about creativity. The large body of cognitive research not only demystifies the creative process by raising it from the dark well of the unconscious, but also implies that the cognitive capacity for creative behavior can be developed in all of us. If we cannot all be great poets or novelists, we can learn to think more creatively. To foster this mode of thinking, we can make the creative writing class a safe place for experimentation and self-expression, a place where unconventional solutions are sought and rewarded. By using probing questions instead of red pencils, we can encourage students to expand their boundaries and explore alternatives.

Student writers are often limited, not because they have no solution, but because they can see only one solution to a narrative problem. We can stimulate and validate our students' inherent creativity by exposing them to the prose and poetry of a variety of contemporary writers, such as John Barth, William Gass, Max Apple, and Richard Shelton, who challenge perceptual and linguistic conventions. We can expand the boundaries of canon to include the work of African and Native Americans and feminist writers like Alice Walker, Tess Gallagher, and

Adrienne Rich whose voices and forms explode traditional conceptions of genre. Finally, we can find comfort in the conviction that thinking creatively is a learned process, and that while the journey from the trite to the startling may be a long one, it can be made.

Creativity as a Personality Trait

A third major current in mainstream creativity research is concerned with the role of personality factors in creative behavior. Efforts to identify a prototypical creative personality have been partially successful. While there is agreement that creative people, for example, tend to be self-confident, autonomous, skeptical, insightful, sensitive, and have high self-esteem, there appears to be not one, but several distinct types of creative personalities. In addition, since these traits commonly occur in uncreative people, their presence is hardly sufficient to account for creative behavior. Finally, despite evidence that men and women create in different ways (Maccoby and Jacklin), personality studies overlook the important issue of gender, an area that remains under-theorized. Current research recognizes that personality factors can't be considered in isolation and probably won't support a comprehensive explanation of creativity.

In spite of these theoretical limitations, personality research suggests some valuable applications to classroom practice. In particular, the collaborative work of George Jensen, a compositionist, and John DiTiberio, a psychologist, is especially relevant. By administering the Myers-Briggs Type Indicator (MBTI), a paper and pencil instrument which assesses personality type in terms of sixteen bipolar dimensions, to writers of various levels of proficiency, Jensen and DiTiberio investigated how personality factors account for variables in writing processes and texts. Even though everyone exhibits a variety of personality styles, individuals tend to prefer one over the other, and this preference is reflected in their writing process.

According to the Myers-Briggs model, *extroverts* generate ideas best by talking about or actually experiencing their material, and they tend to leap into writing with little planning. Because they think better when writing quickly, impulsively, and uncritically, freewriting is a comfortable heuristic for them. Their writing, while close to experience, may be fragmentary and lacking in audience awareness.

Introverts, on the other hand, need time and seclusion for concentration and are at a disadvantage when writing in class or under time pressures. Since their writing reflects an inner dialogue, it tends to be smoother, but less experientially connected than that of extroverts.

Sensing types generate ideas best when they move from a collection of sensory data to abstractions, but this preference may produce concrete coherence without global cohesion. They may need help recognizing and developing underlying implications in their writing.

Intuitive types generate ideas quickly, almost unconsciously, and write quickly, letting one idea trigger the next. They are innovators but frequently need help with revision to clarify ambiguities, complexities, and logical connections.

Thinking types tend to write from distance rather than self-involvement and excel at writing logically, objectively, and analytically. Their writing tends to be well-organized and structurally sound but may lack enlivening personal, concrete references.

Feeling types tend to reflect their personal values, experiences, and subjective thought processes in their writing. Their empathy enables them to make contact with their audience, but they may need help avoiding excessive sentimentality.

Judging types tend to limit the goals and scope of their writing, make organizational and stylistic decisions quickly, and write expediently and emphatically. When revising, they need to re-evaluate decisions that may have been made hastily or arbitrarily and to expand their writing to clarify, qualify, or elaborate their ideas.

Perceiving types tend to select broad topics and to defer writing until they feel thoroughly prepared. Since they pause frequently to consider stylistic and organizational alternatives, perceiving types may need large blocks of time to write productively. Topics may be limited only as deadlines approach, and their first drafts tend to be long, thorough, and often overinclusive.

Jensen and DiTiberio present convincing evidence that writing processes are as individual as our students' personalities and that there are many equally valid ways to write. Although it may be comfortable for us to "teach" the writing process we prefer, we must be aware that radical alterations to students' writing processes can be disconcerting and stressful. Jensen and DiTiberio suggest that writers function best when their early drafts draw upon their preferred writing process style, with later drafts drawing upon unpreferred process styles to round out the composition. Effective teachers will respect their students' preferences and provide relevant intervention at appropriate points in their writing process.

Perhaps more important, Jensen and DiTiberio point out that our own personality typology affects the way we judge and respond to student writing. We tend to prefer writing by students who share our personality style, and this bias may blind us to the strengths of other personality types. It is crucial for us to recognize and appreciate a variety of types and personality styles if we are to nurture and develop each student's latent abilities.

The Interactive Model of Creativity

Within the past decade, scholars and researchers have attempted to account for how social circumstances foster or impede creative behavior. Instead of limiting their consideration to the *intrapersonal* aspects of cognition and personality, researchers have recently begun to recognize the importance of *extrapersonal* situational and cultural influences in determining actual creative production.

One of the most promising constructs to emerge from this shift in perspective is the interactive model proposed by Teresa Amabile. She argues that "creativity is best conceptualized not as a personality trait or a general ability but as a behavior resulting from particular constellations of personal characteristics, cognitive abilities, and social environments" (358). Amabile's model posits three major components of creative behavior:

1. *Domain-relevant skills* include mastery of knowledge about a particular area, the skills necessary to produce in that area, and "talent" for that particular area. According to Amabile, such skills comprise "the individual's complete set of response possibilities" (363). Verbal fluency, interpersonal acuity, and an intimate acquaintance with subject matter, for example, are essential components in the creative writer's repertoire of domain-relevant skills.

2. *Creativity-relevant skills* are the cognitive and personality characteristics that have traditionally been viewed as underlying potentially creative responses. They include cognitive skills such as trying new problem-solving strategies, keeping response options open, and breaking out of routine performance patterns; conducive work styles such as the ability to concentrate for long periods of time and to abandon fruitless strategies; and personality factors such as self-discipline, the ability to delay gratification, perseverance, and the absence of conformity. These creativity-relevant skills comprise what is commonly perceived as the writer's "artistic temperament." Viewed in the behavioral context of Amabile's model, however, they may be more readily influenced by teaching practice than previously expected.

3. The final component, *task motivation,* is specific to a particular task and has both intrinsic and extrinsic elements. Attitudes toward

the task are determined intrinsically by assessing the degree to which the task matches one's interests. On the other hand, one's motivations for undertaking the task are largely determined by external social/environmental factors which constitute the "objective reasons" for undertaking a particular task. For creative writing students, task motivation encompasses the complex interplay of competing forces such as the pleasure and satisfaction they derive from writing, their personal writing goals and interests, and the formal requirements imposed by the creative writing course.

Amabile's interactive model synthesizes the best contributions of earlier approaches. Domain-relevant skills and creativity-relevant skills incorporate essential elements of cognitive and personality theories, and Amabile's notion of task motivation recalls May's "commitment to the creative encounter." At the same time, interactive theory is based on observable and manipulable antecedents of actual creative products. Since she defines creativity as a *behavior,* her model is functionally tied to creative production. Using this model, researchers can measure the effects of environmental factors on objectively judged creative products.

Amabile has focused her own research on task motivation, and specifically on how extrinsic factors may constrain creative production. Her finding that external evaluation or the expectation of evaluation lowers creative productivity is particularly relevant to the goal of fostering creativity in the classroom. In an academic setting it is impossible to escape altogether the onus of grading student creative writing, but each piece of writing need not be graded separately. Portfolio grading and student conferences can ameliorate the evaluation process, and, in addition to their other purposes, journal writing and written responses to outside readings can also serve as supplemental bases for course grades.

Amabile has also demonstrated experimentally that choice in whether or how to engage in a particular problem increases creativity and that expressed interest in an activity is positively related to creative performance. Neither of these findings is particularly surprising; what is novel is her experimental confirmation of the essentially intuitive, humanistic insight that creative writers write best when they engage in writing for its own sake.

If, as Amabile's research suggests, extrinsic factors impair creativity, must we wait patiently for our students to discover for themselves those intrinsic rewards which will unlock their creativity? Are there no extrinsic influences we can bring to bear in the classroom that will positively effect creativity? Fortunately, there is a small, but convincing body of research that concludes otherwise.

In what might be considered an analog to Amabile's concern with the negative effects on creativity of extrinsic factors, over the past two decades Robert Boice has investigated the positive effects of external reinforcements ("Contingency Management in Writing," "Experimental and Clinical Treatments," "Increasing Writing Productivity," "The Neglected Third Factor"). Boice, who works with professors who are experiencing writing blocks, advocates forcing productivity through the use of rewards and punishments, or "contingencies." His studies grew out of his desire to rebut critics who charge that coercing writers to produce predetermined amounts of writing each day will inevitably stifle their creativity.

The results of Boice's research appear to support his contention. In one recent study, which measures creativity in terms of the number of new ideas for writing, his primary conclusion is that "external contingencies that force writing regardless of mood seem to facilitate, not impede, the appearance of creative ideas for writing" ("The Neglected Third Factor" 477). Boice documents experimentally what experienced writers know, that forced writing, rather than stifling creativity, may be necessary to preserve the opportunity for a creative experience.

In order to foster creativity in the writing classroom, then, teachers must maintain a delicate balance. We can impose a regimen of daily writing and insist that our students achieve predetermined levels of productivity. At the same time we must also accept what for some teachers may be an uncomfortable restraint—non-intervention in our students' choices about whether and how to engage in a particular writing task. Journal writing, freewriting, written responses to outside readings, in-class writing activities, and all forms of student-sponsored writing are legitimate options for creative writing students. Until researchers develop a more effective alternative, increased productivity may be our most accessible means of engendering creativity.

Innovative Practitioners

Creative writing teachers do not share the quiet insularity of the research laboratory or the luxury of researchers' sanguine patience while they await future confirmation of tentative results. Right now, perhaps this afternoon, we must face a class that has stubbornly resisted our best efforts to awaken them, the invention exercise that worked beautifully last semester failed miserably yesterday, the student poems we read this morning were as lifeless as dried fish in an Oriental market, our kids are home with the flu, the baby-sitter didn't show up, and it's raining.

The security of a fully developed theory would be as comforting as a pacifier to a fretting baby, but we simply can't wait.

In the press of present exigencies, it is helpful to turn to the work of writer/teachers whose innovations emerge from the laboratory of their own experience. Unlike standard texts on poetry (Jerome, Nims, Wallace), fiction (Burroway; Gardner, *The Art of Fiction;* Knight), and mixed genres (Bishop, Minot) which focus on formal and technical considerations or heuristics and in-class exercises, these innovative practitioners confront the creative process directly. Each is influenced to varying degrees by creativity theory, but their perspective is distinctly untheoretical and determinedly focused on the classroom.

In *Writing Down the Bones: Freeing the Writer Within* and *Wild Mind: Living the Writer's Life,* Natalie Goldberg speaks directly to writers from her experience as an author of fiction and poetry, a Zen Buddhist, and a creative writing teacher. She prescribes large doses of daily practice writing to escape that egocentric, internal editor that makes us want to make what we write sound better. When writers "keep the hand moving," they learn to stay with their original mind and write from it, capturing on paper those "first thoughts" which produce what Goldberg calls "naked writing." Goldberg's approach helps writers and teachers alike hone the creative focus within their writing process.

Gabrielle Rico's *Writing the Natural Way* is a technique-oriented presentation aimed specifically to the creative writing teacher. Based on Rico's study of recent brain research that has differentiated right- and left-hemisphere functions, her book offers a course of writing exercises she has developed to trigger dormant right-brain language abilities. Exercises in word "clustering," "creative tension," and "re-vision" tap complex images, patterns, and designs of non-literal meaning that produce the richness, depth, and originality which characterize "natural writing."

Another method for short-circuiting the cognitive process and sparking the writer's authentic voice is John Schultz's Story Workshop (Shiflett; Schultz, "The Story Workshop Method"; Schultz, *The Story Workshop Reader*). Although Story Workshop directors must undergo formal training, Schultz's method can be usefully adapted by teachers for classroom use. Schultz's techniques rely heavily on the oral, story-telling capacity of language which underlies and predates written communication. Following a prescribed format, workshop directors coach students through a series of exercises designed to elicit immediate connections between the imaginative process ("seeing") and its oral expression ("voice"). Students are urged to "see" each image, to recall and experience the physical sensations associated with each, and to go past the obvious and superficial to the unexpected, surprising words that produce evocative images for the speaker. The "voice" students discover in these immediate, sensory, and unedited oral responses, can then be carried into their writing.

In spite of their different orientations, these innovative practitioners share the goal of engaging student writers in a genuine encounter with their writing. (Goldberg's "naked writing," Rico's "natural writing," and Schultz's "voice" all represent writing stripped of self-conscious artificiality.) They begin with the assumption that imagination, voice, and perception are gifts possessed by everyone, and they are prepared to accept their students where they find them. They enter the classroom armed with insight into their own creative process.

Conclusions

Like any difficult undertaking, research into creativity has been plagued by false starts, contradictory findings, and ambiguous results. In spite of these difficulties, these studies provide the skeleton, at least, of a creative writing pedagogy. Our current understanding of creativity shapes and limits the ways in which we can effectively intervene in our students' creative process and leads inevitably to a clarification of our role as teachers.

Familiarity with creativity research increases our sensitivity to the negative effects of external evaluation; fortifies our tolerance for each student's unique personality style, work habits, and writing process; and prepares us to supplement these preferences appropriately. Our role, then, is that of a skillful midwife rather than a critic/judge.

The often-overlooked factor of productivity provides the writing teacher with a simple, accessible, and manageable key for unlocking the student's natural creativity. Buried in the rich organicity of the writing process is an elegantly simple seed: the most effective teaching tool is the process itself. Our first responsibility as teachers is to nurture our students' productivity. With our focus clarified, we can concentrate our efforts on our most important task—getting our students to write.

References

Amabile, Teresa. "The Social Psychology of Creativity: A Componential Conceptualization." *Journal of Personality and Social Psychology* 45 (1983): 357–76.

Bishop, Wendy. *Released into Language: Options for Teaching Creative Writing.* Urbana, IL: National Council of Teachers of English, 1990.

Boice, Robert. "Contingency Management in Writing and the Appearance of Creative Ideas: Implications for the Treatment of Writing Blocks." *Behavior Research and Therapy* 21 (1983): 537–43.

———. "Experimental and Clinical Treatments of Writing Blocks." *Journal of Consulting and Clinical Psychology* 51 (1983): 183–91.

———. "Increasing the Writing Productivity of 'Blocked' Academicians." *Behavior Research and Therapy* 21 (1982): 197–207.

———. "The Neglected Third Factor in Writing: Productivity." *College Composition and Communication* 36 (1985): 472–80.

Brown, Robert T. "Creativity." *Handbook of Creativity.* Ed. John A. Glover, Royce R. Ronning, and Cecil R. Reynolds. New York: Plenum, 1989. 3–32.

Burroway, Janet. *Writing Fiction: A Guide to Narrative Craft.* 3rd ed. Boston: Little, Brown, 1992.

Gardner, John. *The Art of Fiction: Notes on Craft for Young Writers.* New York: Knopf, 1984.

———. *On Becoming a Novelist.* New York: Harper, 1983.

Goldberg, Natalie. *Wild Mind: Living the Writer's Life.* New York: Bantam, 1990.

———. *Writing Down the Bones: Freeing the Writer Within.* Boston: Shambhala, 1986.

Guilford, John P. "Creativity." *American Psychologist* 5 (1950): 444–54.

Jensen, George H., and John K. DiTiberio. *Personality and the Teaching of Composition.* Norwood, NJ: Ablex, 1989.

Jerome, Judson. *The Poet's Handbook.* Cincinnati: Writer's Digest-F & W, 1980.

Knight, Damon. *Creating Short Fiction.* Cincinnati: Writer's Digest-F & W, 1981.

Maccoby, E. E., and C. N. Jacklin. *The Psychology of Sex Differences.* Stanford, CA: Stanford UP, 1974.

May, Rollo. *The Courage to Create.* New York: Norton, 1975.

Minot, Stephen. *Three Genres: The Writing of Poetry, Fiction, and Drama.* 5th ed. Englewood Cliffs, NJ: Prentice-Hall, 1993.

Nims, John Frederick. *Western Wind: An Introduction to Poetry.* 2nd ed. New York: Random, 1983.

Plimpton, George, ed. *Writers at Work: The Paris Review Interviews.* 7th Series. New York: Viking, 1986.

Poincaré, Henri. *The Foundations of Science.* New York: Science Press, 1913.

Popper, Karl R. *The Logic of Scientific Discovery.* New York: Basic Books, 1959.

Rico, Gabrielle Lusser. *Writing the Natural Way.* Los Angeles: Tarcher, 1983.

Schultz, John. "The Story Workshop Method: Writing from Start to Finish." *College English* 39 (1977): 411–36.

———, ed. *The Story Workshop Reader.* Chicago: Columbia College, 1982.

Shiflett, Betty. "Story Workshop as a Method of Teaching Writing." *College English* 35 (1973): 141–60.

Wallace, Robert. *Writing Poems.* 3rd ed. New York: HarperCollins, 1991.

Woodman, Richard W., and Lyle F. Schoenfeldt. "Individual Differences in Creativity." *Handbook of Creativity.* Ed. John A. Glover, Royce R. Ronning, and Cecil R. Reynolds. New York: Plenum, 1989. 77–91.

10 On Seeing the Green Parrot and the Green Salad

Alice G. Brand
SUNY at Brockport

Despite the persuasive power of Peter Elbow's and Donald Murray's writing pedagogies, expressive writing—wholly legitimate in creative[1] writing—is considered merely instrumental in academic discourse, intended to be left behind as quickly as possible. The romantic "me-nobody-knows" reform of the late 1960s and early 1970s—marked by the supposed gush of feelings into curricula—seemed to dissolve irreversibly into flow chart intelligence and digital models of the writing process. Of course, creative writing programs flourished on campuses all during this time. But they were detached, if not estranged, from academic writing programs, the distinction glaring, the twain rarely if ever meeting.

So work on the glorious and consequential intersection of imaginative and academic writing is a gift, a renaissance in the way of thinking about both modes of writing. Composition specialists have pointed out their curricular and rhetorical similarities (Bishop; Brand, *Therapy;* Moxley). Exemplars of this coupling are, of course, not new. I am referring primarily to professionals who write both creative and scholarly pieces (with generally a preference for and strength in one over the other). These writers have always done both. And we have always known it. We'd be shocked any other way. Somehow they remain faithful to their imaginations but still manage to teach and turn out scholarship, textbooks, reviews, feature articles, and columns (Rosellen Brown, Robert Bly, Stephen Dunn, Nadine Gordimer, Donald Hall, Carolyn Heilbrun, Richard Hugo, X. J. Kennedy, Iris Murdoch, V. S. Naipaul, Joyce Carol Oates, Alicia Ostriker, Adrienne Rich, William Stafford, Alberta Turner, and dozens more). For many years, poet John Ciardi published a column in *The New York Times* and popularized good language on radio. James Dickey advertised poetry writing for the International Paper Company. My sense is that these writers endure the scholarly or commercial endeavors in order to enjoy the creative ones.

Nonetheless, distinctions persist among persons who sit in a wood and write about it, persons who write about the wood from the window, and persons who write about the other two. The difference between writing a novel or poem and analyzing it comes as no surprise. Ernest Hemingway was once to have said, "It is hard enough to write books and stories without being asked to explain them as well. Also it deprives the explainers of work. If five or six or more good explainers can keep going, why should I interfere with them?" That there are some things third-rate writers know that first-rate critics never know is an idea that provides considerable comfort to the rest of us, the great unwashed. But these writers know both.

However, something has happened to creative writing during the recent burgeoning of composition studies. The widening interest of writing specialists—from the body of literary knowledge to that of rhetorical knowledge—has produced a corresponding shift in their scholarly activity. Some, like David Bleich, Richard Marius, and Linda Peterson, seem to move comfortably between composition and literature. For others, literary criticism became composition research (David Bleich's psychology of cultural fantasies became the psychology of subjective criticism, Peter Elbow's Chaucerian contraries became *Embracing Contraries,* Pat Bizzell's American literature became rhetorical literature). But something else happened. By design, default, or sheer professional necessity, imaginative writing seems to have fallen away (or perhaps never was) for composition specialists. Serious fictive or poetic inclinations appear further out of reach emotionally. Whatever creative space once existed has been filled largely with scholarship—or remains a black hole.

The net result is a lost generation of composition specialists cum creative writers. They are an endangered species. I say this more confidently about poets than fiction writers to the extent that I have co-organized the Exultation of Larks at the Conference on College Composition and Communication for several years now. And of the thousands attending the conference, only a handful of writing specialists reads their poems, and much the same handful continues to do so year after year.[2] As a member of the poetry board of *College Composition and Communication,* I have reviewed and seen published in it only a handful of poems since its inception about five years ago.[3] This paucity became utterly real to me when I read Peter Elbow's foreword to my book, *The Psychology of Writing: The Affective Experience*:

> I find myself interested in the various roles Brand plays—especially in relation to that pervasive cultural pattern her work calls attention to that shapes how we see the mind: the linked opposition of thinking versus feeling and hard versus soft. Brand is not just sticking up for what our culture reads as soft (feelings), she does so from a position defined as doubly soft: she is a woman and a published poet. Despite—or because of—this position, she insists on defying these easy oppositions and writing a "hard" book in two senses: she uses a fairly technical, quantitative mode for her research; and the result is not always easy reading. (She also happens to live what I personally see as one of the hardest roles of all, writing program administrator). . . . [H]ers is not a book for people seeking rich and warm poetically nuanced portraits of actual feelings on the hoof. (*xvi*)

The combination of my activities was apparently rare enough to call attention to itself. And not merely because I did research. I am not now talking about ordinary research, since all scholarship involves some form of research. Janice Hays and Anthony Petrosky are serious poets and have engaged in research for years. And there are surely more like-minded souls. But I did quantitative research. I could negotiate dependent and independent variables, standard deviations, correlations, main effects, and F statistics. And because of it, I am perhaps somewhat more alone.

Picture this. If among writing specialists there is one population of poets and if among the same group of writing specialists there is another population of composition researchers, a Venn diagram would demonstrate that even harder to come by is the population of poet-researchers of the sort Peter Elbow meant. They either write creatively or engaged in composition research. They rarely do both. Writing creatively and engaging in quantitative research was even rarer. And this is the point.

As a researcher as well as an administrator I am paid to schedule people, manipulate numbers, group things, see trends, and predict from them. As a poet I spend a lot of time ungrouping things, undoing sense, letting my mind run. But I also have learned to write the academic poem (what I call the cognitive or head poem, also called the workshop poem in creative writing circles) which is like doing research or administration. I leave little to chance. I schedule my time. I do the research: I use my notebooks like microfiche. I count syllables, plan endings, factor in line and stanza breaks, project audience, and estimate impact. I run the material like a business. I can generate text on demand, work up the necessary pathos or reverie or suggestive line of reasoning.

When I am writing from irrepressible feelings, I leave everything to chance. By design I am without design. Meaning comes. And the words come. Or words and meaning come concurrently and randomly. It's nothing that one can necessarily suppress. It is an involuntary impulse, automatic, like a reflex. I am without self-consciousness. Naked and without shame. And how fast I can move from one mind-set to the other depends on how long my weekend is.

But there is an analog here. What I am coming to is a bifurcation—and I use the term advisedly—within us that enables people like me, for example, to work qualitatively and quantitatively, to exercise different parts of their mind. I can scarcely claim originality for this idea—it has only been out of vogue. I think the bifurcation has something to do with the way writing is approached, between the work that we tend first to think through and the work that we tend first to feel through.

For me one way starts from the intellect, from what I call the head. Go no further than the first few pages of this very essay. They are a straight-forward, no-nonsense type of writing. This does not happen only with prose. Here is an example of one of my technically crafted poems, the subject matter and style dictated by establishment tastes:

some Sundays

in the warmer weather we go out for walks
just when nothing moves and the sky is turning
flagstone
we need the clarity of cold
the balm of winter mist
we practice being old and simple
we pick up wood that has fallen into the street
or along other people's sidewalks
it lies lazy
or dead from hard rains or the season or age
the big logs, a cord bought years ago
outlasts the kindling
the twigs, branches, snippets of bark and leaves
we carry them back to replenish the pile
beside the mantle
we know we need to do this to start a fire
when it gets molten cold
as the Upper Peninsula or along vast dark lakes.

Although the poem predates my knowledge of the computer, in retrospect, it felt computer constructed at the time and very self-conscious, plotted, written against the grain, with respect to my search of my notebooks, my calculated selection of the right words, as one might choose ties on a rack, and the methodical and sequential building or modeling from there, as with clay. I thought it through and constructed it, phrase by phrase. It is a cognitive poem, and I am its architect, engineer, and technician.

The other general way to start is from feeling. This writing tends to be created whole at whatever speed it takes for the feelings to make their way into words. It is quick, direct, and unequivocal—what my students say knocks their socks off. Emily Dickinson immortalized reading this type of writing: "If I read a book and it makes my whole body so cold no fire can ever warm me, I know it is poetry. If I feel physically as if the top of my head were taken off, I know this is poetry. . . ." The feelings are so demanding they won't let me off the hook until the words do not merely surface but are emptied out onto paper, all of them.

Here is the opening paragraph of an article that appeared in *Freshman English News* some years ago:

> I think it was the department meeting about the final exam that started me. I was at the kitchen table going over some notes for a class when I heard some ideas (mostly violent ones) loitering in my head. I was arguing with my department. I had the good sense to rush to my typewriter (I don't always have one close at hand). The evening wore on. My son was docked from recreation because of a C-on a biology test. One daughter was rearranging her bedroom furniture for the third time. I got ready for bed and prepared to take a shower when I heard more of the same voice. I was still arguing with the department. This time in the bathroom. My husband keeps note paper on the shelf where he empties his pockets so I quickly wrote down my ideas. Then after my shower I went upstairs and added them to the first pages. More came in the morning while I was still in pajamas. . . . (18)

Then I get down to the business of the article.

Sometimes my writing starts mechanically and then takes on a life of its own. My father used to say, "The appetite comes while eating." The writing comes while writing. I was afraid. Then all of a sudden I found what I had to say and said it no matter what:

> [C]ritics argue that the model uses jargon that gives it the respectability of high science but demonstrates little new explanatory power. After all, how different is the idea of the "agent" or "executive," cognitive terms, from the "individual" or "person," more common words? How different is "retrieving" from "remembering," "reprocessing" from "revising"? How different is "instantiation" from "developing by example." What is gained by calling a weak essay an "inadequate representation"? My concern is not only with what the model omits but what it suggests about people. The cognitive notions of Monitors and Operators

> are not people but incorporeal automatons. Disembodied Editors, not humans, detect flaws. Disembodied Inspectors evaluate performance. These entities have decision-making powers through us, but they are not us. We are circuits. We are transistors, fire alarms, smoke detectors, switching yards, semaphore signals, radar, and PCs. The problem with these metaphors is that they promote a mechanistic view of the human mind. Digital system metaphors are poor if not fearful lies about what happens psychologically when we compose. We may sometimes think of ourselves as if we are computers. But computers do not grow. They do not learn with practice or understand what they do. And computers do not feel. (Brand "Why" 440)[4]

Indeed, the piece does not have to use emotional words to be full of passion.

I have collected batches of odd phrases so interesting that I keep them for years. Once in a while I divide some of them up into three or four piles like a game of solitaire. I say: I want to use this and this and this. And somehow after looking at them for a time, I figure out what to do with them. It is something like the exercises proposed by poets Marvin Bell or Mark Strand, but I don't think of my process that way. Nor do I know why it works. It feels serial and matter-of-fact but probably isn't after a while.

My friend, Carol, heads up administrative computing at a local college and routinely imagines a computer database in her head. This is a premeditated, highly intellectual act of the imagination, duplicated I am sure by master chess players, air traffic controllers, and astronauts. Carol closes her eyes and sees where all the pieces of the intricate puzzle go in some kind of a scaled-down graphic display. She says she has always been able to do this. She also writes poetry and personal essays in whichever form tells her story most effectively. But mostly she writes when intense emotions arouse her. She says, "I can feel two sides of my head. I swear I can feel them. When I have been without words for too long, I've got to take an English course, read a book, or write one." Her emotions thus empower her in an accidental but very bodily way. One story opens, then narrows, like a fan:

> Usually, I think I don't know who you are, but today, Michael called and said that you had taken six months off work, bought yourself a horse, and are leaving for Colorado, where you will begin a ride, on horse-back, from Denver to the west coast. As I have longed often to bicycle freely through Europe, I think I can talk to you because I recognize this lust of yours. My hope is to talk to you about memories, some of them shared, others not. My doubt is that you may think of life as a set of contiguous experiences while for me it is disjoint; a memory here, another

> there like dry leaves that have settled in crisp piles on a fall day and are then caught by small currents and tossed into different piles that look the same, but never are. . . .
>
> I went back to Falconer once. It's one long street, passing, without bothering to wind, in front of one story houses, small shops, and old brick faced buildings. I recognized one corner in the town, knowing, the same way I know that Maple Walnut ice cream tastes good, that if I turned right, and walked two houses, I would be somewhere.

Let me be clear. Be it imaginative or expository writing, the ratios are the same. The hard is to the soft as the cognitive or head poem is to the felt poem, as compulsively methodological writing that makes visible its step-by-step thinking is to more natural, spontaneous discourse. It reduces to something obvious and elementary.

The scientist in me explains that we can envision the mind as whole, 100 percent mind. Let's say it is constituted by the intellect and emotion (an egregious oversimplification) which are in constant interplay or flux. Sometimes the head-feeling ratio—in some proportion equaling 100—is unmistakably skewed toward cerebration, as when we are reporting a laboratory experiment. Other times the ratio is reversed; the skew is weighted toward feeling, as in writing a personal letter. Sometimes things are about 50–50, or even the opposite. A biology report is consumed with feeling, and a personal letter is as dry as the Gobi Desert. These internal adjustments to experience, often minute and undetected, are decidedly adaptive. But they also have their problems.

The most blatant abuse of the thinking-feeling ratio, I think, is a product of the schools. This is an example of what happens when students choose icons:

A Day in the life of . . . Spring

Newly born dappled fawns stir at dawn when
the sun ray's streaked line designs shine upon
early morning's pearly dew the
butterflies flutter by
narrow shallow streams containing fish
spotted mottled sleek darting with a swish
hours pass then it's time at last for spring fever's flings
boyfriends girlfriends old loves new flames
it's still the same tried and true
they mutter stutter tongue-tied dreamy-eyed
looking at one another
hours fly on the wings of time and the mellowed
blue skies lose their yellow hue and later
turn deep and dark except for the shimmer
of the stars diamond brightness

the day is good and gone but for long
tomorrow another day will come and carry on
the life of spring.

Over real meaning:

Southern Fried chicken

I sit here, civilized
eating cold, unrecognizable chicken
in the darkness of some roadside stand.
Surely, I must look a little like a savage,
hunched in the back of a cold, dark cave
biting and tearing through
the flesh of some ancient dinosaur.

There are organic, if not functional, differences between these two poems by Stacy, not only in the texts themselves but in their conception, evolution, and purpose. A Gerard Manley Hopkins look-alike, the first poem is a zircon in which meaning is lost to description. Not one syllable reflects Stacy's thoughts, feelings, or experience. Instead of being cashed in for a grade, the clichés bounce like bad checks. At their worst, students like Stacy simply copy, overwriting mindlessly. They overdose on the showy adjectives that they've been taught characterizes good poetry. Why else would they be required to read it, if not to imitate it? As Patricia Hampl says: "The safety of ornamentation is what they trust, not meaning" (quoted in Kowit).

The other poem she handed in on the same page is the sort that comes in a plain brown wrapper. Unambitious and ordinary, it could easily have been a piece of conversation. Free from grandiose posturing, it has a fundamental truth going for it. At the literal level it is self-conscious—adolescent—but not infantile. Yet on another level it is childlike in Stacy's sense of wonder at (if not revulsion to) herself. Picasso once said: "I used to paint like Raphael. It has taken me a whole life time to learn to paint like a child." In a small way, Stacy came full circle and didn't know it. The childlike simplicity of Stacy's felt poem is wonderfully ignorant; in Picasso's case it is wonderfully artful.

I am particularly sensitive to this situation because I have come around a similar circle. I see my own writing processes caricatured to some extent in Stacy's work. I am not a card-carrying member of creative writers. I was not formally taught to write poetry. I didn't undergo the requisite workshop experience, have the requisite credential or even the New Critical sensibility. I read poetry in school and knew what I didn't like or understand. (Even if I understood it, I generally didn't like it.) But I also did not know what I loved. One virtue of missing that education was that I never learned to distrust my feelings the way academics have—considering only valid responses those that can be defended intellectually (Hugo). It took me a while to figure out that I was a poet primitive.

To make matters worse, nature has been an important operative theme in academic poetry. My especial pet peeve is with pastoral poems that leave humans out. I am a people person. I am a city girl. I only dabble in countryside—stones, fences, barns, woodchucks, sky, and stars—I do not find myself in it. Nor am I moved by it. It is literally out of my line of sight. Then I finally figured it out. The natural writing came *spontaneously* from within, from in-sight. The writing I had to *work at* came, you might say, from out-sight.

But the greatest discovery was that I could do both. I can start with the head and move to the heart, so to speak. Or I can start with the heart and move to the head. I can start from the head or the heart, switch back and forth, and end up saying something that is both meaningful and sensitive. Fervor is everywhere. The work may eventually arrive at the same place—though the course and outcome of any process other than the one we use can never be known for sure. But it is impossible not to wonder.

All of a sudden I feel arrogant and false, as if I believe I write so well my readers can't tell the honest or felt work (good-guy writing) from the dishonest or head work (bad-guy writing). (Not that it necessarily matters?) Of course, utter honesty can generate wrong as well as right writing. I reserve the option to ignore the non sequitur or distraction or to follow it. or to clarify such and such idea. Or to realize that while I can't use it in this essay I can use it elsewhere. That makes me an opportunist by nature. As I think we all should be—under the circumstances.

School is the training ground for producing correct things, and straight thinking is one of them. On one hand, it is healthy because correct thinking encourages students to discipline themselves and reason their way through their ideas. Cognitive or head poems perform necessary functions. They help students know when they are not writing them. Without the cognitive poem they might never recognize the felt poem. On the other hand, there is a certain tragedy to the cognitive poem: it encourages students to conform to, not to question, someone else's criteria. Many academically correct poems and prose writings say little of any consequence and emerge from academically correct emotions (which is to say no emotions). To write pure head poems (a virtual impossibility) is like painting by the numbers or writing what Donald Hall calls the "McPoem" (Adams).

The tradition that informs my vision of academic creativity amounts to the poem we do not feel. But we write them and they are, at times, useful. They keep us honest and practicing when our emotional environment is flat and predictable. They force creative minds to submit to empirical control. And when we want to, we can look at our kitchen tile and see a human profile in the bumps and pits. We can stare at our ceiling and see faces, or we can see crass, white plaster that needs patching. Picasso said it best: "A green parrot is also a green salad and a green parrot. He who makes it only a parrot diminishes its reality." The point is to try to do both.

Not everyone can move back and forth between seeing and imagining with equal agility. While we all mobilize material from thought and feeling in varying proportions and one is likely to prevail at any given moment, there tend to be linear and contextual types. I am lefty and according to the literature we lefties have the competitive edge in this regard. It takes practice, but I believe such mental flexibility has an average if not better chance of being learned.

I hope by this time it is clear that I am not writing strictly about poetry or about research or, for that matter, academic discourse. I am using the thinking-feeling dichotomy to argue for its collapse: "Thought and emotion are not two different things. We analyze our mental processes and say our thought and emotion are two different categories but that's an analytic trick, because we think emotionally and we emote thoughtfully. They're part of the same process" (Dugan, quoted in Ellefson and Waring). This is why the nonscientific and the scientific need each other more than ever before. This is why, too, that attempts to persuade solely through cognitive means generally do not work. When things get stalled, it is because of emotion. When things go well, it is also because of emotion. Head and heart become the same thing. As Roethke says: "I learn by going where I have to go. / We think by feeling. What is there to know?" We all talk about the holistic mind and the healthy blur between the left and right brain, clearly a doomed metaphor for academic and creative activities. At the intersection of those two discourses is a breakdown in the barriers between the cognitive and the affective. We ask people to believe in something regardless of form. Call it multiple or creative intelligence(s) (Gardner).

It has been said that the purpose of poetry is to learn how to feel. As e. e. cummings wrote: "since feeling is first / who pays any attention / to the syntax of things / will never wholly kiss you." John Ciardi put it more plainly: "You can't write what you don't feel." While this is, in a large sense, true, emotions predispose individuals to writing in certain forms and composing in certain ways. This is inescapable. So it is important to learn how it feels when we don't feel.

But be they practical or personal (the personal is mostly practical), the objectives of formal composition and imaginative writing have everything to do with getting to meaning. An important educational goal is helping students become proficient in knowing and communicating their thoughts through the reflexive check of feeling. The pedagogical power of the emotions is too good to waste. An earnest curriculum provides emotional education where we learn to recruit emotions or render them inoperable; where we learn to replace inhibitory or explosive emotions with regulative ones (Jones 91).

Imaginative writing makes a claim as literature on the grounds of beauty, form, and emotional effect. Make no mistake. I am not talking about the effect of writing on readers but on its authors. Good writing of any kind involves the glands, the blood stream, the cortex, our whole mental machinery. My vision of the creative intellect enables us to imagine the salad when we see the parrot. My vision is to make thinking and feeling coextensive, to write from whatever consciousness contains the germ of the other, and each needs cultivating. And if they can be cultivated, just think of the harvest.

Notes

1. Let me at the outset clear up any confusions about the term *creative.* While all written work is in fact "creative" on one level, I use the term *creative writing* to distinguish fiction, poetry, drama, from traditional academic discourse. Those readers sensitive to the term should substitute *imaginative.*
2. Admittedly, writing specialists-cum-poets may be reluctant to read or may not attend the conference.
3. Two factors account for this: While it is unnecessary to be a writing specialist to submit to *College Composition and Communication,* the journal accepts only poems about writing, and reviews are uncompromising.
4. Internal documentation has been removed.

References

Adams, Kate. "Academe's Dominance of Poetic Culture Narrows the Range of American Poetry." *The Chronicle of Higher Education* May 18, 1988: A48.

Bishop, Wendy. *Released into Language: Options for Teaching Creative Writing.* Urbana, IL: National Council of Teachers of English, 1990.

Brand, Alice G. *Therapy in Writing: A Psycho-Educational Enterprise.* Lexington, MA: D.C. Heath, 1980.

———. "On the Teaching of College Comp: Will There Ever Be a Once and For All?" *Freshman English News* 10 (1979): 18–20.

———. *The Psychology of Writing: The Affective Experience.* Westport, CT: Greenwood Press, 1989.

———. "The Why of Cognition: Emotion and the Writing Process." *College Composition and Communication* 38 (1987): 436–43.

cummings, e. e. *Complete Poems.* Bristol, England: McGibbon & Kee, 1973.

Ellefson, J. C., and Belle Waring. "Alan Dugan: An Interview." *The American Poetry Review* May/June 1990: 44–51.

Gardner, Howard. *Frames of Mind: The Theory of Multiple Intelligences.* New York: Basic Books, 1983.

Hugo, Richard. "In Defense of Creative Writing Classes and Nuts & Bolts." *The American Poetry Review* March/April 1979: 21–27.

Jones, R. M. *Fantasy and Feeling in Education.* New York: Harper & Row, 1970.

Kowit, Steve. "Not a Bartender or Safecracker Among Them." *American Book Review* May/June 1986: 14–15.

Moxley, Joseph M., ed. *Creative Writing in America: Theory and Pedagogy.* Urbana, IL: National Council of Teachers of English, 1989.

11 It Is Ourselves that We Remake: Teaching Creative Writing in Prison

Diane Kendig
University of Findlay, Ohio

Since 1984 I have taught one-fourth of my regular university assignment in our prison program. Our writing program there began with two composition courses and has grown—along with the program itself—to include an additional three creative writing courses, a Visiting Writers series, and an extracurricular writers workshop. We did not begin the program with plans to expand the creative writing component. Rather, we were moved to expand the offerings by the talent and needs of the students. In the ensuing years, we have been grateful for the anthologies and critical studies of prison literature that have helped us to understand what teaching creative writing in prison means.[1]

H. Bruce Franklin's *Prison Literature In America: The Victim as Criminal and Artist* has been particularly helpful. It analyzes several themes that run through American prison literature from earliest slave chants up to the literature of the modern prison. It concentrates on the dialectic of two concurrent themes in the literature: "a collective revolutionary consciousness based on the Black historical experience and the loneliness of the isolated convict ego" (261). At the end of his introduction to the expanded edition of the study, Franklin mentions, in passing, that a third theme that drives the teaching of creative writing in prison: "the urgency and difficulty of communicating to the rest of America" (*xxi*). This theme is central, too, to the creative writing classroom in prison.

In our roles as both "the rest of America," and as the intermediaries between the inmates and "the rest of America," creative writing teachers face our own urgencies and difficulties, some of which I would like to discuss here, many of which bear on the teaching of creative writing in general. First, let us consider the urgencies and difficulties that inmate writers face.

The Difficulty of Words

During our first year in medium security, we witnessed the actual physical pain that written communication caused our incarcerated students. One colleague, who has taught English in prison for years, had a student come to her to explain why he could not write a response journal for her literature class. He had made it a practice, he explained, to eat any personal writing in his possession. She was at first unfazed, assuming that "eat" was prison slang for "getting rid of," and then she was shocked to hear the inmate explain that, during his incarceration, he had actually chewed and swallowed every piece of paper on which he had written or received personal writing . To maintain such a diet, one must not produce many meals, and he knew he literally could not swallow what she was asking him to produce.

We saw many examples of similarly fierce and bizarre resistance to putting words down on paper, and we improvised our way toward solutions to such problems. For example, the professor mentioned in the case above held a discussion with the class on the loaded (for them) word "journal," on difficulties they had faced with personal correspondence, and on their suggestions for changing the assignment to make it less threatening.

We also had to educate ourselves in how deeply the tradition of "silencing" is ingrained in the American prison system. The notion of inmate silence was essential to both of the nineteenth-century models of prisons, the Auburn and the Philadelphia (Foucault 237). The main difference was that in the Auburn model the inmates worked and ate together but were not permitted to speak, while in the Philadelphia model inmates were silenced by solitary confinement (238). As late as 1940, one of the special features of Alcatraz was its "no talking" rule (Fuller 3). In such an atmosphere, written communication can be even more dangerous than oral communication because it leaves a record that can be interpreted and manipulated in whatever way the institution chooses. Guards may enter an inmate's cell at any hour of the day or night and perform a "shakedown," at which time anything can be confiscated, including paper.

If we were ignorant at first of the risks our students ran when they wrote, we were educated swiftly by the end of the first semester. In our English department, we often publish student writing, and the need of the first semester of the new prison program seemed like a good publication opportunity, so we circulated about 100 copies of a 22-page publication of writing from three classes—mostly half-page descriptions of the men's families, of simple processes, and of prison life.

The interest of the faculty and the pleasure of our students at the publication was rewarding. The shock came after Christmas vacation when we learned that several of our students had been called in and reprimanded for what they had written.

Among those reprimanded was George, my fifty-year-old basic writing student. George had struggled through the first half of the semester with a case of overgenerality and lack of development that finally dissipated when I suggested he write a plain, one-paragraph description of how to write a "kite" (a memo requesting something in prison). He wrote a well-organized, specific, and satiric paragraph titled "Kiting to See Your Social Worker." For writing this, he was threatened with being shipped out of that medium-security institution to a maximum-security institution.

In addition to the tradition of silence and the punishment for writing that is part of the prison system, there is a third difficulty for the inmate writer in a creative writing class, and that is the pain I referred to at the beginning of this piece. The student's physical pain from having to eat his writing dramatizes the psychological pain that writing can cause. Ethridge Knight, a convict who began writing poetry in prison and then went on to win the National Book Award for Poetry, has spoken most eloquently about that pain:

> [W]hen one is involved in the creative process in prison, one is extremely aware of the pain and suffering of the outer environment (prison itself) and the inner world (one's view of himself). The prisoner seeks to avoid this pain and suffering—by escaping into sex novels, westerns television, bootleg booze and pills. (69)

Students may leave class with an invention exercise and return to the following class with a twenty-page account of a painful and long-repressed memory that the exercise forces them to come to terms with. Their writing sensitizes them to their surroundings, which even in a shiny-new minimum-security prison, can be painful, and which in the horrid depressing ugliness of many facilities, can be worse. Meanwhile, as Knight notes, there are many more opportunities to escape from pain than to create in spite of pain, and since creation is the alternative that is more loaded with danger and risk, it sometimes seems a wonder that anyone writes in prison at all.

The Urgency of Words

Despite all the factors that work against the student inmate's writing, there is a paradoxical urgency to write that is palpable in prison. Two modern writers who have witnessed the urge are Jean-Paul Sartre and Vaclav Havel. Sartre encountered this urgency in "a little poacher" whom he met in prison. Although everyone in the prison knew the man's life story and "the Military Tribunal was able to confirm it. . . . this wasn't enough—the man felt cheated. . . . He then invented the idea of writing it down in order to express it—in other words, to possess it in all its clarity and distinction, and at the same time to let the story take possession of him and so survive—with its author, frozen within it" (30).

Vaclav Havel noted a similar urge during his incarceration: "Almost every prisoner had a life story that was unique and moving. As I listened to these different accounts, I suddenly found myself in something like a 'pretotalitarian' world, or simply in a world of literature" (quoted in Davies 142). Sartre and Havel suggest two urgencies for creative writers in prison: self-control and self-expression, which are not mutually exclusive and often overlap.

Sartre used his fellow inmate as an example of what he believed was everyone's desire to write in order to make experience meaningful. Some of us who teach writing entertain doubts some days that anyone wants to write, but those who teach writing in prison recognize all students in Sartre's line of reasoning: "People everywhere wish their own life, with all its dark places that they sense to be an experience not only lived, but presented. They would like to see it disengaged from all the elements that crush it; and rendered essential by an expression that reduces what crushes them to inessential conditions of their persons" (30).

Prose is especially useful for responding to this urge. Sometimes we see a new student in prison who hands in his life story in addition to the first writing assignment, saying, "I know this wasn't the assignment, but I had to get this down first," or, "I'm sorry. I know this isn't what you wanted, but I couldn't stop. I've been writing this for three days." The "dark places" in those accounts may be childhood, crime scenes, prison, or all of those places and others, but the writer conveys a sense of relief in handing the work over, just at getting the account written for the first time.

Revision is also useful for responding to the urge Sartre describes. Sartre noted of his fellow prisoner's written account that "he wrote it badly. . . . [the] initial desire to say everything results in everything being hidden" (30). Of course Sartre was not a writing teacher accustomed, as we are, to reading rough drafts and to pointing out and questioning the silences. As the stories are revised, the student may have to relive, or even live for the first time, the emotions of grief, self-pride, or shame. At this stage of the process, I am often reminded of Yeats's lines:

> The friends that have it I do wrong
> Whenever I remake a song,
> Should know what issue is at stake:
> It is myself that I remake.

The prison fiction-writing class, then, is one where students are most free to pursue their personal agenda of getting down the past, and it is also the place where they can envision the future. Along with the literature class, it is the place where ethical issues are most hotly debated in the context of the stories we read and the stories the prisoners write. One political science teacher said that "[His] discussion of Marxism lasted ten minutes on campus and two weeks in the prison," and made me realize that while my discussion on ethics in fiction on campus lasts ten minutes, the issue of ethics in fiction at the prison is one raised and discussed by the students throughout the semester.

If writing fiction helps students gain control over their own experience, poetry-writing classes are often best for providing experience in self-expression, or as one inmate put it at the end of the first poetry-writing class: "When I first got in this class, I thought, 'Not me, not sissy poetry stuff. I'll drop during the drop period.' But then I was here, and I was expressing myself, and I liked it. I had never expressed myself before."

As a matter of fact, poetry and other types of creative writing often provide the liberating key between the difficulty and urgency of words. Terry Hermsen, a poet who teaches composition and literature courses at the Ohio State University Marion campus, says, "I use poetry-reading and poetry-writing in my prison composition class because poetry releases the language into a composition class. In prison, where the men are so often betrayed by language, it is more crucial to help them find ways to release the language."

Urgency for the Creative Writing Teacher

The sheer interest expressed by inmates in writers and writing was a prime factor in the expansion of our creative writing program. We had many indications of the respect with which the inmates regarded writers, but the reaction to visiting writers was the most observable. Here are a few reactions of the inmates to one visiting poet's reading:

> I don't know how she does it. If I had to express something like she does, I don't know what I'd do. . . . She really got into the

> poetry, every single word. . . . She is the one that wrote them. I bet that takes a lot of time. And she teaches too. I don't know how she does it.
>
> I thought she was a really great kinda person. She expressed what she felt and didn't care what others thought. . . . Poetry has a special meaning to me as it is self-expression.
>
> I started to look at the faces of the people around me. I have never seen looks like that on inmates before. It was a country-boy-come-to-the-big-city-and-seeing-his-first-skyscraper look.

Richard Shelton, who ran a writing workshop in the Arizona prison system for years, describes two other urgencies for creative writing teachers in prison where they may find "a wealth of literary talent. They have also found that the act of writing creatively and the success and prestige which comes with publication can have a profound effect on the self-image and future behavior of the incarcerated" (*vii–viii*).

I requested to teach a poetry-writing class at the prison based on the talent I had witnessed as word got out that I was a poet and manuscripts came into my possession. By then, I was also motivated by seeing the change and growth which Shelton mentions in the writers I encountered there. The dramatic changes in skills, reasoning, appearance, and self-esteem were positive changes that all my colleagues witnessed, but we writing teachers had the additional incentive of watching "the guys" win many of the college's creative writing awards and national awards such as the PEN Prison Writers Award. They began publishing in little magazines, and one had a chapbook accepted for publication.

One of our most successful creative writers, when asked if he thought creative endeavors empowered inmates to change their lives, answered that success with creative writing helps to create self-esteem, which is a beginning. He continued, "I don't think it's just the writing or the art that does the empowering, but the overall educational process in conjunction with the creative effort—as well as that internal search for meaning and external search for harmony."

To illustrate some of the positive effects of creative writing on the program and the students, I would like to present two types of prison writers that Franklin names: the writer who becomes a prisoner and the prisoner who becomes a writer (243).

Emanuel: The Writer Who Became a Prisoner

Emanuel came into our program in his early thirties; already known as a poet, he placed out of the basic writing class into a literature class.

The teacher of the class, Lu Capra, assigned each student the task of producing a "creative response" to one of the works studied in the class. Among the paintings and jazz compositions in response to ten works studied, four students, including Emanuel, wrote in response to Gloria Naylor's *Women of Brewster Place.* He saw Brewster Place as a metaphor for the prison, and he concluded his poem with these lines: "Yet, though I've died a thousand deaths, I shall live to die a thousand more."

Capra mailed the four student responses to Gloria Naylor, who responded by volunteering to give a reading. To this day, I do not know who was more nervous the night of that reading: Naylor, who chain-smoked; the men, who stopped chain-smoking for once; or the teacher who had had the prison give and then rescind and then give permission for the author to enter several times the previous week. I do know that all the tension faded when the reading began with Naylor reading from the still hand-written copy of *Mama Day.*

Emanuel witnessed the power of words that night: Naylor's words, to be sure, but also the power of his own words which had connected with Naylor in New York and carried her to the vast wasteland of Ohio.

Rick: The Prisoner Who Became a Writer

Rick, in contrast, came to the writers workshop out of the remedial program. His writing teacher recognized that his writing, though mechanically flawed, revealed real talent, suggested he come to the creative writing workshop. One of his early pieces of writing, three pages of single-spaced rhymed quatrains, begins:

> Our love began so innocently
> so many years ago.
> years of hopes and dreams and fears
> let that loves light, brightly glow.

Perhaps evidence of his improvement since this poem is the note he attached to it when I recently asked him for a copy of his early work: "For you let me tear out these few hideous pages from my notebook of the damned" (Rimbaud). In addition to obtaining a bachelor's degree in four years, he also gained success as a creative writer, including the publication of a chapbook titled *Tearing through the Fence.* One of the poems in that book, "The Calling," was written to Emanuel as the two men were leaving the institution.

When I first read the poem, I was galvanized by the race and class issues it raised, especially in these lines:

> . . . in the streets
> where the white man's stick has beat it
> into the stones, pounded it into our souls!
> Yes, my friend, even mine.

As Franklin says, "Afro-American consciousness in prison reaches way out beyond the experience of Black prisoners. Even the term 'Black' sometimes comes to signify a class point of view" (260). The poem concludes with these three stanzas:

> . . . Black Man, Brother, fellow keeper
> of word, of deed, of spirit,
> so few on either side possess the knowledge
> reserved centuries for us:
>
> the calling to arms;
> the naming of things lacking names
> in a world that would rather forget
> about ashes and flames and the names
> of all who've been martyred to them,
> of all who die in them daily,
> of all who'll never know . . .
>
> Chant on, my friend, chant and revive
> the music, the dance, the beat of the heart:
> cast your spells for all to hear,
> and sharpen your tears for those who won't.

In addition to coming to term with the race and class issues that prison represents, this poem celebrates writing itself, just as prison writing amplifies and focuses key issues of creative writing pedagogy in general, including the relation between power and writing; the tension between self-control and self-expression; and the interplay between writing as a mode of liberation and writing as a mode of endangerment.

Notes

1. Although these anthologies are too numerous to mention here and can best be found in Franklin's bibliography, the work of Joseph Bruchac is crucial to anyone who teaches English in prison, especially "Breaking Out With a Pen" and his anthology, *The Light from Another Country.*

I gratefully acknowledge the assistance of the editors Wendy Bishop and Hans Ostrom in the preparation of this manuscript. In addition, I thank three Findlay Colleagues: Rick Gebhardt, for administrative support; Lu

Capra, for generously sharing her experience in prison teaching; and Paul Beauvais, for leading me to Sartre. A special thanks to the students at Lima and Allen (Ohio) Correctional Institutions whose lives have inspired my work.

The earliest notes for this essay come from my presentation at the 1986 convention of the Conference on College Composition and Communication in New Orleans. A version of this essay was presented in a session sponsored by the Interpretation Division at the 1989 Speech Communication Association in San Francisco. I am grateful for the input of those two audiences.

References

Bruchac, Joseph. "Breaking Out With the Pen: Poetry in American Prisons." *A Gift of Tongues: Critical Challenges in Contemporary American Poetry.* Ed. Marie Harris and Kathleen Aguero. Athens: U of Georgia P, 1987. 286–94.

———, ed. *The Light from Another Country: Poetry from American Prisons.* Greenfield Center, NY: The Greenfield Review P, 1984.

Davies, Ioan. *Writers in Prison.* Cambridge, MA: Basil Blackwell, 1990.

Foucault, Michel. *Discipline and Punish: The Birth of the Prison.* New York: Random, 1979.

Franklin, H. Bruce. *Prison Literature in America: The Victim As Criminal and Artist.* New York: Oxford UP, 1989.

Knight, Ethridge. "Prison and the Creative Artist." *Indiana Writes: Writing from the Prisons* (1979): 69–71.

Miller, Richard. *Tearing through the Fence.* Olean, NY: Split Personality, 1989.

Sartre, John Paul. "The Purposes of Writing." *Between Existentialism and Marxism.* New York: Pantheon, 1974. 9–32.

Shelton, Richard. "Introduction." *The Light from Another Country.* Ed Joseph Bruchac. vi–xi.

12 Voice(s) in Writing: Symphony and/or Cacophony

Carl Leggo
University of British Columbia

Writing with no voice is dead, mechanical, faceless. (Elbow 287)

Because the whole notion of "voice" is so mystical and abstract, the term "voice" may have become nothing more than a vague phrase conjured up by English teachers to impress and motivate the masses to write more, confess more, and be happy. (Hashimoto 75–76)

Your authentic voice is that authorial voice which sets you apart from every living human being despite the number of common or shared experiences you have with many others: it is not a copy of someone else's way of speaking or of perceiving the world. It is your way. (Stewart 2–3)

Is not any writer (even the pure lyricist) always a "dramaturge" in the sense that he directs all words to others' voices, including the image of the author (and to other authorial masks)? (Bakhtin 110)

Divorcing voice from [the writing] process is like omitting salt from stew, love from sex, or sun from gardening. (Graves 227)

Invitation

I hope to court contradiction and confusion and consternation in my commitment to shake up and explode the notion of voice in writing, in my interrogation of the rhetorical function and concept of voice, and in my conviction (the only conviction I am ready to defend) that the experience of voice, the device of voice, the personality of voice, the tone of voice, the politics of voice, the intertextuality of voice, the authenticity of voice, the origin of voice, the ubiquity of voice, the energy of voice cannot be conceptualized, schematized, and classified anymore than beach stones can be categorized and labeled.

As a writer I enter my voice into a chorus of voices. I am caught up in the codes and conventions and intertextual connections of the discourse communities in which I operate. I often have the desire to overstep these boundaries, to exert pressure against the walls that inscribe the possibilities of meaning-making in writing. But, at the same time, I am divided by the equally strong desire to goose-step obediently around the parade ground, happy to know at least a modicum of acceptance.

I am born into language, into its rule-governed structures and codes. When I write or read, I am both empowered and constrained by my inevitable involvement in these codes. For example, as a child I knew the structures of story-telling from hearing and reading and writing and telling stories. I reveled in the pleasure of story-making. Nevertheless, my knowledge of the codes was also constraining because I seldom had the confidence to push against the codes, to test their plasticity. In other words, I learned to obey the codes, but failed to interpret them, to translate them in their plurality. No longer a child, I am learning what Roland Barthes understands:

> Writing is that play by which I turn around as well as I can in a narrow place: I am wedged in, I struggle between the hysteria necessary to write and the image-repertoire, which oversees, controls, purifies, banalizes, codifies, corrects, imposes the focus (and the vision) of a social communication. On the one hand I want to be desired and on the other not to be desired: hysterical and obsessional at one and the same time. (quoted in Sontag 419)

Even with encouragement, I too often lack the courage to write with boldness and innovation, and writing with boldness and innovation is precisely the kind of writing I admire and aspire to because I am inspired by Ronald Sukenick's sound advice:

> One of the main purposes of really good writing is to destroy other really good writing, to destroy all the old concepts and formulas that come out of the best of the past. You should destroy them lovingly and with great consciousness and awareness of them, but always with the end in mind of getting beyond them again. (282)

As a young academic eager to be published, I am tempted to write the kind of essays that belie the meaning of essay as "trying." I am tempted to write essays that I don't really want to write, that don't seem especially significant, that are full of complaint and criticism, that croak in somebody's notion of a scholarly, academic voice, that huff and puff with braggadocio, whimper and whine with sibilant sycophancy, and pontificate with proclamations for progress—a sort of bash 'em, trash 'em, hash 'em, flash 'em writing. But in this essay at least I am trying to avoid those rhetorical stances in favor of an interrogative stance that suggests and demonstrates that I have no answers, just questions—questions that are too seldom asked, questions that can lead to more questions and possibly even some answers.

As a poet and a teacher I am constantly reminded that language is a slippery affair. Often (most of the time? all of the time?), I am only partially successful in using words to understand and make sense and communicate. Still I continue to try. Again and again, I have advised my students in both high school and university classes: Write in your own voices, your personal, authentic, sincere voices. But I am not at all sure that I know what I mean by "voice."

Writing is more than the transcription of an inner voice or the expression of a core self in a unique voice. More and more, I find myself reflecting on writing as languishing in language, a dance of oppositions, a labyrinthine journey, a game of Scrabble, a chorus of conflictual voices, an ontological enterprise, a(w)hole and seam(less) web of textuality, (con)fusion, dis-ease, textual intercourse, dispersing dissemination/not determinate destination, a germinating and gestating blank page, glossolalia, textual acrobatics, polyphony, ventriloquism, (a) play.

As Jacques Derrida proposes, "no matter what I say, before all else I am seeking to produce effects" (113). And, as the Dodo observes in *Alice's Adventures in Wonderland,* "the best way to explain it is to do it" (Carroll 32). My purpose is to explore and interrogate the concept and function of voice in writing. I could have written an essay that reviews the literature concerning voice, examines the subject informed by current theoretical perspectives, and proposes a helpful list of pedagogical implications for writing teachers, an essay that posits and promulgates and "proves" a thesis, an essay that rings with echoes of conventional scholarly voices pretending authority and transparency and immutability. Instead, I have written an essay that invites the reader to ask questions about voice. I regard myself as a host in my essay, a host who invites and convenes and caters a party. You are cordially invited to help write the following essay, to interact with the record of my quest/ioning, to engage in your own ongoing quest/ioning.

Quest/ioning

1. What is voice?

2. As a writer do I have a single and consistent voice or multiple and variable voices? Can my voice(s) change from text to text and still

be distinctively mine? Is it ethical to change my voice(s) to meet the expectations of specific audiences and the demands of certain subjects?

3. How can I account for the common experience of hearing an author's voice when I read? Do I hear the author's voice? Does the voice belong to the narrator or the author? When I read a personal letter or an anecdote by a person I know, why am I convinced that the person is almost speaking to me?

4. What is the relation between voice and intention?

5. What is there of desire in voice?

6. As a reader, how much of the experience of voice do I generate as part of my productive encounter with the text?

7. How is voice determined and influenced by the writer's choice of diction, genre, organization, shape, and typography? Is voice related to the texture of language use like brushwork is in painting?

8. How is voice determined and influenced by the demands and prescriptions of writing textbooks?

9. What is the relation between a serious voice and a playful voice? Is a serious voice valorized over a humorous voice? Why or why not?

10. How workable is the advice often given to beginning writers: Write in your own voice? Do beginning writers know what "their own voice" is? Do the people who advise beginning writers, "Write in your own voice," know what "your own voice" is?

11. As a writer, am I trying to find the right words to voice the right emotions and right ideas, or are the right words trying to find the right writer in order to be voiced?

12. How self-conscious is voice? Do I want to be held personally responsible and accountable for all voices in my writing?

13. Why do I experience an insatiable and irrepressible need and desire to voice experience, to give voice(s) to experience, to experience voice(s)?

14. Can voice in writing be developed? How?

15. Why was I offended when a reader commented (several other readers concurred) that one of my stories sounded like a prissy high school English essay?

16. Is the term *voice* used so loosely that it has become useless as a signifier? Is the term *voice* used so loosely that it has become useful as a signifier?

17. Is voice a fundamental technique of order, a framework which guides the reading process? Who or what is in control?

18. What is the relationship between voice and power?

19. In what ways can voices be liberated? Do voices need to be liberated?

20. Is voice socially constructed? How?

21. How does voice help structure writing? How does writing help structure voice?

22. Are some voices more effective than others?

23. Are there people(s) without voices?

24. Is voice borrowed? inherent? inherited?

25. How are voices suppressed? Do all voices have an equal claim to the privilege of being voiced?

26. How are the effects of voice generated? Who generates the effects of voice?

27. Is the tentative, probing voice of questions underrated while the more assured, declarative voice of statements is overrated? Or vice versa?

28. Is a plain, simple voice valorized over a convoluted, obscure voice? Why or why not?

29. What might be the result if beginning writers were advised: Do not write in your own voice?

30. Why do the business writer, the technical writer, the academic writer, the bureaucratic writer, the children's writer, the romance writer, the theological writer, the pornographic writer, the news magazine writer often have different voices? Where do they find their voices?

31. Can writing be voiceless?

32. When I read, do I respond to the voice(s) in the writing in the same way I respond when listening to a speaker's voice(s)?

33. Can voice be defined with definiteness?

34. Does voice emanate from a subject or from a subject position? Does subjectivity emanate from voice?

35. Do all readers hear the same voices? Do readers hear the same voices in texts as their authors hear?

36. To what extent do texts produce and create and construct and contain and control voice(s)?

37. What is the relation between voice in writing and voice in speaking? Is the voice in my writing the same as the voice in my speaking?

38. Do I hear the same voices every time I read a text? Do I hear the same voices when I write a text and when I read the text?

39. What voice(s) characterize(s) writing that is clear, unified, coherent, and emphatic?

40. Can voice be summarized with a few descriptors, such as "poignant," "satirical," "sentimental," "bold"?

41. Is there an impersonal, logical, rational, linear, objective, public, theoretical voice? Is there a personal, intimate, subjective, private, exploratory, emotional voice?

42. Is the voice I experience or perceive in a text the same voice I explain I have experienced or perceived?

43. How is voice connected to connotation?

44. How is voice connected to personal experience?

45. Could voice be experienced in reading a randomly generated sequence of letters of the alphabet?

46. What is the effect of contravening the generic conventions which govern voice in technical writing?

47. Does it matter if readers of my poems hear voices different from those I hear?

48. How is voice related to psychoanalytic processes?

49. How is voice related to the texture, color, and size of the paper on which writing is printed?

50. How does knowledge of an author's biography influence the voices heard in her writing?

51. How is voice related to spelling and grammatical correctness?

52. How is voice related to dialects?

53. How is voice politically determined?

54. How is voice historically determined?

55. Is voice an element in a fiction that posits writing as a communication between two people?

56. How is a writer's voice validated, confirmed, authorized, legitimized?

57. Can a voice be original? How?

58. Does the concept of voice necessitate the concept of audience?

59. How can a voice be trustworthy? Reliable? Is a trustworthy, reliable voice more valued than an untrustworthy, unreliable voice? Why or why not?

60. What is an "authentic" voice? How can I write with an authentic voice? Do I have only one authentic voice? Is the authentic voice immutable? Why is the authentic voice valorized? What is an inauthentic voice? Is the current notion of what constitutes an authentic writing voice no more than a culturally constructed and sanctioned and promoted rhetorical device which is currently popular and may be replaced by a new fashion?

61. How can readers be guaranteed that the voice in writing is honest and sincere? Why do we regard an honest and sincere voice as important?

62. Why do many writing teachers prioritize a kind of writing voice over other kinds? Should some voices be prioritized over other voices? Why or why not?

63. How is voice related to scription, the manual activity of writing with a pen or pencil or typewriter or word processor?

64. As a writer am I an echo of others' voices, or do I have a voice of my own?

65. How much do I want to call attention to voice? Why?

66. How much is the unique voice just clever, done once, and therefore noniterable?

67. How is voice related to the illusion of presence? What is the effect of diminishing the illusion of presence?

68. What is the origin of my voice?

69. Do I find a voice by rebelling against the voices of others?

70. Am I granted/given/awarded a voice by others?

71. What is it possible to say? What is it possible to hear?

72. Why is my interjected voice (my inserted and grafted and thrust voice) strident and loud and critical?

73. Why is my voice when it repeats and quotes and echoes the voices of others considered unoriginal?

74. If a text has (a) voice(s), does the text also listen?

75. Because trees must be cut down in order to make paper in order to provide a site for my voice, to allow my voice to perform, is that a waste of trees?

76. Am I like Huckleberry Hound, who advertised his circus act: THE MAN WITH A THOUSAND FACES? (When Huckleberry Hound displayed his faces, one after the other, the thousand faces—at least the part of the thousand he showed; I lost count—were all the same.

The Man with a Thousand Faces had one face.) Am I the writer with a thousand voices which are one voice?

77. Does it really matter if the voice of a poem is identified with an anonymous poet, a poet about whom much is known or little is known, a speaker constructed in the poem by the poet and constituted or actualized by the reader?

78. Must the voice in writing be unified and seamless? Why not schizophrenic?

79. What is the relation between voice and silence?

80. Are voices costumes worn for particular functions and purposes? Are voices like clothes, different clothes appropriate for different occasions? Do tastes concerning voice change? Do we determine by cultural consensus what constitutes acceptable voices in writing?

81. Is voice a weapon in an arsenal? A tool in a tool chest? An instrument in an orchestra?

82. What is the motivation for writing, for inserting my voice in the chorus of voices?

83. Why am I compelled to make the voice in my writing seem logical, witty, erudite, imaginative, complex? Am I successful?

84. Is there a universal feminine language, style, practice, voice? Can there be one feminine language, style, practice, voice?

85. Does the notion of a woman's voice iron out the differences in women's experiences?

86. Is voice related to the body? How?

87. Is it useful to label voice as masculine or feminine? Why or why not?

88. In what ways have women's voices been muted?

89. Can voice be patriarchal or man-centered? How?

90. What is a dominant voice?

91. Have women's voices been suppressed by a male-determined, male-dominated hierarchy that favors linear, logical prose to personal, exploratory prose?

92. Is the typical feminine voice autobiographical, confessional, sensitive, intuitive, personal, emotional, natural, anti-authoritarian, close to experiences of the body? Is such a description of "the typical feminine voice" just one more way of ghettoizing and muting women's voices?

93. Is there a danger of constructing a feminine voice which is identified only by its difference from a masculine voice instead of by its cooperation and involvement and interaction with a masculine voice?

94. How do the experiences of race, culture, and class influence a woman's voice? a man's voice? Would a black, working-class, lesbian writer have the same kind of voice as a white, college-educated, heterosexual woman writer?

95. What is the relationship between women's voices and men's voices? Can the voices be transposed?

96. Is a woman's voice historically/socially constructed or genetically constructed?

97. Is the mode of questioning—tentative, indefinite, open, probing—closer to a feminine voice than a masculine voice? Does this question signify a masculine questioner?

98. Is voice like a thumbprint—unique, one in the universe?

99. Is voice mimetic and/or metonymic and/or metaphorical?

In/Conclusion

In "Invitation" I presented myself as the host of a party. The party has been going on for a long time and will continue for a long time. "In/Conclusion" signifies no more than the temporary absence of my interjected voice (perhaps as one at a party would be absent while visiting the washroom), an absence imposed for the sake of convenience—in this case the need to impose a boundary on a project that will not cease because it is limitless and inexhaustible. During my absence you are invited to answer the following multiple-choice quiz:

Circle the correct answer:

Voice Is

1. Persona
2. Naturalness
3. Driving force
4. Stance
5. Point of view
6. Code
7. Style
8. Rhetorical device

9. Rhythm
10. Authority
11. Truth
12. Figure
13. Self
14. Mask
15. Unity
16. Essence
17. Tone
18. Mood
19. Sincerity
20. Personal imprint
21. Creativity
22. Ideological construction
23. Warmth
24. Energy
25. Liberation
26. Ventriloquism
27. All of the above
28. None of the above
29. Some of the above
30. I don't know

A Note from the Washroom in Which the Author, Who Cannot Bear to Be Absent from the Party, Confesses the Irrepressible Didacticism of a Fervent Agnostic

As I grow older, I also grow less and less sure about "truth." Most days the only conviction I am willing to profess publicly and loudly is the agnostic's declaration, "I do not know." And yet, this agnostic stance does not prevent my earnestly seeking answers. I am a tireless questioner on a quest. When I say "I do not know," I am not confessing a weary exasperation or a confused resignation. Instead, I am singing a lyric of celebration. In fact, I profess that I do not know because I do not want to know. On those occasions when I have been convinced that I knew the answers, I then zealously tried to propagate the answers so that others would know too. In effect, I energetically wanted to evangelize the world with the truths I possessed. I now regard that kind of approach as dangerous because it leads to formulaic activities and responses constrained by standards that are arbitrarily awarded too much authority for inclusion and exclusion.

And yet I am a writer and a teacher, and, as a writer and a teacher, I am didactic. Absent from the party, I am trying to complete the multiple choice quiz (as I hope you are), and I want to circle item thirty, "I don't know"; but I also want to circle item twenty-seven, "All of the above"; while item twenty-eight, "None of the above," is tantalizing, too. But in the end I choose not to answer the quiz at all, at least not yet. My question/ing will continue.

In the meantime, based on my ninety-nine questions about voice, I have generated nine commandments (I am not presumptuous enough to propose ten commandments) which I live by and which I share with my students. Of course, I am constantly interrogating these commandments and generating more questions. But these are commandments that I recommend be pinned on the refrigerator door and read daily and lived by until there are other commandments with more promise for nurturing successful experiences with writing.

NINE COMMANDMENTS

1. Revel in the multiplicity of voices.
2. Experiment playfully and earnestly with voices.
3. Listen to the multitude of voices of other writers.
4. Explore the effects of different voices.
5. Weave your voices into the chorus of voices.
6. Learn the voices unique to discourse communities.
7. Question connections between voices and selfhood.
8. Celebrate the voices you hear in your writing.
9. Write in voices filled with desire.

Having propagated these nine commandments about writing and voice for several years in secondary and university classes, I have learned three general and practical lessons:

1. Some students revel in the liberation they experience in their writing which is frequently outrageous, risk-taking, experimental, fun, subversive, life-enhancing.

2. Some students fear the liberation they are offered and write writing that is predictable and monotonous like a fast-food hamburger.

3. Some students do not care about liberation or lack of liberation. They do not care about writing. They have probably never heard their voices or the voices of others.

My experience suggests that I will always have students with these three attitudes. My hope is that with my approaches to writing, more of my students will adopt the first attitude, and grow in confidence and skill and power as writers who can sing in a multitude of voices. As a teacher and a writer, steeled with agnosticism, I always live with hope.

References

Bakhtin, Mikhail. *Speech Genres and Other Late Essays.* Trans. Vern W. McGee. Ed. Caryl Emerson and Michael Holquist. Austin: U of Texas P, 1986.

Carroll, Lewis. *The Complete Illustrated Works of Lewis Carroll.* London: Chancellor, 1982.

Derrida, Jacques. *The Post Card: From Socrates to Freud and Beyond.* Trans. Alan Bass. Chicago: U of Chicago P, 1987.

Elbow, Peter. *Writing with Power: Techniques for Mastering the Writing Process.* New York: Oxford UP, 1981.

Graves, Donald H. *Writing: Teachers and Children at Work.* Exeter: Heinemann, 1983.

Hashimoto, I. "Voice as Juice: Some Reservations About Evangelic Composition." *College Composition and Communication* 38 (1987): 70–80.

Sontag, Susan, ed. *A Barthes Reader.* New York: Hill and Wang, 1982.

Stewart, Donald C. *The Authentic Voice: A Pre-Writing Approach to Student Writing.* Dubuque, IA: Wm. C. Brown, 1972.

Sukenick, Ronald. Interview. *Anything Can Happen: Interviews with Contemporary American Novelists.* Ed. Tom LeClair and Larry McCaffery. Urbana, IL: U of Illinois P, 1983. 279–97.

IV Rethinking, (Re)Vision, and Collaboration

13 Crossing the Lines: On Creative Composition and Composing Creative Writing

Wendy Bishop
Florida State University

We need to be crossing the line between composition and creative writing far more often than we do. In fact, we may want to eliminate the line entirely. To support this claim, I hope to describe what it has felt like to enter the creative writing classroom as a composition specialist and the world of composition studies as a creative writer, before suggesting that we rethink undergraduate writing curriculums and revise graduate education for writing teachers.

To begin, consider this undergraduate's journal entry, discussing creative writing and composition:

> I'm really confused here. What's the difference between the two? Most of the time I use the two words interchangeably. . . . For all I know, it is a grave sin to use one for the other. If I think really hard, I can see a line of distinction begin to form between the two ideas. Is creative writing stuff that is done for fun, and composition stuff that the teacher makes you do? That's what it meant in elementary school, and later. Composition was writing about a specific topic, picked out by the teacher and had to be a certain length and certain form. Creative writing was anything you felt like putting down on paper. My creative writing was most often poetry, or a short story. Composition was an essay. So it's fun stuff vs. required stuff. Then I wrote a paper that was required, and it turned out to be fun. What??!? Yes, and it was an English (ugh! don't say it!) term paper. I chose my own topic, so I wouldn't get bored with it. Something totally off the wall, so fascinating that its appeal overwhelmed my intense hatred of term papers. It was on parapsychology.

This student, Fran, found composition a dreary, teacher-imposed task and creative writing something done to pass time, for fun.[1] In her world view, students in creative writing classes seemed launched on a teacherless field-trip and students in composition classes entered a kind of academic prison. Fran was confused when she realized that the distinction between fun stuff and required stuff, creative writing and composition, broke down when she chose and wrote on her own topic, parapsychology. Equally important, from the view of the two writing professions, Fran doesn't make nearly as much of the genre distinction as her teachers make—that is, that creative writing results in poetry and stories, non-nonfiction, while composition results in essays, nonfiction (terms I use intentionally to highlight problematic distinctions). Finally, there's a hint of guilt in Fran's story: she had fun, became engaged, and even learned in a composition class only when she broke the rules.[2]

My second story moves from unintentional to intentional confusion. A first-year college writer calls home to talk to her mother, a former director of composition and a friend of mine. Composing her first college paper, this writer, Lee, was resistant. She told her mother that she didn't like the first-year writing teacher, the assignment, or the grade she received (a C) and reported current first-year lore that claimed a first-paper grade would be a student's end-of-semester class grade.

For the second paper, students were asked to go off campus and interview someone about his or her work and writing. Lee didn't have time, didn't want to—knew she was going to get a C. But, a week later, Lee reported that she had received a B− on the interview paper and strong teacher encouragement. Then, she explained to her mother that she had *invented* the interview and that during a revision conference for this paper the teacher asked Lee about a detail relating to her imagined "real" interviewee. "I'll go back and ask him," Lee assured her teacher. And, real interviews or not, Lee was encouraged by her improving class performance; she made a high B on her third paper and the same for her final class grade.

The semester after this story unfolded, I continued to reflect on Lee's experiences, for I believed that they would be replicated by students enrolled in my own writing program—again and again. First-year writing, for Lee, was no fun; she was disengaged, at least until she redefined her assignment by turning in a piece of "imaginative" writing for the required factual interview. Genres seem to have little to do with her new success with writing.

In a third and final story, this one from the creative writing side of the line, we see that confusion can result in self-doubt. Despite Fran's assumption that creative writing is the fun stuff, writing with which we're more readily engaged, students who enroll in creative writing classes for the first time may have to overcome an overwhelming sense of unworthiness. Since creative writing is usually an elective class, those who elect it may be English majors, more steeped than fellow students in the traditional canon.[3]

If creative writing is the class in which literature is made, as an English-studies-influenced student tends to think, she or he will wonder: Am I good enough to make literature with a capital L? Frank writes in his class journal:

> I think I was misleading myself for a very long time. I had so many grand ideas about writing that I had forgotten that you have to write to be a writer. . . . [Now,] instead of pondering over ideas and waiting for the perfect one, the one to make me famous, I take small ideas and make them good ones. I just recently finished a short story that I am very proud of. It was 8 pages long, the longest one I had ever written. It had scenes, summaries, dialogue. I love it. I didn't really ever think I had it in me. I was putting so much pressure on myself to write the masterpiece that all of my writing was overdramatic, didn't say anything and was shallow. I have learned to write in stride, write for myself & let my ideas flow. Although I really do picture my audience as I write, I now write with much less apprehension and try not to make them my cornerstone.
>
> I have realized that just by sitting down and writing many different ideas just pop into your head. It is as if you turn on a hose that has been lying out in the sun. You expect cold water to come out & then are amazed that you get scalded by the water that has been heating in its length.

For some of us, a ready response to Frank's entry is to shake our heads and think he's more than a little misguided. Famous? A masterpiece? For, depending on our feelings about who should be encouraged to pursue "creative" writing, we may find Frank's hose metaphor an indication of promise or a prediction of mediocrity.

As I moved as a teacher between these worlds of composition classes and creative writing classes, my pedagogy in each became more similar. However, because the culture I inhabited—English Studies—didn't support such commonalties in instruction, I hadn't examined very well my growing beliefs that it was more productive to cross the line than to create a separate teaching persona on either side. If there was limited use in making so many distinctions between the areas, I needed to understand why I continued to make some of them and what was at stake.

I was formally trained to teach composition. I was not formally trained to teach poetry. However, I write poetry and not compositions, at least not the type of essays—in the modes—that I was first hired to teach to my students. Jim Corder is one of the few composition teachers I know of who regularly reports his attempts to write essays with his students although theorists now often advocate such a practice. And

Corder admits to the difficulty of the enterprise; sometimes he even cheats, recycling old papers and creating pastiche compositions so as always to be there with students as a fellow author.[4] Most writing teachers, however, don't write with their students, if they write much at all. When we do write, it seems safe to say, we don't produce the type of writing we ask students to produce. Lynn Bloom argues that: "teachers of writing should write literary nonfiction, assuming that is what we teach, and we should publish what we write.... writing regularly should be as much a part of the teacher's activity as meeting class, and as unremarkable" (87). Additionally, like me, many of the new teachers of writing that I train never took first-year writing, having tested out of those classes and wandered back into the fold via literature and creative writing; therefore, we have underdeveloped personal schemas for those classrooms.

These attitudinal and experiential problems compound. While graduate students in creative writing programs inevitably see themselves as writers, M.A. and Ph.D. candidates in English literature traditionally have prepared themselves for lives as "scholars," defined by their abilities to read. Undergraduates' careers as students of great literature may ill-prepare them for naming themselves writers as graduate students. "The problem for many of us," explains Harvey Kail, "is that authors became our heroes long before we began to think of ourselves as writers willing to compete with those heroes for a reader's attention" (89). And Patricia Sullivan's study of graduate-level literature instruction shows that writing abilities are usually assumed and not taught, deficits being attributed to problems in the student not to problems with English graduate education.

While it's easy to imagine readers who resist my claims with the simple counter-claims that they do write and teach, these readers would be ignoring the toll taken on many of their colleagues by teaching loads, department assignments, institutional attitudes, and personal life—constraints that work to keep the majority of writing teachers from publishing or even from viewing themselves as authors. Mimi Schwartz found this to be true to a surprising degree. She opens *Writer's Craft/Teacher's Art* in this way:

> This book began on Martha's Vineyard three years ago, with this question: "How many of you consider yourself writers?" I was teaching a two-week seminar on writing to twenty-five writing teachers from twenty states, mostly from English Departments.... Two hands went up. "What about the rest of you?" I asked, somewhat surprised... "We're not good enough... famous enough... creative enough.... What we write—memos, letters,

> articles, reports, diaries, grants—that doesn't count," said the Noes. (*ix*)

These writers did not feel that their academic writing was valid or valuable. And clearly, academic writing may be as distinctly unpleasurable for some teachers as composition is for many of their students since academic writing is, to a degree, as compulsory within institutional life as is first-year writing for a first-year student. Compulsion has the same counterproductive results, both constituencies avoid writing; Maxine Hairston suggests that "at least two-thirds of college professors publish nothing after the dissertation" ("When Writing" 62).

These, then, are just a few of the problems that arise. Many teachers don't write; those who do write, specialize. Creative writers compose primarily imaginative work and composition instructors excel at the academic essay or, more likely, the memo and class handout. Graduate-level tracking into creative writing or academic writing has been strenuous and successful. And creative writing teachers with an unhealthy sense of author hero-worship may transmit those feelings to a student like Frank, who for a long time saw writing primarily as the act of producing a masterpiece in order to gain fame. And composition teachers may tend to perpetuate the conservative writing class Fran mentioned—students writing only on teacher-specified topics of restrictive length and form. This will be particularly likely if these teachers have underdeveloped writers' identities, experience negative institutional pressures (either they must write and/or they're given no opportunity to write), and have never experienced first-year writing from the inside—as students or as teachers who write with their students.

It is important to emphasize that teachers participate in a complicated acculturation process within departments of English. As graduate students, many progress through the various strands of English studies looking for a home. For instance, I started in creative writing, quickly added literature, discovered and moved into rhetoric and, all the while, kept up my interests in all my earlier types of writing and reading. I wanted to connect my knowledge of writing and reading, discovered in the separate "strands," but was not encouraged to do so. I don't think, from conversations with colleagues, that mine is simply a naive academic Bildungsroman—there is rarely an easy initiation into English studies. But I have been able to begin sorting my confusions with the help of the institutional histories and professional critiques that are becoming more available.

One examination of the lines that divide us has been provided by Robert Scholes in *Textual Power.* Scholes describes how the institution of English studies has always valued the consumption of texts (interpretation and reading) over the production of texts (all writing) and that in the four-tiered textual hierarchy of the traditional English department, creative writing ranks as pseudo-literature (literature in the wings) and is valued over composition (pseudo-nonliterature). Both, in turn, are subservient to literature because literature calls for interpretation, the highest ranked form of consumption. In spite of these apparently stable, ranked positions, however, creative writing developed with composition.

The two writings were in unison at the turn of the century, after which, according to Doug Meyers, composition became a routinized operation for teaching the large numbers of students to write.[5] Robert Connors traces an equally efficient institution-serving movement, claiming, "Narration and description seceded to become the nuclei of creative writing courses, and argumentation, finding itself more of an orphan in English Departments, took refuge in Speech departments and became largely an oral concern for many years" (30). From a creative writing historian's or composition historian's point of view, composition was left with the stripped-down expository, non-fiction, essay form that we now recognize, while literary composition was viewed generally as unsuitable for "the masses" who weren't qualified to appreciate or practice literary art: "It was foundations of grammar and usage that students required" (Meyers 103). The lessons here are obviously political ones; fundamentals precede art and art writing is for the elite (endlessly, the white, literate, at least middle-class kind),[6] and composition writing is for those who need nothing more than *basic* literacy (although what that is no group has yet been able to agree upon).

There are conflicts here of class. There is an issue of genres being asserted to represent class interests. But actual writers—student writers—don't fall neatly into categories. I point to Fran, Lee, and Frank, to the ways they found that one genre is not more valuable than another for learning about writers and writing; specifically, Frank, in a creative writing class, is as engaged with his work as is Fran, writing her self-chosen term paper on parapsychology in a composition class. Because they are engaged with their writing, choosing topics and using writing to learn more about themselves and their worlds, Fran and Frank are writers-more-than-students. However, when students remain students-more-than-writers, when instruction is top-down, for their own good, they quickly become disenfranchised.

Often students believe essay writing is a chore. They also believe in what I'll call the myth of "free creativity" in creative writing classes, as expressed here by Bill: "In creative writing, I feel that there is no set guidelines. It leaves room for experimentation and you can go into any angle or direction. In expository prose you have set guidelines of what you must write and how you should write it." This "free creativity" belief is as devastating for the creative writing class as it is for composition classes. When students arrive in creative writing classes with dichotomous attitudes—composition is no fun, creative writing therefore must be fun—creative writing classes can appear surprisingly restrictive since novice writers are often expected to learn conventions like the intricacies of formal verse or plotting and point of view rather than simply given free rein to "find some exotic, fun, brilliant way to say things," as Ashley had hoped.

No doubt, students are confused about the relationship between composition and creative writing because English studies, as a profession, is confused. Early in his history of the subject, Meyers defines creative writing:

> As it is loosely applied today, creative writing seems to denote a class of compositions once simply called fiction. . . . As such it is a makeshift, omnibus term for poems, novels, novellas, short stories, and (sometimes) plays; for the invented as opposed to the historical; for the imaginary in contradistinction to the actual; for the concrete and particular as distinguished from the thorny and abstract. In short, for non-nonfiction. . . . (2)

The textual creations Meyers catalogs as fixed genres will be found by many current compositionists (and literary theorists) as convenient, contingent, and situated. The historical must be discovered through the ideologically based author; the actual can only be apprehended through the representations of language and constructed texts; and the thorny and abstract may provide valid, but (currently) not sanctioned, ways of learning about the concrete and particular.

Essentially, our categorical systems work to maintain order within our communities. And our communities—to maintain and preserve order—insist that we adhere to our categories and their hierarchies. When genres blur, it is necessary to remind ourselves that categories are *constructed* and that genres are *defined: "Genre,"* Scholes reminds us, "refers to things regularly done and *style* to a regular *way* of doing things" (2).

English studies is not the only academic field that is considering these problems. Particularly relevant is the situation of ethnographers, who are entertaining critiques of one-hundred-fifty years of field-research, purporting to detail the "real" life of other cultures. Anthropologist Clifford Geertz explains:

> . . . [the idea] that the writing of ethnography involves telling stories, making pictures, concocting symbolisms, and deploying tropes is commonly resisted, often fiercely, because of a confusion, endemic in the West since Plato at least, of the imagined with the imaginary, the fictional with the false, making things out with making them up. The strange idea that reality has an idiom in which it prefers to be described . . . leads on to the even stranger idea that, if literalism is lost, so is fact. (140)

Discussing the construction of ethnographic narratives, certain anthropologists argue that ethnographic reporting involves "telling" the life of the researcher as much or more as reporting the life of the studied culture. Influenced by current critical theory, these scientists acknowledge the subjective and ideological nature of their profession, based as it is on human experience. Human science, then, becomes more similar to than dissimilar from humanistic study; field notes are texts, and text *are interpreted* by highly trained, skilled, but situated authors. Those exploring these views challenge anthropology's original values, those of positivistic research, an empiricism grounded in "true" facts and "pure" data.[7]

It would seem that the strands of English studies—literature, composition, and creative writing—are also laboring under, and have actually even helped to establish and maintain, similar self-limiting ideas of the "true" relationship of fact and fiction: if literalism is lost, is fact? What of the imaginative reality of Fran's fabricated composition interview? Would we do better to consider the degree to which non-nonfiction writing always evolves out of its composer's fact-filled existence and the degree to which non-fiction is shaped by its composer's judgments, desires, and imagination?

Whether we sanction it or not, when fact and fiction do blend, we need other ways of looking at and of teaching writing.

These considerations return me to the writing classroom. As a composition teacher, I was trained to have the unique ability to grade individual first-year texts. I learned to invoke the generic "college-level" rubric (essentially thesis, development, organization, mechanics) that my teacher preparation class and textbooks taught me. And I rarely doubted my abilities to rank what might seem a bewildering array of "essays." I could identify not only superior and inferior examples of writing but every range in-between.

From my earliest moment teaching poetry writing, however, in spite of my own experience with the genre—which included far more practice with the form and far more reading in it—I was sure that it is impossible to evaluate (grade) the single poem, and I have never done so. Although

I know a few individuals who grade single pieces of "art" writing, most do not. And never would I grade my student's first poem, although early in my teaching I was regularly required to grade first freshman essays in freshman composition. And, oddly, in creative writing classes the *adequate* story or poem (call it average or C-level) was rarely discussed and never assumed to be a normal base for future growth.

Although I now grade all writing classes—composition and creative writing—by the portfolio method, as a writing program administrator and institutional representative, I must note that I still sanction more controlling attitudes and practices toward first-year writing and writers. Certainly, I *am* liable to certain state, university, and program mandates and constraints. But also, I suspect that I agree to institutional pressures in part because I have never taken first-year writing and never had regularly to produce those pieces of "student writing." As I wrote this essay, I changed that situation, and the process of meeting the deadlines and writing demands of my own advanced composition class *as I taught it* proved sobering, informative, and tough. It also prompted me to improve my classroom design.

By writing and rewriting this essay, by writing with, for, and to my writing students, I'm exploring the degree to which I am a product of my own literary education, taught to value the "fictional" work (pseudo-literary text) over the essay (pseudo-non-literary text), and I still find myself in situations where I may talk about the average essay although it remains impossible (not-creative-writing-field-sanctioned) to hold serious discussions about the *average* poem or story. All this despite my willingness to tell you that I believe writing in each genre to be more similar to writing in other genres than it is different from them.

I am, of course, influenced by what Linda Brodkey calls the "scene of writing." In the modern scene of writing, the artist is locked into a garret, writing masterpieces alone. Brodkey warns of the danger of this image: ". . . those who teach as well as those who take composition [and all writing] courses are influenced by the scene of writing, namely, that all of us try to recreate a garret and all that it portends whether we are writing in a study, a library, a classroom, or at a kitchen table, simply because we learned this lesson in writing first" (397). One result of this lesson is an overvaluation of—a worship of—Literature. Over and over, we come to non-nonfiction with "the attitude of the exegete before the sacred text" (Scholes 16).

Not surprisingly, the "scene of writing" and its image of "solitary genesis," as Valerie Miner calls it, affects our students' views of texts. They quickly learn that the most *valuable* texts are puzzles; they learn to solve puzzles in literature classes and they come to creative writing hoping to learn puzzle-construction, to escape to a garret and reappear hours later with a soon-to-be-acknowledged masterpiece. The role of author is seductive, as you've seen from Frank's journal entry and, no doubt, from the responses of your own creative writing students. And the roles as apportioned leave nothing to composition classes except the predictable drudgery of delivering unpuzzling texts to uncomplicated readers. No wonder neither students nor their teachers look forward to such a workplace.

It is possible to point out that institutions have rigid and self-maintaining categorical systems—field coverage, composition *or* creative writing, fact *or* fiction, and so on. It is less easy to discover how these systems work within research agendas—say the ones of the composition community. Classic studies in composition research often compared and contrasted the basic and the expert (non-fiction) writer. Difficult areas—student engagement (or lack of it), individual talent, cognition and creativity, writer's affect—were generally considered out of bounds for research projects, influenced as such projects were by the positivistic research tradition. Even today, there are few studies of "creative writers" and there is little encouragement to conduct such studies.[8] As compositionists model the writing process, what will be known when we claim to present this thing we call the *non-fiction writing process?*

Creative writing as a composition research area, then, is generally ignored in spite of cross-the-line pedagogical raiding; compositionists have borrowed effective teaching methods from the creative writing workshop—particularly group-response sessions and portfolio evaluation—improved on those borrowings and gone beyond them.[9] Seldom discussed are the basic commonalities of writing a poem and writing an essay. That is, many teachers in both writing areas deny commonalities while a few teachers are exploring connections. Anthony Petrosky feels that, despite surface differences, the processes of poetry and essay writing are productively similar (209). Marie Ponsot and Rosemary Deen believe all students of writing are creative, that they are always writing literature, and that writing processes have basic commonalities:

> [S]tudent writing is literature, that is, free and disinterested, a product of imagination and thought. In our experience and the experience of those we know, there is no essential difference between writing a poem and writing an essay, except, as we must often say, that writing a poem is easier, its conventions being so much clearer and more plentiful. (65)

Their claim that essays are more difficult to compose may seem hard to believe until we remember those teachers of composition who rarely themselves write first-year compositions. So, for many of us, perhaps, writing a poem would be easier than writing an essay since we are well schooled, if literature majors, in the conventions of poetic form. We are also taught in that school never to view student writing as Literature (despite what that vision promises for the project of responding to students' drafts). Literature is what is past, what is old. Ponsot and Deen, however, redefine literature through language, claiming, "What[ever in a text] we pay attention to is literature" (68) and then show how this definition helps both teacher and student: "When we name and praise the literature in a student's writing, she sees, sometimes for the first time, what she had done. Then she sees that what she has originated is not peculiar to her but is part of her culture" (68).

Ponsot and Deen's claim does not advocate chaos, but it does alert us to complexity. Critical and discourse theories constantly complicate our definitions of literary writing (as the primary imagination [Coleridge]; aesthetic [Rosenblatt], poetic [Britton et al.], discursive [DeQuincy; Langer]; and so on).[10] Reader-response theory persuades that meaning does not reside solely in the text, inserted once and for all by authorial agency. Meaning is constructed by authors in conjunction with a reading and a reader. And several theorists have provided readings of texts as non-literary-seeming as lists left on blackboards (Fish) to computer instructions and phone booth directions (Winterowd, *The Rhetoric*), in order to show that literary texts are those *to which we pay attention in particular ways and by community-sanctioned agreement.* In fact, our response to and interpretation of a first-year theme will change over time. In his essay "The Drama of the Text," W. Ross Winterowd reads a twenty-five-year-old student theme in three ways: "Between 1965 and the present, the paper changed radically. . . . it has become sexist. . . . It has been, successively, (1) an inadequate structure, (2) an inadequate statement of selfhood, and (3) a perfectly normal exemplar of a pseudo-genre" (22–23).

That students can see the literature within their own writing in order to understand text-building is not a radical notion if we use current theories of texts to let us understand that Literature with a capital *L* is primarily a canonized set while writing literature with a small *l* may be thought of as writing in order to understand genre conventions, writers' choices, readers' responses: the exhilarating act of experiencing textuality, as defined by Scholes and commented upon by others.

What is lost by these views? Certainly the idea that not everyone can be a writer, for everyone should be able to learn to see the texts within his or her texts. We also come closer to understanding student writing practices. Imagine, as I have been doing lately, the vast network of first-year writing instruction as we know it today. Consider that for years we may have been reading a wealth of "imaginative" and "creative" essays even when we assigned them and evaluated them as non-fiction work. It is also possible then to visualize the infinity of shaped "family stories" and "true experiences" that comprise the beginning compositions of generations of creative writing students (and comprise the published texts of many of their teachers, myself included). The old, limiting distinctions, I maintain, were given primacy because they helped keep our selves and our academic territories well and safely sorted.

These days, we might ask for research agendas that help us to take a closer look at genre expectations and their influence on composing. I think we must note, for instance, the way the essay is moving back into the three-genre literature anthology and ask what it means when two recent books from a "composition" press focus on *Literary Nonfiction* and *The Rhetoric of the "Other" Literature.* This movement, I believe, may represent either a bridge between Literary Studies and Composition Studies or a movement on one side (Literature) to co-opt the power rhetoric has gained in English departments when "[T]he 'literature of fact' is being rehabilitated within the literary establishment, and rhetoric is being repatriated after nearly a century of exile from the literary establishment" (Winterowd *ix*).

Or, it may represent a movement on one side (Composition) to assert a primacy for itself as strong as that asserted in Literary Studies: "[T]hat literary nonfiction, by its nature, reveals to us the complexity and power and rhetorical possibilities of language—and that the complexity and power and possibility of language ought to be the unifying concern of rhetoric and composition as a discipline" (Anson *xxiv*). The latter may be a significant political move in composition, an area that has traditionally felt undervalued, members of which still debate the wisdom of a suggestion that first-year programs leave English departments and create academic programs of their own (Hairston, "Breaking"). The moves on either side seem, however unfortunately, to be revisiting old categories and ways of viewing English Studies and simply looking to reapportion power.

In several of the scenarios I've sketched above, claims are being raised formally that we can (and should) read non-fiction as non-nonfiction. To me, these claims suggest that some of the deepest categorical assumptions of our writing classrooms and writing research models may be simplistically exclusionary; we have assumed, due to our own English studies institutional hierarchy, that comparing nonfiction to non-nonfiction is like comparing apples to oranges. Maybe.

Maybe, though, we have talked ourselves into using a single lens, the wrong lens, one out of several possible category systems. What if non-fiction is apples and non-nonfiction is apples, too, and both must be looked at that way and/or categorized in other ways?

To start, I believe we should teach "creative" writing in the first-year program, as has been done at my school for many years with good effects—particularly on student and teacher attitudes—and no reported harm. Students are well prepared for future academic writing when they explore creativity, authorship, textuality, and so on, *together, all at once.*[11] In fact, I suggest that they are more prepared to think about and perform the complicated act of writing when they study this way. Many of our students pick up conflicting understandings about textuality from traditional courses, the ones that define writing or reading very narrowly and focus on skills rather than on active learning and process, or that offer only a naive theory of texts (if any). Understanding writing as a subject, I believe, aids the development of written products. And, certainly during the college years, if not earlier, a well-developed metacognitive and metalinguistic understanding of the demands of writing and reading enables a student to develop flexible responses to class-assigned or self-assigned writing tasks.

Next, in our classrooms, the results of writing research should be welcome beside the testimonial of expert (and/or famous) writers. Equally, we should read and study the best, most exciting, most creative texts in all genres (this includes scientific and technical texts), whether the authors of such texts have invested more heavily in fact or fiction. We should remember, also, that when conducting a writing class, we are convening a discussion among writers who happen to be students. We should consider the extent to which "literary interests" have defined the creativity quotient of other kinds of writing (usually as zero). When we see the individuals on our rosters as writers-more-than students, we distance ourselves from the demeaning, disempowering concept of "student writer" with its inevitable implications of eternal deficiency. Our students aren't writers the day they are finally hired as writers in the workplace or the day they publish in "professional" forums. They are writers whenever they write, and they will believe us when we say so only when we acknowledge their rights through our course designs and our attitudes toward their work.

Finally, throughout their graduate education, prospective teachers should be trained as writers, composing extensively and gaining an introduction to the many discourses of English studies (and when feasible to the discourses of fields outside English). While doing this they should receive help and encouragement. Teachers shouldn't need to apologize for having a writing strength or a weakness ("I'm never going to be a poet"; "I can't write a critical essay to save my life"; "I don't think of myself as a [creative] writer"; "I write, but I guess the type of writing I do isn't creative") as long as they are willing to explore writing in the same manner and along the same dimensions that I'm suggesting for first-year college writers: as a complex human endeavor, requiring practice and analysis, involving beliefs and emotions, resulting in failure and success. Teachers don't have to profess writing, but they should experience it, and that experience, as any graduate of National Writing Project training will attest, is life-changing. It's possible, I guess, to teach writing without ever having felt like a writer, but shouldn't we insist that it be otherwise?

Anyone interested in writing and reading in academic settings will have realized by now that a wealth of issues and questions can be raised on both sides of the line that seems to divide composition from creative writing; I tend to believe that our categories don't suffice and that questions—now—are essential. And our questions need to move into both territories from this disturbing spot in no-person's land where we reside, together with Fran and Lee and Frank. For instance, there is much to be asked, too, about the world of creative writing instruction. Why is the institutional history of creative writing the last to be written? In the creative writing class, why do we devalue critical theory and writing research? In what ways does it hurt us to find out that the muse can have regular habits and hours and that our writing processes can be illuminated, adapted, enhanced, and changed? What do we gain when we lose complete authority over our texts? And finally: Who is served by the assumption that the academy taints "creative" writers and that composition taints "creative" writers even worse than the generic "academy"? It isn't a sin, as Fran worried, to ask these questions. Surely, it's time to find more answers and then to return, renewed, to our work.

Notes

1. The names of those I quote are fictional at their own request.

2. The issue of rules and rule-breaking in writing classes is explored more fully in Bishop "Teaching the Process."

3. For more on the problems of undergraduate creative writing see Bishop "Teaching" and *Released into Language* and Ostrom.

4. See Corder's "Asking for a Text."

5. For extensive composition-studies histories of the development of writing instruction in American universities, also consult Berlin.

6. See Eagleton and Graff *Professing.*

7. For more on discussions of fact and fiction in ethnographic reporting, see Bishop "I-Witnessing."

8. Published exceptions include those by Armstrong, Brand, and Tomlinson.

9. Robert Brooke's recent book provides great theoretical insight into why workshops are successful and what they are actually doing for student writers.

10. These categories are discussed in Winterowd's *The Rhetoric.*

11. See for instance, Graff's *Beyond.*

Works Cited

Anderson, Chris. *Literary Nonfiction: Theory, Criticism, Pedagogy.* Carbondale, IL: Southern Illinois UP, 1989.

Armstrong, Cheryl. "A Process Perspective on Poetic Discourse." Paper presented at the Annual Meeting of the Conference on College Composition and Communication. New York, NY, March 29–31, 1984. ERIC Document Reproduction Service No. ED243108.

Berlin, James A. *Rhetoric and Reality: Writing Instruction in American Colleges, 1900–1985.* Carbondale, IL: Southern Illinois UP, 1987.

———. *Writing Instruction in Nineteenth-Century American Colleges.* Carbondale, IL: Southern Illinois UP, 1984.

Britton, James, et al. *The Development of Writing Abilities 11–18.* London: Macmillan, 1975.

Bloom, Lynn Z. "Finding a Family, Finding a Voice: A Writing Teacher Teaches Writing Teachers." *Writer's Craft, Teacher's Art: Teaching What We Know.* Ed. Mimi Schwartz. Portsmouth, NH: Boynton/Cook Publishers, 1991. 55–68.

———. "Why Don't We Write What We Teach and Publish It?" *Journal of Advanced Composition* 10.1 (1990): 87–100.

Bishop, Wendy. "I-Witnessing in Composition: Turning Ethnographic Data into Narratives." *Rhetoric Review* 11.1 (Fall 1992): 147–58.

———. *Released into Language: Options for Teaching Creative Writing.* Urbana, IL: National Council of Teachers of English, 1990.

———. "Teaching the Process of Creative Writing." Symposium on K–12 Creative Writing Instruction. Ed. Joseph Moxley. *Design for Arts in Education* 93.2 (November/December, 1991): 27–34.

———. "Teaching Undergraduate Creative Writing: Myths, Mentors, and Metaphors." *Journal of Teaching Writing* 7 (1988): 83–102.

Brand, Alice. *The Psychology of Writing: The Affective Experience.* Westport, CT: Greenwood Press, 1989.

Brodkey, L. (1987). "Modernism and the Scene(s) of Writing." *College Composition and Communication* 49: 396–418.

Corder, Jim W. "Asking for a Text and Trying to Learn It." *Encountering Student Texts: Interpretive Issues in Reading Student Writing.* Ed. Bruce Lawson, Susan Sterr Ryan, and W. Ross Winterowd. Urbana, IL: National Council of Teachers of English, 1989. 89–98.

Connors, Robert. "The Rise and Fall of the Modes of Discourse." *The Writing Teacher's Source Book.* 2nd ed. Ed. Gary Tate and Edward P. J. Corbett. New York: Oxford UP, 1988. 24–34.

Fish, Stanley. "Literature in the Reader: Affective Stylistics." *Reader Response Criticism: From Formalism to Post Structuralism.* Ed. Jane Tompkins. Baltimore: Johns Hopkins UP, 1980. 70–100.

Eagleton, Terry. *Literary Theory: An Introduction.* Minneapolis: U of Minneapolis P, 1983.

Geertz, Clifford. *Works and Lives: The Anthropologist as Author.* Stanford, CA: Stanford UP, 1988.

Graff, Gerald. *Beyond the Culture Wars: How Teaching the Conflicts Can Revitalize American Education.* New York: W.W. Norton, 1992.

———. *Professing Literature: An Institutional History.* Chicago: U of Chicago P, 1987.

Hairston, Maxine. "Breaking our Bonds and Reaffirming Our Connections." *College Composition and Communication* 36 (1985): 272–82.

———. "When Writing Teachers Don't Write: Speculations about Probable Causes and Possible Cures." *Rhetoric Review* 5 (1986): 62–70.

Kail, Harvey. "A Writing Teacher Writes About Writing Teachers Writing (About Writing)." *English Journal* 75 (1986): 88-91.

Meyers, David Gershom. *Educating Writers: The Beginnings of "Creative Writing" in the American University.* Northwestern University, 1989. DAI Order Number 9009673.

Miner, Valerie. "The Book in the World." *Creative Writing in America: Theory and Pedagogy.* Ed. Joseph Moxley. Urbana, IL: National Council of Teachers of English, 1989. 227–36.

Petrosky, Anthony. "Imagining the Past and Teaching Essay and Poetry Writing." *Encountering Student Texts: Interpretive Issues in Reading Student Writing.* Ed. Bruce Lawson, Susan Sterr Ryan, and W. Ross Winterowd. Urbana, IL: National Council of Teachers of English, 1989. 199–220.

Ponsot, Marie, and Rosemary Deen. *Beat Not the Poor Desk: Writing—What to Teach, How to Teach It, and Why.* Upper Montclair, NJ: Boynton/Cook, 1982.

Ostrom, Hans. "Undergraduate Creative Writing: The Unexamined Subject." *Writing on the Edge* 1.1 (1989): 55–65.

Rosenblatt, Louise. *The Reader, the Text, the Poem: The Transactional Theory of the Literary Work.* Carbondale: Southern Illinois UP, 1978.

Scholes, Robert. *Textual Power: Literary Theory and the Teaching of English.* New Haven, CT: Yale UP, 1985.

Schwartz, Mimi, ed. *Writer's Craft, Teacher's Art: Teaching What We Know.* Portsmouth, NH: Boynton/Cook Publishers, 1991.

Schwartz, Mimi. "Wearing the Shoe on the Other Foot: Teacher as Student Writer." *College Composition and Communication* 40.2 (1989): 203–209. Printed in *Creative Writing in America: Theory and Pedagogy.* Ed. Joseph Moxley. Urbana, IL: National Council of Teachers of English, 1989. 227–36.

Sullivan, Patricia A. "Writing in the Graduate Curriculum: Literary Criticism as Composition." *Journal of Advanced Composition* 11.2 (Fall 1992): 283–99.

Tomlinson, Barbara. "Cooking, Mining, Gardening, Hunting: Metaphorical Stories Writers Tell About Their Composing Processes." *Metaphor and Symbolic Activity* 1.1 (1986): 57–79.

Tomlinson, Barbara. "Tuning, Tying, and Training Texts: Metaphors for Revision." *Written Communication* 5.1 (1988): 58–81.

Wilbers, Stephen. *The Iowa Writers' Workshop: Origins, Emergence, and Growth.* Iowa City: U of Iowa P, 1981.

Winterowd, W. Ross. "The Drama of the Text." *Encountering Student Texts: Interpretive Issues in Reading Student Writing.* Ed. Bruce Lawson, Susan Sterr Ryan, and W. Ross Winterowd. Urbana, IL: National Council of Teachers of English, 1989. 21–34.

———. *The Rhetoric of the "Other" Literature.* Carbondale: Southern Illinois UP, 1990.

14 Voices from the Writing Center: Risky Business/Safe Places

Julie Neff
University of Puget Sound

When faculty think of writing centers, they most often think of the academic conference—writing advisor and student sitting at a table, struggling to tame a thesis sentence or to organize an essay on the French Revolution. What they do not see in their mind's eye is the writing advisor and student "clustering" at the blackboard to expand the student's thinking, role-playing a scene from a narrative that includes dialogue, or reading a poem aloud to listen for rhythm and emphasis. Writing center advisors do help students in traditional ways with writing, but they also use techniques borrowed from creative writing to help students write vividly and convincingly in all academic areas.

For creative writers, the writing center provides a haven, a safe place for them to receive feedback on a story, play, or poem. The center is a place for experimenting with writing and for taking chances. For example, in the center, writers can try out plot lines before they have to commit to them completely. Writers can also work on dialogue or check the believability of a setting before the piece is finished enough for review by a writing group.

Here is but one anecdote from the writing center at the University of Puget Sound that shows how creative writing conferences work: A student writer brought a short story to a writing conference asking the writing advisor (a student trained to work in the center) for feedback. After spending several minutes reading the story, the advisor stopped and said, "I love the story, but I don't believe page one."

"Why?" the student asked.

"Because I can't see it. You tell me I'm in an expensive office, but I can't tell you what it looks like." The writing advisor put her pencil down and closed her eyes. "Does it have windows? Where is the light coming from? What kinds of expensive art objects are you talking about? I can't see them."

The writing advisor asked the student to describe the "expensive art objects." In this case, the student did not know what they were or how they looked, nor had he thought about the size of the room or the placement of windows. But through conversation, questioning, and drawing a sketch of the room, he began to see for himself how the description of the office setting for his story was crucial to the theme of the story.

The center conference is, in many ways, similar to the workshop setting in the way it provides feedback and audience reaction for the writer. But the writing conference also provides support for the writer that goes far beyond what is typically available in a workshop. In a workshop, the writer may receive 20–30 minutes of attention, while the center's advisor is able to devote the best part of an hour to any one student writing project. In many centers, students may have more than one session per week.

Because the writing advisors are trained readers, they are more likely than peer respondents in a writing group to ask the hard questions of the writer, and they are more likely to give useful, specific feedback. Writing advisors are not timid, and they will say, "I don't get this." The writing advisors are also a confidential source of feedback, however. They will never say to other students, "You wouldn't believe how corny that poem was."

The writing conference also provides some necessary distance from the creative writing course, and, with distance, the social dynamics of the conference change. In "Peer Tutoring and the 'Conversation of Mankind,'" Kenneth Bruffee notes: "Some of us had guessed that students were refusing the help we were providing because it seemed to them merely an extension of the work, the expectations, and above all the social structure of traditional classroom learning." The writing center conference is disconnected from the social structure of the classroom and many writers will be more open talking to someone who will not be grading their work. The more open and comfortable students are the more likely they are to ask tough questions and the more receptive they are likely to be to criticism. The time of faculty members, who have dozens of students, is also limited. Even if they have several office hours a week there is seldom time for in-depth conferences.

Writing advisors also know that even though the writing is creative the writer does not have total freedom from conventions. The writing advisor has the knowledge and the handouts, to explain how punctuation, for instance, might be used to create the desired effect. ("What would be more effective here, a dash or a colon?") He can also explain how and why word choice or sentence construction affects him as a reader. The writer has choices to make, and the writing advisor can help the reader see the choices and more importantly the implications of those choices. It takes time to draw out a writer, time that the professor or the writing group often does not have.

But students who are involved in other kinds of academic writing can also benefit from writing advisors who know creative writing techniques. Freshmen enrolled in English 101 courses, for example, are often the beneficiaries of the creative writing techniques used in the center. The narrative assignment, the first assignment in many composition classes, is particularly difficult for students who have been trained in the five-paragraph essay or have taken Advanced Placement English in high school. Already these students have lost touch with their own voices, have trouble with dialogue, and tend to over-intellectualize even the simplest experience.

The writing conference, a requirement for many students taking introductory writing courses, might take the students through free-association exercises, mind-mapping, or focused free writing so that they can get in touch with their own voices. The writing advisor might talk about point of view and ask the student to draw sketches to help the student see the scene she is attempting to describe. One writing advisor, Shirley Schultz, a Politics and Government major at Puget Sound, describes her conferences:

> I often found it helpful to take notes, allowing the student to free-associate ideas and facts—in short, everything she knew about the subject. Clustering ideas in loose groups was much more useful than strict outlining; I encouraged it as a precursor or alternative to outlining. Then, after the student wrote and wrote and wrote, outlining could be used as a means for final organization of what was written.

Creative and academic writing, then, can share remarkably similar generative stages.

Students further along on their papers may have difficulty including dialogue; others have trouble moving from "telling" to "showing." One student wrote about her home state of Alaska, but lack of specific detail kept the reader at a distance from the experience. She brainstormed with a writing advisor about the scene, using all of her senses; by the time she finished, she had a half page of detail that was not found in the original. "Now I can see why you couldn't see," she told the writing advisor.

Because writing advisors apply "creative writing techniques" to many conferences in the center, advisors are trained in invention strategies. One session is devoted to Gabrielle Rico's version of prewriting techniques called "clustering," where a nucleus word evokes clusters of associations. The student writing advisors learn that the first stage of writing is chaos, and properly so. They learn to press writers for the image; rather than saying that Marcia was messy, show it: "As usual, her blouse was dotted with remnants of lunch. Today the cafeteria must have been serving cream of asparagus soup."

According to another student writing advisor, "All kinds of academic papers can benefit from creativity: I found that with students, and in my own writing, creativity is the key to *any* good paper—after all, what professor wants to read thirty identical essays?"

The student writing advisors also learn that writer's block usually results from trying to pursue the contradictory modes of creating and critical thinking simultaneously rather than sequentially. Invention techniques are intentionally structured to force writers out of critical thinking into a creative mode. When writers can be convinced to reserve editing during this phase, they learn they really can judge better at a later time, that writing *is* recursive. Additionally, advisors learn to combat the illusion of total freedom from form by demonstrating techniques of strong nouns and verbs, of punctuation as choreography, of showing, not telling—techniques that add power to writing.

Students who are themselves creative writers can be a tremendous asset to the writing center. They bring a spark to the center that many of the finest academic writers do not have. Because creative writing techniques can enhance much of the conferencing that goes on in the center, it is important to have creative writers make up at least part of the staff.

Directors who want to involve creative writers need to recruit them. Faculty who teach creative writing will know who the best candidates are. However, the best writers may not be the best writing advisors. Typically, the best advisors are those who love to write and share their writing, those who work well with others in groups and are good listeners.

Every writer needs a reader, and the role of the writing center is to provide the thoughtful, insightful, trained readers for the writers of fiction, academic papers, or poetry. The line between expository writing and creative writing is often blurred; nowhere is this distinction more blurred than in the writing center.

References

Bruffee, Kenneth. "Peer Tutoring and the 'Conversation of Mankind.' " *Writing Centers: Theory and Administration.* Ed. Gary A. Olson. Urbana, IL: National Council of Teachers of English, 1984.

Schultz, Shirley. Letter to the author. 5 September 1992

15 Voices from the Writing Center: Storytelling in the Writing Center

Beverly Conner
University of Puget Sound

A year ago, when I became the first creative writing teacher in the Center for Writing and Learning at the University of Puget Sound, I naturally had some concerns about this new venture. A couple of them, I now realize, indicated my own misconceptions of the role of the writing center: Would I find myself confined to explaining rules of grammar and punctuation? And would I be working primarily with basic writers? Other concerns had to do with writing across the curriculum: Even though I teach composition in addition to creative writing, how would I feel when faced with a Rhodes or Fulbright application from a senior in biology or a graduate admissions essay from a student in occupational therapy?

As it has turned out, I was in for a marvelous time, working with students from freshman composition to applicants for fellowships and scholarships to short story writers to graduate students—a degree of variety I would never have encountered in the classroom alone.

As teachers of creative writing, we are used to walking that fine line between encouraging students to reach more deeply into themselves for writing that is vivid and truthful and, on the other hand, helping them revise with an unsentimental rigor for clarity and impact. Our methods are diverse: brainstorming with student writers; teaching invention techniques, scene, dialogue, narrative, point of view, and voice; helping students with writer's block; structuring small writing groups; and scheduling an infinite number of one-on-one writing conferences.

These skills translate well to the writing center. One of my first appointments in the center was with a senior applying to graduate school for an MAT program. She brought in a draft of her personal essay in answer to a question which asked, in effect, "Tell us in one double-spaced, typewritten page why you would make the greatest teacher who ever lived!" Understandably, she was trapped between modesty (really her intuitive feel for the correct tone) and her wish to impress. As a result, her draft was filled with abstract language, inflated diction, and clichés. It essentially described a generic applicant.

As we talked, however, I discovered she had worked as a classroom aide under a teacher she considered especially creative, and from this teacher's example she had envisioned the kind of classroom she herself would one day like to establish. I suggested we put down our pencils and just chat about that classroom experience. What did she remember? Any specific events or activities? Don't worry about the essay, I told her, just talk to me. She could remember nothing in particular. Time passed. She thought hard. "Oh," she said dismissingly, "maybe the Snake Man." I perked up and pressed. "Not much to tell, really. He just brought some snakes in for the kids to handle."

"How many? Three? Ten?"

"No, he had about—oh, I'd say twenty-five snakes with him."

"Do any of those snakes stand out in your memory today?"

"Now that you bring it up (note that I didn't bring up anything), yes. An albino python—pure white and ten feet long!"

I doubt her admissions committee will soon forget the image of a ten-foot albino python or the applicant who described it as evidence of the lively classroom she hoped one day to create. It was just a matter of brainstorming and of using that ancient prewriting technique of "speaking," really of letting the stories do their work, of showing rather than telling (as creative writing students are used to hearing!).

Writing advisors often become readers for graduate or professional school applications and applications for fellowships like the Marshall, Mellon, Fulbright, or Rhodes. These statements are often gray; that is, they convey no vivid images, no colorful language, nothing the reader can remember once she has put down the paper.

"Memorable—that's what these applications need to be," said Jannie Meisberger, Assistant Director of the Honors Program and Graduate Fellowship Advisor. But most of them are not. It is often difficult to distinguish one essay from another because they sound impersonal and disinterested. When you've read a few, they seem to blend together and none of them stands out.

Using our understanding of creative writing to inform what we recommend that writers include in these essays can often make the difference. One Fulbright candidate who was majoring in biology wrote in her personal statement that she was influenced by her mother, who was a musician. The sentence communicated an idea, but the sentence was flat, lifeless. In a conference, the writing advisor asked her to describe a particular time when she was inspired by her mother. The advisor pushed her to use all of her senses to describe the situations in some focused free writing. The revision was memorable because it was vivid: "My mother, a musician and painter, taught me to see beauty in any number of settings (wet gloppy sand, bass notes on a piano, or the angelfish in our aquarium). She also taught me how to make the detailed and comprehensive observations basic to good science." The essay came to life because we could see and feel the images that the biology student brought into the statement.

I worked with a senior who turned out to be our Fulbright winner, as well as with many freshmen and sophomores applying for our Pacific Rim study-abroad program. The task was the same: to get the essence of the individual onto the page. In fact, without some sort of evidence, why should a reading committee believe a student who claims to be adaptable or quick-witted or emotionally sturdy enough for the rigors of travel abroad? After reading students' bland attempts at describing previous travel experience in such applications, I ask them something like, "So you never had any problems while traveling? No mishaps? No misadventures?" "Oh, sure," they'll say, "lots of stuff went wrong." "Tell me about one such time," I'll say, and we're off and running into "stories" that show courage and compassion and initiative and great senses of humor. "Write that story," I'll say, "and the committee will know who you are without your jumping up and down, yelling, 'I'm wonderful and smart and brave' " (which, students will agree, lacks something in tone).

A major project in the writing center is working with graduate students enrolled in our School of Occupational Therapy. These students are required to write a great deal of material at a professional level, so their application essays are carefully reviewed. About twenty desirable candidates are admitted provisionally, with the stipulation that they rewrite their application essays to the satisfaction of both the writing center and the School of Occupational Therapy.

In every case, we start by eliciting information on the writer's background in science, internships, work experience, etc. In other words, what happened to these students to bring them to this particular field, and even more importantly, what made them think they would be good at it? Inevitably, they arrive at a compelling piece of evidence that shows how OT came to be their chosen vocation. One student had a friend critically injured in an auto accident who now travels abroad in her wheelchair, thanks to physical and occupational therapy. Another knew a couple who had been married forty years when the husband was felled by a stroke. The student watched the wife's joy when her husband could button his shirt by himself again after extensive therapy.

Once these OT students turned in their rewrites (and some students rewrote four or more times), we then had the opportunity to look at grammar and punctuation (the areas I had originally feared I'd spend all my time on). In many cases, mechanics had improved merely by writers getting involved with their own material. Students realized they were in charge of punctuation, for example, and came to see it as a tool to direct the reader. And as these graduate students faced the potential impact of their own writing, their attitudes toward writing became much more positive.

In a similar vein, after having spent two or three years writing economics or history or political science papers, students often have internalized the academic style and have given up their own voices. The role of the writing center is to help them rediscover voice and to overcome the constraints of academic writing through freewriting, clustering, or other kinds of reflection. Through this reflection, the students are able to get in touch with the concrete images that can make writing alive and authentic. Additionally, these same students are often helped by seeing their academic papers in terms of "story," by realizing that introductory paragraphs, especially, are frequently narratives and that most essays contain narrative paragraphs of chronological organization. This view helps to demystify the writing process and can clarify structure.

Recently, a student came to the writing center with a highly polished introductory paragraph for an essay in a comparative religion course. She had been unable to move beyond this well-written opening (which she had rewritten nearly a dozen times) and was as blocked as any student I've encountered. She froze over suggestions to freewrite or to cluster. Nor did talking about the possible causes for her block relieve her panic; she seemed unable to release her grip on perfection, even for a fledgling rough draft. In this case, I asked her to forget her essay for the moment and to pretend I was an intelligent eighth-grader to whom she was telling the story of the historical clash between Islam and Christianity. Conversationally, relieved not to be pressed to write, she relaxed enough that a well-considered narrative tumbled out of her. Clearly, she had a grasp not only of the events but also of their significance. I took notes as she spoke, and when she had finished I handed her an outline of what she had just said and asked if she'd like to add to it, to fill in any gaps I'd left. After she made a few additions, I asked whether she could draft or freewrite a second paragraph by following the outline. Her body language had changed; with a grin, she began to write and drafted the next two paragraphs, made further adjustments to the outline, and left the conference a considerably happier student, knowing what direction her first draft would take.

In many cases, the writing conference itself is a kind of narrative about writing, and sometimes we even have a cast of characters, especially when one of our Occupational Therapy graduate students is somewhat resistant to the writing task that has been set for him or her. The student may see herself as protagonist, the Occupational Therapy admissions committee as "villain," and the writing center staff member as a sort of white knight riding to the rescue. Of course, we don't really talk about it in such terms, but the challenge is to shift the "power" from both the committee and the center onto the writer herself.

At other times the unintentional narratives of students' lives spill across the hour, as when one student revealed that her interest in OT came as a result of a rock-climbing accident two years before. It had been by no means sure she would regain the use of her legs after surgery to implant metal rods in her back. She knew first-hand the grueling hours of physical and occupational therapy. It was a stunning story, and I urged her to incorporate it in the personal essay she was revising, but she had left it out from an intuitive feeling that she didn't want to be "known by her accident." She still felt that way strongly, that it was almost a cliché in OT circles that physical misfortune drew students to the profession. This was a case of a conference composing itself into a narrative which needed to be released but not necessarily into the essay; in this case, the story's being told led to the informed choice by the writer to withhold it from her essay. She told me I was the only person at school who knew, and it was only when she left at the end of our hour together that I realized she still walked with a limp.

Indeed, just as I originally misperceived the role of the writing center, other teachers of creative writing may wonder whether the center offers undergraduate writers anything that the workshop doesn't already provide. But few teachers or workshops are able to offer fifty minutes of undivided attention to both the writer and the work. Ideally, the workshop and the writing center can work in tandem by giving the writer a chance in the writing conference to develop ideas or techniques or address problems identified in the workshop. A further link would be to provide a place for creative writing groups to meet. Currently, one of our student writing advisors who is enrolled in advanced fiction writing is using the center to hold extra meetings with her classroom writing group.

Scene and anecdote are powerful writing tools, often overlooked by the student writer. And the principle of "showing rather than telling" holds as true for essays as for imaginative writing. In fact, "story" is the creative writing teacher's stock in trade and makes us a valuable resource in the writing center. As writing groups and writing conferences of all sorts compose themselves into narratives, perhaps they form one more hedge against the chaos of the world, a buttress composed of our minds, of first drafts, and of the stories we all have to tell.

16 Voices from the Writing Center: It's Okay to Be Creative—A Role for the Imagination in Basic-Writing Courses

Lea Masiello
Indiana University of Pennsylvania

. . . You can fashion everything
From nothing every day, and teach
The morning stars to sing. . . .
W. B. Yeats, "A Prayer for My Son"

I look at that piece of writing, and I say, 'That ain't me.' but I like it better than anything else I've ever written. I needed to write that.
Jerry Shields, student

The job of any writing instructor is to bring a person/writer back to the moment of confrontation and invention.
Rosaly Roffman, teacher/poet

We often think of basic-writing courses as providing instruction in basic "skills," such as composing complete sentences, punctuating sentences accurately, and structuring the college essay. However, we do students a terrible disservice when we emphasize skills in a basic-writing course; instead, we need to emphasize the development of identity and confidence. Imaginative invention activities can be used in basic-writing courses to build identity and confidence very successfully, and these activities will be especially effective when combined with support from peer tutors in a writing center.

A student, Tom, commented on the role of the imagination to the development of identity in an essay responding to Annie Dillard's imaginary travels through Pittsburgh history in her book, *An American Childhood.* Tom eloquently explains exactly why imaginative writing belongs in basic-writing courses:

> I too was interested in the French and Indian War when I first read about it. Stories such as these are exciting and hold a sense of mystery to them. As a child, nothing is stronger than your imagination. Your imagination can protect you, it can take away the pain, and it can bring you closer to your true self.

As students develop their abilities to write college essays, they should be drawing upon their imaginations to write effectively—with voice and style; we should never assume that basic writers cannot write expressively. Indeed, they often have strengths as expressive writers, though they may perform weakly as academic writers because of their lack of experience as readers and writers in general. I have found that bringing creatively written texts into the classroom sparks students' development as writers and thinkers.

I believe in using whole readings in a basic-writing course. I have used, with great success, *Beloved, The Color Purple,* and Dillard's *An American Childhood.* Although these works are challenging for my students, they have been willing to learn new ways of reading and responding in order to value books. I ask students to read and respond based on their own experiences that are similar to or different from the authors'. Thus, students learn it is acceptable to read and enjoy a work without endorsing everything about it. *An American Childhood* is about gaining identity, "waking up," as Dillard names it, and I begin exploring this book by asking students to write about how they "wake up." Then we can move from the literal idea of waking up to Dillard's metaphor and consider the many ways in which people are shaken into consciousness. This book is especially effective here at Indiana University of Pennsylvania because many students are from the Pittsburgh area, and Dillard writes specifically about growing up in a Pittsburgh neighborhood that was once upper-middle class and is now a "drive-by" shooting zone. When students write about this neighborhood as it exists now, they connect and disconnect with Dillard's writing; they see how her identity formation was linked to specific sidewalks, streets, neighbors, and libraries that have changed but still continue to influence the identities of the people who grow up there. When they note these changes, the students grab hold of those aspects of their neighborhoods that do influence their ways of making meaning out of the world.

As we look carefully at how Dillard discovered ways to make meaning out of rocks, bugs, parents, schools, and friends, we can turn back to these very ordinary parts of our lives and re-envision our experiences. Dillard is full of surprises: having students read and respond to short passages from *An American Childhood* resulted in stylistic growth in their own writing. I found that asking students to focus on and respond to short descriptive sections led to unsolicited stylistic imitation when writing about their own similar experiences. For example, after responding to Dillard's descriptions of the aftermath of a tornado that included a violent fireball that sprouted like a water fountain and a melting power line that made a loud crackling hiss like a snake, Jason wrote expressively and clearly about his own experiences during a severe thunderstorm. Although I never suggested he should imitate Dillard's descriptions, his style shows the influence of her patterns of narration and comparison:

> On a bright sunny afternoon in the summer, I was mowing the grass and noticed the sky being sallowed by dark blue storm clouds. Soon after I looked at the sky, the sun was blocked by the clouds. I tried to mow the grass as fast as I could to finish before it started to rain. I heard a clash of thunder that gave me a signal to stop mowing. I looked over my shoulder as the wind blew grass cuttings across my face and saw the clouds rolling towards me. The clouds were twice as dark than I remember seeing them before. The clouds combined together looked like a steep avalanche of destruction on the town.

Jason's writing demonstrates that when we encourage basic writers to be creative, and when we reinforce their successes, we help strengthen the overall development of their writing abilities.

To grow as writers, students such as Jason need to discard previously over-learned and applied rules and discover new ones. Many basic writers feel bound by writing conventions—they know too many rules that begin with "don't": don't begin a sentence with *and,* don't use *I,* don't write more than eight sentences in a paragraph. Such rules bind writers; creative invention activities release them. Pat Hartwell illustrates the difference between a static model of writing and a dynamic one in his text, *Open to Language* (31–33). His synthesis of the static model describes exactly what I must struggle against when working with my students:

> Writing for writing classes is artificial and mechanical. It has no relevance to the real world. One writes down what one already knows, with special attention to the correct way to express it. One is never rewarded for one's effort, and one's grade is always beyond one's conscious control. As a result, one learns nothing from writing; it's simply a matter of showing the instructor what you already know. (32)

If I want to help students formulate new dynamic models of writing, I must start over with their writing processes. We engage in playful invention activities that contradict a rule-governed approach to writing that has caused them to focus on their erasers and errors rather than their thinking and expression. Writers have to revise their understanding of what it means to write and what it means to be a writer, notions that are at the core of personal and intellectual growth as well as essential to the development of writing abilities. Writing topics that stretch students' imaginations often produce the writing they value the most and recognize as their best work. For example, I have asked students to write about a "talisman," describing it, telling the story of how they received it, and explaining its significance. We began by reading a *Time* magazine story about the "Iceman," a 5,300-year-old corpse found in the Alps in almost perfect condition, with his tools and an item that could only be identified as a "talisman" nearby. Challenged by this concept of a talisman and by the Iceman's mysterious belongings, the students struggled to fit the concept into their lives, but eventually all identified an important object—such as trophies, diplomas, and pictures—and told their stories. I found that the Iceman's story, along with the mysterious word "talisman," gave students a freedom to write narratives with dialogue and description that surprised me. Tamara Green began her story with a conversation that set the tone of her writing:

> "Ooh! Grandma this is gorgeous," I recall saying to my Grandma Clara as she presented me with a ring. It was truly stunning. It had a rich deep golden colored stone in the center with a shiny brilliant gold band that housed the stone. "Hi Grandma, how are you doing?" I said to her that evening when she came to visit me. While I was setting on the front porch of my house, she told me I was a young lady and needed to have a "good" piece of jewelry. I was only fifteen years old, but she thought I was a young lady—no longer than a day ago I was fist-fighting with a boy over a basketball in the schoolyard.

Introducing poetry and prose that break rules shows students that "real" writers do startling things and, eventually, they feel they can too. In "A Prayer for My Son," Yeats emphasizes his positive hopes about his child's future creativity, just as writing teachers must emphasize the "can" aspect of becoming a writer. Roffman also echoes "A Prayer for My Son" in her discussion of the moment of confrontation and creativity: "The creative writing activity is confrontational—it's making a mark—making something out of nothing." Any act that begins with "nothing"—as writing does—can be frightening. But one act of making something builds confidence students need in getting through that first confrontation with the "nothing" sitting in front of them on the page, and imaginative invention activities help writers create discourse that is immediately interesting, although very rough. First, the writer rewards herself through her effort and success; in a tutorial, the tutor furthers that reward by confirming that "something," however rough, was initiated.

Introducing creativity into a basic-writing course introduces additional complications into a pedagogy for nurturing basic writers. The comments above from Jerry Shield, an adult student enrolled in a basic-writing course, and from Rosaly Roffman, a teacher/poet, illustrate the essential tension among creativity, teaching writing, and identity. All writers must face the moment of confrontation that Roffman identifies, whether they are writing college essays or poetry, enrolled in an advanced creative writing workshop or a first-semester composition course. When we work with students—as I do in the classroom and in the writing center at Indiana University of Pennsylvania—who test into basic-writing courses, the tension increases: most students who place into our basic-writing courses have not had any school personnel encourage their creativity or tell them what they *can* do. Instead, they have been told in school that they can't write and aren't writers. But as college-level writing teachers, we can take the approach that our students are writers—though not necessarily fluent in any preferred literary or academic genre—and we can recognize whatever identities they have as writers to further our goals of developing their confidence levels, personal and academic identities, and their abilities to write fluently.

I have found that this positive endorsement and recognition, along with an individualized and self-paced approach to instruction, enables me to meet my students where they are as writers. For example, I recently worked patiently with one student who consistently submitted highly poetic prose for me to grade as an essay. It was simply impossible for me to assess and grade his creative writing about his love for his girlfriend. I met with him individually to discuss ways to move his writing toward the essay form, and he was discouraged and disappointed that what he felt was his style was not acceptable for a graded essay. Because I allow students to submit revisions repeatedly and receive new grades on any essay following a successful revision, I could wait until he found a way to merge his style with the college essay, and he eventually did. With assistance and encouragement from a writing center tutor whom I hired specifically to nurture creativity in writers, he found a way to integrate his poetic expression into his narrative and descriptive passages, and he was extremely satisfied and proud of the results. I felt that the support he received from his tutor was instrumental in gaining confidence to adapt his poetic voice to an essay.

I am very sensitive to the fact that I had created a conflict for this writer: he must choose whether or not to change an important part of his voice and thus, change himself. Although I believe that his decision to change and the change itself would help him grow in many ways, I was firmly committed to staying away while he wrestled with his decision. If I had forced him to change, he would have only decided to write in order to please me, and therefore he would have lost identity rather than gained it. When I stayed away, he owned the conflict, the decision, and the change. My role as an authority in the classroom ensures that my involvement with his conflict would have been counterproductive to the development of his writing abilities. I hope that this stance leads to positively challenging classes "which recognize the positive uses of conflict and struggle and which teach the process of repositioning" (Lu 910).

Because writing center tutors are closer to the conflicts that my undergraduate students are experiencing in their approaches to writing, they are more able to convince my students that they can learn to write academic essays and still maintain their creativity. Many basic writers fear that if they cave in to the structural demands of the college essay, they must abandon the voice and stylistic expression that they feel is uniquely theirs. Because they associate their voice and expression with the only writing identity they have, we must find a way to maintain those elements while they work toward the college essay.

I work closely with our writing center tutors as they work with my students who are struggling with remaking their writing lives. I teach both tutors and writers mini-scripts for learning to talk with each other so that they can clarify their expectations at the beginning. For example, I tell my students, "When you go to the writing center tonight, say to your tutor, 'I need to work on developing my descriptions,' " and I tell the tutors, "Ask my students what they'd like to work on tonight. I'm spending class time talking about using comparisons in writing descriptions." After introductory tutorial sessions, tutors and students develop their own communication styles that work far better than those I share with them. Tutors provide the encouragement that new writers need for the risk-taking that accompanies this massive change in the students' approach to writing. When the tutor says, "I like this sentence here about why you like your friend—it's very expressive—but I need more descriptions about your friend," the writer does not think, "I have to change everything!" but "If I just add a little more here it will be better. I guess I can do that."

While students are struggling with their identities as writers, I, as a teacher, struggle with a commitment that seems contradictory to me and to the students: nurturing the creative writer while instructing the college-essay writer. The students I have worked with in basic-writing courses usually do not have confidence in their abilities to become writers of any kind; they associate failure, humiliation, frustration, and fear with the writing process, and cannot begin to imagine how an English course might cause them to experience success with writing, much less enjoyment. However, when I work with such students in the writing center, I am aware of a paradox: although my students are sure they cannot be successful in a school writing course and thus do not have a positive academic "writing identity," they may have had very positive experiences in high school as writers, or they may write privately in journals or notebooks, and thus do think of themselves as writers, but only in a private, creative realm. Unfortunately, students often perceive that these two modes of writing—creative and academic—are incompatible, and instruction in one cancels out any nurturing of the other.

Because I, as the instructor, represent the educational forces associated with failure and all the "don't" rules, it is difficult for students to trust my encouragement to "be creative." They will, however, listen to their peers who assist them in the writing center. Therefore, I rely on the peer tutors to nurture creativity.

Because writing centers encourage individualization and "self-pacing," a strong tutorial component in a basic writing course that includes creative writing activities and encourages multiple revisions helps developing writers control their decisions to use the conventions of college discourse. Our acceptance of their writing identities enables us to move them towards discovering what constitutes good writing without forcing them to abandon the writing identities they have, however unrealistic those identities may appear to be. Writing centers can be instrumental in supporting first-year college students as they take risks in this discovery process, and especially in supporting the creative writer inside many basic writers as they accommodate their writing styles to academic conventions.

We need to remember how difficult the first year of college is. Freshman are learning how to survive in a new environment that is puzzling, hostile, overwhelming, and demanding. They need all the extra support they can get. Tamara Green entered IUP through a special admissions program, and on her first day of summer classes in a presummer program, she found the writing center, and has been in every day since. Through a special work-study program for freshmen, I could hire Tamara to work in the writing center, with the hope that she will move from general assistance to tutoring within a year.

Tamara is a good student, with a clear sense of direction and motivation, yet even for her, the year's task is momentous. For her, however, writing is part of her way of coping, and she chooses her topics to help express her concerns. During the first week of classes, she wrote "Circus," an essay comparing college life to circus performance. She wrote,

> I feel as if I'm the center of attraction. I am Binky, the buffoon from the cartoon Garfield . . . I'm a student in the big top of IUP. My special feat is juggling my classes, social life, and work with my eyes closed. My class schedule builds up to be a trapeze act. It appears that I must bounce from building to building throughout the day . . . Achieving the Dean's List is my overall objective as a student. I plan on doing this by intense studying, working, and knowing when to just take a dive into a bucket of water ten feet off the ground, to ensure that I won't become the rambling deranged person that cleans the elephant stalls.
>
> It may be that college is a three ring, big-top circus for me this year, but hopefully by my senior year I may well be the Ringmaster of the big top.

I am sure that Tamara has found a "home" in the writing center, and I know that her presence here comforts and encourages other new students who are looking for a place to write. The easy way in which she gets along with the rest of our staff makes an important statement to other basic writers: you can be yourself here; you can take risks.

Writing center tutors can be instrumental in building these bridges for underprepared students, between their school and personal identities, by urging them to discover and utilize their creativity. The writing center is an ideal environment for trying on the role of a writer—someone who reads, listens, rewrites, and makes a portfolio. By leading basic writers through their "moments of confrontation," tutors can help them productively immerse themselves in the struggle of writing—an immersion that must occur for writing to be satisfying. The pedagogy associated with assisting underprepared students in writing centers focuses on their strengths, develops their self-confidence, allows them to retain ownership of their work, attends primarily to global rather than surface features, and draws upon their native linguistic competencies. My students recognize the writing center tutors as their peers, and they know that these folks will help them feel in some way that they are writers, a feeling that the basic writer hasn't yet fully internalized. I can depend upon the tutors to help convince my students that, as Roffman explains, creative writing can be inclusive and available to everyone, not just the advanced students, but the "basic writers" too. Peers can show other students how they can think of themselves as writers by modeling the interactions that writers have when they share their work and collaborate on revisions. Thus, the tutors act out Roffman's conviction that "It is important to move people away from the idea 'I have to be a this or a that to be a writer.' "

We will force creative writing underground in the writing center and lose opportunities to contribute to our students' growth as learners and human beings unless we work consciously to get it to the forefront of our practice and program development. And, particularly in basic-writing programs, the perception of a desperate need to provide instruction in formal conventions may make us feel that nurturing creativity is superfluous. However, nurturing creativity is essential to developing strong writing identities, and without such an identity, basic writers will continue to avoid writing and/or remain disengaged from their ideas and expression. Our goal must be to help students find a way to see themselves as writers and to make that part of their identities.

References

Hartwell, Patrick. *Open to Language.* New York: Oxford UP, 1982.

Lu, Min-Zhan. "Conflict and Struggle: The Enemies or Preconditions of Basic Writing?" *College English* 54.8. December (1992): 887–913.

Roffman, Rosaly. Personal Interview, Indiana, PA, September, 1992.

Yeats, William Butler. "A Prayer for My Son." *The Poems of W. B. Yeats: A New Edition.* Ed. Richard J. Finneran. New York: Macmillan, 1983. 212.

17 Oral Literature in the Teaching of Creative Writing

Maxine Clair
George Washington University

I decided to consider oral literature in teaching creative writing primarily as a way to address the issue of marginalized voices in American literature. Recently the Ford Foundation, along with universities across the country, committed resources to counteract the reality that in college curricula the literature of Chicana, Latino, Asian-American, African-American, and Native-American women is excluded or marginalized more often than the literature of any other group. My aim, as a participant in the Ford Foundation Project, was to transform my curriculum to embody more works by women of color as the exemplary texts my students read.

Early on I recognized the futility of merely including more poems and stories by these writers. Students merely became indifferent to a larger number of texts. What my readers needed were new reference points, referential experiences with which to read and appreciate these works. Since many of the voices—particularly those of Hispanics, Native Americans, and African Americans—resonate with oral tradition, and since our aesthetic judgments are informed not only by an analysis of the work before us, but also by an understanding of that work's background or origins, orality seemed a good place to begin. My hope was that students would develop an appreciation for the ways in which culture is celebrated within oral literature, that they would discover complexities of language and music inherent in oral forms. I expected students to understand that there are elements to be valued in the oral just as there are in the written, and that the extent to which the poet or storyteller is successful at retaining those valued elements is a measure of excellence. It was a reasonable expectation.

Primary among the mistaken beliefs for many beginning writers is that writing poems and stories means being suddenly inspired and, with little more than desire, creating a masterpiece in one draft. Wrapped up in this fantasy are romantic writing habitats, dreams of entirely innovative genres and themes, brilliant agents, and six-figure advances.

As we try to dispel mistaken beliefs, teachers take on the responsibility of charging students with the more realistic task of learning to write by beginning, stumbling, running ahead, falling back, and beginning again. The complexity of such a task is seldom lost on students. However, there are at least three particular aspects of creative writing that can be illuminated when students examine oral literature. These three aspects are challenges for students and teachers alike.

Apart from likes and dislikes, undergraduate creative writing students are seldom aware of aesthetic criteria that separate "good" from "not-so-good" literature, and they lack the critical vocabulary to discuss these criteria in workshops. The first challenge, then, is to distinguish and understand elements of literature, those we weigh when we assign aesthetic value.

A second challenge is to establish and broaden the writer's sense of audience. Wendy Bishop in her study *Released into Language,* discusses reader/writer relationships and refers to students who have a limited sense of audience as the "underground writers," those who write cryptic, spur-of-the-moment, indecipherable pieces.

A third challenge, the initial impetus for using orality, is to motivate students to transcend prejudice in the appreciation of "other" voices. Most beginning creative writers are in their first two years of college, having arrived from neighborhoods of culture where world views are often homogenized. Consequently, students often resist tolerance for the literary strivings of any "others." If students are ever to write poems important to themselves, they must sooner rather than later discover what they believe. It will shape moral imperatives that will ultimately empower their poems.

Based on discourse theory, social science, and psycholinguistics, the model of exposing students to oral literature before they write—giving them the experience of orality both as creators and consumers—can redefine a rightness in literature that is concrete.

Although the term *oral literature* is most frequently associated with non-literate simplicity, it is a product of both non-literate and literate societies, ancient and contemporary, distant and local. Certainly orality has suffered from the fact that most investigations of literature are based on the assumption that "literature" necessarily means "written." Ruth Finnegan, the pre-eminent orality scholar, sees this as a central problematic assumption in determining the validity of oral work: "Over the last centuries of European history, written modes have been taken as *the* paradigm for education, scholarship, and artistic activity, a dominant cultural view widely accepted even beyond the narrow circle of academics. What was written was to be valued and analyzed; and what was not written was not worth scholarly study."

This view persists on university campuses in this country as well. But oral literature is not an aberrant phenomenon in human culture. One could recall the nearly clichéd reference to the epic poetry of Homer, but certainly move on to that of recent oral poets in Yugoslavia or the Soviet Union. One could look at the 450-line panegyric, the praise poem of the famous nineteenth-century Zulu warrior, Shaka, or the emotional verse of preachers in contemporary America. One could recite ballads and even some folksongs.

By definition, literature is intellectual expression conveying some truth perceived by the poet and expressed in terms intelligible to the poet's audience. Literature also is associated with the sense that its form of expression can be recognized as possessing its own inner truth. When one considers both oral and written expressions together, the functions of literature can be associated equally with each and affirms the use of both in the teaching of creative writing.

In an in-class lesson that begins with the first day of class and lasts over several class meetings, students hear lectures on the foundations of oral literature, witness live performances by performance poets, and are exposed to audio/video tapes of oral literature by various authors and performers. Students are then required to examine details of their own individual backgrounds and, from a fusion of those details, to create an *oral presentation.* Movements and music are allowed, but only as integral parts of the presentation, not as mere accompaniment. Students are encouraged to rely on memorization and embellishment (true to the oral tradition), but they are allowed to use notes. There is little that is labeled right or wrong in this exploration, including form. No genre labels are imposed—poetry, prose, fiction, nonfiction are not delineated.

Although the results are discussed in more detail later in this paper, students were able to associate particular aspects of oral presentations with corresponding concepts in written literature. Students discovered a depth to their own knowledge about craft that was useful in their discussion of the written work they were asked to criticize later in workshop.

For example, most teachers and writers will agree that voice is a conceptual element of poetry. Various terms—-style, speaker's presence, tone, persona—are sometimes used interchangeably, if not always accurately, for the concept of voice. In oral presentation, the voice is embodied, an aural experience that dramatizes the speaker's attitude with all the nuances physical presence can bring. In one instance of actual performance, students-as-audience had the experience of one of their own, a young woman of mixed heritage, performing an oral composition in three voices, each from a different ethnic tradition and attitude, each competing for the position of dominance within the one personality. The young woman, born in America, had a British father and an Irish mother. As each separate personality emerged, it had its own discourse—from a lilting, lyrical rendering with an Irish accent, to a stern, formal, pedantic voice, and on to a casual and direct delivery punctuated with colorful idioms.

During the discussion that followed, the concept of voice was explored using the presentation as a reference point. In this instance, students had the opportunity to construct or recall the original application of the concept of voice. Such an experience facilitated the transfer of their understanding to the new, "written" situation.

In one of Vygotsky's psycholinguistic explorations, *Thought and Language*, he outlines experimental studies of how we form concepts, how the mental elaboration of sensory material gives birth to the concept. Although most of his work is directed at thought formation in children, he emphasizes the fact that ". . . we [adults] form and use concepts correctly in concrete situations, but we find it strangely difficult to express [those] concepts in words."

From a simple experiment, he explains the three-stage mental activity that translates sensory material: A subject is given blocks as objects of his activity. They are wooden blocks varying in color, shape, height, and size. On the underside of each, not seen by the subject, one of four nonsense words are written.

The first step toward formation of a concept occurs when the subject puts the blocks together in an unorganized heap. This heap is formed by objects linked by chance in the subject's perception. In an analogous situation in a creative writing workshop tone, style, attitude are undifferentiated in the mind of the listener, yet labeled "voice" outside of the listener's awareness.

The second major phase on the way to forming a concept is "thinking in complexes." In a complex, the wooden blocks are united in the subject's mind not only by the subject's impressions, but also by bonds actually existing between the objects. The examiner turns up one of the blocks, reads its nonsense name to the subject, and asks the subject to select like blocks. The subject, by degrees, obtains a basis for discovering to which characteristics the words refer. In an analogy for creative writing, the listener would witness variations in pitch, variations in intensity, physical gestures, style, tone, emphasis on particular words, facial expressions that would be variously labeled, some with the label "voice."

In the final phase, potential and advanced concepts are formed on the basis of similar impressions or similar functional meanings. In the experiment, as soon as the subject makes the discovery that words refer to characteristics of the blocks, words come to stand for definite kinds of objects, and new concepts for which the language provides no names are thus built up. The subject is then able to complete the task of separating the four kinds of blocks indicated by the nonsense words.

If the "voice" label is used whenever a certain sound, tone, manner, style, or attitude of expression is conveyed in the oral presentation, then voice becomes a concept in the mind of the listener. As for our student writers, they have formed the abstract concept of *oral* voice long before they entered a classroom. However, in creative writing the new concrete situation presents itself—that of transferring the understanding of the oral concept to the written page.

Vygoytsky goes beyond the fact that we (adults) form and use a concept quite correctly in a concrete situation but find it strangely difficult to express that concept in words. He says that the verbal definition will, in most cases, be much narrower than one might have anticipated from the way we used the concept. But he says, most emphatically, that the greatest difficulty of all is the application of a concept to the new concrete situation.

This is the critical juncture where the original concept must be recalled in dramatic detail from the oral delivery, and it is this oral review that facilitates the transition to the new situation, the written page. It follows that mental elaboration on the oral, dramatized material facilitates a fuller understanding of some of poetry's other elements such as rhythm, sound, music, perhaps even imagery. With oral presentations, students necessarily created their own instructive experiences.

For the writer, establishing the sense of audience is a challenge. Since the oral presentation is the initial one made in workshop, audience is integral to an approximation of success. Students come to understand and value audience and retain that understanding when they begin to compose on the page. Borrowing from the discourse theorists, and using the writer-text-reader current model that informs writing, we as teachers can create situations where the author witnesses audience frustration and the author is in turn confronted with deciphering her or his own compositions.

Again I refer to *Released into Language,* where Bishop asserts that in transactional writing workshops (writer on one side, text in the middle, and audience (reader) on the other side) teachers must first believe in the potential of all writing students. Employing the oral strategy for introducing writer and text to audience allows for the focus to be shared with text, author, and audience.

In an exemplary presentation, one student narrated what sounded much like a ballad, recounting unique details of his family and slowly outlining his place in it—all within the framework of riding the ocean's surf, sometimes buoyant, sometimes overwhelmed. With audience participation, he went into the telling refrain of ". . . and the water rushes over me, the water rushes over . . ." Waves became a metaphor for buoyant and overwhelming family experiences.

Bishop suggests that in this shared context, teachers are aiming for student empowerment. Clarence Major explains why empowerment is desirable:

> Most students in college today aren't going to have an opportunity to be in touch with who they are and where they come from in such an intense way ever again as they will in a workshop. They will go into different kinds of things: business, engineering, the sciences; but (it is hoped) they will remember how important it was to create a wedding of that voice that was theirs and that history that was theirs.

It is just this respect for individual difference that brings students to face the third challenging aspect of living that is reflected in their writing—that of prejudice. In the writing class, students distill experience, reshaping ideas to a satisfactory product. Unfamiliar with formal literary criticism, beginning writers rely on their own world views as they make evaluations. When student writing is the focal point of instruction, students bring the same assumptions about life to bear on the work of other writers. Race, gender, and class prejudices notwithstanding, too often students fail to consider that basic differences in ideas about the nature of reality engender differences in literary constructs. Too often subjective biases determine what is aesthetically correct.

The inclusion of more poems and stories by and about "other" peoples will do little to ensure appreciation or evoke understanding. But when students create their own oral literature, they are required to explore their own traditions without having to consider a "permanent record" of their ideas. Nor are they required to suddenly elevate their language to the "poetic."

They explore family rituals—preparing meals, taking meals, preparing for bed, household tasks, etc. They go in memory and imagination to celebrations, ceremonies—weddings, funerals, parties, picnics, etc.

They recall places, foods, tales, stories, jokes, songs, languages, and accents of the "old folks" and distant kin; the embarrassments, fears, woundings, and triumphs. They are reminded that forgotten attitudes arise when they lapse into old patterns of speech, sing old songs, or view old photographs.

In this exercise, results often exceed the most optimistic expectations of the students' originality and scope. Students can create imaginative, ingenious compositions in which they demonstrate widely varied examples of oral literature from widely varied perspectives. It becomes obvious that oral literature exists in performance, and it attempts to remain faithful to the culture in its expression. The necessary bridge of speaker and audience is more accessible, and style and opportunity for improvisation arises from the combination spontaneously. Borrowing from Allport's *Nature of Prejudice,* writing classes form a new "in-group" where each member of the class has a legitimate place. At least on the face of it, prejudice is mitigated by knowledge and reason.

Here is a brief summary of a few of the events: As audience, students considered a powerful delivery in the persona of an observer at Auschwitz, where the shawled narrator asks of God, "Were you there? Did you, too, breathe deeply, bravely inhaling the fumes?" Students were visibly moved. There was no mistaking the bitterness in the speaker's tone. Another student livened things up with rhythms combined in a children's whimsical, hand-clapping ditty and a poem of protest. Students could witness African American vernacular which embodies such tropes as enumeration, virtuoso naming, signifying, and improvisation. Students had to consider the language of *poi* and *pancit* in a Filipino household with aunts stirring the pots; they were invited into imaginary homes with rice paper windows, and into Buddhist temples. A tale of Little Bear was told, complete with Native American circle of flames (votive candles), and the existence of family crests in suburban America was revealed, and more.

When one hears these and imagines the rest—the embellishments of smells, blues harmonicas, laughter—one understands William Stafford's words: "The kind of process we are talking about is native to everyone, kids with their hopscotch and so on. Everyone. Everyone I've ever met, everyone, has what to me is the essential element of what we're talking about. They may not write what they call poems, but they make remarks they like better than other remarks. They have that lipsmacking realization of differences in discourse" (80).

When students experience the Shaker call and answer, the Irish chants—the diversity of cultures—they begin to address their limitations. What in a writing class are too often abstract pronouncements can become suggestions, innuendo, and concrete images.

When the class moves from this oral tradition to the written, we acknowledge certain tradeoffs. In the transition, language becomes more representational and relies on other skillful manipulations for success. What there is to be gained is a world unto itself. But in the imagination of the maker and the seer, the oral persists.

References

Allport, Gordon. "Formation of In-Groups." *The Nature of Prejudice.* New York: Harper, 1954.

Bishop, Wendy. *Released into Language: Options for Teaching Creative Writing.* Urbana, IL: National Council of Teachers of English, 1990.

Bunge, Nancy. *Finding the Words: Conversations with Writers Who Teach.* Athens: Swallow-Ohio UP, 1985.

Finnegan, Ruth. *Oral Poetry: Its Nature, Significance, and Social Context.* New York: Cambridge UP, 1977.

Stafford, William. *Writing the Australian Crawl: Views on the Writer's Vocation.* Ann Arbor: U of Michigan P, 1978.

Vygotsky, Lev. *Thought and Language.* Cambridge: Massachusetts Institute of Technology P, 1986.

18 Without a Net: Collaborative Writing

Linda Tomol Pennisi
Vermont College

Patrick Lawler
Onondaga Community College

Table Tennis

> *"When you get there*
> *you can't see him*
> *but you know he is waiting*
> *on the other side of the net."*
> *"The Midnight Tennis Match," Thomas Lux 248–50*

When Man Ray and Marcel Duchamp first met in Ridgefield, NJ, they didn't have a common language with which to communicate. Duchamp could barely speak English while Man Ray knew nothing of French—so they played tennis, a game made more appealing because they slaved without a net. Though their game lacked the grammar of the game, it still contained its own language. Man Ray would call out the score while Duchamp would shake his head in agreement.

To potluck suppers, my mother often brought Pittsburgh cake, a recipe given to her by an old Hungarian woman from, of course, Pittsburgh. There was a loose structure to those meals—each woman signed her name next to a category: salad, vegetable, dessert, on a clipboard in the church vestibule. What resulted was a meal which represented thirty or so different families. When placed together on the buffet table, though, these often basic dishes were transformed. They spoke of something larger—an agreement of cooperation. If the spaces for cakes were already taken, my mother would bring potato salad or pickled beets.

In some ways the dada tennis match captures some of the quintessential aspects of collaborative writing. A writer arrives in a collaborative situation with a different language—her language. Because two writers reassemble the world in their individual writings, when they write collaboratively they require a third language to touch that world, to open that world, to reflect that world. And frequently it is better to play without the traditional net, without the previous restraints and old limits we have placed around our own individual writing efforts where we may have unconsciously delineated and restricted the areas of inquiry, the style, the language. This is a time to take risks, a time to be more intuitive, a time to charge a net that isn't there.

It is so, too, that the writer in the collaborative situation brings her own voice to the table. Here, however, instead of relying on old recipes—metaphors revolving around bowls of ripened fruit or the delicate curve of an egg—she hears someone speaking of tennis. She is relieved the game is to be played without a net. She finds her way in a volley of words.

Collaborative writing is like having another self. Even in composing this document, a third person emerges. We speak of "we do this," of "we do that" as if the individual "I" became a third "we," and the "I's" become someone else in the process. It is as if this document and, by implication, the collaborative writing classroom were written from the omniscient point of view but without an omniscient observer.

She imagines a clay court outside her kitchen window. As she heaps peaches and grapes onto a dinner plate, she watches him warm up and sees that he too is tentative. She carries the fruit outside with her, placing it on the edge of the court. He serves the word "spark"; she returns a peach.

Doubles

> *"Doubles is much more of a challenge than singles."*
> *(Billie Jean King)*

Such is the mixture of collaborative writing. In the conventional writing class, we will encourage our students to avoid mixed metaphors, but in a collaborative situation there are only mixed metaphors. The mix of metaphors creates the sparks, the synapses; the words, like neurons, connect. The authors of this piece have been involved in a number of writing situations together as teacher/student, student/teacher, co-collaborators, colleagues in the writing process. We've brought our food to the court; we've cooked our language in invisible pots.

Having been influenced by Bruffee, Abercrombie, Gere, and Vygotsky (among others), we have designed classroom situations which encourage interaction. Though we feel the permutations of such exercises are innumerable, we have included some collaborative projects with which we have been involved. We have divided these into group writing on the micro level (where students provide inspiration to one another concerning language) and group writing on the macro level (where students not only participate in the language of the group, but also influence larger aspects of structure, themes, issues).

Micro Level:

Group Poem—Each student writes the second line of a first line provided by the instructor. (First lines can be taken from published poems or created by the instructor.) Students sit in a circle, each providing a line and then passing it to the next individual. The poem is finished when it reaches the person who started the process. The instructor now has a number of poems to consider. She can concentrate on the function of first lines, on the value of surprise in poetry, on the issue of closure, and certainly on the images that are created by the students.

Voice/Box—Students, with some direction, write down a list of interesting words or images. (They can be working on this for several weeks before the assignment is given.) Word lists are cut up into strips of paper, placed into a box, and passed around the classroom. Students select five or six words or images and are asked to write a poem using them. (This also works well with titles. Students write down titles. They are placed in a box, and then selected. Students write poems based on selected titles.)

Response Poems—Each student writes a poem in response to another student's poem. After the second poem is considered, the original poet writes a poem in response to the second poem. This process continues throughout the semester. Students can pick up on an image, a theme, a word, and use this as a spring board into their own poems (a la Stafford/Bell).

Macro Level:

The Living Newspaper—Students select an issue (the environment, racism, the homeless, feminism). Using the newspaper as a source of inspiration, students begin to write about their issue collectively with the idea of having the pieces performed at the end of the semester. Students work with poetry, prose, and drama, incorporating music, mime, dance, etc.

The Personas Poems—Students create a character in small groups of 3 or 4, by answering 20–25 questions asked by the instructor

(Describe the last dream the person had. What is the person's occupation? What kind of music does she like?). The small groups, after creating the character, begin to write in the voice of that character. Often they begin to grow as writers because they are more willing to experiment with language, subject matter, and form when they are free to write in another voice. (See Roque Dalton.)

Creating a Novel—Students in small groups create a character by answering 20–25 questions asked by the instructor (see examples in previous exercise). Once the characters are created, the class creates situations in which they can interact. An interweaving of characters occurs as the class makes decisions concerning genre, plot, style, etc. Chapters are collaboratively written and shared with the class. (See Ken Kesey.)

Such situations allow for powerful opportunities to explore the creative process in a nonthreatening, enriching atmosphere where every participant is there for support. Also, the critique has a broader lens. Instead of focusing on the individual, it can explore social, cultural, and gender issues. These exercises can challenge a student to grasp more and say more than she could individually. Writing is not viewed as an act separate from the context in which it occurs.

Charging the Net/Changing the Net

> *"Writing free verse is like playing tennis with the net down."*
> (*Robert Frost*)

The writer in the collaborative environment continually expands herself, not only to allow the entrance of new material as she does in the traditional classroom, but to accommodate the new "selves" she develops in relation to the collaborative experience. At her discretion, her own voice slows to a trickle or loops back upon itself to allow the entrance of other voices—from outside and from within. Thus, an internal process of collaboration begins, with each voice asserting its influence—at other times relinquishing it to other voices. The response is an effusion of voice unrestricted by her own, but resonating with it. Whereas in the traditional writing class we encourage a student to discover her own voice, in the collaborative environment we consider the complexity of voices and the contexts within which individual voices speak/write.

Mikhail Bakhtin has described hell as a place where there is no third person, no listener. For those involved in a creative collaborative experience, there is always a listener, someone pouring you a mirror out of herself. This is far more than narcissistic. It is actually as if you could keep writing until you become a window—letting in everything. It is writing outside the cocoon of consciousness. It is writing inside the body of another. The I is plural. Polyphonic.

Poetry is monologic according to Bakhtin, unlike novelistic discourse where there is "social heteroglossia," diversity and stratification, the proliferation of discursive frames. Bakhtin is responding to the Romantic aesthetic where the individual poet's individual voice captures the rare and exquisite air that shapes a whole culture or a whole generation. But this voice is separate from the community it describes. Because of genius or a unique vision or obsessions or pain, the poet is distinguished from all others. This is very different from the Eskimo carving a gigantic walrus tusk, who, when asked by an interviewer what he was making, responded, "I don't know. I'm trying to find out what's inside." Bakhtin is referring to the poet as myth maker or truth maker. He is referring to the poet as creator (Daedalus/Icarus), not the poet as the finder of what's inside. Thus, when he says poetry is the "sealed off utterance," he is talking about the voice of the Romantic poet. But collaborative poetry can release those other voices, allowing for a fuller interaction between discursive frames. We keep writing until we become a window.

Resistance to the collaborative process, when it occurs, usually does so in relation to what we have described as macro-level exercises. Whereas the very structure of micro-level exercises provides balance and maintains individuality within the framework of collaboration, macro-level exercises require compromises and relinquishment of individual agenda and voice. Presenting itself in two forms—silence and dominance—resistance can intrude upon the spirit of collaboration. One must also acknowledge the issue of control in the collaborative classroom and the potential for silencing those voices that speak in opposition to the dominant voice of our culture (white, male, heterosexual). Because the dominant voice may silence the voice of the other in the creative process, participants in the collaborative activity must be aware of potential abuse and must be cautious in creating spaces for the silent and the silenced. By relinquishing her role of authority within the group, by becoming instead "participant," the instructor can renounce the traditional hierarchical structure of the classroom. From within the circle of writers, she can more effectively encourage the one who is silent, as well. And when the silent one speaks, she can pour a mirror from herself that reflects the value of what is being said. Thus, she sets the stage for true collaboration—an environment where every voice streams into every other voice.

This issue of the dominant voice and authority can be presented in another manner. Francisco Varella ("Laying Down a Path") says 80 percent of the information involved in an act of perception comes from the brain. The world then becomes a "perturbation on an ongoing buzzing of internal activity, which can be modulated but not instructed" (47). If we see as we have been trained to see, if we see that which already falls within our current conceptual framework, how do we create possibilities for change, opportunities to oppose this lithic resistance? Collaboration is one answer because it allows for more of the world to enter us. Collaboration presents an occasion for questioning issues of authority and author-ity. And it introduces intertextuality, blurring the boundaries (mine, yours, and ours)—while approaching trans-textuality or metatextuality.

Paradoxically, as the writer experiences a heightened sensitivity to issues of control, she simultaneously experiences a loosening of control, an opening which releases her into unknown waters. Such journeying leads, of course, to discovery. The writer who has previously avoided anger in her work, may suddenly be caught in a persona's whirl of rage. As she learns to work within the rage of another, writing from the experience of anger becomes less foreign and thus becomes available to her in her own work.

Because they replace mimetic representation, because they rely on context and contestation, because they explore the layers of voice, collage/ montage/ pastiche are most rewarding as compositional facets of collaboration. When writing about Brecht, Walter Benjamin describes the impact of montage as when "the superimposed element disrupts the context in which it is inserted" (266). This is more than a feature of collaborative writing; it is the theme. The techniques of collage/ montage/ pastiche are not meant to be reflections of reality; rather they are interventions in an effort to change reality.

However, this use of the collaborative situation to access new waters also works in reverse. The collaborative persona leads the writer into new space, yet she returns to something familiar—some stylistic technique, a metaphor, her own language, perhaps, to understand it. Thus as she is carried away, she moves toward herself. As she listens to her voice in relation to the voice of another, she comes to know it, to recognize it as her own.

Again, we mix our metaphors—nets and new water. Suddenly, we have a fishing metaphor. Perhaps there is a fishing boat lost in a turbulent sea, and we only have these words by Antonio Machado:

Four are the useless things
a man in the sea has found:
anchor, rudder, oars,
and fear of being drowned.
(167)

Mixed Doubles

". . . there was no turning back but the end was in sight"
("The Tennis Court Oath," John Ashbery)

Two Inuit women will stand very close.
They will chant so the sounds of each
will enter the voice of the other.

Such is the nature of the collaborative enterprise. Where there were two voices suddenly there are four. And where there was solitude suddenly there are connection and relationship. Natalie Goldberg says in *Writing Down the Bones,* "So writing is not just writing. It is also having a relationship with other writers" (80).

Two Inuit women will stand very close.
They will chant so the sounds of each
will enter the voice of the other.
Each of them will sing in two voices
simultaneously because the sound
of one is echoed in the other's mouth.

Ultimately, in the convergence of voices the feast flourishes. A tableful of opposites: text and subtext, version and subversion, critique and desire. A language to shake up the house it is served in. A sensuous language. A language to be tasted. "I enwrap the other in my words" (Barthes 73). We feed the other through the words. Fluid, vibrant words found in someone else's mouth.

Two Inuit women will stand very close.
They will chant so the sounds of each
will enter the voice of the other.
Each of them will sing in two voices
simultaneously because the sound
of one is echoed in the others mouth.

Instead of one voice sounding the loss
of connection, clarity, community,
listen to the celebration in the throat.

And let us not forget the tennis players: the tennis players, who came with different languages. Because of the nature of this netless game, they come away with more words than they could have dreamed of alone.

> Two Inuit women will stand very close.
> They will chant so the sounds of each
> will enter the voice of the other.
> Each of them will sing in two voices
> simultaneously because the sound
> of one is echoed in the others mouth.
>
> Instead of one voice sounding the loss
> of connection, clarity, community,
> listen to the celebration in the throat.
> Acquire the songs of another;
> release the songs of the self.
> There is a choir in the mouth.

References

Abercrombie, M.L.J. *The Anatomy of Judgment.* New York: Basic; Harmonsdworth, England: Penguin, 1960.

Barthes, Roland. *A Lover's Discourse: Fragments.* Trans. Richard Howard. New York: Hill and Wang, 1978.

Benjamin, Walter. "The Author as Producer." *The Essential Frankfurt School Reader*. Ed. A. Arato and E. Gebhardt. New York: Urizen, 1978.

Bruffee, Kenneth. "Collaboration and the Conversation of Mankind." *College English* 46 (1973): 635–52.

———. "Collaborative Learning: Some Practical Models." *College English* 46 (1973): 447–54.

Dalton, Roque. *Clandestine Poems.* Ed. Barbara Paschke and Eric Weaver. Trans. Jack Hirschman. Willimatic, CT: Curbstone, 1990.

Gere, Ann Ruggles. *Writing Groups: History, Theory, and Implications.* Carbondale: Southern Illinois UP, 1987.

Goldberg, Natalie. *Writing Down the Bones: Freeing the Writer Within.* Boston and London: Shambhala, 1986.

Knox-Quinn, Carolyn. "Collaboration in the Writing Classroom: An Interview with Ken Kesey." *College Composition and Communication* 41 (1990): 309–17.

Levon, O. U. *Caverns.* Introduction by Ken Kesey. New York: Penguin Books, 1990. A composite novel—the result of an experiment Kesey conducted with a creative writing class at the University of Oregon.

Lux, Thomas. "The Midnight Tennis Match." *The American Poetry Anthology.* Ed. Daniel Halpern. New York: Avon Books, 1975.

Machado, Antonio. "Proverbs and Songs." *Antonio Machado.* Ed. Alice Jane McVan. New York: The Hispanic Society of America, 1959.

Stafford, William, and Marvin Bell. *Annie-Over.* Rexburg, Idaho: Honeybrook Press, 1988.

Varella, Francisco. "Laying Down a Path." *Gaia/A Way of Knowing: The Political Implications of the New Biology.* Ed. William Irwin Thompson. Hudson, NY: Lindisfarne Press, 1987.

Vygotsky, L. S. *Mind in Society: The Development of Higher Psychological Processes.* Ed. M. Cole, V. John-Steiner, S. Scribner, and E. Souberman. Cambridge, MA: Harvard UP, 1978.

———. *Thought and Language.* Ed. A. Kozulin. Cambridge, MA: Massachusetts Institute of Technology P, 1986.

19 Reading the Creative Writing Course: The Teacher's Many Selves

Patrick Bizzaro
East Carolina University

By this time it must be obvious: a course in writing is simultaneously a course in reading. Besides learning how to read various assigned texts, students must learn how to read their teachers . . . through syllabuses, reading assignments, and writing assignments. What's more, students in creative writing courses must learn how to read each other's texts as well as the texts of each other's readings. As a result, teachers must be conscious of teaching their students how to respond to comments, the teacher's as well as other students'. As teachers, we must spend less time telling our students what they should do when they write and more time showing them who they can be.

Apprenticeship Relationships: The "Overly Influential" Teacher

Among other benefits that accrue when students are helped to read in their creative writing courses is the realization by both teacher and student that traditional classroom interaction and methods of evaluation foster apprenticeship relationships that often result in the teacher's appropriation of student writing. Depending on the kind of relationships established by teachers with their students—which I believe depends largely on the methodology teachers employ in reading and interpreting student texts (see Bizzaro 1992)—teachers can lengthen or shorten the time span involved in a master-to-apprentice relationship. In any case, there is no substitute for the teacher's and student's recognition that they are in such a relationship.

After all, there is little doubt apprenticeship relationships exist; they have even influenced the development of renowned literary figures. As one example, Richard Hugo describes their affects in his discussion of Theodore Roethke's dominance over his students:

> Roethke, through his fierce love of kinds of verbal music, could be overly influential. David Wagoner, who was quite young when

> he studied under Roethke at Penn State, told me once of the long painful time he had breaking Roethke's hold on him. (29)

Those who have considered the problems inherent in the writing teachers' authority over their students wonder how writers ever manage to set themselves free. William Stafford describes the predicament as follows: "You can become a lost soul in literature just as surely as you can in any activity where you abandon yourself to the decisions of others" (78).

In considering such influence, Stafford makes some distinctions between possible teacher-student relationships worthy of consideration here:

> ... [S]uppose you had a chance to work with someone who would correct your writing into publishability. This person would be efficient, knowing, memorable, valid: an accomplished writer. In the company of this person you could go confidently into the center of current acceptance; you would quickly learn what brings success in the literary scene.
>
> Now suppose another kind of associate. This one would accompany you as you discovered for yourself whatever it is that most satisfyingly links to your own life and writings. You would be living out of your own self into its expression, almost without regard to the slant or expectation or demands of editors and public.
>
> Let there be no mistake about it: a large and significant, and I believe most significant, group of writers today would prefer the second kind of company.

One of the goals of the creative writing teacher should be to become this second kind of company, showing students not how to change individual texts, but introducing students to the many selves writers might become. To do so, however, teachers must relinquish power in the classroom, abdicate authority granted them through tradition and privilege. The liberation of students begins with the teacher's willingness to undermine his or her authority in the classroom by using that very authority to do so.

How can this seemingly contradictory activity take place? Barbara Waxman offers some clarification when she writes:

> If we create in our classrooms what Giroux calls an "emancipatory authority," one that is committed to social empowerment and ethics, then we will see ourselves not just as technocrats who distribute knowledge and values, but also as morally concerned teachers who conceptualize and raise questions about our curricula and the methods that enable students to develop both humanity and sociopolitical *savoir faire.* (149)

There is no doubt that the one area where we establish our relationship with our students—as either master or "emancipatory authority"—is in our appraisal and judgment of their writing ability, usually involving evaluation of one text at a time, but leading to generalizations about a student's overall writing skill.

New Criticism: Privileged Readings and Teacher Mastery

Since the publication of Charles Cooper and Lee Odell's *Evaluating Writing* (1978), the most innovative thinking about evaluation has focused chiefly on the politics of evaluation and on the necessity for reconsidering our methods of evaluation, largely from a theoretical perspective (see Anson 1989; Atkins and Johnson 1985; Brannon and Knoblauch 1982; Crowley 1989; Donahue and Quandahl 1989; Faigley 1989; Lawson, Ryan, and Winterowd 1989; Moran and Penfield 1990; Moxley 1989; Sommers 1982; and White 1988). As Tilly Warnock summarizes from what has been written, "While we may seem to have turned our attention from product, a New Critical approach, to process, perhaps biographical, historical, developmental, intentionalist, we wonder. Our practices in responding to texts still seem tied to New Criticism's concern for unity and intensity of words-on-the-page . . ." (67).

For nearly forty years, the New Criticism alone has had a place of unquestioned authority in its relationship to the reading and evaluation not only of canonical literature, but of student texts as well. Undoubtedly, because so many students receiving advanced degrees between the Second World War and the end of the Vietnam Era have backgrounds as literary specialists, the New Critical methodology that they were given in graduate school persists in their methods of reading and evaluating what they read. Well known is the theory that in the post-World War II period, when university professors were anxious about having their political preferences called into question, the New Criticism, by virtue of its elevation of the text as the authority for meaning, made the study of literature apolitical and, as a result, safer than innocent membership in certain social clubs.

But, as William E. Cain (1984) notes, "Politics cannot be avoided in literary study, and we should not pretend otherwise" (*xiv*). We might add to this that politics cannot be avoided in the classroom, and we should not pretend otherwise. For surely the politics of the classroom make teachers, as exemplary readers, authorities for determining meaning, not only in literary texts, but in student texts as well.

To permit themselves this privilege, teachers give assignments, offer observations, and employ teaching strategies that make New Critical estimations possible. For example, the looming question at a recent meeting of the National Testing Network was "how in assessing writing do we build into writing prompts the stimuli that evoke what we desire from students?" (quoted in Wolcott 1987, 41). By and large, we continue to view writing as a text-centered discourse and assign tasks that can be evaluated as though meaning exists in the text itself. Again, to cite Cain in *The Crisis in Criticism:*

> What we have is a curious phenomenon. The New Criticism appears powerless, lacking in supporters, declining, dead or on the verge of being so. No one speaks on behalf of the New Criticism as such today, and it figures in critical discourse as the embodiment of foolish ideas and misconceived techniques. But the truth is that the New Criticism survives and is prospering, and it seems to be powerless only because its power is so pervasive that we are ordinarily not even aware of it. (10)

Among the influences on current methods for evaluating student writing, text-based commentary—including New Criticism and its adaptations, the Analytic Scale and Primary Trait Scoring—is, perhaps, the most influential. For instance, most of the poets who comment on students' texts in Alberta Turner's *Poets Teaching: The Creative Process* (1980) focus chiefly on the text. Turner's introduction—in which she gives an overview of the teaching methods used by 32 well-known poets—suggests wide use of exactly this traditional perspective on reading and writing as text manipulations.

> Studying writing [is] a process of sharpening perception: awareness of all the connotations of a word, of all the rhythms of an emotion, of all the possible clashes among images, awareness of clichés and how to avoid them or use them so that they become effective allusion. . . . (1)

While most teachers of creative writing can see the wisdom of such an approach to evaluating writing, they must certainly see as well the kind of relationship between teacher as master and student as apprentice that accompanies such a view of the teacher as final authority. Turner continues, "To the student-poet as artificer the teacher-poets give (or rather offer) advice from their own experience as artificers" (15). This experience alone is the teachers' authority. And this authority is reinforced by the New Critical methods so widely used by teachers in examining student writing, creative and otherwise.

The New Criticism arose as a method for commenting on literature and approaches literary texts as finished products, ones that can be analyzed for the relationship among their parts without regard for the author's intentions, the reader's responses, or the biographical and historical backdrop. The goal of the New Criticism is to determine a text's meaning by offering close analysis or close reading intended to approach the text as final authority for such determinations. Current methods of evaluation, especially those advocated in Cooper and Odell's *Evaluating Writing,* differ from the New Criticism chiefly on what might be done to the text. For the commentator on student writing, the text is uniquely suited to evaluation since it is viewed as an incomplete work, often in need of correction. Of the New Critical perception of student texts, Edward White writes, "Such texts exist in general in order to be criticized" (291), especially when held alongside what Nancy Sommers calls an "ideal text."

This major difference aside, the New Criticism and current thinking about evaluating student writing hold a great many elements in common. First, at the epistemological center of both systems is the belief that meaning arises not from ideology or logic, but from analysis of the structure of norms that direct—in fact, are—the reader's experience of the text. Use of New Critical values in evaluating student writing requires students to believe that the teacher's reading of the text, as the meaning rendered by an exemplary reader, is the text as it really exists. Second, both systems derive their standards for evaluation from the reading of numerous other texts of the kind under examination. The New Critics refer to these standards as "norms," which enable us to focus on the work itself, according to Lynn (1990), "rather than the author, the reader, the historical context" (102); composition theorists refer to such standards as "features": "the separate elements, devices, and mechanisms of language" which enable us to make "judgments about the quality of writing" (Lloyd-Jones 1977, 33). Third, by thus appealing to their familiarity with other texts, commentators are able to remain objective and scientific, basing analysis on their experience of the text rather than on personal opinion. A classroom driven by the New Criticism places emphasis on the teachers' authority which arises, as Wendy Bishop (1990) says, because teachers are "much more widely read in the conventions and history of literature" than are their students (141). And, as White notes, "On the positive side [the New Criticism] urged readers of student writing to attend to the texts that the student produced rather than to the student's social class, appearance, or moral predispositions" (286). Fourth, since the text is seen as a system of formal elements which can be manipulated in the process of revision to achieve certain other specific effects, critical and evaluative statements can be fairly specific since they must be made on the basis of these norms. And, finally, meaning arises in both from a "close reading," which reveals how the formal elements of the text work together and whether a piece of writing has certain characteristics "that are crucial to success with a given rhetorical task" (Cooper and Odell 32). As Mark Schorer writes in "Technique as Discovery": "[T]echnique is the only means [the writer] has of discovering, exploring, developing his (sic) subject, of conveying its meaning, and, finally, of evaluating it" (quoted in White 286). Joseph M. Moxley (1989) states clearly the goal of most efforts at adapting New Critical methods to the evaluation of student writing: "Ultimately, our goal is to teach students to adopt the critical role writers assume when they ask questions about their work" (40).

One well-known drawback to the adaptations of New Critical methods and emphases to the reading and evaluating of student writing is text appropriation. An unwanted though mostly unavoidable by-product of using text-based methodology, appropriation results when teachers do what seems most natural and instinctive in the traditional classroom: quickly provide students who have not had adequate reading experiences with the information they need to write poetry. Composition theorists, including Sommers and Brannon and Knoblauch, have argued that such appropriation is unwanted since it takes the authority for writing away from students, subordinating them to the authority of their master-teachers. We often call the relationship in which appropriation occurs an "apprenticeship relationship."

But it is true to the experiences of most creative teachers that, on the whole, students enter creative writing courses without relevant reading and writing skills. From this perspective, text appropriation seems a natural consequence of conscientious teaching. Teachers have the opportunity (as plumbers might with their apprentices) to say, "Move over and let me show you how I would do it." Appropriation of the text (or of the pipe wrench), from this viewpoint, offers two distinct advantages. For one, it assumes that the expert-practitioner knows better than the apprentice does what needs to be done by giving first consideration to experience in making the needed repairs. For another, since such a view suggests that beginners merely lack information that, once obtained, will enable them to perform like their teachers, many expert-practitioners believe students will carry over into subsequent tasks skills learned by observing the teacher. Though writing and plumbing are hardly the same kinds of activities, they offer similar problems to the novice: an inexperienced writer will have no more luck writing something called a poem than an inexperienced repair-person, unfamiliar with the "rules" (if, indeed, any exist), would have repairing a dishwasher. For this reason, most students willingly relinquish control of their texts to teachers who, if they do not actually know the rules, are at least perceived by students as knowledgeable.

Perception of Knowledge and Identity Negotiation

This very perception is problematic, however, if the teacher hopes to be included among those Stafford might describe as "the second kind of company." Robert E. Brooke (1991) notes that "[f]or students to use their classroom experience to move from understanding themselves as students to understanding themselves as writers requires a shift in perceived context, a shift in how they understand the classroom where they are acting" (143). To make such a shift, students must learn how to act out nontraditional roles in the classroom rather than simply those they have learned through other school experiences. Brooke continues:

> Such a reconceptualization does not happen by itself, of course. To make such a shift, people require some sort of mark or cue, some sort of indication that the other participants in the situation are also changing their understanding of the activity. (14)

Such cues are vital to changing roles in the classroom. Without them students will continue to operate in terms of normal classroom expectations. If teachers want students to explore other possible identities in the classroom, the teachers themselves must provide students with signals to do so. Without "explicit cues to the contrary," the traditional apprentice-to-master relationship of examinee-to-examiner will dominate classroom relationships (Brooke 144).

The difficulty in offering such cues—especially if the mode of interpretation and evaluation is New Critical—is excellently portrayed by Lawson, Ryan, and Winterowd:

> If we believe that the locus of interpretation is *in* the student paper, then we must also believe that there is determinate meaning, something the student intended from the outset to say. This notion assumes that teachers can recognize . . . the thoughts their students are trying to express and assist them in improving ideas or communication. (*xiii,* emphasis mine)

From this perspective, the teacher knows better than the student what the student intends to say and gives advice about how to say it that the student must follow. In such comments we seem to say to students, implicitly or explicitly, "I, the teacher, am an exemplary reader. Your job as student is to please *me*. If I can't be moved by your text, you better take my advice on *how* to move me."

But how might a teacher, interested in designing a classroom based on emancipatory authority, signal to students that other roles are possible? Brooke argues that "[s]tudents need to experience a shift in how teacher and students interact, a change in the nature of student roles, if they are not to become fixed in the roles their past schooling leads them to expect" (144). The critical issue confronted by Brooke in his study of identity negotiation in writing workshops is how a class might be constructed by a teacher to enable students to play non-traditional roles and thereby assume identities as writers. To determine how best teachers might empower students in this negotiation, Brooke carefully studies three kinds of class formats and concludes:

> By observing the roles available in our own classrooms, we can describe how our students are learning and the kinds of selves we are helping them to become. Such observation, finally, offers us teachers a choice: what roles will we promote? what sorts of selves will we help our students to develop? The choice is, of course, ours, and aspects of our culture's future depend on the choices we will make. An identity negotiations perspective can make these choices clear; the rest is up to us, our students, and the kinds of writing classes we create. (155)

In reconsidering our roles in interacting with students, we must begin with Brooke's challenge: that we look closely at what we have created in our classrooms and determine, on the basis of what we see, the roles we are encouraging our students to play both as writers and readers.

Relating to Students, Relating to Texts: Helping Students Negotiate Identity

The most formative activities performed by teachers in signaling to students possible relationships are those related to the reading, interpreting, and evaluating of the students' writing. From this perspective, the New Critical values and emphases, in granting authority to the teacher as exemplary reader, promote the teacher-student relationship granted by tradition and privilege. In short, the student serves an apprenticeship, unbounded by time limits. The apprenticeship, as we have seen, may continue indefinitely, and no one is quite certain how a writer breaks free of the master-teacher to assert individual identity as a writer.

From this perspective, it seems a moral imperative that, as teachers of creative writing, we make every effort to relate to students and to their texts in nontraditional ways. In light of this belief, I am now ready—at least temporarily—to reconsider my own comment of just a year ago: ". . . introductory students will continue to learn best in the time available in a semester if the teacher employs strategies—perhaps, among others—inherited from the New Critics" (Bizzaro 1992, 173). Rather, we must model for students the various selves they might become as readers and writers. Like our students, and perhaps because of them, we must negotiate identities during the writing course. From this perspective, the best teachers of writing are not necessarily the best writers or best readers, as we have long and perhaps erroneously assumed. Rather, the most successful teachers are apt to be those who are best able to adapt to texts their students write and model the various roles their readings require of them. It seems logical to assume that the best teachers of writing are those who can play various roles in the classroom, who are capable of adopting numerous personas, and who are willing to experiment with authority both in student texts and in classroom interaction.

To this end, we must reconsider our usual method of reading, interpreting, and evaluating student writing. New Criticism offers us a way of noting text-based changes that *must* be made in student poems since the teacher is the exemplary reader and ultimate authority in the classroom. The "star" system, upheld at most universities, which asserts curiously that the best known and most well-published authors are, in fact, the best teachers of writing simply serves to reinforce the belief that the best way to learn how to write is to do what the teacher says. In the master-classroom, where workshops are conducted by renowned writing stars, revision of a text is a matter of learning to read the poem or story or creative non-fiction essay as the teacher has read it and of manipulating the text to the teacher's satisfaction.

In recent years, however, this method of reading the classroom has been challenged. Edward White, who advocates the use of literary critical methods in evaluating student writing, enables us to better understand the contradictions abounding currently in our profession. If we do not always employ the New Criticism when we read canonical literature, *real* literature, but do employ it when we confront students' literature, we are encountering student texts, as White says, "as if our confusion about evaluation is somehow bound up with a confusion about the nature of the student text, an odd form of literature created for the sole purpose of being criticized" (95). But this confrontation resonates throughout the university and involves matters of selfhood for teachers: if we treat student texts with the respect usually reserved for "real" literature, we as teachers somehow diminish *our* importance in the classroom.

Nonetheless, if we hope to create in our classroom an emancipatory authority and do so by modeling other possible identities for our students to negotiate, we must consider the critical issue at stake here, the issue of privilege: What if the usual authority for meaning (i.e., the text)—*and therefore, the guidelines for reading and the advice to students about revising (i.e., manipulating the text)*—exists somewhere else, as it does when we employ alternative literary-critical methods (e.g., reader-response criticism, deconstruction, feminist criticism, Marxist criticism, etc.)? If it does, the traditional argument for authority in the classroom—by virtue of tradition and privilege—will no longer apply, and authority will inevitably become decentralized. Teachers employing alternative critical lenses for examining student writing will eventually become authorities on how to disperse authority rather than authorities on how to read individual texts.

What will happen to texts written in our classes if we do not require students to make them conform to certain norms or contain within them certain rhetorical features, as we traditionally do? Clearly, the evaluation of student writing poses a problem in reading. Among other things, we will be required in writing courses to teach our students, and in some cases ourselves, how to be better readers, to empower them to see texts—their own and others'—differently, to devise a plan for their own writing not just from the perspective of author, but now from the point of view of a first reader—from one of many possible first readers—who can see the text better by having been shown how to view it through various critical lenses.

Most importantly, by viewing texts in this way, by having their texts read differently by their teachers, students will be able to negotiate identities in the classroom different in type from identities the traditional "master" class requires of them. To that end, teachers' comments on student texts might cover a range of distances, from the long-range perspective of teacher-authority in text-based commentary to the up-close-and-personal perspective of shared authority in reader-response methods. Classroom interaction might reflect the changing relationship these theories advance between teacher and student, enabling teachers to negotiate for themselves and model for their students the various identities their theories promote.

By enabling students to play various roles in relationships with their teachers, their texts, and their peers' texts, teachers might employ various literary-critical theories in reading their students' writing both at different stages in the writing process and at different stages in the writers' growth toward maturity and independence. By offering such readings, teachers simultaneously offer a solution to the prison of apprenticeship in creative writing courses by signaling to their students that other relationships, besides the traditional one of examiner to examinee, might be developed in the classroom.

In addition to the New Criticism, teachers might employ reader-response criticism, deconstruction, feminist criticism, or Marxist criticism to provide students with the cues they need to begin negotiating new identities as writers in the classroom. Each of these theories enables students to see that alternative relationships are possible in the classroom since each of these methods takes a different slant on the authority for the reading of student as well as professional writing. While teachers are reading and evaluating student poems, in process, by adapting literary-critical theory to the students' texts, they are simultaneously inviting students to interact with them differently.

These signals concerning changing roles in the classroom provide a heretofore unexplored avenue of escape from the prison-house we honor and fear, the New Critical approach to the student text. Naturally, models for such evaluation must be developed before most teachers will comfortably employ them. Still, with more and more emphasis on the use of portfolio evaluation in creative writing courses, teachers will be called upon to focus increasingly on their students' writing processes. Once teachers begin to focus on the kinds of comments they can make about student writing *in process,* they will see the necessity and have the opportunity to read differently. By employing the rich and interesting readings of student creative writing fostered by using literary-critical theories, teachers will simultaneously present themselves differently to their students and, in so doing, signal students that relationships other than (or, at least, in addition to) apprenticeship relationships are possible in the classroom. And this, it would seem, is a goal worthy of our most focused efforts.

References

Anson, Chris M. *Writing and Response: Theory, Practice, and Research.* Urbana, IL: National Council of Teachers of English, 1989.

Atkins, G. Douglas, and Michael L. Johnson, eds. *Writing and Reading Differently: Deconstruction and the Teaching of Composition and Literature.* Lawrence: UP of Kansas, 1985.

Bishop, Wendy. *Released into Language: Options for Teaching Creative Writing.* Urbana, IL: National Council of Teachers of English, 1990.

Bizzaro, Patrick. "Interaction and Assessment: Some Uses of Reader-Response Criticism in the Evaluation of Student Writing in a Poetry Writing Class."

The Writing Teacher as Researcher. Ed. Donald Daiker and Max Morenberg, 256–65. Portsmouth, NH: Boynton/Cook, 1989.

———. "Some Applications of Literary Critical Theory to the Reading and Evaluating of Student Poetry Writing." *Poets' Perspectives: Reading, Writing, and Teaching Poetry.* Ed. Charles R. Duke and Sally A. Jacobsen, 154–74. Portsmouth, NH: Boynton/Cook, 1992.

Brannon, Lil, and C. H. Knoblauch. "On Students' Rights to Their Own Texts: A Model of Teacher Response." *College Composition and Communication* 33 (1982): 197–222.

Brooke, Robert E. *Writing and Sense of Self: Identity Negotiation in Writing Workshops.* Urbana, IL: National Council of Teachers of English, 1991.

Cain, William. *The Crisis in Criticism: Theory, Literature, and Reform in English Studies.* Baltimore: Johns Hopkins UP, 1984.

Cahalan, James M., and David B. Downing, eds. *Practicing Theory in Introductory College Literature Courses.* Urbana, IL: National Council of Teachers of English, 1991.

Cooper, Charles R., and Lee Odell. *Evaluating Writing: Describing, Measuring, Judging.* Urbana, IL: National Council of Teachers of English, 1977.

Crowley, Sharon. *A Teacher's Introduction to Deconstruction.* Urbana, IL: National Council of Teachers of English, 1989.

Daiker, Donald, and Max Morenberg, eds. *The Writing Teacher as Researcher: Essays in the Theory and Practice of Class-Based Research.* Portsmouth: Boynton/Cook, 1989.

Donahue, Patricia, and Ellen Quandahl, eds. *Reclaiming Pedagogy: The Rhetoric of the Classroom.* Carbondale: Southern Illinois UP, 1990.

Duke, Charles R., and Sally A. Jacobsen, eds. *Poets' Perspectives: Reading, Writing, and Teaching Poetry.* Portsmouth, NH: Boynton/Cook, 1992.

Faigley, Lester. "Judging Writing, Judging Selves." *College Composition and Communication* 40 (1989): 395–412.

Hugo, Richard. *The Triggering Town: Lectures and Essays on Poetry and Writing.* New York: W.W. Norton & Company, 1979.

Johnson, Barbara. "Teaching Deconstructively." *Writing and Reading Differently: Deconstruction and the Teaching of Composition and Literature.* Ed. Douglas Atkins and Michael L. Johnson, 140–48. Lawrence: UP of Kansas, 1985.

Kaufer, David, and Gary Waller. "To Write Is to Read Is to Write, Right?" *Writing and Reading Differently: Deconstruction and the Teaching of Composition and Literature.* Ed. G. Douglas Atkins and Michael L. Johnson, 66–92. Lawrence: UP of Kansas, 1989.

Knoblauch, C. H., and Lil Brannon. "Teacher Commentary on Student Writing: The State of the Art." *Freshman English News* 10 (Fall 1981): 1–4.

Knoper, Randall. "Deconstruction, Process, Writing." *Reclaiming Pedagogy: The Rhetoric of the Classroom.* Ed. Patricia Donahue and Ellen Quandahl, 128–43. Carbondale: Southern Illinois UP, 1989.

Lawson, Bruce, Susan Sterr Ryan, and W. Ross Winterowd, eds. *Encountering Student Texts: Interpretive Issues in Reading Student Writing.* Urbana, IL: National Council of Teachers of English, 1989.

Lloyd-Jones, Richard. "Primary Trait Scoring." *Evaluating Writing: Describing, Measuring, Judging.* Ed. Charles R. Cooper and Lee Odell. Urbana, IL: National Council of Teachers of English, 1977.

Lynn, Steven. "A Passage into Critical Theory." *Conversations: Contemporary Critical Theory and the Teaching of Literature.* Ed. Charles Moran and Elizabeth F. Penfield, 99–113. Urbana, IL: National Council of Teachers of English, 1990.

MacDonald, John D. "Guidelines and Exercises for Teaching Creative Writing." *Creative Writing in America: Theory and Pedagogy.* Ed. Joseph M. Moxley, 83–88, Urbana, IL: National Council of Teachers of English, 1989.

Minot, Stephen. "How a Writer Reads." *Creative Writing in America: Theory and Pedagogy.* Ed. Joseph M. Moxley. Urbana, IL: National Council of Teachers of English, 1989. 89–95.

Moran, Charles, and Elizabeth F. Penfield, eds. *Conversations: Contemporary Critical Theory and the Teaching of Literature.* Urbana, IL: National Council of Teachers of English, 1990.

Moxley, Joseph M. *Creative Writing in America: Theory and Pedagogy.* Urbana, IL: National Council of Teachers of English, 1989.

Onore, Cynthia. "The Student, the Teacher, and the Text: Negotiating Meanings through Response and Revision." *Writing and Response: Theory, Practice, and Research.* Ed. Chris M. Anson, 231–60. Urbana, IL: National Council of Teachers of English, 1989.

Schorer, Mark. "Technique as Discovery." *Hudson Review* 1 (1948): 67–87.

Shaw, Margaret L. "What Students Don't Say: An Approach to the Student Text." *College Composition and Communication* 42 (1991): 45–54.

Shelnutt, Eve. "Notes from a Cell: Creative Writing Programs in Isolation." *Creative Writing in America: Theory and Pedagogy.* Ed. Joseph M. Moxley, 3–24. Urbana, IL: National Council of Teachers of English, 1989.

Smith, Dave. "Passion, Possibility, and Poetry." *Poets Teaching: The Creative Process.* Ed. Alberta Turner. New York: Longman, 1980. 173–90.

Sommers, Nancy I. "Responding to Student Writing." *College Composition and Communication* 33 (1982): 148–56.

Stafford, William. *Writing the Australian Crawl: Views on the Writer's Vocation.* Ann Arbor: U of Michigan P, 1978.

St. John, David. "Teaching Poetry Writing Workshops for Undergraduates." In *Creative Writing in America: Theory and Pedagogy.* Ed. Joseph M. Moxley. Urbana, IL: National Council of Teachers of English, 1989. 189–93.

Summers, Hollis. "Shaking and Carving." *Poets Teaching: The Creative Process.* Ed. Alberta T. Turner, 87–92. New York: Longman, 1980.

Turner, Alberta T., ed. *Poets Teaching: The Creative Process.* New York: Longman, 1980.

Warnock, Tilly. "An Analysis of Response: Dream, Prayer, and Chart." *Encountering Student Texts: Interpretive Issues in Reading Student Writing.* Eds. Bruce Lawson, Susan Sterr Ryan, and W. Ross Winterowd. Urbana, IL: National Council of Teachers of English, 1989. 59–72.

Waxman, Barbara Frey. "Feminist Theory, Literary Canons, and the Construction of Textual Meanings." *Practicing Theory in Introductory College Literature Courses.* Ed. James M. Cahalan and David B. Downing. Urbana, IL: National Council of Teachers of English, 1991. 149–60.

White, Edward. *Teaching and Assessing Writing.* San Francisco: Jossey-Bass, 1988.

Wolcott, Willa. "Writing Instruction and Assessment: The Need for Interplay between Process and Product." *College Composition and Communication* 38 (1987): 40–46.

Young, David. "Group I." *Poets Teaching: The Creative Process.* Ed. Alberta T. Turner. New York: Longman, 1980. 20–25.

20 The MFA Graduate as Composition Instructor: A Self-Analysis

David Starkey
Francis Marion University

In June 1988, when I left my position as a claims examiner for a Los Angeles insurance company, I only knew that I wanted to write and that I wanted desperately to earn a living in a way that didn't involve so much deception. The previous February, I had spoken with a guidance counselor at the university where I'd received a master's degree in English literature. He said to imagine for a moment that all obstacles had been overcome: what was my ideal situation? I told him I saw myself in a small college—maybe in the South—wealthy and teaching creative writing. He nodded and, in the parlance of the times, advised, "Go for it."

To my disappointment, I learned that by February the deadline for application to a majority of the MFA programs had already passed. Nevertheless, I found eight or nine schools I could still apply to and in a few months was tentatively accepted to most of them. I chose the one that paid the most for the least amount of work, handed in my resignation, bought a word processor, and moved to a city 1700 miles away.

Like all graduate teaching assistants at the university, I was automatically enrolled in English 7915, Teaching Composition. It wasn't that the course was poorly taught or that the material presented wasn't useful—I now refer often to the reading packet—but I had come to school to be a *writer.* Being a TA was simply a way to make (barely) enough money to live. This attitude was widespread among the MFAs, or "Mother-Fucking Artists" as the first of many party flyers would defiantly have it. Consequently, there was an enduring undercurrent of resentment between the creative writing students and the Director of Freshman English. The students felt the Director never gave them a chance to prove themselves, and rumor had it that the Director thought all MFAs were flakes.

Having recently become astute at office politics, I managed to stay out of this controversy. Anyway, I was so frightened of teaching that I clung to every word of *practical* advice the Director offered in her seminar. "When we command a theoretical framework which explains our activities, we are better able to evaluate student performance, revise courses, and justify our work to interested parents and administrators," admonished Erika Lindemann, among others—but I paid scant attention to composition experts (9). I wanted to know how to fill up my class hour with whatever activities would take the focus off of me as teacher. Most MFA teaching assistants weren't as nervous as I was—in fact, they were an affable lot—but rarely did anyone I know show much interest in becoming an excellent teacher of freshman writing. We briefly lamented the thick-headedness of composition students, then dove back into our own work. Those few who went on to take the advanced class in composition studies seemed to do so mostly out of last-minute panic: they suddenly realized how dim their job prospects actually were.

TAs were only required to teach one course a semester, and with my energy focused on writing poetry it took me an academic year before I realized what an unsuccessful teacher I was. I remember in the late spring of 1989 thinking how long my classes seemed, how precariously they were constructed. Keeping eighteen-year-olds engaged in a textbook that *I* read with little interest was an arduous task. They sighed and looked at their watches. I dreaded the thought of another year teaching.

Partly because my Freshman English mentor used workshops exclusively, and partly because I attended several creative writing workshops a week, I decided to try an approach with which I was more familiar. The transformation was marvelous. Students had a stake in the day's work, discussion was fluid, voices were raised—the class seemed to care. I told others in the MFA program about my success, and they were enthusiastic about the results in their own classes. Perhaps the chief reason for our excitement was that the workshop seemed to run itself, cutting down on our preparation and giving us more time for our own work. Later, when interviewing for teaching positions, I returned again and again to my triumph in the workshop. It was about the only thing I had to say when I was asked how I taught composition.

The job search is a stressful time for any graduate student, but for an MFA it is often demoralizing. The days are long past when college administrators say, as the president of Bard College remarked to Theodore Weiss in the early 1970s, "I know . . . poets are the most desired in the academy" (149). Creative writing faculty are beginning to realize they can no longer wildly exaggerate the value of what they do. In his otherwise enthusiastic *Peterson's Guide* introduction to graduate writing programs, James McMichael includes the caveat, "academic budgets remain so tight that the holder of a Master of Fine Arts or Doctor of Philosophy degree in writing will not easily find a job as a teacher" (1431). However, when one lives daily with the hype that creative writing programs manufacture, it is difficult not to believe that somewhere out there comfortable employment as a writer-in-residence awaits. My own adviser suggested that I apply for every job I saw, even if it seemed out of my reach. There was always a chance that I might be just what they were looking for.

I scoured the MLA *Job Information List,* and in the fall and early winter of 1989 sent out nearly fifty letters of application. My vitae was seven pages long. That December in Washington, DC, I had two interviews, both for instructor positions teaching composition. I was lucky. Several people in the program didn't have any. Even our "star," a man who has gone on to win a $20,000 NEA grant, ended up at a two-year branch campus, teaching composition along with creative writing. One of the members of his thesis committee told me that the letter she wrote for him was the best letter of recommendation she'd ever seen written for anyone.

Neither of my interviews resulted in a job offer, so in late March I was in Chicago for something I'd only recently heard of: "4 Cs." By this time I had reworded my cover letter to highlight my experience teaching composition. Unfortunately, at the convention it became clear to me, and to my interviewers as well, that I knew next to nothing about the subject. Moreover, I discovered that I would rather wander aimlessly around the Loop, cuffed by the bitter cold Lake Michigan wind, than sit in on any of the sessions. From my window in the Hilton Hotel room I couldn't afford, I stared out at the bright lights, remembering fondly the expensive Los Angeles restaurants—Perino's, the Pacific Dining Car—where corrupt doctors had treated me to lavish meals.

It wasn't until the first of June that I had an on-campus interview at the college where I now work. For me, finding a place in an English department had become the only criteria by which I could measure my success as a writer. ("I'm not much of a teacher," I informed my parents, "but it's the only way to make it in this business.") Luckily, the campus interview was largely considered a formality. I was polite and deferential. I gave my now highly polished spiel about the workshop and got the job.

My first semester teaching full-time I had a class of unruly students, many of whom knew each other from high school. They talked incessantly and quickly disabused me of the notion that the workshop was a cure-all. Less than a month into the course, I abandoned it, but was hard pressed to find something to take its place. As punishment, I made my class do grammar exercises. I grumbled and read the Thompson/Winnick biography of Frost, taking solace in the fact that the great poet's students evidently ignored him, too.

The next semester I was allowed to teach the beginning poetry workshop, which I tried to run as a graduate workshop: my MFA program made no provision for graduate students to teach creative writing. Naively assuming that my students were bursting with poetry they could hardly wait to write down, I discussed invention activities only in passing, and their poetry reflected this neglect. Quite simply, I was unprepared for the job I thought I'd been trained to do.

Sometime during my second year teaching full-time, when I was again teaching the poetry workshop, it occurred to me that there was an important connection between what I'd been striving so vigorously to do—teach creative writing—and what I'd been so diligently trying to avoid—teaching beginning composition. I realized at the age of twenty-nine that, as Susan Miller wrote when I was a freshman in high school, "[w]hile the requirements of Freshman Composition may seem more rigid than in a Short Story [or Poetry] Writing Class, the basic creative processes are, in fact, the same. Rather than being the specialized activity of a special kind of person, creativity is an ordinary process that you engage in every day" (33).

My hard-won revelations probably seem obvious to any decently trained high school English teacher, but I have every reason to believe that the majority of MFA graduates now working in universities could tell stories very much like my own. And there are many more who decided they possessed a worthless degree and gave up looking for employment in the academy. They are a very bitter lot, and they have every right to be.

What went wrong?

The Associated Writing Programs is the organization most directly responsible for keeping graduate creative writing programs alive. The *AWP Chronicle,* along with *Poets & Writers* magazine, is where MFA students turn to keep up with the latest trends, contests, and books. Although the *Chronicle* occasionally runs a dissident article, nearly every page contains an ad or an essay which implies that all good writers also have good jobs teaching creative writing. Novelist Bret Lott recalls, "The job I got when I came out was teaching remedial English. . . . But it's the hope of MFAs that if they're going to be in academia, they're going to teach creative writing, and to write to get published. But it's not reality" (55). Even Liam Rector, the organization's executive director, admits, "a serious revision of writing programs is in order. It's not a time to think about proliferation and the McFranchise that grows out of the McPoem. . . ." (56). Nevertheless, as numerous critics have pointed out, proliferation and "McFranchising" are exactly what MFA programs need in order to be considered "healthy," in order to keep their faculty employed.

And it is precisely because so much attention in graduate creative writing is focused on publishing and landing that rare but cushy job (with plenty of time to write) that so little effort is spent providing MFA students with what will likely be their most marketable skill: the ability to teach composition. Eve Shelnutt finds that "the marked absence [in the *AWP Chronicle*] of essays about the *teaching* that creative writers do within English departments underscores a passivity" about innovative methods of instruction. "The assumption could easily be," Shelnutt goes on, "that most teachers of creative writing find the workshop format effective because it is the only format they know" (16).

Joseph Moxley, who writes about both composition and creative writing, maintains that "by focusing primarily on revising and editing, the workshop fails to address prewriting strategies. Given that many professional writers such as Donald Murray report that they spend as much as 85 percent of their time searching for ideas and rehearsing possible alternatives, our omission of prewriting strategies is troublesome" (1). Surely "troublesome" is a grave understatement. It is inexcusable for creative writing teachers to ignore the many advances that rhetoric and composition researchers have made, but tenured faculty have little incentive to "muck about" in composition theory. As Shelnutt points out, they are too busy defending their own citadels to spend time in the castle of anyone else.

Sometimes, when I am angry, faced with a teaching problem I feel I ought to be able to handle but can't, I think that the MFA should be abolished altogether. Most bright young poets and fiction writers can learn the basics of their crafts as undergraduates. And if students want to study creative writing in depth, there are a burgeoning number of Ph.D. programs where they can develop their talents as writers *and* spend time learning how to teach. The commitment that it takes to get a Ph.D. might filter out those who enroll in MFA programs simply to mark time.

Of course too many people have too much at stake for that to happen in the near future. A more sensible solution would be for the MFA to be divided, like most Ph.D. programs, into different tracks. One track would emphasize the writer's own development; questions of academic employment would be immaterial. Many students come to graduate school simply wanting to improve their writing, and for them a curriculum could be designed emphasizing workshops and literature classes in their genre of interest. When they go on—like the people I knew—to take jobs as waiters or house painters or poodle groomers, there would be no shame involved. These graduates could carry on their careers as writers outside the university without carrying the onus of failure. The other track, which might require a year or more of extra work, would emphasize pedagogy. Students who wanted to make teaching in higher education a career would focus from the outset on writing theory and praxis. Rather than taking the cowardly "cross your fingers" attitude now prevalent, creative writing and composition faculty would be expected to rigorously prepare students in this track for the job market. Obviously no guarantees could be offered, but at least these MFA graduates would feel confident in themselves knowing that they were capable instructors of English.

One problem immediately apparent is the uncertain position composition programs still hold in the English department. With theorists like Stephen North suggesting that writing programs need complete autonomy in order to survive, closer ties between creative writers and composition specialists seems unlikely. Yet, as Andrea Lunsford has pointed out, "compositionists" have traditionally invited others inside their field, encouraging newcomers "to challenge divisions between disciplines, between genres, between media" (9). Writing Program Administrators are in an ideal position to facilitate a fresh exchange between teachers of writing. The challenge will be to overcome the long-standing distrust and fear creative writers have developed towards anyone outside their inner circle. The rewards, though, for students and teachers of writing at all levels, are potentially immense.

Coda

A central tenet of the Associated Writing Programs' philosophy is that universities should regard the MFA as a terminal degree. As it stands now, this is a fantasy for any writer without substantial publication credits or an extensive network of influential friends. Few graduate students have had time to amass the former and—outside of elite places like the Iowa Writers' Workshop—fewer still have access to the latter. Unless departments take a hard look at their graduate writing programs, ads like those I have begun to see in the *Chronicle of Higher Education* are likely to proliferate: "English Instructor. MAs only. No MFAs."

References

Fitzpatrick, Kathleen, and David Starkey. "An Interview with Bret Lott and Liam Rector, May 5, 1989." *New Delta Review* 7.1 (Winter 1990): 41–56.

Lindemann, Erika. *A Rhetoric for Writing Teachers.* New York: Oxford UP, 1987.

Lunsford, Andrea A. "The Nature of Composition Studies." *An Introduction to Composition Studies.* Ed. Erika Lindemann and Gary Tate. New York: Oxford, 1991. 3–14.

McMichael, James. "Writing." *Graduate Programs in the Humanities and Social Sciences.* Ed. Theresa C. Moore and Raymond D. Sacchetti. Princeton, NJ: Peterson, 1987.

Miller, Susan. *Writing: Process and Product.* Cambridge, MA: Winthrop, 1976.

Moxley, Joseph M. "Creative Writing and Composition: Bridging the Gap." *AWP Chronicle* (Vol. 23, No. 2), 1, 7–11.

North, Stephen M. *The Making of Knowledge in Composition: Portrait of an Emerging Discipline.* Upper Montclair, NJ: Boynton/Cook, 1987.

Shelnutt, Eve. "Notes from a Cell: Creative Writing Programs in Isolation." *Creative Writing in America.* Ed. Joseph M. Moxley. Urbana, IL: National Council of Teachers of English, 1989.

Weiss, Theodore. "A Personal View: Poetry, Pedagogy, Perversities." *The American Writer and the University.* Ed. Ben Siegel. Newark: U of Delaware P, 1989. 149–58.

V Creative Writing and the 21st Century

21 The End of Books

Robert Coover
Brown University

In the real world nowadays, that is to say, in the world of video transmissions, cellular phones, fax machines, computer networks, and in particular out in the humming digitalized precincts of avant-garde computer hackers, cyberpunks, and hyperspace freaks, you will often hear it said that the print medium is a doomed and outdated technology, a mere curiosity of bygone days destined soon to be consigned forever to those dusty unattended museums we now call libraries. Indeed, the very proliferation of books and other print-based media, so prevalent in this forest-harvesting, paper-wasting age, is held to be a sign of its feverish moribundity, the last futile gasp of a once vital form before it finally passes away forever, dead as God.

Which would mean of course that the novel, too, as we know it, has come to its end. Not that those announcing its demise are grieving. For all its passing charm, the traditional novel, which took center stage at the same time that industrial mercantile democracies arose—and which Hegel called "the epic of the middle-class world"—perceived by its would-be executioners as the virulent carrier of the patriarchal, colonial, canonical, proprietary, hierarchical, and authoritarian values of a past that is no longer with us.

Much of the novel's alleged power is embedded in the line, that compulsory author-directed movement from the beginning of a sentence to its period, from the tip of the page to the bottom, from the first page to the last. Of course, through print's long history, there have been countless strategies to counter the line's power, from marginalia and footnotes to the creative innovations of novelists like Lawrence Sterne, James Joyce, Raymond Queneau, Julio Cortazar, Italo Calvino, and Milorand Pavic, not to exclude the form's father, Cervantes himself. But true freedom from the tyranny of the line is perceived as only really possible now at last with the advent of hypertext, written and read on the computer, where the line in fact does not exist unless one invents and implants it in the text.

"Hypertext" is not a system but a generic term, coined a quarter of a century ago by a computer populist named Ted Nelson to describe the writing done in the nonlinear or nonsequential space made possible by the computer. Moreover, unlike print text, hypertext provides multiple paths between text segments, now often called "lexias" in a borrowing from the prehypertextual but prescient Roland Barthes. With its web of linked lexias, its networks of alternate routes (as opposed to print's fixed unidirectional page-turning) hypertext presents a radically divergent technology, interactive and polyvocal, favoring a plurality of discourses over definitive utterance and freeing the reader from domination by the author. Hypertext reader and writer are said to become co-learners or co-writers, as it were, fellow-travelers in the mapping and remapping of textual (and visual, kinetic, and aural) components, not all of which are provided by what used to be called the author.

Though used at first primarily as a radically new teaching arena, by the mid-1980s hyperspace was drawing fiction writers into its intricate and infinitely expandable, infinitely alluring webs, its green-limned gardens of multiple forking paths, to allude to another author popular with hypertext buffs, Jorge Luis Borges.

Several systems support the configuring of this space for fiction writing. Some use simple randomized linking like the shuffling of cards, others (such as Guide and Hypercard) offer a kind of do-it-yourself basic tool set, and still others (more elaborate systems like Storyspace, which is currently the software of choice among fiction writers in this country, and Intermedia, developed at Brown University) provide a complete package of sophisticated structuring and navigational devices.

Although hypertext's champions often assail the arrogance of the novel, their own claims are hardly modest. You will often hear them proclaim, quite seriously, that there have been three great events in the history of literacy: the invention of writing, the invention of moveable type, and the invention of hypertext. As hyperspace-walker George P. Landow puts it in his recent book surveying the field, *Hypertext:* "Electronic text processing marks the next major shift in information technology after the development of the printed book. It promises (or threatens) to produce the effects on our culture, particularly on our literature, education, criticism and scholarship, just as radical as those produced by Gutenberg's movable type." Noting that the "movement from the tactile to the digital is the primary fact about the contemporary world," Mr. Landow observes that, whereas most writings of print-bound critics working in an exhausted technology are "models of scholarly solemnity, records of disillusionment and brave sacrifice of humanistic positions," writers in and on hypertext "are downright celebratory. . . . Most poststructuralists write from within the twilight of a wished-for coming day; most writers of hypertext write of many of the same things from within the dawn."

Dawn it is, to be sure. The granddaddy of full-length hypertext fictions is Michael Joyce's landmark "Afternoon," first released on floppy disk in 1987 and moved into a new Storyspace "reader," partly developed by Joyce himself, in 1990.

Joyce, who is also the author of a printed novel, *The War Outside Ireland: A History of the Doyles in North America with an Account of their Migrations,* wrote in the on-line journal *Postmodern Culture* that hyperfiction "is the first instance of the true electronic text, what we will come to conceive as the natural form of multimodal, multi-sensual writing," but it is still so radically new it is hard to be certain just what it is. No fixed center, for starters—and no edges either, no ends or no boundaries. The traditional narrative time line vanishes into a geographical landscape or exitless maze, with beginnings, middles, and ends being no longer part of the immediate display. Instead: branching options, menus, link markers and mapped networks. There are no hierarchies in these topless (and bottomless) networks, as paragraphs, chapters, and other conventional text divisions are replaced by evenly empowered and equally ephemeral window-sized blocks of text and graphics—soon to be supplemented with sound, animation and film.

As Carolyn Guyer and Martha Petry put it on the opening "directions" to their hypertext fiction "Izme Pass," which was published (if "published" is the word) on a disk included in the spring 1991 issue of the magazine *Writing on the Edge:*

> This is a new kind of fiction, and a new kind of reading. The form of the text is rhythmic, looping on itself in patterns and layers that gradually accrete meaning, just as the passage of time and events does in one's lifetime. Trying the textlinks embedded within the work will bring the narrative together in new configurations, fluid constellations formed by the path of your interest. The difference between reading hyperfiction and reading traditional printed fiction may be the difference between sailing the islands and standing on the dock watching the sea. One is not necessarily better than the other.

I must confess at this point that I am not myself an expert navigator of hyperspace, nor am I—as I am entering my seventh decade and thus rather committed, for better or for worse, to the obsolescent print technology—likely to engage in any major hypertext fictions of my own. But, interested as ever in the subversion of the traditional bourgeois novel and in fictions that challenge linearity, I felt that something was happening out (or in) there and that I ought to know what it was: if I were not going to sail the Guyer-Petry islands, I had at least better run to the shore with my field glasses. And what better way to learn than to teach a course in the subject?

Thus began the Brown University Hypertext Fiction Workshop, two spring semesters (and already as many software generations) old, a course devoted as much to the changing of reading habits as to the creation of new narratives.

Writing students are notoriously conservative creatures. They write stubbornly and hopefully within the tradition of what they have read. Getting them to try out alternative or innovative forms is harder than talking them into chastity as a lifestyle. But confronted with hyperspace, they have no choice: all the comforting structures have been erased. It's improvise or go home. Some frantically rebuild those old structures, some just get lost and drift out of sight, most leap in fearlessly without even asking how deep it is (infinitely deep) and admit, even as they paddle for dear life, that this new arena is indeed an exciting, provocative, if frequently frustrating, medium for the creation of new narratives, a potentially revolutionary space, capable, exactly as advertised, of transforming the very art of fiction even if it now remains somewhat at the fringe, remote still, in these very early days from the mainstream.

With hypertext we focus, both as writers and as readers, on structure as much as on prose, for we are made aware suddenly of the shapes of narratives that are often hidden in print stories. The most radical new element that comes to the fore in hypertext is the system of multidirectional and often labyrinthine linkages we are invited or obliged to create. Indeed the creative imagination often becomes more preoccupied with linkage, routing, and mapping than with statement of style, or with what we would call character or plot (two traditional narrative elements that are decidedly in jeopardy). We are always astonished to discover how much of the reading and writing experience occurs in the interstices and trajectories between text fragments. That is to say, the text fragments are like stepping stones, there for our safety, but the real current of the narratives runs between them.

"The great thing," as one young writer, Alvin Lu, put it in an online class essay, is "the degree to which narrative is completely destructed into its constituent bits. Bits of information convey knowledge, but the juxtaposition of bits creates narrative. The emphasis of a hypertext (narrative) should be the degree to which the reader is given power, not to read, but to organize the texts made available to her. Anyone can read, but not everyone has sophisticated enough methods of organization made available to them."

The fictions developed in the workshop, all of which are "still in progress," have ranged from geographically anchored narratives similar to "Our Town" and choose-your-own-adventure stories to parodies of the classics, nested narratives, spatial poems, interactive comedy, metamorphic dreams, irresolvable murder mysteries, moving comic books, and Chinese sex manuals.

In Hypertext, multivocalism is popular, graphic elements, both drawn and scanned, have been incorporated into the narratives, imaginative font changes have been employed to identify various voices or plot elements, and there has been a very effective use of formal documents not typically used in fictions—statistical charts, song lyrics, newspaper articles, film scripts, doodles and photographs, baseball cards and box scores, dictionary entries, rock music album covers, astrological forecasts, board games, and medical and police reports.

At our weekly workshops, selected writers display, on an overhead projector, their developing narrative structures, then face the usual critique of their writing, design, development of character, emotional impact, attention to detail, and so on as appropriate. But they also engage in continuous on-line dialogue with one another, exchanging criticism, enthusiasm, doubts, speculations, theorizing, wisecracks. So much fun is all of this, so compelling this "downright celebratory" experience (as Mr. Landow would have it), that the creative output, so far anyway, has been much greater than that of ordinary undergraduate writing workshops, and certainly of as high a quality.

In addition to the individual fictions, which are more or less protected from tampering in the old proprietary way, we in the workshop have also played freely and often quite anarchically in a group fiction space called "Hotel." Here, writers are free to check in, to open up new rooms, new corridors, new intrigues, to unlink texts or create new links, to intrude upon or subvert the texts of others, to alter plot trajectories, manipulate time and space, to engage in dialogue through invented characters, then kill off one another's characters or even to sabotage the hotel's plumbing. Thus one day we might find a man and woman encountering each other in the hotel bar, working up some kind of sexual liaison, only to return a few days later and discover that one or both had sex changes.

During one of my hypertext workshops, a certain reading tension was caused when we found that there was more than one bartender in our hotel: was this the same bar or not? One of the students—Alvin Lu again—responded by linking all the bartenders to Room 666, which he called the "Production Center," where some imprisoned alien monster was giving birth to full-grown bartenders on demand.

This space of essentially anonymous text fragments remains on line and each new set of workshop students is invited to check in there and continue the story of the Hypertext Hotel. I would like to see it stay open for a century or two.

However, as all of us have discovered, even though the basic technology of hypertext may be with us for centuries to come, perhaps even as long as the technology of the book, its hardware and software seem to be fragile and short-lived; whole new generations of equipment and programs arrive before we can finish reading the instructions of the old. Even as I write, Brown University's highly sophisticated intermedia system, on which we have been writing our hypertext fictions, is being phased out because it is too expensive to maintain and incompatible with Apple's new operating system software, System 7.0. A good portion of our last semester was spent transporting our documents from Intermedia to Storyspace (which Brown is now adopting) and adjusting to the new environment.

This problem of operating-system standards is being urgently addressed and debated now by hypertext writers; if interaction is to be a hallmark of the new technology, all its players must have a common and consistent language and all must be equally empowered in its use. There are other problems too.

Navigational procedures: how do you move around in infinity without getting lost? The structuring of the space can be so compelling and confusing as to utterly absorb and neutralize the narrator and exhaust the reader. And there is the related problem of filtering. With an unstable text that can be intruded upon by other author-readers, how do you, caught in the maze, avoid the trivial? How do you duck the garbage? Venerable novelistic values like unity, integrity, coherence, vision, voice seem to be in danger. Eloquence is being redefined. "Text" has lost its canonical certainty. How does one judge, analyze, write about a work that never reads the same way twice?

And what of narrative flow? There is still movement, but in hyperspace's dimensionless infinity, it is more like endless expansion; it runs the risk of being so distended and slackly driven as to lose its centripetal force, to give way to a kind of static low-charged lyricism—that dreamy gravityless lost-in-space feeling of the early sci-fi films. How does one resolve the conflict between the reader's desire for coherence and closure and the text's desire for continuance, its fear of death? Indeed, what is closure in such an environment? If everything is middle, how do you know when you are done, either as reader or writer? If the author is free to take a story anywhere at any time and in as many directions as she or he wishes, does that not become the obligation to do so?

No doubt, this will be a major theme for narrative artists of the future, even those locked into the old print technologies. And that's nothing new. The problem of closure was a major theme—was it not?—of the "Epic of Gilgamesh" as it was chopped out in clay at the dawn of literacy, and of the Homeric rhapsodies as they were committed to papyrus by technologically innovative Greek literates some twenty-six centuries ago. There is continuity, after all, across the ages riven by shifting technologies.

Much of this I might have guessed—and in fact did guess—before entering hyperspace, before I ever picked up a mouse, and my thoughts have been tempered only slightly by on-line experience. What I had not clearly foreseen, however, was that this is a technology that both absorbs and totally displaces. Print documents may be read in hyperspace, but hypertext does not translate into print. It is not like film, which is really just the dead end of linear narrative, just as 12-tone music is the dead end of music by the stave.

Hypertext is truly a new and unique environment. Artists who work there must be read there. And they will probably be judged there as well: criticism, like fiction, is moving off the page and online, and it is itself susceptible to continuous changes of mind and text. Fluidity, contingency, indeterminacy, plurality, discontinuity are the hypertext buzzwords of the day, and they seem to be fast becoming principles, in the same way that relativity not so long ago displaced the falling apple.

Finding Your Way in Hypertext: A Guide to the Software

Hypertext fiction software, including Storyspace, guide and HyperCard, as well as Expanded Books (which are print texts converted to an electronic medium and thus not true multilinked hypertext), are generally available in computer stores.

For information about Guide (MS-DOS and Macintosh), write to Owl International Inc., 2800 156th Avenue Southeast, Bellevue, WA 98007.

For information about HyperCard, an Apple product, write to the Claris Corporation, 5201 Patrick Henry Drive, P.O. Box 58168, Santa Clara, CA 95052.

For information about Expanded Books, write to the Voyager Company, 1351 Pacific Coast Highway, Santa Monica, CA 90401.

For information about Storyspace, write to Eastgate Systems, P.O. Box 1307, Cambridge, MA 02238. Eastgate Systems not only manufactures Storyspace software but publishes, in computer disk form, hypertext fictions and poetry, including "Afternoon" by Michael Joyce, "King of Space" by Sarah Smith, "Victory Garden" by Stuart Moulthrop, "The Perfect Couple" by Clark Humphrey, and "Sucker in Spades" by Robert DiChiara, and will soon bring out "Uncle Buddy's Phantom Funhouse" by John McDaid, "Quibbling" by Carolyn Guyer, and "Its Name Was Penelope" by Judy Malloy. Eastgate is also planning to publish an online hypertext journal for short fiction, poetry, and criticism, with new work by Rob Swigart, William Dickey, and Jim Rosenberg scheduled for early issues.

For fictions written in Judy Malloy's Narrabase format (a random shuffle of grouped lexias), write to Narrabase Press, Box 2340, 2140 Shattuck, Berkeley, CA 94704.

The Art Com Electronic Network (ACEN) on the Well (Whole Earth 'Lectronic Link) puts out such experimental computer text pieces as "Diagram Series" by Jim Rosenberg, "The Heart of the Machine" by Ian Ferrier, and "The First Meeting of the Satie Society" by John Cage. For more information, write to the Well, 27 Gate Five Road, Sausalito, CA 94965.

Another hypertext network, similar to ACEN though more like an online art movement (its founder, Nancy Kaplan, explains that it was originally "a small group of people who stumbled across each other in the predawn of interactive fiction time . . . in my kitchen in Ithaca, N.Y., in November of 1988"), is TINAC (Textuality, Intertextuality, Narrative and Consciousness, and/or This Is Not a Conference). For more information, write to Nancy Kaplan, University of Texas at Dallas, School of Arts and Humanities, Richardson, TX 75083-0688.

The three major online electronic journals publishing information about interactive writings are *Postmodern Culture, EJournal,* and *Leonardo Electronic News.* For more information about *Postmodern Culture,* write to the co-editors, John Unsworth and Eyal Amiran, Box 8105, Raleigh, NC 27695. For information on *EJournal,* write to the editor, Ted Jennings, *EJournal,* State University of New York, Albany, NY 12222. For *Leonardo Electronic News,* write to Leonardo, the International Society for the Arts, Sciences and Technology (ISAST), 672 South Van Ness Avenue, San Francisco, CA 94110.

Several print journals have published or plan to publish articles on hypertext fiction and a few are beginning to add disks of fiction and nonfiction in hypertext format. The spring 1991 issue of *Writing on the Edge* (published at the Campus Writing Center, University of

California, Davis, CA 95616) featured eight printed articles and two hypertext fictions on disk ("WOE" by Michael Joyce and "Izme Pass" by Carolyn Guyer and Martha Petry). The magazine *Perforations* is publishing a special issue on hypertext, entitled "After the Book." For information, write to Richard Gess, Cataloging Department, Woodruff Library, Emory University, Atlanta, GA 30322-2870. (This issue may turn up in the Storyspace catalogue as well.)

There are also a number of books on hypertext. Among them are George Landow's *Hypertext* (Johns Hopkins University Press); *Hypermedia and Literary Studies*, edited by Mr. Landow and Paul Delany (MIT Press); Ted Nelson's *Literary Machines* (Mindful Press, Sausalito, CA); and Jay David Bolter's *Writing Space: The Computer, Hypertext, and the History of Writing* (Lawrence Erlbaum Associates, Fairlawn, NJ).

Hypertext is now being used in literature and writing courses in Austria, Denmark, England, Scotland, Japan, and Norway. In this country, hypertext workshops and seminars have been or are being conducted at New York University, Illinois Wesleyan, Brown, Cornell, Syracuse, Yale, George Mason, Carnegie Mellon, Michigan Tech, San Francisco State, and San Jose State, the University of Rochester, the Universities of Oregon, North Carolina, and Texas (Austin and Dallas campuses), Georgia Tech (where the hypertext fiction pioneers Stuart Moulthrop and Jay David Bolter now teach) and, not least, Jackson Community College in Michigan, the home base of Michael Joyce, one of Storyspace's co-developers (along with Bolter and John B. Smith) and the author of the landmark 1987 hypertext fiction *Afternoon*.

22 Riding the Bus in Silicon Valley: Building Virtual Worlds

Sarah Sloane
University of Puget Sound

I have always known
That at last I would
Take this road, but yesterday
I did not know that it would be today.

Ariwa No Narihira
Ninth-century Japan

Journal

July 13, 1992

I am riding a Number 22 bus along El Camino Real at dusk, heading towards the Stanford computer science bookstore in Palo Alto, California. On the bus, an old woman who has spent the day picking apricots tells her seat companion to get over her fear of flying: "Ahh, there's nothing to it. You're here, you're there. And if anything's going to happen, it's going to happen whether you're up there or down here." Her eyes are large and watery under thick glasses. The two women talk about how hard it is to make it on social security, how they have to keep working just to pay the utilities, put food on the table. They look out the window at the franchises and stores; they sit in silence for a while. "You look good for seventy," one of them says. Above them, on the curve of ceiling over their bus window, Narihira's words float on a poster: *I have always known that at last I would take this road, but yesterday I did not know that it would be today.* I sit with my own cheek pressed against the glass, looking out at the street fading in twilight.

Two miles away, past the composite roofs of El Camino Real, the Association of American Artificial Intelligence is holding its annual convention (AAAI–92) in downtown San Jose. Earlier today I spoke to an audience of programmers and researchers in artificial intelligence about ways new narrative theories might describe and inform the story structures of interactive fiction. We talked among ourselves a great deal about how we might create stories in the future, about the differences between characters and agents, about whether building *Star Trek's* holodeck was a possibility in our lifetime. Now, on the bus, I am weary and hoarse, happy to escape the crowds of the convention. Inside and outside the bus, the light fades. A gibbous moon rises over Minton's Lumber Supply, the moonlight waxy and close, the deserted lumberyard's stucco walls a friable pink in the twilight. Caltrain speeds by in the other direction and I head to the computer store in silence, my thoughts a muddle of ideas about writing, reading, and interactive fiction. I ride the bus in the midst of ordinary conversations, thinking thoughts about our extraordinary world. The road passes under the wheels.

And as the road passes, I think about how my own history has led me to this moment on the bus; I think about histories and chronologies in general. I know, for example, that the hotel I am staying in during this conference is one that is built on the ruins of a Chinatown burned down a hundred years ago. I know that history is what keeps everything from happening at once, keeps nineteenth-century Chinese bachelors from taking their coffee in the Fairmont lobby. The day I was born the Russian Sputnik sailed overhead, and the United States' "Space Age" began. I know what a mix of timing, chance, and perseverance has led me to sit in a conference hotel, eat party mix with programmers, and write about building virtual worlds. I know that the kinds of stories I have been hearing about all day in the workshop are strange computer-supported stories that may lead to a new dimension of narrative, a dimension different from what happens on paper or in hypertext or in text-based. I think about stories with three-dimensional interfaces, interactive stories, stories you "read" with eyephones and datagloves. I sit on a bus watching a woman read a magazine. I think about my own future and the future of stories.

I realize how much we order our place in the universe by the stories we tell; realize that the old women on the bus are versions of my own self, down the road. And as I see the bus itself being overtaken by Caltrain, I think of my own destination, the computer store, and I realize it is a destination I never would have even looked for just ten years ago. I know I am a member of a transitional generation, a woman writing on the cusp between print narrative and machine narrative. Even on my most ambivalent days, I still feel lucky to be in this historical position, this place from which to observe the transmogrification of print culture into something dreamlike, nascent, new. I sink back into my bus seat and daydream about where I was a year ago: back then I was writing a dissertation, revising to the laughtrack of David Letterman, caffeinated and determined and overwhelmed by the endless loop of self-referentiality as I wrote at a computer about how computers are affecting authorship, textuality, and reading. Here, let me paste in some of those ideas of a year ago.

Notes toward a Dissertation

July 5, 1991

Interactive fictions, or stories read on a computer in which the reader takes on the role of a central character and writes into an evolving narrative, run the gamut from hypertext fictions to MUDs (multi-user dungeons), from adventure games to the large-scale mainframe-based stories such as those under development by the Oz project at Carnegie Mellon University's School of Computer Science. In all these interactive fictions, or virtual world narratives, traditional notions of authorship and meaning are endlessly deferred, and textual stability could hardly be more challenged. Typically written in the second person, most interactive fictions comprise a genre of playful and combinatory fictions that allow readers to engage the text in limited co-authorings. Typically, through the agency of a keyboard, readers type short sentences or phrases that appear on the screen and direct a computer program to select sometimes random responses.

Interactive fiction such as the stories under development by the Oz project at Carnegie Mellon go far beyond the more common hypertext fictions written in Storyspace or Intermedia (see Coover's article in this volume) and should be distinguished from this more limited genre. Hypertext fictions are usually based on giving the reader a series of choices; they use plot branching and do not require readers to type phrases and sentences to interact with the characters and the plot. The interactive fiction of the Oz project, on the other hand, uses recent advances in artificial intelligence to model characters and settings more richly and to allow the reader far more license in examining and interacting with the creatures of the invented world. For example, the Oz project is currently developing a program that guides the behavior of Lyotard, a cat. Owing to the complexity of the underlying programs, the textual descriptions of Lyotard's behavior are unpredictable. The cat character, in a sense, has a mind of its own, and further, the reader is treated as just another character by the program (Schneider, 1992).

These kinds of interactive fictions, in general, provide a scene that is postmodern: heteroglossic and fragmentary, occasionally nihilistic, disjointed. Within this scene, interactive fiction evokes new sets of reader and writer activities that challenge our conventional sense of what an author is and what we do when we read. Let me first talk about who these new authors are and how the notion of a solitary author scribbling away in a garret is no longer (if it ever was) an entirely reliable portrait of a writer's activity.

Members of the Oz project, located primarily in Wean Hall within the School of Computer Science at Carnegie Mellon University, are engaged in an interdisciplinary effort to create dense, rich interactive fictions that will provide participants "with an experience of living in a simulated world and interacting with simulated people, or fictional characters, in dramatically interesting virtual worlds." Dr. Joseph Bates, currently a research professor in the School of Computer Science at Carnegie Mellon, directs the Oz project research group, a group comprised mainly of graduate students in computer science as well as faculty and students in the departments of English and drama. In a private conversation with me last winter, Bates said that the reason he embarked on this project was that he "wanted to build [his] dreams and have someone else be in that world."[1]

I have known Joe Bates for almost seven years now, and have worked with his Oz project members in constructing narrative theories to guide the interactive stories they are creating. In many conversations and presentations at conferences such as AAAI, Bates has explained that the interactive fiction project at Carnegie Mellon plans to use existing artificial intelligence technology to improve the state of the art of interactive fiction and build dramatic worlds that users can engage in in a variety of ways. According to Bates, the immediate and long-term goals of Oz are complementary efforts to create a medium beyond "static stories," or paper-and-print stories, and to create stories that are active and interactive. The overall goal of the Oz project is to create "constructed yet unpredictable worlds" and to provide users with rich experiences of these worlds, most immediately through a text-based interface and, eventually, through graphics and an oral interface (virtual reality). In more general terms, Bates sees the Oz project as a place to study mind—the analysis and synthesis of mind. As Bates recently stated in an e-mail message addressed to members of his research group:

> My long term goal for Oz is to provide modern IF [interactive fiction] technology in a sufficiently well-packaged form that individuals or small groups can build worlds. . . . [O]ur main goals

> should be the development of science/art and the accompanying technology, the eventual packaging of our technology for individuals, and keeping our research group open to ideas and comfortable for all who want to pursue this research.[2]

Specifically, members of the project team are pressing forward on these areas of research by building a prototype of an interactive mystery novel (*Tea for Two*) and dealing with questions of modeling as they arise. Their goals over the next five years are to accumulate a large "library" of settings, characters, and plots (and other "meta-knowledge" that will direct the arrangement and editing of this library) that writers and artists can recombine and tailor to create new works of interactive fiction. They see possible applications for this technology—and the narratives and narrative techniques it facilitates—in entertainment and in training in interpersonal skills. Most important, Bates is committed to including creative writers and artists in a collaboration with computer scientists to design together the shape and range of stories and storytelling techniques in interactive fictions and virtual worlds. In a recent interview, Bates states:

> It's important to bring in the artists . . . or the technologists will just go with it. The technologists have to be there too, because the artists can't imagine these things effectively, but eventually I hope it will be possible to get rid of the technologists, so that someone living off the coast of Maine will be able to wake up at two in the morning, build an alternative world and go back to sleep. (Schneider 24)

The goal of the Oz project over the next ten years is to move beyond text-based interactive fiction systems and to contribute to making "synthetic realities" (or, more commonly, virtual realities), that is, three-dimensional simulated environments enhanced by computer-generated sounds and graphics and encountered through eyephones and a dataglove. In these three-dimensional simulations, Bates proposes, narration will be replaced by animation; text generation will be replaced by speech generation; and parsing will be replaced by speech understanding. In short, the researchers of Oz plan to move beyond a pure text interface and to invent an interface with facilities for speech, animation, and gestures, guided cooperatively by program and user. Bates's organization of a "Synthetic Realities Workshop" at the 1990 Association of American Artificial Intelligence (AAAI–90) meeting and the AAAI–92 Artificial Intelligence and Interactive Entertainment workshop marks his team's efforts towards building a community of researchers to collaborate on making synthetic reality systems available to computer users.

To realize their long-term goal of realistic and dramatic computer simulations, researchers at Carnegie Mellon University are currently involved in modeling "world parts," including objects and settings, parts of minds, sets of linguistic rules, and narrative and dramatic theories by using the Common Lisp Object System on Mach/Unix workstations. While interested in the narration of these worlds, the primary focus of the Oz project's current research is to build "the simulations behind the interface, which we call the deep structure of virtual reality." Thus, members of the research group participate in modeling different parts of the programs that make up Oz by collaborating and corresponding over the electronic mail network that links their offices. The subject of their discussions is the ongoing production of an Oz synthetic reality and its pure text-based interface, a physical world simulation, character models, a natural language generator and understander, and theory of drama, all written in Lisp.

A Reader's Interlude: Explaining Lisp

To help his research team's daily work, Bates has divided the work necessary to realize the Oz project's ambitious long-term vision into six sets of questions or problems: how to simulate the physical world, how to simulate the minds of characters, how to design the user interface, how to build a working theory of drama, how to design the world-building environment, and how to facilitate artistic use of the system. The answer to each of these questions depends in part on using a high-level programming language, Lisp, to create working models of character and world.

Since many of you readers are like me and have only a passing knowledge of programming languages, let me pause to explain how Lisp interacts with other languages to provide the illusion of complex interaction on the computer's screen. Building "rich, deeply modeled underlying worlds" (Bates and Smith 9–10) with which the reader-user will interact involves writing several layers of instructions for the computer. At the lowest level, the level of "the real machine," a programmer composes a program in machine language, "the long strings of 1s and 0s that are all the hardware can really understand" (Johnson 16). This built-in program is called an interpreter or a compiler and can "write things on the screen and cause the other hardware (e.g., the chips of the memory and processor) to behave in selected ways" (Johnson 16). In the Oz project, programmers run a higher-level program called "the Lisp system" that, for all intents and purposes, transforms any "real machine" into a machine that can run Lisp programs. (In general, Lisp programs not only perform reasoning tasks, "but are actually intended as theoretical models of how humans perform those tasks." (Anderson, Corbett, and Reiser 2). Oz uses the Lisp programming language to model the descriptions and behavior of objects (including the bodies of characters) and provide a common sense model of the physical world. Once within the Lisp system, these programmers run another, higher-level program called Oz. Oz includes a framework for running a collection of other programs (called the "agents" of the world) that are written in other languages, usually called the "architectures" of the agents.

In brief, and in the jargon of computer scientists, Bates's model of the Oz architecture can be understood as a high-level description of a system of hierarchically related programs operating together on several levels to create collaboratively a rich simulation of a world populated by deeply simulated objects and characters. The reader interacts with these layered programs through a computer keyboard and the terminal screen. Each of the six areas of inquiry currently engaging researchers at Oz subsumes many smaller problems or areas of research that inform the ultimate shape of the layered program design.

One of the most important goals of the Oz project is to give authors or artists a set of tools and a library of settings and characters that will help them create interesting interactive stories. According to Bates, the work to simulate the physical world is ultimately intended to "provide just enough of a physical reality to let authors construct interesting characters and stories" (Bates "Synthetic"). Right now, the process of composing simulated objects in the physical world involves writing Lisp code, debugging that code, and then testing the object through a user's interaction with it.

End of Reader's Interlude and Back to the Task—and Page—at Hand

Writers and programmers involved in Oz are tackling questions of how to model mind and identity as well as what voice or array of voices to give the narrators of these worlds. Simulating the minds of independent characters within the model of the physical world is clearly more challenging than modeling relatively static objects. A jug is easier to describe than a shy person. Currently, Bates uses two frameworks for designing the minds (i.e., the computer programs that simulate mind) of characters, although these models are expected to change quickly. One is a goal-driven reactive planner called HAP, and the other is based on the Prodigy planner.[3] The ultimate goal of the researchers involved in this aspect of Oz is to represent explicitly and deeply, the beliefs, goals, plans, and emotions of synthetic characters who, according to Bates, will be able to discuss their mental lives (if they so choose).[4]

Once inanimate objects, animate objects, settings, and plots have been designed and described in Lisp, a narrative voice needs to describe the interactions of the user with the invented world to the participant. The user interface, which connects human agents to the simulated world, is an area currently being explored by Mark Kantrowitz of the Oz project. The Oz interface is based on "Glinda," a natural language generator designed by Kantrowitz, a graduate student at Carnegie Mellon. Kantrowitz characterizes Glinda as the "natural language generation module" of Oz. Kantrowitz's work hopes eventually to approximate and extend Hovy's experiments in rhetorical transitions. Specifically, the work on natural language text generation in the Oz project is linked to "Pauline" (Planning and Uttering Language in Natural Environments), a project completed at Yale University as Eduard Hovy's Ph.D. thesis in 1987. Pauline is a text generator that has the facility to rhetorically alter output. According to Kantrowitz, Pauline is capable of saying the same thing in many ways to achieve various effects,[5] a capacity he hopes to exploit in his own work with Glinda and the virtual worlds created by other programmers of Oz.

One of the most interesting problems that Bates and his researchers are tackling is how to develop a computational model of how drama and stories work. Developing the narrative and dramatic theories that will be implemented in Oz is aided by "live" improvisational experiments in drama, conceived and coached by Margaret Kelso, among others, and informed by the work on dramatic theory begun by Brenda Kay Laurel in her 1986 dissertation, "Toward the Design of a Computer-Based Interactive Fantasy System." Laurel relies on Aristotle's *Poetics* in her dissertation as a means of understanding and generating plot, character, spectacle, and creating an automated playwright. Laurel's encapsulation of Aristotle is one source of Oz's working theory of drama and the source of their conception of plot structure as comprised of complication, climax, and resolution. The central issue in the project's discussions is how to reconcile the creative tension between a scripted plot and unpredictable users; how to allow the user/reader/agent to have real effect on quality and sequence of event and narration. The current model of Oz is negotiating gingerly between the two poles in this tension, a negotiation that will eventually have important ramifications for the reader's experience of the narrative progression in stories written by the project team.

Careful discussion and implementation of a particular theory of drama will precede a reader's satisfying engagement with his computer screen and with his puppet or her avatar in graphics-based virtual worlds. The proportion of reader control and selection of event, sequence, and quality of encounter will shift according to which dramatic theory is ultimately chosen to guide Oz's constructions; the degree to which the reader experiences ethical culpability or even general responsibility for events will shift as well (see Benedikt for an interesting discussion of related issues).

Beyond these important questions of how to model objects and characters, how to narrate the invented world, and developing an adequate theory of plot and drama, it bears emphasizing again that Bates is concerned that the technology that he is building be used by artists, and that its development be guided by the needs of artists and writers building worlds. He hopes to have the population of Oz users grow as the system develops, and he hopes they will assist in constructing a substantial library of world parts. Bates's goal is to have artists develop the potential of interactive fiction as a new art form and to guide the development of Oz. For the next several years, however, collaborating with the members of the Oz project will mean that artists learn to program in Lisp as well as learn how to build complex systems. Now you know why I have taken up the study of Lisp.

August 1, 1992

Brave New World

The Oz project and other projects exploring MUDs, computerized narratives, and virtual worlds (including Autopoesis at Rennsalaer Polytechnical Institute and the Narrative Intelligence group at Massachusetts Institute of Technology Media Lab) raise serious questions about the shape human stories will take in the future, questions about composing processes and electronic publishing, questions about whether we are seeing the beginning of the end of the book. Does the nonlinearity of my own account, its mix of formal and informal discourse, relate more to an approaching deadline, postmodernity, or to the new elasticity of textual material composed on a computer? Is the book just a delivery system? And will this delivery system be replaced by the computer and the new stories and forms it can engender? Will *Gulliver's Travels* be superceded by some version of *The Lawnmower Man?* Will Nintendo modestly propose to replace Swift, and will the book, indeed, die? And what will story lose or gain by the death of the book? Even more pressing to us as teachers and writers—if the book is dying, the author is in his death throes, and the computer is becoming the preferred system to deliver stories in the future—is the question of what a creative writing teacher will become in the twenty-first century. How will she intervene in these new "creative" processes?

Let's first take a radical view of what writing and teaching writing in a bookless future might look like. Writing itself may come to be a new kind of manipulation of a different set of symbols—programs, icons, alphabets of synaesthetic, multimedia experience that will make Joris-Karl Huysmans's *Against Nature* seem tame. Writers or authors or composers or users will have the opportunity to completely reconfigure reality—and to build body representatives in graphics-based texts that may or may not be anything like the user herself. The definition of text itself will expand to include virtual worlds, computer graphics, robotic rhetoric, the postmodern bricolage of advertisements, urban images, graffiti, moving billboards, computer screens embedded in a wall. And as our definition of text expands, so will our rhetorics need to assess the newly possible grammars of images, icons, graphics, sounds, the three-dimensional interface, the textual invitations of computers.

The notion of singular authorship, a notion questioned and discarded by current research in composition (including Lunsford and Ede 1991) is replaced by a vision of collaborative writing communities that include programmers, authors, network specialists, and interface designers. These communities currently speak Lisp. And these collaborative writing communities construct layered, interactive texts that, to some extent, must predict the reader's input. Suddenly, the writer who wishes some modicum of control over the presentation of her fiction, and the teacher who wishes to help her in this endeavor, must also meddle with the delivery system. She need not concern herself only with developing a character, describing a place, or expressing an idea—she must program, and she must concern herself with what kind of voice and role to assume in these newly visible interactions with the reader. To some extent, these are familiar questions of craft, and contemporary readers and writers are well acquainted with the possibilities of unreliable narrators. However, the new writer of interactive fictions will be faced with a set of questions which are generated by a kinetic medium that will need several architectures of fiction and a stable of critics to inform and understand it. Because of the ways Oz and other builders of virtual worlds open up questions of textuality, authorship, and the notion of story, all preconceptions about creating story need to be reexamined.

And the role of the creative writing teacher may expand to encompass these demands for a new critical understanding of how the reading writing relationship is changed in this new medium.

In short, interactive fiction projects like Oz dramatically alter traditional understandings of writing story. Creative writing students of the future might upload and download the programs underlying their virtual worlds from writers, well-known and unknown, all over the country. Creative writing teachers might initially become facilitators, choreographers, or guides to the network, to programming, to the new practices and metaphors of building a story, rather than simply showing students how they might write a new world. Even that familiar and elusive hallmark of success in MFA programs, publication, might change in meaning. In a century where any writer might have access to any reader over a computer network, publication will no longer become the indicator of success and status it sometimes is now; publication will be the right of every composer who downloads his virtual world on the Internet.

In other words, whole new sets of questions about the writing of fiction arise for the communities of people who read, write, and script the fluid textual artifacts called interactive fiction. The creative writing teacher interested in experimenting with programming and with designing stories for these new delivery systems will probably have to start class with the premise that writing is a collaborative activity. (It always has been, of course, with much editorial intervention and co-writing, but interactive fictions make this notion even clearer.) The teacher will have to demonstrate a new textual enterprise shared by writers, programmers, publishers, and readers. The creative writing teacher's role will become one of demonstrating different composing processes within each of these intersecting communities, as well as one of demonstrating how to negotiate among the communities. The classroom will become a workshop of writing partners co-writing and corresponding with computers, using laptops and e-mail, and mastering Lisp and other high-level programming languages to create this new interactive art form. The students' readings, especially at the early stages, will include theories that help them look up from the page (and all the ways the print and paper metaphors drive our electronic writing practices) and into the world (because the page might disappear in their lifetime). Peer editing groups might become group tours through virtual worlds, a guided artistic critique of characterization and setting that could be altered with the wave of a dataglove.

Face it: ambivalent as we are, reluctant as we are, we may be among the last few generations who trouble to write ideas on a page. We might become teachers who are better off teaching our students graphic design and courses in visual rhetoric than talking about anaphora or pacing. We might be better off looking for the virtual-world corollaries to classical rhetorical terms than talking solely about point of view. Throw away this book. The novel is dead, the author is dead, and now, it grows clearer, the book is dead. The creative writing teacher will need to prepare for a bookless future.

However. Let me hasten to claim I am merely being provocative. There is another, less radical, view possible of how computer fictions might ingratiate themselves into our lives, and this less radical view is the one I propose here, the one that I more truly believe. Certainly for the next fifty years, at any rate, students and teachers of story will continue to look at the paper-based artifact called "book" and examine how the symbols contained within its pages question, create, constrain, and enhance the lives of their readers. Our jobs as teachers will remain the same as they have always been: We will guide our students into critical understandings of the myriad texts that surround them daily, helping them in rhetorical and narrative analyses that will help their own readings, help them understand the methods that underlie a text's creation, and help them write their own scripts and worlds. But our understandings of reading, writing, and text will probably change a great deal and will no longer be confined to studies of paper and ink. The critical techniques, the grammars of understanding story, will certainly survive for some time, and maybe for all time. Books will probably coexist peacefully as another format for story, quaint, perhaps anachronistic, a bit of an antique, but nonetheless able to satisfy some users. Some readers will still prefer to hear stories on the page, in the way that some riders prefer the bus when a plane could get them there in half the time.

We're riding a bus together right now. Half-heard conversations float overhead as we circle the block, meander through the postmodern city, heading for who knows what brave new world. Right now the technologists are creating the hardware and software of the next medium; they're drying the papyrus and grinding the ink for the next generation of writers. But what will happen when the artists pick up these new tools? What stories will they create, what voices will be silenced? Who will have access to the new pens and paper, and who will be denied? How will the computer medium of interactive fiction itself constrain what might be said? And what will the teacher be doing? Send me letters, send me faxes, send me e-mail, and let me know.

August 29, 1992

Flashback

Eleven years ago, I was a student living in Edinburgh, Scotland, writing poems, thinking about how to live the writer's life. I was renting a room in a meditation center, a great old house near Arthur's Seat, occupied by cranky Sufi mystics and followers of Bagwhan Shree Rajneesh who used to practice "active meditation" and dance around in the room above the kitchen, making the dining table shake. Sesame seeds shook in their bowl when they danced upstairs. Lonely, unclear, I attended the dream group held by Winifred Rushforth, a retired doctor in her nineties who attended her bible on a regular and rigorous schedule throughout the day. Once, at her dream group, I sat in a circle and listened to a nun tell her story of a dream inhabited by twelve yellow dolls, sat listening near the grainy photograph of Carl Jung and Winifred Rushforth standing together—two great thinkers, one alive, one dead, captured within the frame of a photographic print. We talked about what the dolls could have meant, talked about months, hours, the cycles of time we live within. Another time, a woman had a dream about a bus. And Winifred said, when you dream of a bus, you are dreaming of the omnibus, of all people. When you board a bus in your dream, you are joining with all of humanity. You are commingling, connecting, indicating a direction. You are turning the driving over to the collective unconscious. You may find yourself traveling in directions you didn't anticipate, on nonlinear journeys and readings that simultaneously illuminate and confuse. This is how I remember what she said, anyway. And nowadays, whenever I ride a bus, I look around at the other passengers and wonder what journey we have jointly undertaken, under what moon, toward what shared horizon.

References

Anderson, John R., Albert T. Corbett, and Brian J. Reiser. *Essential LISP.* Reading, MA: Addison-Wesley, 1987.

Bates, Joseph. *OZ Project: Overview and Schedule 1989–1992.* Unpublished document, Carnegie Mellon University Computer Science Department, 1989.

Bates, Joseph. "Synthetic Realities." Unpublished draft, Carnegie Mellon University Computer Science Department, 1987.

Bates, Joseph, and Sean Smith. *Towards a Theory of Narrative for Interactive Fiction.* Carnegie Mellon University Computer Science Department Technical Report #CMU-CS-89-121, published at Carnegie Mellon University, February 20, 1989.

Benedikt, Michael, ed. *Cyberspace: First Steps.* Cambridge: Massachusetts Institute of Technology, 1991.

Bolter, Jay David. *Writing Space: The Computer, Hypertext, and the History of Writing.* Hillsdale, NJ: Erlbaum, 1991.

Johnson, George. *Machinery of the Mind: Inside the New Science of Artificial Intelligence.* New York: Random House, 1986.

Laurel, Brenda Kay. *Toward the Design of a Computer-Based Interactive Fantasy System.* Diss. The Ohio State University, 1986.

Laurel, Brenda. *Computers as Theatre.* Reading, PA: Addison-Wesley, 1991.

Laurel, Brenda Kay, Ed. *The Human-Computer Interface.* Reading, PA: Addison-Wesley, 1991.

Lunsford, Andrea, and Lisa Ede. *Singular Texts, Plural Authors: Perspectives on Collaborative Writing.* Carbondale & Edwardsville: Southern Illinois UP, 1990.

Rheingold, Howard. *Virtual Reality.* New York: Simon and Schuster, 1991.

Ronell, Avital. *The Telephone Book: Technology, Schizophrenia, Electric Speech.* Lincoln: U of Nebraska P, 1989.

Schneider, Michael. "The Oz Project or Virtual Reality with Aristotle at the Joy Stick." *Carnegie Mellon Magazine* 11.2 (Winter 1992): 23–24.

Woolley, Benjamin. *Virtual Worlds: A Journey in Hype and Hyperreality.* Cambridge, MA: Blackwell, 1992.

Notes

1. Private conversation, December 9, 1990.

2. E-mail message sent 6 March 91 12:40:24 EST to interactive-fiction group from Joseph Bates. Subject: Kinds of Worlds.

3. Sean Smith and Joseph Bates, *Toward a Theory of Narrative for Interactive Fiction* (Technical Report CMU–CS–121, published at Carnegie Mellon University on February 20, 1989), 9–10.

4. Bates, Oz Project Overview, 1.

5. Kantrowitz's summary of Hovy, *Overview of Natural Language Text Generation,*(class lecture given at Carnegie Mellon University, November 6 and 8, 1990), 12.

Afterword—Colors of a Different Horse: On Learning to Like Teaching Creative Writing

Wendy Bishop
Florida State University

I've often felt an outsider to creative writing "society" and insecure about my forays into that particular café. I need to testify to my own education, though, because it is the mis-educational parts of that experience that drive me to improve instruction. "How do you inscribe difference without bursting into a series of euphoric narcissistic accounts of yourself and your own kind?" Asks Trinh Minh-ha, author of *Woman Native Other.* "Without indulging in a marketable romanticism or in a naive whining about your condition? . . . Between the twin chasms of navel-gazing and navel-erasing, the ground is narrow and slippery. None of us can pride ourselves on being sure-footed there" (28).

I am not sure of being sure-footed, but I have talked to others about teaching creative writing who feel as I do. We were in creative writing classrooms a lot, but didn't feel supported there. Some of us were simply muddling along, trying to right the wrongs we felt were done to us by our own previous teachers. Some of us had internalized a destructive self-doubt: that it wasn't just teaching that our poet or fiction teachers disdained, maybe it really was us, the young aspiring writers in their classes, that they dispaired of.

What, if anything, had been withheld from some of us? Has anything changed? Where are we going as teachers? It is time to look around and see what has been made, to find a language in which to express divergent perspectives, to avoid (if possible) narcissism, romanticism, and whining. With my Capricorn goat-feet, I hope to stay somewhat sure-footed as I investigate this difficult terrain, for, oddly, I feel that I had to *learn to like* teaching creative writing.

Learning to Learn

I had two obvious credentials for writing poetry. I had family stories that needed telling, and a way with words after I developed a childish agoraphobia, determined to escape family fights not by moving out into the world, but by moving into books, becoming a consumer of words, more words, more words until they finally had to be returned in kind, in elementary school poems that angled for teacher approbation. What fifth grade teacher could resist the seventeen rhyming quatrains of "The Grunion Run" and fail to honor me? Certainly I became addicted to the distinction of being the family "smart one," "reader," and finally "writer." Easily, I gave in to my addiction. As the sounding board for my high school girlfriends, I wrote "portraits" of each as gifts, and, as I widened my audience, soon won high school writing competitions and published for the first time.

Now, part of me has been schooled to find something horrible in this confession, for later, in college, I was trained to see writing, poetry, art—as art, nothing more. To allow art to serve me, to help me understand myself, to make me feel good, was to tarnish somehow the profession with schoolgirlishness. At the time of my college education (and perhaps still) New Criticism held sway. The canon was strong and entering it was the (impossible) goal; art that *felt* or *helped* was wrong.

"Instead of moving the audience and bringing pressure to bear on the world," explains Jane Tompkins, "the work is thought to present another separate and more perfect world. . . . The imputation that a poem might break out of its self-containment and perform a service would disqualify it immediately from consideration as a work of art. *The first requirement of a work of art in the twentieth century is that it should* do *nothing*" (210, emphasis added). Of course, and I didn't know this then, the Do-Nothing School of Art was a strategic move to keep insiders safe and outsiders safely out. The still hotly debated issue of art as political action illuminates the insider/outsider struggle. And the outsider struggle has been most evident for women and for those not raised in the canon. Canonical arguments are convenient diversions away from larger problems, like those pointed out by Mike Rose in his book *Lives on the Boundary:* "Although a ghetto child can rise on the lilt of a Homeric line—books *can* spark dreams—appeals to elevated texts can also divert attention from the conditions that keep a population from realizing its dreams" (237).

"And writers at the margins," says Toni Cade Bambara, "are more likely to link thought and body, writing to the body, the writer to the community, writing for dear life. A writer like any other cultural worker, like any other member of the community, ought to try to put her/his skills in the service of the community" (quoted in Minh-ha 9–10).

The problem for the sixties and seventies was class, remains class, classes—how did so many, from so many places, of so many colors, with so many unrecognized strengths and too easily labeled deficiencies, enter the academic realm? Open admissions policies produced waves of irreconcilable Otherness.

As a senior in college in 1974, I asked my boyfriend to take a poetry workshop with me; he said "yes" but didn't show up on the first day of class. Here I am, then, in a college writing workshop for the first time. I'm assigned a riddle poem. I buy a book of Old English verse. I write. I recapture my early writing successes under the guidance of an involved woman teaching assistant who praises and encourages us. We can tell that she dearly loves poetry. Somehow, she has already learned to like teaching creative writing, perhaps because she is *not* a creative writer (though later she leaves the university, Ph.D. complete, unable to get tenure-line work in the Bay Area). I double my art major to English; spend a fifth undergraduate year finishing my creative writing major, entering, as I envision it, classes full of word making and book reading; imagining I've come home.

Then, after being a good student in several undergraduate workshops, I am let into graduate school where the distinction of being the quiet brainy child who read books was negated in a matter of months. In a theory class, I thought I was listening to a foreign language (and I was). In a poetics class, I already lacked several hundred years of preparation. I was surprised to find my undergraduate confidence and excitement draining away. I didn't know that I wasn't able to be a poet because I was a woman. The Master Poet I studied under claims: "Poets, like people in love, always behave badly, except on occasion" (Shapiro 55). If I were to behave badly, then I would not be let into the club of women who swelled the workshops, the conferences, the famous writers' lunches, professors' trysts. In the role of a bad girl—one wanting respect and attention for her writing—I would not be contributing to, I would be asking of. And that would not do. To begin with, there was not enough room in the world for great poets of the first rank. Competition was necessarily fierce for the few places in the pantheon for women who were writers (writers who were women?). It was understood: If you make it, you're a poet; if you fail, you're a woman poet. "Exceptionalism," Nadya Aisenberg and Mona Harrington point out in their book *Women of Academe* "condemns the voices of most women to silence" (143).

In my first-year graduate workshops, young men and women sit in a half-circle around a famous white-haired poet. He smokes a pipe, pages through our work, drops matches, and doesn't intervene during our remarks to each other. No comments beyond the significant twitch of an eyebrow or speedy movement to the next text.

I thumb the *Norton Anthology of Modern Poetry* to figure out what poets write about. I am embarrassed by the women—Sylvia and her anger, and Anne and her body. I mention loudly that I never want to be called a woman poet. I never mention that I have bought all of Anne Sexton's books and read them, yet rarely buy the assigned others: Wordsworth floated outside my experience—a young man's life, what was that to me? I say none of this in class, although I write a lot, like the women of academe in Aisenberg and Herrington's study who "prefer the written to the spoken voice, because in this form they can project authority and influence without engaging in confrontations that raise confusing issues of appropriate response" (74).

Although I didn't know I couldn't be a poet, I did know I felt terrible when it came to my voice. I stumbled if I read aloud. Attending poetry readings, I'd see *real* poets: How could I impress in the manner of William Everson, Robert Bly, or Gary Snyder—low, vibrant voices seducing audiences with words?.

As a fellowship student at a summer writer's conference, I was momentarily mentored. The poet reviewing my manuscript suggested that I not publish under the name "Wendy." I obeyed him, in my insecurity using W. S. Bishop for five years.

During that time, I wrote about my family. My young loves. A chapbook, compiled for me by a willing small press editor, seemed to be composed primarily of those of my poems that had the word *thigh* in them.

My second year of graduate workshops consisted of hours of meeting with a group of other aspiring poets not to be taught. Our egos grew to the degree that they were not sated. Cliques, competitiveness—some of us thrived, at a cost. Deborah Churchman, interviewed John Hopkins creative writing faculty and students in the mid-1980s to find:

> In most programs, weekly seminars tear through students' works line by line, giving criticism that may or may not be constructive. "You're generally naked here," said Professor Barth, ". . . and if you've botched it, it's there for all to see." "It was fiercely competitive," said Miss Robison of her year at Johns Hopkins, "though now those students are like family. But it took pounds off me." (43)

We spent our time waiting for our Master Poet to say: "This is good." We read his books and liked his work. He was a poet. He did not teach us, we assumed, because we were not ready, worthy, or worth it. He told us stories of his own battles. If we stayed, we built our own armor, were launched into the world from indifferent degree committees.

"What are you going to do now?"

"Submit my book to The Yale Series of Younger Poets."

Polite embarrassed silence.

For fifteen years, I submitted my manuscripts in anger. And never won. I proved my masters right instead of learning from them. And it was bred in the bones that my growing joy in teaching as a graduate student was one more mark of non-achievement. Here is my Master Poet's verse on teaching:

Creative Writing

English was in its autumn when this weed
Sprang up on every quad.
The Humanities had long since gone to seed,
Grammar and prosody were as dead as Aztec.
Everyone was antsy except the Deans
Who smelled Innovation, Creativity!
Even athletes could take Creative Writing:
No books, no tests, best grades guaranteed,
A Built-in therapy for all and sundry,
Taking in each other's laundry.
No schedule, no syllabus, no curriculum
No more reading (knowledge has gone elsewhere).
Pry yourself open with a speculum
And put a tangle in your hair.

(Shapiro 27)

This teacher, in the years I studied with him, returned no annotated texts, gave no tests, shared no grading standards, kept to no schedule or syllabus, designed no curriculum. That's the way it was: master knows, disciples wait for enlightenment. Follow the rules, the Poet suggests:

Rules live in masterpieces.
Get them to read the masters, let them
Learn some humility for art;
Let them copy, let them imitate,
Memorize models, learn languages,
Above all master their own.

(Shapiro 56)

But over the years, I would learn to distrust rules like these: learn the master plots; imitate the masters; aim for clarity, coherence, and correctness. Trinh Minh-ha suggests, "Clarity is a means of subjection, a quality both of official, taught language and of correct writing, two old mates of power: together they flow, together they flower, vertically, to impose an order (16).

Learning to Teach

Although teaching creative writing at the university where I first began to do so was an assignment of honor, I viewed my first classes with some terror. I could not demand emulation, even if I had believed emulation was the solution, which I didn't. "It's not a question of teaching without theory," Francois Camoin suggests, "—we can be goats and monkeys in the halls and at department parties, but in workshops the students want more from us than 'Be like me. Write,' which is not very useful advice, finally" (1.4).

At first I was barely able to keep a step ahead of my students, whether opening my first grammar handbook to "grade" my first set of essays or reading anthology poems for the first time in a blur the night before attempting to teach them. Finally, I stopped trying to stay ahead, I fell back, I was with my students, and I developed the exciting idea of learning together that I have never left. The classroom—that I needed to make over into a success story—became my haven. If being a poet meant teaching badly—I suppose so I could stay home and wait for my poems—then I couldn't do it.

In the first place, it was boring and unproductive to stay home and wait for poems. My poems, I knew, arrived because I willed them into being—due for a class, generated by a need to learn my life and share it, prompted by self-imposed exercises because working with words was so damn pleasurable in itself. And anyway, I wanted to write stories, novels, essays, too, any and everything. I hated writers' conference panels on: "The possibility of creative writers succeeding in *two* genres." I remember with some anger the colleague who told me he didn't think he *believed* in the prose poem.

After a few quarters, I had some teaching success, but I didn't yet know how well creative writing could be taught, because teaching it well had built-in risks. For example, it was okay to teach, but not to say that writing could be taught. When I said: "Here's what I did; it worked," I seemed to become a conversational pariah. And, not unexpectedly, my Master Poet still didn't agree with me—in my head or in his published poems:

> Creative Writing classes are the pits,
> Yet by some osmotic-symbiotic-
> Empathetic catalysis people learn,

> At least the two percent with talent learn.
> The others do their own spontaneous thing.
> Surrealism as a rule.
> The worst start all their poems with I
> And end with me. And nobody reads.
> How did they get this far? Who let them in?
> Are these rooms holding-pens?
>
> (Shapiro 55)

I started with different questions. Why hadn't we been let in before (women, minorities, lower-classes)? Why was I given and asked to give out so many rules? Why was I supposed to read books that signified nothing to me but a world that excluded me, folded me down, hid me away? Why were the benefits of workshops extolled or assumed, and the dangers never examined? As Lynn Domina, earlier in this volume, noted:

> Writing about what you know about often implies writing about what other members of the workshop will not know about, which is easily enough dealt with, if what you know about is running a dairy farm or swimming competitively or communicating with an Australian via short-wave radio, less easily dealt with if what you know about is prostitution or incest or addiction, and much less easily handled if what you know about is anger at your exclusion from a culture by white people or by wealthy people or by men or by heterosexuals, who are all your classmates and/or your teacher.

Why were only two percent of human beings talented? Were they? What was at stake?

> "Even after I began to recognize these incursions into peoples' texts/stories/lives as colonizations," says Katharine Haake, "I kept it up, not knowing what to replace it with. Over time, I began to realize that what students need to know is not how to 'fix' any given story, but how to read, instead, the conventions of the discourse—in general, any discourse, and in particular, a fictional literary narrative text. Where a writer decides to locate herself and her work within the context of these conventions is a decision that should not involve the teacher. I am not saying not to 'advise' students; I am saying to respect who they are, and also to trust their decisions."

Clearly, I could not teach the way I had been taught. At a teaching loss, I analyzed my own poems and made assignments for students from self-assignments that had worked for me. I also looked sideways, stealing from my composition classes—for I had received some training to teach composition—repaying my thefts, a little, with what was developing in my creative writing workshops. Nowadays that's less new. Rex West says, "As I see it, if someone walks past my classroom and can't tell whether I'm teaching expository or creative writing, that's a good sign" (Turkle et al. 4.27). But in 1981, cross-fertilization between composition and creative writing just wasn't done, though I did it. If my composition students were benefiting from sharing drafts—comparing an early draft with a later one—I borrowed that for my poetry workshops, sharing my own, realizing that I had *never* seen my own teachers' work in draft.

Robert Scholes puts the classroom and real-life divide that is indicated here in perspective when he reminds us:

> [A]ll who write, whether in an ivy-covered study or a crowded office, are involved in a process that moves from practice to earnest, beginning with dry runs, trial sessions, rough drafts, scratchings out, and crumpled sheets in the wastebasket. There is, then, something inescapably academic about all writing, whether in school or out of it, and many a text begun in school has finished in the world. The "real" and the "academic" deeply interpentetrate one another. (10)

In my own education, I was not offered the commonalties between ivy-covered study and crowded office that Scholes describes, but I started to explore commonalties in the classes I taught. If, in poetry workshop, poems were never graded poem by poem, then the method would suffice for essay writing, too. If I was already trained in essay conferencing, then I would need to have poetry students in my office doing the same. I asked creative writing students to read a draft aloud and talk about it. Soon I asked for portfolios that showed the process of writing poems and stories. I tried to learn where (creative) writers' ideas came from, what they didn't understand, what they did. I attempted praising development, change, and risk, and, better, I figured out how to reward these attributes by articulating my assessments beyond a grade.

As I began to see creativity as more than a two-percent issue, I found genre and writer's myths twin tyrants in the workshop, lingering on to trick me and my students into self-hatred long after my Master was a ghost in the corner of my classroom, sleeping mostly, if awake a trifle condescending or amused. Fighting myths and received ways of doing things meant asking difficult questions and assuming difficult (nontraditional) views, as Robert Scholes does when he claims:

> We must help them to see that every poem, play, and story is a text related to others, both verbal pre-texts and social sub-texts, and all manner of post-texts including their own responses, whether in speech, writing, or action. *The response to a text is itself always a text.* (20)

As Trinh Minh-ha does when she asks:

> Why view these aspects of an individual which we imply in the term "writer" or "author" as projections of an isolated self and not of our common way of handling texts? (Minh-ha 35).

As Katherine Haake points out when she explains:

> We could be a long time debating, for example, such a question as whether we write the writing, or the writing writes us.

And despite what could be seen as a series of triumphs—a first-generation college student, Army-brat from the suburbs, becomes a writer and teacher of poetry and composition, I still felt an outcast from creative writing. *I could claim* that I write many genres, speak theory and pedagogy and art; *it could be claimed* that I let my energies be sapped and diffused between teaching and parenting and writing. Worse, I am not a name poet and haven't published a book with a university press, yet I inhabit an academic system where that matters. Instead, I have published several books of writing about writing and find, ironically, that I'm still subdued by genre. We all know that in the Do-Nothing School of Art a book of elegant verse is worth more than many hard-working books of pedagogy or criticism. Trinh Minh-ha captures my feelings:

> Accumulated unpublished writings do stink. They heap up before your eyes like despicable confessions that no one cares to hear; they sap your self-confidence by incessantly reminding you of your failure to incorporate. For publication means the breaking of a first seal, the end of a "no-admitted" status, the end of a soliloquy confined to the private sphere, and the start of a possible sharing with the unknown other—the reader whose collaboration with the writer alone allows the work to come into full being. Without such a rite of passage, the woman-writer-to-be/woman-to-be-writer is condemned to wander about, begging for permission to join in and be a member. (8–9)

Are we policing *quality,* or *society,* with our stiff publication competitions, with our focus on measurable products and our neglect of intangible and multiple processes? The amount of unproductive competition and anti-pedagogical thinking in this field strikes me oddly since it often comes from those who also rail at anti-intellectual thinking. In my experience, creative writers continue to be exceptionally worried about the taint of the academy where a majority of them live. Francois Camoin recalls, "I remember watching William Least Heat Moon take off his boots at a convention in St. Louis, and talk about squelching his feet into the mud of life. Who would ever have thought that he had a Ph.D. in Renaissance Lit.? Who'd have thought that he would be so ashamed of it? (1.2)

And yet, and yet, it is by training in rhetoric in composition after my training in creative writing and by writing pedagogy that I've come to find myself as a writer, I've learned to like teaching creative writing, and, finally, in doing so, been freed to like my own.

Learning to Like Teaching Creative Writing

I'm hoping for nothing less than to change our profession, so that the parts of it which proved incredibly valuable for me and others like me are not lost to the kind of anger and difficulties you can hear in my story: "[T]he lure of teaching for many women," Aisenberg and Harrington found, "is the desire to reinvoke the transformational experience, their own experience of growth and change, for others. It is not, that is, simply an extension of the nonintellectual gifts of mothering transplanted to another, professional, scene, but something far more radical—women invoking change in others" (39).

To keep the affirmation in my daily life, I've had to rewrite the story of learning and teaching creative writing as I'm trying to do here. The story of my own workshop education was, in many ways, like this one, narrated by Peter Elbow:

> We write something. We read it over and we say, "This is terrible. I *hate* it. I must work on it to improve it." And we do, and it gets better, and this happens again and again, and before long we have become a wonderful writer. But that's not really what happens. Yes, we put it in a drawer and vow to work on it—but we don't. And next time we have the impulse to write, we're just a *bit* less likely to pick up the pen. (199).

That's the type of workshop education that derives from the critical, doubting, winnowing, elite form of the master-teacher workshop. But the workshops we need to develop—and I think there are many ways to orchestrate them—read like this story, again narrated by Elbow:

> What really happens when people get to write better is more like this: We write something. We read it over and we say, "This is terrible. . . . But I like it. Damn it, I'm going to make it good enough so that others will like it too." And this time we *don't* just put it in a drawer, we actually work hard on it. And we try it out on other people too—not just to get feedback and advice but, perhaps more important, to find someone else who will like it. (199–200)

Peter Elbow's retellings of the story of the growth of writers echoes all the way back through my confessional history. Something in that terrible poem "The Grunion Run" made me like it. The sheer pleasure of having gotten from beginning to end in rhyme. Because I didn't keep it hidden in a drawer, I found a teacher who could like it too. And while my story is also one of sheer dogged insistence in the face of poor teaching, proving that it is possible to buck the odds and learn alone, my productive writing addiction was actually generated in that first undergraduate poetry workshop where my work was liked. I was not making a McPoem; I was making me.

Elbow argues that liking work allows us to be more demanding of the writer. He also suggests that good writing teachers feel able to like student writing. If they like students' work, they can be more demanding. If they're more demanding, the work improves. Liking creates a positive chain reaction.

If we enter the creative writing class expecting to limit the size of the playing field, keep closed the floodgates on "too much damn writing," we certainly will. Conversely, if we enter with expectation, appreciation, and excitement, we have the possibility of engendering intrinsic rewards in writers and demanding vast amounts of high quality work from them. What writer would work hard to fail, to be dubbed uncreative, to not publish or converse in a public forum? Whenever we set up doubtful and doubting classes, we encourage our students in their inwardness, their paranoia, their grievances, their narrow world view; we keep them in the limited therapeutic state of writing to fix the past instead of the perhaps equally therapeutic but more important state of writing to construct the future. "Shake syntax," exclaims Trinh Minh-ha, "smash the myth, and if you lose, slide on, *unearth* some new linguistic paths. Do you surprise? Do you shock? Do you have a choice?" (20)

The benefit of liking our students is manifold, for we talk to them and learn from them and celebrate their progress rather than bar it. Truly, they are not going to displace us before our time. Rather than two percent with talent, there are probably only two percent of our students who will follow us into this profession. To the degree that we like their work and know we're orchestrating learning, to that same degree we can raise our class standards, asserting the truth: improvement in writing results from long-term, serious attention to writing, from drafting, response, reading, pushing, experimenting, and succeeding *even just a little bit.*

The benefit of liking our teaching is manifold. Primarily, we don't feel our class time is stolen from our writing time. If we write with our students in class, write about our classes, read theory and writers with an eye to developing the students in class and the student in ourselves, we develop an ecologically sound system for our writing lives. We find other teachers to share with rather than complain to. We find our students own small successes cause as much celebration as our own small successes. We tend not to procrastinate in responding to student texts; we like their texts better because they are better texts and because ours is no longer the only valuable opinion or suggestion.

The benefit of liking our colleagues, our English departments, our professional organizations, is manifold. For a new generation of creative writer-teachers, it is becoming easier to teach with involvement and distinction. Unfortunately, many others of us—those who are one, two, and even three generations older than currently enrolled MA, MFA, and Ph.D. students—matured in a climate that did not encourage pedagogical and theoretical thinking about creative writing, an upbringing I've woven together in this essay through my own personal testimony and the contrapuntal voices of writers I admire.

Change in this climate has only come lately, though I hope it will continue rapidly. Only in the last five years has the Associated Writing Programs started hosting annual workshops and sessions focusing on pedagogy, and teachers who do not teach at the graduate level have started to discuss undergraduate creative writing instruction during the meetings of a special interest group at the Conference on College Composition and Communication and are developing a strong voice in that organization. In the same five-year period, the book lists of the Poets and Teachers' Collaborative, Boynton/Cook Heinemann Publishers, and the National Council of Teachers of English have increased greatly, responding to a growing interest among readers in creative writing pedagogy and theory by publishing a number of collections of note. And finally, within the last five years, we have regularly heard discussions of new undergraduate and graduate course listings that explore and feature the intersection of creative writing, composition, theory, and pedagogy.

I'd like to argue now that this pedagogical change needs to be undertaken more actively in all degree programs in creative writing. Learning to teach better is tough, exhilarating, and possible. I'm talking here about the need I see for a deep revision of what it means to teach and learn creative writing, a reprioritization of products and processes, a curriculum that investigates itself, that denounces old premises, topples myths, renames, and reaffirms: "Substantial creative achievement," Trinh Minh-ha suggests, "demands not necessarily genius, but acumen, bent, persistence, time" (7). We can start fostering acumen and bent by instituting pedagogy seminars; we can give to teaching and learning the persistence and time they require. Here is the response of a graduate student to one creative writing pedagogy seminar.

> Quite frankly, I think this should be a required course—part of the MFA program requirements. Many of us would like to go out and get a job teaching—but without having thought a great deal about teaching creative courses, so we end up doing the same thing we did in our courses in school. Pretty sad. Some people may find out they don't want to think about their craft in this way, and that is useful too. They'll steer away from teaching.

How well do we know our graduate students? How willing are we to let them carve out careers different from the dominant (and often unattainable) one of "star" writer. Our students will be teaching under conditions and in locations we can only speculate on. How do we prepare a teacher to teach creative writing in nursing homes, hospitals, and prisons? Much support is needed for much is at stake. Diane Kendig found:

> One colleague, who has taught English in prison for years, had a student come to her to explain why he could not write a response journal for her literature class. He had made it a practice, he explained, to eat any personal writing in his possession. She was at first unfazed, assuming that "eat" was prison slang for "getting rid of," and then she was shocked to hear the inmate explain that he had actually chewed and swallowed every piece of paper he had written or received personal writing on during his incarceration. To maintain such a diet, one must not produce many meals, and he knew he literally could not swallow what she was asking him to produce. (11.2)

A writer, as a cultural worker, does put his/her skills in the service of communities that are difficult to support.

And a pedagogy seminar does not take valuable time *away* from the study of literature or the practice of craft: it can address theory, research, and practice; it can and should include writing and workshopping; it should address what we know and what we need to know—how to design courses, how to grade; it should take a student and a teacher beyond the boundaries of what they themselves have experienced into investigations of alternatives, into deeper understandings of students, into broader examinations of cultures, politics, and institutional systems.

Often, our graduate students are trained to teach composition and benefit from that training. Now they need to be taught to teach writing both generally and specifically, to examine the "creative" in creative writing. Today, the separation between composition and creative writing programs is still so firm that the two fields rarely converse except in the overtaxed brain of the university teaching assistant. Too often, this TA learns that those professors she studies under believe little overlap does or should exist between these fields, with a resulting puzzlement similar to the Irish individuals in this story:

> When a sufficient number of specialists are assembled on a college faculty, the subject of which each knows only a small part is said to be covered, and the academic department to which they all belong is regarded as fully manned. In ancient Ireland, if legend is to be trusted, there was a tower so high that it took two persons to see to the top of it. One would begin at the bottom and look up as far as sight could reach, the other would begin where the first left off, and see the rest of the way. (Erskine, quoted in Graff 111)

I'd like to question the division of our writing programs so that some individuals are assigned views of the bottom half of the tower—exposition—and others are assigned the top half of the tower—imagination. Encouraged to talk about their field and to view themselves as teaching professionals in that field, allowed to evaluate models of teaching and question received wisdom, creative writers turned students of pedagogy grow into individuals who can see and appreciate the entire tower.

I want to offer some testimonials, because I see myself as the mirror here:

> A writing *for* the people, *by* the people, and *from* the people is, literally, a multipolar reflecting reflection that remains free from the conditions of subjectivity and objectivity and yet reveals them both. I write to show myself showing people who show me my own showing. (Minh-ha 22)

After a pedagogy seminar, these graduate students showed me my own showing. They felt:

- That students can be trained to critique each other's work rather than left to "catch on," as is expected in a standard workshop.
- That invention exercises are as important for creative writing students as they are for composition students.
- That there is no comparing graduate (trained) and undergraduate (untrained) writers. I'm not sure I want to work with untrained writers.
- That it's harder to neglect an intriguing bit of invention that's already on paper than it is an abstract idea in your head. Being forced to invent in a prescribed way is useful and enlightening in

spite of my resistance to prescription. I can produce something worth showing to people in only one week. I can share early drafts.

- That, as instructor, it is important to participate also. It's important to sit around a big table, to read aloud samples, to try various workshop formats and share students' reactions, to provide unguided holistic response to writing.
- That there is sexism in the field.
- That it is possible to deal with student writers' block.
- That I'm sensitive about my own creative efforts and felt exposed sharing spontaneous work.
- That what it all boils down to for me, is that students get the respect they deserve in classrooms.

I don't think it matters what we're teaching—literature, composition or creative writing—what we're helping students to achieve is the ability to empower themselves thorough language. When we understand this, the tools—literature, essays or poems or stories or criticism—take on an equal weight: one is no more primal than the other. What is most important is that students experience language, discover it, and clarify their relationship to it.

These changes—to encounter writer/teachers like this—to Hans and me (who met many years ago in one of the workshops of the Master poet and remet some years later and began to collaborate on rethinking our workshop experiences)—seem as rapid and surprising as second-wave feminism must have seemed to first-wave feminists. So Hans and I and others who shared in this collection hope, that as a profession, we have finally moved from feeling the need to be horses of a different color—individuals steeped in a romantic creative writing culture that valorized the hard-drinking, sweet-talking, solitary, and usually male author. The romantic creative writing culture sanctions the star system without the underlying capital to support that system (most authors we know, lifelong, will make very little money, directly, for their work) and a set of cultural stances that encouraged us to inhabit rigid positions that made us feel unrealistically exalted and more often not very valuable, as we've tried to explain.

These attitudes linger, hopefully, more truly in the minds of those who once suffered from the classroom and publishing climates created by such thinking; we have indications that the day-to-day learning life of younger creative writers is more tolerant and informed, or that it could be if we honored teaching and offered courses to prepare those writers who continue on in the academy. That they should continue is fine by us since there's a pretty good life to be had here. The stunningly notable increase in interest in creative writing, practice and instruction, indicates that we are ready to reconceptualize this field and all creative practitioners not as writer **or** teacher, not as famous or failed, not as infamous or boring, not as first or second rank, not as contributing to a glut of creative work and therefore *never* contributing to a conversation about art through art. In this, we also reconceive our metaphor—we aim toward different distinctions, not to be a product only, a horse of different color, but to become part of a process, a work and thought community that generates the colors of a different horse, creative writing in new hues and configurations, a collaborative and energetic intellectual and creative project undertaken inside and outside universities, alone at home and together in the classroom.

References

Aisenberg, Nadya and Mona Harrington. *Women of Academe.* Amherst: U of Massachusetts P, 1988.

Camoin, Francois. "The Workshop and Its Discontents." In this volume.

Churchman, Deborah. "Fertile Time for Creative Writing: More College Courses Every Year." *New York Times* 8 Jan. 1984: 42–43.

Domina, Lynn. "The Body of My Work Is Not Just a Metaphor." In this volume.

Elbow, Peter. "Ranking, Evaluating, and Liking: Sorting Out Three Forms of Judgment." *College English* 55.2 (Feb. 1993): 187–206.

Graff, Gerald. *Professing Literature: An Institutional History.* Chicago: U of Chicago P, 1987.

Haake, Katherine. "Teaching Creative Writing If the Shoe Fits." In this volume.

Kendig, Diane. "It Is Ourselves that We Remake: Teaching Creative Writing in Prison." In this volume.

Minh-ha, Trinh T. *Woman, Native, Other.* Bloomington: Indiana UP, 1988.

Rose, Mile. *Lives on the Boundary.* New York: Penguin, 1980.

Scholes, Robert. *Textual Power: Literary Theory and the Teaching of English.* New Haven, CT: Yale UP, 1985.

Shapiro, Karl. *The Old Horsefly.* Orono, MA: Northern Lights, 1992.

Tompkins, Jane. "The Reader in History: The Changing Shape of Literary Responses." *Reader-Response Criticism.* Ed. Jane Tompkins. Baltimore: John Hopkins UP, 1980. 201–32.

Turkle, Ann, Julene Bair, Ruth Anderson Barnett, Todd Pierce, and Rex West. "Life in the Trenches: Perspectives from Five Writing Programs." In this volume.

Selected Resources for Teaching Creative Writing

Wendy Bishop
Florida State University

Katharine Haake
California State University, Northridge

Hans Ostrom
University of Puget Sound

Collaborative Learning

Bruffee, Kenneth A. "Writing and Reading as Collaborative or Social Acts." *The Writer's Mind: Writing as a Mode of Thinking.* Ed. Janet L. Hays and others. Urbana, IL: National Council of Teachers of English, 1983.

Bruffee, Kenneth A. "Collaborative Learning and the Conversation of Mankind." *College English* 46 (1984): 635–52.

Ede, Lisa, and Andrea Lunsford. *Singular Texts/Plural Authors: Perspectives on Collaborative Writing.* Carbondale: Southern Illinois UP, 1990.

Elbow, Peter, and Pat Belanoff. *Sharing and Responding.* New York: Random, 1989.

Gere, Ann Ruggles. *Writing Groups: History, Theory, and Implications.* Carbondale: Southern Illinois UP, 1987.

Harris, Joseph. "The Idea of Community in the Study of Writing." *College Composition and Communication* 40 (1989): 11–22.

Harris, Muriel. *Teaching One-to-One: The Writing Conference.* Urbana, IL: National Council of Teachers of English, 1986.

Weiner, Harvey S. "Collaborative Learning in the Classroom: A Guide to Evaluation." *College English* 48 (1986): 52–61.

Critique

Bishop, Wendy. "Teaching Undergraduate Creative Writing: Myths, Mentors, and Metaphors." *Journal of Teaching Writing* 7 (1988): 83–102.

Bogan, Don. "Beyond the Workshop: Suggestions for a Process-Oriented Creative Writing Course." *Journal of Advanced Composition* 5 (1984): 149–162.

Bullock, Richard, John Trimbur, and Charles Schuster, eds. *The Politics of Writing Instruction: Postsecondary.* Portsmouth, NH: Boynton/Cook, 1991.

Chestek, Virginia L. "Teaching Creative Writing: An Emphasis on Preparation." *Freshman English News* 15 (1986): 16–19.

Delany, Samuel R., Allan Gurganus, Marianne Hauser, Richard Howard, Peter Klappert, and Honor Moore. "The Gay/Lesbian Writer in Context: The University, The Writing Community, The Marketplace." *AWP Chronicle* 22.5 (March/April 1990): 1–10.

Haake, Katharine, Sandra Alcosser, and Wendy Bishop. "Teaching Creative Writing: A Feminist Critique." *AWP Chronicle* 22 (Oct./Nov. 1989): 1–6.

Moxley, Joseph. "Tearing Down the Walls: Engaging the Imagination." *Creative Writing in America: Theory and Pedagogy.* Ed. Joseph Moxley. Urbana, IL: National Council of Teachers of English, 1989. 25–46.

Newlin, Paul. "Creative Writing in the Traditional English Department." *ADE Bulletin* 78 (Summer 1984): 24–28.

Ostrom, Hans. "Undergraduate Creative Writing: The Unexamined Subject." *Writing on the Edge* 1.1 (1989): 55–65.

Saunders, Scott Russell. "The Writer in the University." *ADE Bulletin* 99 (Fall 1991): 21–28.

Shelnutt, Eve. "Notes from a Cell: Creative Writing Programs in Isolation." *AWP Chronicle* 22.4 (Feb. 1990): 1, 4–11.

Smith, Frank. "Myths of Writing." *Language Arts* 58 (1981): 792–98.

"Special Issue: The Workshop." *Mississippi Review* 19.1 &2 (1990): 290–337.

Tanner, Ron. "How to Be an Artist in the Anthill of Academe." *AWP Chronicle* 23.5 (March/April 1991): 1, 8–11.

Discourse Theories

Anderson, Chris, ed. *Literary Nonfiction: Theory, Criticism, Pedagogy.* Carbondale: Southern Illinois UP, 1989.

Bishop, Wendy. *Released into Language: Options for Teaching Creative Writing.* Urbana, IL: National Council of Teachers of English, 1990.

Bahktin, Mikhail. *The Dialogic Imagination: Four Essays.* Ed. Michael Holquist. Trans. Caryl Emerson and Michael Holquist. Austin: U of Texas P, 1981.

Barthes, Roland. "The Death of the Author." *Image, Music, Text.* Ed. Stephen Heath. London: Hill & Wang, 1977.

Booth, Wayne. *The Rhetoric of Fiction.* Chicago: U of Chicago P, 1961.

Crowley, Sharon. *A Teacher's Introduction to Deconstruction.* Urbana, IL: National Council of Teachers of English, 1989.

Crusius, Timothy W. *Discourse: A Critique and Synthesis of Major Theories.* New York: MLA, 1989.

Eagleton, Terry. *Literary Theory: An Introduction.* Minneapolis: U of Minneapolis P, 1983.

Forster, E. M. *Aspects of the Novel.* New York: Harcourt, 1927/1947.

Foucault, Michel. "What Is an Author?" *Textual Strategies: Perspectives in Post-structuralist Criticism.* Ed. J. V. Harari. Ithaca, NY: Cornell UP, 1979. 49–50.

Gass, William. *Fiction and the Figures of Life.* New York: Knopf, 1970.

Gross, Harvey. *Sound and Form in Modern Poetry.* Ann Arbor: U of Michigan Press, 1973.

Graff, Gerald. *Beyond the Culture Wars: How Teaching the Conflicts Can Revitalize American Education.* New York: Norton, 1992.

Hoffman, Michael, and Patrick Murphy, eds. *Essentials of the Theory of Fiction.* Durham, NC: Duke UP, 1988.

James, Henry. *The Art of Fiction and Other Essays.* Ed. Morris Roberts. London: Oxford UP, 1948.

Kundera, Milan. *The Art of the Novel.* New York: Grove, 1986.

Lakoff, George, and Mark Johnson. *Metaphors We Live By.* Chicago: U of Chicago P, 1980.

LeFevre, Karen Burke. *Invention as a Social Act.* Carbondale: Southern Illinois UP, 1987.

Miller, Susan P. "The Student's Reader Is Always a Fiction." *Journal of Advanced Composition* 5 (1984): 15–19.

Moi, Toril. *Sexual/Textual Politics: Feminist Literary Theory.* London: Methuen, 1985.

Perloff, Marjorie. "Theory and/in the Creative Writing Classroom." *AWP Newsletter* (Nov./Dec. 1987): 1–4.

Rimmon-Kenan, Slomith. *Narrative Fiction: Contemporary Poetics.* London: Methuen, 1983.

Scholes, Robert. *Textual Power: Literary Theory and the Teaching of English.* New Haven, CT: Yale UP, 1985.

Smith, Barbara Herrnstein. *Contingencies of Value: Alternative Perspectives for Critical Theory.* Cambridge, MA: Harvard UP, 1988.

Spellmeyer, Kurt. "A Common Ground: The Essay in the Academy." *College English* 51.3 (March 1989): 262–76.

Stitt, Peter. "Writers, Theorists, and the Department of English." *AWP Newsletter* (Sept./Oct. 1987): 1–3.

Winterowd, W. Ross. *The Rhetoric of the "Other" Literature.* Carbondale: Southern Illinois UP, 1990.

Institutional Histories and Critiques

Aisenberg, Nadya and Mona Harrington. *Women of Academe: Outsiders in the Sacred Grove.* Amherst: U of Massachusetts P, 1988.

Applebee, Arthur N. *Tradition and Reform in the Teaching of English: A History.* Urbana, IL: National Council of Teachers of English, 1974.

Baker, Houston A., Jr. *Black Studies, Rap, and the Academy.* Chicago: U of Chicago P, 1993.

Berlin, James A. *Rhetoric and Reality: Writing Instruction in American Colleges, 1900–1985.* Carbondale: Southern Illinois UP, 1987.

———. *Writing Instruction in Nineteenth-Century American Colleges.* Carbondale: Southern Illinois UP, 1984.

Elbow, Peter. *What Is English?* New York: MLA, 1990.

Greenblatt, Stephen, and Giles Gunn. *Redrawing the Boundaries: The Transformation of English and American Literary Studies.* New York: MLA, 1992.

Graff, Gerald. *Beyond the Culture Wars: How Teaching the Conflicts Can Revitalize American Education.* New York: Norton, 1992.

———. *Professing Literature: An Institutional History.* Chicago: U of Chicago P, 1987.

Knoblauch, C.H., and Lil Brannon. *Rhetorical Traditions and the Teaching of Writing.* Portsmouth, NH: Boynton/Cook Heinemann, 1984.

Lunsford, Andrea, Helene Moglen, and James F. Slevin, eds. *The Future of Doctoral Studies in English.* New York: MLA, 1989.

Meyers, David Gershom. *Educating Writers: The Beginnings of "Creative Writing" in the American University.* Unpublished dissertation, Northwestern University, 1989. Dissertation Abstracts International Order #9009673.

Morton, Donald, and Mas'ud Zavarzadeh, eds. *Theory/Pedagogy/Politics: Texts for Change.* Urbana: U of Illinois P, 1991.

Murphy, George, ed. *A Short History of Writing Instruction: From Ancient Greece to Twentieth Century America.* Davis, CA: Hermagoras Press, 1990.

Ohmann, Richard. *English in America: A Radical View of the Profession.* New York: Oxford UP, 1976.

———. "English In America, Ten Years Later." *ADE Bulletin* 82 (Winter 1985), 11–17.

———. "Literacy, Technology, and Monopoly Capital." *College English* 47.7 (1985): 675–89.

Watkins, Evan. "Intellectual Work and Pedagogical Circulation in English." *Theory/Pedagogy/Politics: Texts for Change.* Ed. Donald Morton and Mas'ud Zavarzadeh. Urbana, IL: U of Illinois P, 1991. 201–22.

Wilbers, Stephen. *The Iowa Writers' Workshop: Origins, Emergence, and Growth.* Iowa City: U of Iowa P, 1980.

Journals

Deckert, Andrew J. "Keeping a Teacher's Writing Journal." *English Journal* 77 (Feb. 1988): 48–50.

Fulwiler, Toby, ed. *The Journal Book.* Upper Montclair, NJ: Boynton/Cook, 1988.

Newman, Judith M. "Sharing Journals: Conversational Mirrors for Seeing Ourselves as Learners, Writers, and Teachers." *English Education* 20 (Oct. 1988): 134–56.

Rainer, Tristine. *The New Diary: How to Use a Journal for Self-Guidance and Expanded Creativity.* Los Angeles: Jeremy P. Tarcher, 1978.

Pedagogy

Selected Classroom/Workshop Textbooks

Behn, Robin, and Chase Twichell, eds. *The Practice of Poetry: Writing Exercises from Poets Who Teach.* New York: HarperPerennial, 1992.

Bishop, Wendy. *Working Words: The Process of Creative Writing.* Mountain View, CA: Mayfield, 1992.

Bly, Carol. *The Passionate, Accurate Story: Making Your Heart's Truth into Literature.* Minneapolis: Milkweed Editions, 1990.

Brooks, Gwendolyn, Keorapetal Kgositsile, Haki R. Madhubuti, and Dudley Randall. *A Capsule Course in Black Poetry Writing.* Detroit: Broadside P, 1975.

Brown, Bill and Malcolm Glass. *Important Words: A Book for Poets and Writers.* Portsmouth, NH: Boynton/Cook, 1991.

Brown, Stewart, Mervyn Morris, and Gordon Rohlehr, eds. *An Anthology of Oral and Related Poetry from the Caribbean.* London: Longman, 1989.

Burke, Carol, and Molly Best Tinsley. *The Creative Process.* New York: St. Martin's, 1993.

Burnays, Anne, and Pamela Painter. *What If? Writing Exercises for Fiction Writers.* New York: HarperCollins, 1990.

Burroway, Janet. *Writing Fiction: A Guide to Narrative Craft.* 3rd ed. Boston: Little Brown, 1992.

Cahill, Susan, ed. *New Women and New Fiction: Short Stories Since the Sixties.* New York: NAL, 1986.

Charters, Ann, ed. *The Story and Its Writer: An Introduction to Short Fiction.* 3rd ed. New York: St. Martin's, 1990.

Conlon, Faith, and Rachel Da Silva, eds. *The Things that Divide Us: Short Stories by Women.* Seattle: Seal Press, 1985.

DeMaria, Robert. *The College Handbook of Creative Writing.* New York: HBJ, 1991.

Drury, John. *Creating Poetry.* Cincinnati: Writer's Digest, 1991.

Duke, Charles R., and Sally A. Jacobsen, eds. *Poets' Perspectives: Reading, Writing, and Teaching Poetry.* Portsmouth, NH: Boynton/Cook Heinemann, 1992.

Dunning, Stephen, and William Stafford. *Getting the Knack: 20 Poetry Writing Exercises 20.* Urbana, IL: National Council of Teachers of English, 1993.

Elbow, Peter. *Writing with Power:Techniques for Mastering the Writing Process.* New York: Oxford UP, 1981.

———. *Writing without Teachers.* New York: Oxford UP, 1977.

Erdoes, Richard, and Alfonso Ortiz, eds. *American Indian Myths and Legends.* New York: Pantheon, 1984.

Fadiman, Clifton, ed. *The World of the Short Story: A Twentieth Century Collection.* Boston: Houghton Mifflin, 1986.

Fussell, Paul. *Poetic Meter and Poetic Form.* Revised ed. New York: Random, 1965, 1979.

Gibbons, Reginald and Susan Hahn, ed. *Fiction of the Eighties: A Decade of Stories from Triquarterly.* Evanston, IL: Northwestern University P, 1990.

Goldberg, Natalie. *Writing Down the Bones: Freeing the Writer Within.* Boston: Shambhala, 1986.

———. *Wild Mind: Living the Writer's Life.* New York: Bantam, 1990.

Guthrie, A. B., Jr. *A Field Guide to Writing Fiction.* New York: HarperCollins, 1991.

Hampl, Patricia, ed. *The Houghton Mifflin Anthology of Short Fiction.* New York: Houghton, 1989.

Hollander, John. *Rhyme's Reason: A Guide to English Verse.* New Haven, CT: Yale UP, 1989.

Hickey, Dona J. *Developing a Written Voice.* Mountain View, CA: Mayfield, 1993.

Hills, Rust. *Writing in General and the Short Story in Particular: An Informal Textbook.* New York: Bantam, 1979.

Hoeper, Jeffrey D., and James H. Pickering, eds. *Poetry: An Introduction.* New York: Macmillan, 1990.

Ibieta, Gabriella, ed. *Latin American Writers: Thirty Stories.* Boston: St. Martin's, 1993.

Johnson, David. *Word Weaving: A Creative Approach to Teaching and Writing Poetry.* Urbana, IL: National Council of Teachers of English, 1990.

Kirby, David. *Writing Poetry: Where Poems Come From and How to Write Them.* Boston: The Writer, 1989.

Koch, Kenneth. *I Never Told Anybody: Teaching Poetry in a Nursing Home.* New York: Random, 1977.

———, ed. *Sleeping on the Wing: An Anthology of Modern Poetry with Essays on Reading and Writing.* New York: Random, 1981.

McMillan, Terry, ed. *Breaking Ice: An Anthology of Contemporary African-American Fiction.* New York: Penguin, 1990.

Madden, David, ed. *A Pocketful of Prose: Vintage Short Fiction.* New York: HBJ, 1992.

———. *Revising Fiction: A Handbook for Fiction Writers.* New York: New American Library, 1988.

Meyers, Jack and Roger Weingarten, eds. *New American Poets of the 80's.* Green Harbor, MA: Wampeter, 1984.

Minot, Stephen. *Three Genres: The Writing of Poetry, Fiction, and Drama.* 5th ed. Englewood Cliffs, NJ: Prentice-Hall, 1993.

Murray, Donald M, ed. *The Literature of Tomorrow: An Anthology of Student Fiction, Poetry, and Drama.* New York: Holt, Rinehart and Winston, 1990.

Nagler, Michael, and William Swanson, eds. *Wives and Husbands: 20 Short Stories about Marriage.* New York: NAL, 1989.

Nims, John Frederick. *Western Wind: An Introduction to Poetry.* 2nd ed. New York: Random, 1983.

Oates, Joyce Carol, and Robert Atwan, eds. *The Best American Essays: 1991.* New York: Ticknor and Fields, 1991.

Ochester, Ed, and Peter Oresick, eds. *The Pittsburgh Book of Contemporary American Poetry.* Pittsburgh: U of Pittsburgh P, 1993.

Ostrom, Hans, ed. *Lives and Moments: An Introduction to Short Fiction.* Ft. Worth: Holt, Rinehart, and Winston, 1991.

Padgett, Ron. *Handbook of Poetic Forms.* New York: Teachers and Writers Collaborative, 1987.

Pack, Robert, Sydney Lea, and Jay Parini, eds. *The Bread Loaf Anthology of Contemporary American Poetry.* Middlebury, NH: University Presses of New England, 1985.

Pack, Robert, and Jay Parini, eds. *The Bread Loaf Anthology of Contemporary American Essays.* Middlebury, NH: UP of New England, 1989.

———. eds. *Poems for a Small Planet: Contemporary American Nature Poetry.* Middlebury, NH: UP of New England, 1993.

Pickering, James H., ed. *Fiction 100.* Sixth ed. New York: Macmillan, 1992.

Poulin, A. Jr., ed. *Contemporary American Poetry.* 3rd ed. Boston: Houghton Mifflin, 1980.

Ravenel, Shannon, ed. *The Best American Short Stories of the Eighties.* Boston: Houghton, 1990.

Reed, Ishmael, Kathryn Trueblood, and Shawn Wong, eds. *The Before Columbus Foundation Fiction Anthology: Selections from the American Book Awards, 1980–1990.* New York: Norton, 1992.

Scholes, Robert, Nancy R. Comley, and Gregory L. Ulmer. *Textbook: An Introduction to Literary Language.* New York: St. Martin's, 1988.

Shelnutt, Eve. *The Writing Room: Keys to the Craft of Fiction and Poetry.* Marietta, GA: Longstreet Press, 1989.

Smith, Dave, and David Bottoms, eds. *The Morrow Anthology of Younger American Poets.* New York: Quill (Morrow) 1985.

Sommers, Nancy, and Donald McQuade, eds. *Student Writers at Work and in the Company of Other Writers.* 3rd ed. Boston: St. Martin's, 1989.

Stern, Jerome. *Making Shapely Fiction.* New York: Norton, 1991.

Trimmer, Joseph, and C. Wade Jennings, eds. *Fictions.* Second Edition. San Diego: Harcourt, Brace, Jovanovich, 1989.

Turco, Lewis. *The New Book of Forms: A Handbook of Poetics.* Hanover, NH: UP of New England, 1986.

Turner, Alberta. *To Make a Poem.* New York: Longman, 1982.

Vendler, Helen, ed. *Voices and Visions: The Poet in America.* New York: Random, 1987.

Wallace, Robert. *Writing Poems.* 2nd ed. Boston: Little, Brown, 1987.

Washington, Mary Helen, ed. *Black Eyed Susans/Midnight Birds: Short Stories by and About Black Women.* New York: Doubleday, 1989.

Warnock, John, ed. *Representing Reality: Readings in Literary Nonfiction.* New York: St. Martin's, 1989.

Willis, Meredith Sue. *Personal Fiction Writing: A Guide to Writing from Real Life for Teachers, Students, and Writers.* New York: Teachers and Writers Collaborative, 1984.

Young, Diana, ed. *The Situation of the Story: Short Fiction in Contemporary Perspective.* Boston: Bedford/St. Martin's, 1993.

Works that Support and/or Complicate the Classroom/Workshop

Bertagnolli, Olivia, and Jeff Rackham, eds. *Creativity and the Writing Process.* New York: John Wiley & Sons, 1982.

Caywood, Cynthia L., and Gillian Overing, eds. *Teaching Writing: Pedagogy, Gender, and Equity.* Albany: State U of New York P, 1987.

Coda: Poets and Writers Newsletter, eds. *The Writing Business: A Poets and Writers Handbook.* New York: Pushcart Press/Norton, 1985.

Elbow, Peter. *Embracing Contraries: Explorations in Learning and Teaching.* New York: Oxford UP, 1986.

Gardner, John. *The Art of Fiction: Notes on Craft for Young Writers.* New York: Knopf, 1984.

Gebhardt, Richard C. "Fiction Writing in Literature Classes." *Rhetoric Review* 7.1 (1988): 150-155.

Hugo, Richard. *The Triggering Town: Lectures and Essays on Poetry and Writing.* New York: Norton, 1979.

Koch, Kenneth. *Wishes, Lies and Dreams: Teaching Children to Write Poetry.* New York: Harper & Row, 1970.

Lloyd, Pamela. *How Writers Write.* Portsmouth, NH: Heinemann, 1987.

Madden, David. *Revising Fiction: A Handbook for Fiction Writers.* New York: New American Library, 1988.

McKim, Elizabeth, and Judith W. Steinbergh. *Beyond Words: Writing Poems with Children.* Green Harbor, MA: Wampeter Press, 1983

Moxley, Joseph, ed. *Creative Writing in America: Theory and Pedagogy.* Urbana, IL: National Council of Teachers of English, 1989.

———. "Symposium on Creative Writing in the K–12 Curriculum" (Eve Shelnutt: "Creative-Writing Pedagogy: What the Specialist Can't Do"; Anthony Petrosky: "The State of Poetry in the Schools"; Alan Ziegler: "A High School Summer Writing Program"; Wendy Bishop: "Teaching the Process of Creative Writing.") *Design for Arts in Education* 92.3 (1991): 9–34.

Murray, Donald. *Expecting the Unexpected: Teaching Myself—and Others—to Read and Write.* Portsmouth, NH: Boynton/Cook, 1989.

———. *Learning by Teaching: Selected Articles on Writing and Teaching.* Upper Montclair, NJ: Boynton/Cook, 1982.

———. *A Writer Teaches Writing.* Boston: Houghton, 1968.

Meyer, Sam. "Prose by Any Other Name: A Context for Teaching the Rhetoric of Titles." *Journal of Advanced Composition* 8 (1988) : 71–81.

Ponsot, Marie, and Rosemary Deen. *Beat Not the Poor Desk: Writing—What to Teach, How to Teach It, and Why.* Upper Montclair, NJ: Boynton/Cook, 1982.

Preminger, Alex, Frank J. Warnke, and O.B. Hardison, Jr., eds. *The Princeton Encyclopedia of Poetry and Poetics.* Princeton: Princeton UP, 1974.

Shor, Ira, ed. *Freire for the Classroom: A Sourcebook for Liberatory Teaching.* Portsmouth, NH: Boynton/Cook, 1987.

Schwartz, Mimi. "Wearing the Shoe on the Other Foot: Teacher as Student Writer." *College Composition and Communication* 40.2 (1989) : 203–09.

Shapiro, Karl, and Robert Beum. *A Prosody Handbook.* New York: Harper and Row, 1965.

Shiflett, Betty. "Story Workshop as a Method of Teaching Writing." *College English* 35 (1973): 141–60.

Smith, Frank. *Writing and the Writer.* New York: Holt, Reinhart, and Winston, 1982.

Spreading the Word: Editors on Poetry. Columbia, SC: Bench Press, 1990.

Stafford, William. *Writing the Australian Crawl: Views on the Writer's Vocation.* Ann Arbor: Michigan UP, 1978.

———. *You Must Revise Your Life.* Ann Arbor: Michigan UP, 1986.

Stegner, Wallace. *On the Teaching of Creative Writing.* Hanover, NH: UP of New England, 1988.

Tsujimoto, Joseph I. *Teaching Poetry Writing to Adolescents.* Urbana, IL: National Council of Teachers of English, 1988.

Weathers, Winston. "Grammars of Style: New Options in Composition." *Rhetoric and Composition: A Sourcebook for Teachers and Writers.* 3rd ed. Ed. Richard L. Graves. Portsmouth, NH: Boynton/Cook, 1984. 200–214.

Theory and Issues of Marginalization

Baker, Houston A., Jr. *Blues, Ideology, and African American Literature: A Vernacular Theory.* Chicago: U of Chicago P, 1984.

Belenky, Mary Field, Blyth McVicker Clinchy, Nancy Rule Goldberger, and Jill Mattock Tarule. *Women's Ways of Knowing: The Development of Self, Voice, and Mind.* New York: Basic, 1986.

Bolker, Joan. "Teaching Griselda to Write." *College English* (1979): 906–908.

Bridwell-Bowles, Lillian. "Discourse and Diversity: Experimental Writing within the Academy." *College Composition and Communication* 43.1 (Oct. 1992): 349–68.

Brodkey, Linda. "Modernism and the Scene(s) of Writing." *College Composition and Communication* 49 (1987): 396–418.

Brooke, Robert. *Writing and Sense of Self: Identity Negotiation in Writing Workshops.* Urbana, IL: National Council of Teachers of English, 1991.

Bruchac, Joseph. "Breaking Out with a Pen: Poetry in American Prisons." *A Gift of Tongues: Critical Challenges in Contemporary American Poetry.* Ed. Marie Harris and Kathleen Aguero. Athens, GA: U of Georgia P, 1987. 286–94.

Caywood, Cynthia L., and Gillian Overing, eds. *Teaching Writing: Pedagogy, Gender, and Equity.* Albany: State U of New York P, 1987.

Cherry, Kelly. "When All Is Said and Done, How Literary Theory Really Affects Contemporary Fiction." *New Literary History* 21 (1989–1990): 111–20.

Chiseri-Strater, Elizabeth. *Academic Literacies: The Public and Private Discourse of University Students.* Portsmouth, NH: Boynton/Cook, 1991.

Dean, Terry. "Multicultural Classrooms, Monocultural Teachers." *College Composition and Communication* 40 (1989): 23–37.

Eagleton, Mary, ed. *Feminist Literary Theory: A Reader.* Oxford: Basil Blackwell, 1986.

Elbow, Peter. "Methodological Doubting and Believing: Contraries in Inquiry." *Embracing Contraries: Explorations in Learning and Teaching.* New York: Oxford UP, 1986. 253–300.

Flynn, Elizabeth. "Composing as a Woman." *College Composition and Communication* (1988): 423–35.

Franklin, H. Bruce. *Prison Literature in America: The Victim as Criminal and Artist.* New York, Oxford UP, 1989.

Gabriel, Susan L., and Isaiah Smithson. *Gender in the Classroom: Power and Pedagogy.* Urbana: U of Illinois P, 1990.

Gates, Henry Louis, Jr. *The Signifying Monkey: A Theory of African-American Literary Criticism.* New York: Oxford UP, 1988.

Gilligan, Carol. *In a Different Voice: Psychological Theory and Women's Development.* Cambridge, MA: Harvard UP, 1982.

Harkin, Patricia, and John Schilb, eds. *Contending with Words: Composition and Rhetoric in a Postmodern Age.* New York: MLA, 1991.

Harris, Marie, and Kathleen Aguero, eds. *A Gift of Tongues: Critical Challenges in Contemporary American Poetry.* Athens, GA: U of Georgia P, 1987.

Heilbrun, Carolyn G. *Writing a Woman's Life.* New York: Norton, 1988.

Marks, Elaine, and Isabelle de Courtivron, eds. *New French Feminisms: An Anthology.* Amherst: U of Mass P, 1980.

Moraga, Cherrie, and Gloria Anzaldua, eds. *This Bridge Called My Back: Writing by Radical Women of Color.* New York: Kitchen Table, Women of Color Press, 1983.

Rich, Adrienne. *On Lies, Secrets, and Silence: Selected Prose, 1966–1978.* New York: Norton, 1979.

Ronald, Kate, and John Volkmer. "Another Competing Theory of Process: The Students'" *Journal of Advanced Composition* 9 (1989): 81–96.

Scheffler, Judith A. *Wall Tappings: An Anthology of Writings by Women Prisoners.* Boston: Northeastern UP, 1986.

Schultz, Lucille M., Chester H. Laine, and Mary C. Savage. "Interaction among School and College Writing Teachers: Toward Recognizing and Remaking old Patterns." *College Composition and Communication* 39 (1988): 139–53.

Spellmeyer, Kurt. "Foucault and the Freshman Writer." *College English* 51.7 (Nov. 1989): 715–29.

Tobin, Lad. *Writing Relationships: What Really Happens in the Composition Class.* Portsmouth, NH: Boynton/Cook, 1993.

Torgersen, Eric. "Loving (Hating) the Messenger: Transference and Teaching." *AWP Newsletter* (November 1988): 1, 12, 14–15.

Warren, Kenneth W. *Black and White Strangers: Race and American Literary Realism.* Chicago: U of Chicago P, 1993.

Weiler, Kathleen. *Women Teaching for Change: Gender, Class, and Power.* South Hadley, MA: Bergen and Garvey, 1987.

Teachers as Learners

Dahl, Karin L. *Teacher as Writer: Entering the Professional Conversation.* Urbana, IL: National Council of Teachers of English, 1992.

Fontaine, Sheryl I., and Susan Hunter, eds. *Writing Ourselves into the Story: Unheard Voices from Composition Studies.* Carbondale: Southern Illinois UP, 1993.

Rodriguez, Richard. *Hunger of Memory.* Boston: Godine, 1981.

Rose, Mike. *Lives on the Boundary: A Moving Account of the Struggles and Achievements of America's Educational Underclass.* New York: Penguin, 1989.

Schwartz, Mimi. *Writer's Craft, Teacher's Art: Teaching What We Know.* Portsmouth, NH: Boynton/Cook, 1991.

Writers on Writing

Anthony, Carolyn, ed. *Family Portraits: Remembrances by Twenty Distinguished Writers.* New York: Penguin, 1991.

Bellamy, Joe David, ed. *The New Fiction: Interviews with Innovative American Writers.* Chicago: U of Illinois P, 1974.

Berg, Stephen, ed. *In Praise of What Persists.* New York: Harper Colophon, 1984.

Brans, Jo. *Listen to the Voices: Conversations with Contemporary Writers.* Dallas: Southern Methodist UP, 1988.

Bunge, Nancy. *Finding the Words: Conversations with Writers Who Teach.* Athens, OH: Swallow Press-Ohio UP, 1985.

Coles, Robert. *The Call of Stories: Teaching and the Moral Imagination.* Boston: Houghton Mifflin, 1989.

Coltelli, Laura, ed. *Winged Words: American Indian Writers Speak.* Lincoln: U of Nebraska P, 1990.

Dembo, L.S., ed. *Interviews with Contemporary Writers: Second Series, 1972–1982.* Madison: U of Wisconsin P, 1983.

Dembo, L.S., and Cyrena N. Pondrom, eds. *The Contemporary Writer: Interviews with Sixteen Novelists and Poets.* Madison: U of Wisconsin P, 1972.

Gardner, John. *On Becoming a Novelist.* New York: Harper and Row, 1983.

Huddle, David. *The Writing Habit: Essays.* Salt Lake City: Gibbs-Smith/Peregrine Smith, 1991.

McCaffery, Larry, and Sinda Gregory. *Alive and Writing: Interviews with American Authors of the 1980s.* Urbana: U of Illinois P. 1987.

Murray, Donald. *Shoptalk: Learning to Write with Writers.* Portsmouth, NH: Boynton/Cook Heinemann, 1990.

Packard, William, ed. *The Poet's Craft.* New York: Paragon House, 1987.

———. *Poets at Work: The Paris Review Interviews.* London: Penguin Books, 1989.

———. *Writers at Work.* 3rd and 4th series. New York: Viking, 1967, 1976.

———. *Women Writers at Work: The Paris Review Interviews.* London: Harcourt, 1979.

Ruddick, Sara, and Pamela Daniels. *Working It Out: 23 Women Writers, Artists, Scientists and Scholars Talk about Their Lives and Work.* New York: Pantheon, 1977.

Schroeder, Eric James, ed. *Vietnam, We've All Been There: Interviews with American Writers.* Westport, CT: Praeger, 1993.

Shapiro, Nancy Larsen, and Ron Padgett, eds. *The Point Where Teaching and Writing Intersect.* New York: Teachers & Writers Collarobative, 1983.

Stein, Gertrude. *How to Write.* New York: Dover, 1975.

Sternberg, Janet, ed. *The Writer on Her Work.* Norton, NY: 1981.

———. *The Writer on Her Work, Volume II: New Essays in New Territory.* New York: Norton, 1991.

Strickland, Bill, ed. *On Being a Writer.* Cincinnati: Writer's Digest, 1992.

Todd, Janet, ed. *Women Writers Talking.* New York: Holmes and Meier, 1983.

Turner, Alberta, ed. *Fifty Contemporary Poets: The Creative Process.* New York: Longman, 1977.

———. *Poets Teaching: The Creative Process.* New York: Longman, 1980.

Waldrep, Tom, ed. *Writers on Writing.* New York: Random, 1985.

———. *Writers on Writing.* Vol. 2. New York: Random, 1985.

Weiss, Jason. *Writing at Risk: Interviews in Paris with Uncommon Writers.* Iowa: U of Iowa P, 1991.

Woolf, Virginia. *A Writer's Diary.* New York: Harcourt Brace Jovanovich, 1953.

———. *A Room of One's Own.* New York: Harcourt Brace Jovanovich, 1957.

Writing Apprehension, Writing Response, and Evaluation

Beavan, Mary H. "Individualized Goal Setting, Self-Evaluation, and Peer Evaluation." *Evaluating Writing: Describing, Measuring, Judging.* Ed. Charles R. Cooper and Lee Odell. Urbana, IL: National Council of Teachers of English, 1977. 135–56.

Belanoff, Pat, and Marcia Dickson, eds. *Portfolios: Process and Product.* Portsmouth, NH: Boynton/Cook Heinemann, 1991.

Bizzaro, Patrick. "Evaluating Student Poetry Writing: A Primary Trait Scoring Model." *Teaching English in the Two-Year College* 17 (1990): 54–61.

———. "Interaction and Assessment: Some Uses of Reader-Response Criticism in the Evaluation of Student Writing in a Poetry Writing Class." *The Writing Teacher as Researcher: Essays in the Theory and Practice of Class-Based Research.* Ed. Donald Daiker and Max Morenberg. Portsmouth, NH: Boynton/Cook, 1989. 256–65.

———. *Responding to Student Poems: Applications of Critical Theory.* Urbana, IL: NCTE, 1993—forthcoming.

Cooper, Charles R., and Lee Odell, eds. *Evaluating Writing: Describing, Measuring, Judging.* Urbana, IL: National Council of Teachers of English, 1977.

Daly, John A. "Writing Apprehension." *When a Writer Can't Write: Studies in Writer's Block and Other Composing-Process Problems.* Ed. Mike Rose. New York: Guilford Press, 1985. 134–165.

Elbow, Peter. "Trustworthiness in Evaluation." *Embracing Contraries: Explorations in Learning and Teaching.* New York: Oxford UP, 1986. 217–32.

Fuller, David. "A Curious Case of Our Responding Habits: What Do We Respond to and Why?" *Journal of Advanced Composition* 8 (1988): 88–96.

Knoblauch, C.H., and Lil Brannon. "Teacher Commentary on Student Writing: The State of the Art." *Freshman English News* 10 (Fall 1981): 1–4.

Lawson, Bruce, Susan Sterr Ryan, and W. Ross Winterowd, eds. *Encountering Student Texts: Interpretive Issues in Reading Student Writing.* Urbana, IL: National Council of Teachers of English, 1989.

McAndrew, Donald. "Writing Apprehension: A Review of Research." *Research and Teaching in Developmental Education* 2 (1986): 43–52.

Murray, Donald M. "The Essential Delay: When Writer's Block Isn't." *When a Writer Can't Write: Studies in Writer's Block and Other Composing-Process Problems.* Ed. Mike Rose. New York: Guilford, 1985. 219–26.

"Portfolio Assessment: An Annotated Bibliography." *The Quarterly* 10 (October 1988): 23–24.

Rose, Mike, ed. *When a Writer Can't Write: Studies in Writer's Block and Other Composing-Process Problems.* New York: Guilford, 1985.

———. "Rigid Rules, Inflexible Plans, and the Stifling of Language: A Cognitive Analysis of Writer's Block." *College Composition and Communication* 31(1980): 389–400.

White, Edward. *Teaching and Assessing Writing.* San Francisco: Jossey-Bass, 1985.

Yancey, Kathleen Blake, ed. *Portfolios in the Writing Classroom: An Introduction.* Urbana, IL: National Council of Teachers of English, 1992.

Ziegler, Alan. " 'Midwifing the Craft'—Teaching Revision and Editing." *Creative Writing in America: Theory and Pedagogy.* Ed. Joseph Moxley. Urbana, IL: National Council of Teachers of English, 1989. 209–25.

Index

Editors

Wendy Bishop teaches writing and rhetoric at the Florida State University. She is the author of *Second Nature* (Tideline, 1980), *Something Old, Something New* (Southern Illinois UP, 1990), *Released into Language* (NCTE, 1990), *Working Words* (Mayfield, 1992), and editor of *The Subject Is Writing* (Boynton/Cook Heinemann, 1993). She has contributed poems, stories, essays, and reviews to numerous magazines and journals. With Hans Ostrom, she collaborated on *Water's Night* (Maraposite, 1991). A poetry chapbook, *Time in the Southwest,* is forthcoming from Jumping Cholla Press. Currently, she is a member of the board of directors of the Associated Writing Programs.

Hans Ostrom is associate professor of English at the University of Puget Sound. He has also taught at Gutenberg University in Germany, and in 1994 he will be a Fulbright Fellow at Uppsala University in Sweden. His published work includes the novel *Three to Get Ready* (1991), *Lives and Moments: An Introduction to Short Fiction* (Holt, Rinehart, 1991) and *Langston Hughes: A Study of the Short Fiction* (Twayne, 1993). He has won a fiction prize from *Redbook Magazine* and poetry prizes from the University of Houston and the Chester H. Jones Foundation. With Wendy Bishop, Ostrom collaborated on *Water's Night* (1992), a poetry chapbook. He is a member of the National Book Critics Circle.

Contributors

Julene Bair is a graduate of the Iowa Writers' Workshop and at the time of this writing was finishing a master's degree through Iowa's Nonfiction Writing Program. She has had essays and stories published in *Iowa Woman, Plainswoman,* and the *North Dakota Quarterly.* She was a finalist in the 1991 *Missouri Review* essay contest, and, in 1990, "Distances," a story based on her childhood in western Kansas, won a contest sponsored by the Writers' Workshop and *Midwest Living.* Also in 1990, Julene won one of the University of Iowa's Outstanding Teaching Assistant Awards. She is currently working on a book entitled *House Dreams,* a memoir.

Ruth Anderson Barnett received her MFA from the Program for Writers at Warren Wilson College in January 1993. She is a full-time instructor of composition, literature, and poetry writing at Grossmont Community College in El Cajon, California, a suburb of San Diego, where she has taught for 21 years. Her poems have appeared in *Beloit Poetry Journal, The Florida Review,* and the *Arizona Quarterly.* She is married and has a 26-year-old son.

R. M. Berry won the 1984 Fiction Collective Award for his collection of stories, *Plane Geometry and Other Affairs of the Heart* (1985). A graduate of the MFA and Ph.D. programs at the University of Iowa, he teaches critical and narrative theory and fiction workshops at the Florida State University in Tallahassee, Florida. His fiction and reviews have appeared in *American Book Review, Apalachee Quarterly, Carolina Quarterly, Illinois Writers Review, Iowa Review, Massachusetts Review,* and *West Branch.* His recently completed novel is titled *Leonard DA Vin Is Dying.*

Patrick Bizzaro's poetry, which has appeared in six chapbooks and over one hundred magazines, has been awarded the Madeline Sadin Award from the *New York Quarterly* and the *Four Quarters* Poetry Prize from La Salle University. In addition, he has published articles on composition and the teaching of writing in *College Composition and Communication, Language Arts,* and *Teaching English in the Two-Year College* as well as essays in numerous other NCTE affiliate journals. He is co-author of *Writing with Confidence: A Modern College Rhetoric* and *Concise English Workbook,* both from D.C. Heath. His literary scholarship includes articles on Jane Austen, William Blake, and Percy Shelley as well as a book on contemporary author Fred Chappell and over three dozen articles and book reviews on contemporary poets and poetry. He teaches at East Carolina University where he serves as Director of Writing Across the Curriculum and co-director of the Coastal Plains Writing Project.

Alice G. Brand is professor of English and director of composition at SUNY Brockport. Among her credits are poetry and essays published in *The New York Times, New Letters, Nimrod, Minnesota Review, Kansas Quarterly, Paintbrush, Literary Review,* and *The Cape Rock.* She has won regional and national poetry competitions, and has published two collections of poetry, *As It Happens* (Wampeter Press) in 1983 and *Studies on Zone* (University of Missouri-Kansas City, BkMk Press) in 1989. She is a three-time Yaddo fellow.

François Camoin teaches Creative Writing at the University of Utah and in the Vermont College Program. His books include *Benbow and Paradise, The End of the World Is Los Angeles, Why Men Are Afraid of Women, Deadly Virtues,* and *Like Love But Not Exactly,* a collection of stories recently published by the University of Missouri.

Maxine Clair is author of *Coping with Gravity,* poems, (Washington Writers Publishing House, 1988), and a fiction chapbook, *October Brown* (Time Press, Baltimore, 1992). Currently, she teaches at the George Washington University in Washington, D.C.

Beverly Conner teaches creative writing, composition, and literature at the University of Puget Sound in Tacoma, Washington. She has published poetry and short fiction and has led creative writing workshops. She has also presented at both national and regional conferences on composition and is a former director of Prelude, a national award-winning freshman orientation program in writing and critical thinking. In addition to teaching, Conner is also a faculty writing advisor in the Center for Writing and Learning at Puget Sound.

Robert Coover was born in Iowa in 1932. His first novel, *The Origin of the Brunists,* was the winner of the 1966 William Faulkner Award. He is the author of many novels, short stories, and plays, including *The Universal Baseball Association, J. Henry Waugh, Prop.; The Public Burning; Gerald's Party; Pinocchio in Venice; A Night at the Movies;* and *Pricksongs and Descants.* His articles and reviews have appeared widely and he has won numerous awards and fellowships: The Brandeis Citation for fiction; an American Academy of Arts and Letters award; the Rea Award for the Short Story; and Rockefeller Foundation, Guggenheim Foundation, and National Endowment for the Arts fellowships. Coover lives with his wife, Pili, in Providence, Rhode Island, where he teaches at Brown University.

Lynn Domina has published poetry, fiction, and reviews in a variety of periodicals, including *The Southern Poetry Review, Poetry Northwest, The Indiana Review, Prairie Schooner,* and *The Northwest Review.* She received an MFA from the University of Alabama, where she edited *The Black Warrior Review,* and she has taught literacy in the Cook County Jail in

Chicago, and writing and literature at The College of St. Francis in Joliet, IL, and Lewis University in Romeoville, IL. Currently, she is a student in the doctoral program in English at SUNY—Stony Brook.

Gayle Elliott is a Ph.D. candidate in creative writing at the University of Wisconsin—Milwaukee where she teaches creative writing, women's literature, and composition. She has presented papers at the AWP National Convention, the University of Wisconsin Women's Studies Conference, and the 1991 and 1992 Midwest Feminist Graduate Student Conference. A former fiction editor of *The Cream City Review,* she is currently working on a collection of her own short stories entitled *Revival.* Her story, "The Family Circle," was recently nominated for a Pushcart Prize by *Writer's Forum* editor Alexander Blackburn.

Eugene K. Garber has published over sixty short stories, a number of which have been anthologized in such places as *Best American Short Stories* (1977), *The Paris Review Anthology,* and *The Norton Anthology of Contemporary Fiction.* Two of his collections have won national competitions: *Metaphysical Tales*--the Associated Writing Programs Short Fiction Award (Missouri Press, 1981) and *The Historian*—the Triquarterly William Goyen Award(Milkweed Editions, 1993). "*My Kinsman Major Molineux*: Some Critical Probes" appeared in *Literature in the Classroom* (NCTE, 1990). From 1978 to 1985 he directed the Capital District Writing Project, a site of the National Writing Project.

Katharine Haake is the author of *No Reason on Earth* (Dragon Gate, 1986), a collection of short stories. She has been anthologized in *New Women's Fiction and Writing in a Nuclear Age,* and her stories have appeared in *The Iowa Review, Mississippi Review, The Minnesota Review, Witness,* among many others. An associate professor of English at California State University, Northridge, she has presented papers and led workshops on creative writing teaching at national meetings of Associated Writing Programs and the Conference on College composition and Communication.

Diane Kendig's books include a collection of poems, *A Tunnel of Flute Song* (Cleveland State Poetry Center) and one of translations, *And a Pencil to Write Your Name* (Bottom Dog). She has won an Ohio Arts Council Artist Grant and a Fulbright Award, and she has been a fellow at Yaddo. Kendig is assistant professor of English at The University of Findlay in Ohio.

Patrick Lawler's collection of poetry *A Drowning Man Is Never Tall Enough* was published by the University of Georgia Press in 1990. He has been awarded fellowships by the New York State Foundation for the Arts and the National Endowment of the Arts. Currently, he is a creative writing teacher at Onondaga Community College and an assistant professor at SUNY College of Environmental Science and Forestry, where he teaches Environmental Writing and Environmental Literature. In addition, he has had poetry and fiction appear in over fifty journals, including *American Poetry Review, Central Park, The Iowa Review, Shenandoah, The New*

York Times Literary Review, Nimrod, and *Northwest Review.* He has published an essay about the teaching of creative writing in *Western Ohio Journal.*

Carl Leggo is assistant professor in the Department of Language Education at the University of British Columbia where he teaches courses in writing and communication skills and issues of gender. His poetry and fiction have been published in journals across Canada and the United States, and in New Zealand and India. Presently, Leggo is completing two manuscripts of poetry, tentatively titled *Growing Up Perpendicular on the Side of a Hill* and *I Do Not Find It Easy to Be a Human Being.* His most recently published essays about composition and rhetoric have appeared in *English Quarterly, Language Arts, Phenomenology and Pedagogy,* and *Rhetoric Review.*

Lea Masiello is professor in the English department at Indiana University of Pennsylvania. She has worked in writing centers since 1974 and continues to develop programs for underprepared students. She has most recently published *Write at the Start: A Guide for Integrating Writing into Freshman Seminar Courses* (The Freshman Year Resource Program, University of South Carolina, Columbia, SC).

Joseph M. Moxley is associate professor of English at the University of South Florida. He edited *Creative Writing in America: Theory and Pedagogy* and has published articles on teaching creative writing in such journals as the *AWP Chronicle.*

Julie Neff is Director for the Center for Writing and Learning at the University of Puget Sound. Neff was president of the National Writing Centers Association and served six years on the Executive Board. She has also been editor of the *Washington English Journal* and has presented at the Pacific Coast Writing Centers Association Conference, CCCC, and NCTE regional and National conferences. Neff contributed a chapter to *Writing Centers in Context: Twelve Case Studies,* edited by Joyce Kinkead and Jeanette Harris and published by NCTE.

Jay Parini, a poet and novelist, is professor of English at Middlebury College. His books include *Anthracite Country, Town Life, The Last Station,* and *Bay of Arrows.* He is a recent Guggenheim Fellow and is currently writing a biography of John Steinbeck.

Linda Pennisi received her BA in English from Le Moyne College in Syracuse, N.Y. She is presently enrolled in the MFA program at Vermont College. Her poetry has been accepted for publication in literary magazines such as *Paintbrush, Nightsun, The Spoon River Quarterly, The Panhandler,* and *The Midwest Quarterly.*

Todd Pierce holds a master's degree in English Composition and Literature from Oregon State University and is presently an MFA (fiction) student at the University of California at Irvine, where he teaches undergraduate fiction and expository writing courses. His stories and nonfiction have most recently appeared in *Amelia* and *Nimrod.* Currently he is at work on a novel.

Jan Ramjerdi is assistant professor at California State University, Northridge, teaching creative writing. She is a former student of Eugene Garber's at the University of Albany (SUNY) where she received her Doctor of Arts degree in May 1992. Her poetry and fiction have appeared in *Denver Quarterly, PRISM International, Mid-American Review, 13th Moon,* and *The Little Magazine.* She is a 1992 winner of the AWP Intro Award in Poetry.

Linda Sarbo teaches writing and is enrolled in the Ph.D. program at the University of South Florida (USF). In 1991 and 1992 she received University and College Poetry Prizes awarded by the Academy of American Poets, and her poems have appeared in such literary magazines as *New Collage, Tampa Bay Review,* and *Sandhill Review.*

Sarah Jane Sloane is currently assistant professor of English at University of Puget Sound. Her research interests include rhetoric and technology, narrative theory, and gender and writing. She has published poems in several journals, including *Bananas* (London), *Sun Dog,* and *The Valley Women's Voice.* Her dissertation, a study of how interactive fiction changes our understanding of the reading-writing relationship, won the 1991 Hugh Burns Dissertation Award from *Computers and Composition.* Currently, she is working on a book about how interactive fiction and virtual realities change the reading-writing relationship.

David Starkey teaches writing at Francis Marion University and is associate director of the annual Francis Marion Writers' Conference. His poems are collected in *Koan Americana* (Colonial Press) and are forthcoming in a second book and chapbook (*Adventures of the Minor Poet* [Signal Books] and *A Year with Gayle, and Others* [Runaway Spoon Press]). His poems, reviews, interviews, essays, and short fiction appear regularly in literary journals; he is a Pushcart Prize nominee and recipient of First Prize Awards in Poetry (1989 and 1990) from the Academy of American Poets Poetry and Louisiana State University.

Ann Turkle earned her Ph.D. in Creative Writing from Florida State University. She has accepted the position of Director of Communication Skills at Warren Wilson College where she received her MFA from the Program for Writers in 1988. The recipient of a 1986 Vermont Council on the Arts grant for her fiction, Ann's work has recently appeared in *The Hiram Poetry Review, Sundog: The Southeast Review,* and *Yankee Magazine.* She is also an editor of *Apalachee Quarterly*, a Tallahassee-based literary journal. She is at work on a novel, *Dakota Commonplace.*

Rex West received his master's degree from Oregon State University. Currently a Ph.D. candidate in the Creative Writing Program at Florida State

University, he is a teaching assistant and coordinator of the 1993 Richard Eberhard Poetry Contest (sponsored by FSU). Rex is also poetry editor for the small press journal *Fathoms* in Tallahassee, Florida. His work has appeared most recently in *Gaia.*